Courting Democracy in Mexico

Party Strategies and Electoral Institutions

This book is perhaps the most comprehensive explanation to date of Mexico's gradual transition to democracy, written from a novel perspective that pits opposition activists' postelectoral conflicts against their usage of regime-constructed electoral courts at the center of the democratization process. It addresses the puzzle of why, during key moments of Mexico's twenty-seven-year democratic transition, opposition parties failed to use autonomous electoral courts established to mitigate the country's often violent postelectoral disputes, despite formal guarantees of court independence from the Party of the Institutional Revolution, Mexico's ruling party for seventy-one years preceding the watershed 2000 presidential elections. Drawing on hundreds of author interviews throughout Mexico over a five-year period and extensive original archival research, the author explores choices by the rightist National Action Party and the leftist Party of the Democratic Revolution between postelectoral conflict resolution through electoral courts and traditional routes – mobilization and bargaining with the Party of the Institutional Revolution authoritarians. He argues that these mobilizations divided the ruling party and facilitated the National Action Party's watershed presidential victory in 2000.

Todd A. Eisenstadt is Assistant Professor of Government at American University, where he directs the four-year "Mexico Elections Project" with the United States Agency for International Development and the University of New Hampshire. Formerly an assistant professor of political science at the University of New Hampshire, Eisenstadt has been a visiting scholar at Harvard University's David A. Rockefeller Center for Latin American Studies and the Center for U.S.-Mexican Studies at the University of California, San Diego. He also spent two years as a Visiting Professor at El Colegio de México, in Mexico City. His current research focuses on comparative electoral reform, on the role of international development assistance in political development, and on public opinion of Mexico's indigenous communities regarding integration with the Mexican state. He is the author of several articles on Mexico's political development in journals such as *Democratization*, the *International Political Science Review*, and *Latin American Politics and Society* and is a past recipient of Fulbright, National Security Education Program, and Rotary International Foundation fellowships. A frequent consultant on democracy and governance matters, Dr. Eisenstadt was an award-winning police-beat reporter for the *Nashville Tennessean* newspaper and a congressional researcher on foreign affairs issues before receiving his Ph.D. in political science from the University of California, San Diego, in 1998.

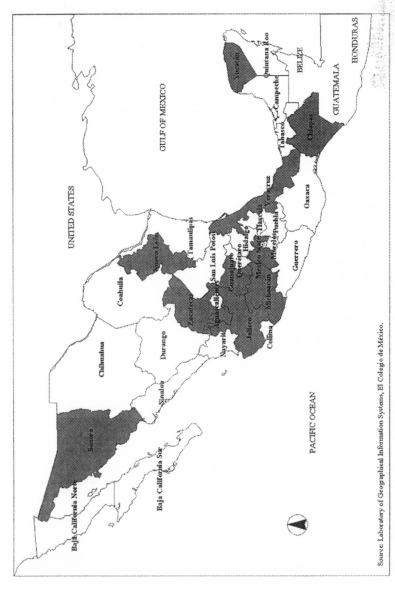

Source: Laboratory of Geographical Information Systems, El Colegio de México.

Map of Mexico Indicating the Ten States in Statistical Sample.

Courting Democracy in Mexico

Party Strategies and Electoral Institutions

TODD A. EISENSTADT
American University

CAMBRIDGE UNIVERSITY PRESS
Cambridge, New York, Melbourne, Madrid, Cape Town, Singapore, São Paulo

Cambridge University Press
The Edinburgh Building, Cambridge CB2 2RU, UK

Published in the United States of America by Cambridge University Press, New York

www.cambridge.org
Information on this title: www.cambridge.org/9780521820011

First published 2004
This digitally printed first paperback version 2007

A catalogue record for this publication is available from the British Library

Library of Congress Cataloguing in Publication data

Eisenstadt, Todd A.
Courting democracy in Mexico : party strategies and electoral institutions / Todd A.
Eisenstadt.
    p. cm.
Includes bibliographical references and index.
ISBN 0-521-82001-4
1. Elections – Mexico – History – 20th century.   2. Political parties – Mexico – History –
20th century.   3. Election law – Mexico.   4. Democratization – Mexico.   I. Title.
JL1292.E36   2003
324′.0972–dc21   2003043473

ISBN-13 978-0-521-82001-1 hardback
ISBN-10 0-521-82001-4 hardback

ISBN-13 978-0-521-03588-0 paperback
ISBN-10 0-521-03588-0 paperback

To my parents, Melvin and Pauline Eisenstadt

Their love, support, civic spirit, and engagement with ideas have provided a deep well of identity and inspiration that I will draw upon for my entire life.

Contents

Figures and Tables

Acknowledgments

Prior to the 1990s, the lack of credible data rendered the study of elections in Mexico more of an art than a science. Three reasons were lucidly stated by Bruhn (1997, 333):

First, since one party won every election, many scholars questioned the usefulness of the effort to construct "models" of the vote. Second, most analysts believed that pervasive fraud marked Mexican elections, inflating vote results even when the outcome would have been the same with or without manipulation.... Third, the limitations of demographic data made the validity of independent variables questionable....

Each of these reasons made information shortcomings insurmountable for the period prior to the mid-1980s, and created challenges for researching later federal elections and, especially, municipal elections.

Mere imprecision of information occasionally gave way to obfuscation of the facts by officials, as I sought a disaggregated presentation of the 1988 federal electoral results, including opposition poll coverage data, to improve the accuracy of my calculations. The task seemed quite simple, as Baez Rodriguez (1994) asserted that the "close to 55 thousand acts from these elections are available, through a computerized retrieval system, in the National Archive (21)." However, inquiries to more than a dozen high-level officials involved in Salinas's electoral certification, the Chamber of Deputies' Electoral College of 1988, and the Baez Rodriguez book project, rendered only a written admission by the director of the Central Historical Archive that "we do not have said items in this institution, and thus cannot provide them for your consultation" (personal communication from Hector Madrid Mulia). Even if copies of these acts had been located, it is widely believed that they would have been altered from the originals. They remain extremely controversial more than a decade after Carlos Salinas (1988–94) took office under the postelectoral cloud of 1988. The experience taught me that even at the federal level, there would be no gleaning of data from Mexico's pretransition period; that data variance since the late 1980s would have to suffice.

If the politization of electoral data hindered scholars of federal elections, they were even more of a hindrance in studying local races, for which researchers could never get full information. And if it was difficult just to get electoral results, it was even more of a challenge to gather information about postelectoral conflicts and their legal and extralegal resolutions. This by way of apologizing in advance for some of the unavoidable data-collection shortcomings of this work and most others seeking to measure indices of political opening in semiauthoritarian regimes. Needless to say, I alone am responsible for any errors in this text.

I have racked up a huge number of intellectual debts in the course of writing this book, which are easy to acknowledge but hard to repay. First, I thank the advisors of the dissertation from which this book finally emerged. My doctoral advisor and thesis chair, Wayne Cornelius, has offered continuous support and encouragement every step of the way. My image of him during our 1994 observation of Mexico's federal elections is the one that sticks with me; seeking shelter in concrete pipes from pouring rain that had washed out one of the largest slums of the Valley of Mexico, he nonetheless insisted we continue patrolling polling stations for signs of electoral fraud, and gauging voter turnout. A foremost authority on Mexican politics and a true believer in field research, his insistence on rolling up sleeves pervades this work. Co-chair Stephan Haggard impressed upon me the imperative of striving to extend the comparative purchase of my study. A masterful and dedicated theorist, he constantly pushed me to revise. Elisabeth Gerber made statistics accessible, encouraged me to represent problems in quantitative terms, and enthusiastically saw my work through. Her ease in transferring concepts to equations helped me out of several jams. I am also thankful to dissertation committee members James Holston, Matthew Shugart, and Peter H. Smith, who exposed me to a wide range of approaches, but with similarly exacting standards. Robert Pastor generously offered his perspectives as a renowned researcher of electoral institutions and democratic transitions, and as an expert policy practitioner and electoral observer.

University of California, San Diego's (UCSD) political science department was a great place to study, and the university's Center for

U.S.-Mexican Studies kept my theoretical work honest through constant exposure to premier scholars and practitioners of Mexican politics. El Colegio de México provided a collegial atmosphere where I could finish my dissertation among the company of distinguished social scientists. In particular, I thank María Celia Toro, María del Carmen Pardo, Jean-François Prud'homme, and Anna Covarrubias for making the Center for International Studies such a welcoming place and Soledad Loaeza, whose enthusiasm and profound knowledge of Mexican political parties inspired me. Exemplary scholars and policy makers Sergio Aguayo, Alonso Lujambio, and Juan Molinar Horcasitas opened doors for me at crucial moments early in my field research, allowing me improved access to sensitive information, and guided my instincts in discerning what information was essential. A talented friend from my undergraduate year on a Rotary Foundation fellowship at Colegio de México, Pedro González Caver, graciously agreed to translate this work into Spanish.

As this book was being completed, several new colleagues at American University made a remarkable effort to welcome me there. I again thank Robert Pastor, who helped me get off to a great start at the Department of Government, Diane Singerman for her timely reassurance, and William LeoGrande and Saul Newman for their patience and good humor during the complications the move presented. Sponsored research administrators Andy Shepard and Cindy Corriveau at the University of New Hampshire, and Liz Kirby at American University helped ensure a seamless transition. Also, I would like to thank Christine Dunn, Lewis Bateman, and Cambridge University Press for guiding me through the publication process and for patiently helping to refine a manuscript into a book.

The University of New Hampshire (UNH) also offered a receptive environment and encouraged my research during much of the write-up stage. John Kayser, Lawrence Reardon, and Clifford Wirth have been particularly exemplary colleagues, and I thank them. Finally, Harvard University's David Rockefeller Center for Latin American Studies afforded me one more round of research and rewriting under the best conditions imaginable. John Coatsworth, Jorge Dominguez, Steven Levitsky, and Steve Reifenberg were particularly welcoming there.

A comparative politics workshop organized at UCSD by Peter Smith in 1996–7 served as a forum for presenting work in progress where colleagues Octavio Amorim Neto, Jorge Buendía, Antonio Ortíz Mena, and Alain de Remes also reviewed extensive sections of the manuscript, as did Jonathan Hartlyn, Fabrice Lehoucq, and Andreas Schedler. Related papers were improved by many other readers, including Joel Barkan, Araceli Burguete, Peter Burnell, Gretchen Casper, Sylvia Gómez Tagle, Richard Katz, Bolivar Lamounier, Juan Linz, Michael Malley, Reynaldo Ortega Ortíz, Shelley Rigger, Luis Miguel Rionda, Ashutosh Varshney, María Cristina Velásquez, Jeffrey Weldon, and several anonymous reviewers.

Several institutions funded portions of this work. UCSD's Center for Iberian and Latin American Studies and the UC-MEXUS Foundation offered critical predissertation grants to assess the project's feasibility during short visits to Mexico in 1993 and 1994. The Fulbright Commission and National Security Education Program (NSEP) funded research in Mexico City and several states in 1995–6, and the NSEP and UC-MEXUS funded follow-up state visits in 1996 and 1997. El Colegio de México funded research and conference-related travel in 1998. Without the United States Agency for International Development (Grant 523-A-00-00-00030-00), the final updates in 2000, 2001, and 2002 would not have been possible. Two enterprising officials at the U.S. embassy in Mexico's USAID Democracy and Governance Division – Jene Thomas and Jill Pike – deserve mention for their dedication and knack for well-directed "hands-on" project planning to get the most out of foreign assistance funds. They have provided useful criticism, public-service role models, logistical support, and, most importantly, friendship. Additionally, Jene Thomas stewarded me through the intricacies of federal government grantsmanship with patience, humor, good advice, and great command of an amazing amount of information. I am thankful.

My field research benefited from increasingly cooperative relations with the Electoral Tribunal of the Judicial Power of the Federation (TEPJF), where presidents Fernando Ojesto and José Luis de la Peza granted my research assistants and me full access to the electoral court archives, and Magistrate Jesús Orozco, International Coordinator Raúl Avila, former Statistics Director Macarita Elizondo, and Information Services Director Jorge Tlatelpa were particularly giving of time and expertise. Two other libraries, that of Mexico's Federal Electoral Institute and the U.S.-based Clifton White Resource Center of the International Foundation for Electoral Systems (IFES), also generously offered assistance. Rafael de la Torre García, former public affairs director of the Interior Secretariat's National Center for Municipal Development (CEDEMUN) also provided data, as did Maribel Méndez de Lara, former coordinator of advisers for the Federal Solicitor General for Agrarian Concerns. Political scientist José Antonio Crespo of the Centro de Investigación y Docéncia Económicas (CIDE), where I was graciously received as a visiting scholar during my first year of field research, granted me access to his unique collection of all of Mexico's state electoral codes during the 1990s. A special debt is also owed to UCSD colleague Alain de Remes, who shared his database of otherwise unmanageable local electoral data. Hundreds of electoral authorities and party leaders at the national level and in Mexico's states also offered extensive assistance and access to information, and while they cannot all be mentioned here, many of those interviewed are cited in the bibliography. Several research assistants also helped make this project possible. Special thanks are due to electoral court research coordinators Carla Barba and Amilcar Peláez Valdés, dedicated law students whose well-directed and frequent questions improved the research design and data collection. Also, I thank graduate students Paloma Bauer de la Isla and Xiaoming Zhang, and former undergraduate assistant Karen García Valdívia, for extensive help tracking down bibliography and entering data.

Perhaps the most important support I have received, for this project and all others, has come from my family. My interest in studying politics resulted from childhood dinner table discussions with my parents Melvin and Pauline Eisenstadt and my brother Keith, who have always encouraged civic awareness and inquiring skepticism. Most importantly, they provided a caring home and made every opportunity available. This book is a tribute to their example and inspiration, and to the generosity and tenaciousness of their own parents, whose difficult immigrant journeys are remembered. I also thank my cousin Laurel Kaufer, whose dining room table doubled as my office for a week while I formatted my dissertation. During the course of my doctoral program, I was lucky to be welcomed at my in-laws' dinner table, where I was received as one of their own. But my greatest joy of all was reacquaintance with my wife Mireya at UCSD's Center for U.S.-Mexican Studies in 1996. I could not have found a more loving, thoughtful, and compassionate lifelong mate (nor a better editor).

A generational transition occurred as I wrote this book. My father-in-law Carlos passed away, but not before meeting his new granddaughter, Natalia, who has made sacrifices for this book that I hope to make up to her and to her forthcoming sibling.

Courting Democracy in Mexico

Party Strategies and Electoral Institutions

Electoral Courts and Actor Compliance: Opposition-Authoritarian Relations and Protracted Transitions

> Indeed, you won the elections, but I won the count.
>
> attributed to Nicaraguan dictator Anastasio Somoza (1896–1956)[1]

Before citizens in authoritarian regimes can hand-cast free ballots in fair elections, they often must vote with their feet. In pre-2000 Mexico, disgruntled opposition activists contested fraudulent elections by launching street mobilizations and building occupations. Before they entrusted their grievances to electoral commissions and courts, they took to the streets. This book documents the rise of Mexico's opposition party activists and how they gradually channeled their postelectoral contestation off the streets and into the courtrooms. Mexico's protracted transition from the longest reigning one-party authoritarian regime in the world to a multiparty democracy culminated in 2000 with Mexico's first executive branch alternation since 1929.

This is a book about the quarter century of national and local elections preceding the 2000 watershed. However, unlike most work on elections, it considers social movements surrounding elections as much as the contests themselves. Courting democracy in Mexico was hardly a straightforward story about the translation of preferences into votes and votes into seats. Rather, it was a "stop and go" process through which opposition parties *did* negotiate increasing spaces of participation, but rarely at the ballot box. Elections, especially local elections, served largely as preliminary summations of forces – starting points for the postelectoral negotiation of opposition party participation in public administration subordinate to

---

[1] Cited in *The Guardian*, June 17, 1977 (referenced in *Microsoft Bookshelf 98*).

the ruling Party of the Institutional Revolution (PRI) authoritarians, the longest continuous one-party state in the world. The PRI-state's electoral stranglehold was finally broken due to the patience of opposition parties on the right and the left, and these parties' willingness to challenge the PRI through informal institutions (bargaining tables), instead of or in addition to the formal institutions (electoral commissions and courts) established by the PRI-state to mediate disputes. The gradual replacement of these seemingly anomalous informal institutions by formal legal institutions – those usually associated with democratization and the advent of "free and fair" elections – is the subject of this book.

I argue that most of the groundwork for Mexico's watershed 2000 national elections, won by the National Action Party (PAN), the country's consistent opposition party since 1939, was laid locally, through a series of postelection power struggles by which the PAN and other opposition party losers contested races at bargaining tables where they extracted concessions from the PRI-state for demobilizing quietly. Through most of Mexico's democratic transition (1977–2000), the PAN and the more recent leftist Party of the Democratic Revolution (PRD) were rarely allowed to win on an electoral playing field skewed by the PRI-state. But these persistent regime opponents did make small inroads – forcing the PRI-state to accept a PRD town council member here, or an interim PAN governor there. The most important manifestations of this democratization from the regions to the center were visible at the federal level, where the opposition party–negotiated autonomous electoral institutions allowed increasingly competitive parties (and especially the PAN) to actually be pronounced as winners in elections where they garnered the most votes.

After thousands of postelectoral conflicts claiming hundreds of lives, outgoing President Ernesto Zedillo's controversial but bold decision to publicly congratulate the PAN's Vicente Fox on election night in July 2000 helped ensure a serene postelectoral environment, where no real challenges, legal nor extralegal, were launched against the legitimacy of President-elect Fox. For the first time ever, Fox's victory was ratified by the Electoral Tribunal of the Judicial Power of the Federation (TEPJF) rather than by the horse-trading Electoral College of newly elected congressional members who for decades had ratified their own elections.

In contrast, Mexico's 1988 presidential race was fraught with so much controversy that even as President Carlos Salinas assumed office, doubts persisted about whether he had actually won the election. Oversight of that election was conducted by an electoral commission headed by the PRI-state's Interior Secretary and irregularities abounded, including burned ballots floating in rivers by the hundreds, and a blackout of the vote-tallying computer. The politically driven Electoral College (the incoming congress that certified its own elections) cut deals, granting "victories" to five opposition vote total runner-ups (after withholding certification of thirteen PRI victories to negotiate outcomes) and obstructing scrutiny of dubious presidential results (Gómez Tagle 1994, 93, 137). Runner-up Cuauhtémoc Cárdenas launched weeks of postelectoral mobilizations that threatened to unite the conservative PAN with his leftist movement and teetered on the brink of violence. For several days in July 1988, the future of the regime hung in the balance.

This book offers a comprehensive treatment of how the authoritarian PRI-state after 1988 deftly walked the line between allowing opposition inroads, but not too many, and constructing independent electoral institutions on demand from the PAN and from international critics, but without really using them, at least initially. This work seeks to provide a "window" on the battles between the PRI-state and two growing opposition parties from the localities on up, and to demonstrate how the opposition parties – particularly the PAN – benefited in the long term from exploiting formal electoral institutions as part of a range of options that also included resolving postelectoral conflicts using informal institution bargaining tables. Mexico's first electoral courts in the early 1990s, however powerful they were on paper, accustomed their users to the norm of electoral justice while allowing them to fall back on old habits of negotiating postelectoral conflict spoils in exchange for the compliance of electoral losers from the PAN or the PRD. By a new taxonomy of informal institutions in the developing world, these bargaining tables were substitutive informal institutions (Helmke and Levitsky 2002), competing directly with formal institutions.

Because some of the weakest courts in practice had been constituted on paper as the strongest, no discernible pattern existed from which a new institutionalist could readily determine which courts would be used and which would be abused. Meanwhile, throughout the period of this study, opposition party competitiveness grew and disputes between the PRI-state and growing opposition over notoriously fraudulent elections continued to be resolved in the streets and in the courtrooms, simultaneously. Postelectoral conflicts usually involved "sit ins" outside municipal buildings or the buildings' outright occupation, and often included violent confrontations lasting weeks or even months, prompting efforts by the PRI-state – often "sweetened" by offers of side payments – to persuade them to desist. In the most conflictive states, postelectoral conflicts could absorb more than a quarter of a state legislature's business, and "waste" much of a governor's term arbitrating postelectoral disputes rather than setting more transcendent policies.[2] Local elections were not for determining who would govern. This decision was made with the selection of the PRI's internal candidate for a given office. However, local elections were for the opposition to register dissent, size up their forces in a manner threatening to the authoritarians, and gather information about PRI-state forces.

Parting from this idea that elections in transitional Mexico were for much more than counting votes, this book has three broad aims. First, it specifies the role of postelectoral conflicts and their accompanying informal bargaining tables in advancing Mexico's electoral opening even before the advent of formal electoral courts. Second, it argues that contrary to the pacted democratization model, protracted transitions to democracy occur under special conditions, and it proposes late twentieth century Mexico as an exemplar protracted transition. Third, it demonstrates that even when credible formal institutions (here electoral courts) are created, political parties respond more to long-standing political grievances than to the codification of formal electoral institutions. That is, the causes of postelectoral conflicts occurring in nearly 15 percent of Mexico's local races over a twelve-year statistical sample (1989–2000) run much deeper than just elections. The "electoralist fallacy" described by Schmitter and Karl (1991), whereby observers consider nations to have democratized solely on the basis of having staged apparently free and fair elections, must be applied in "electoral authoritarian" regimes as well as in democracies. The implications of this last finding, that historical grievances matter more than electoral laws, are important for scholars of democratization and specialists in economic and political development alike.

---

[2] The legislative effort dedicated to resolving municipal postelectoral conflicts is measured as the percentage of the legislature's total decree "output" (including laws) addressing transfer of municipal power. For example, during the Chiapas 1991 legislative calendar, 23 percent of the total of 69 decrees pertained to municipal power transfers (Chiapas State Legislature 1995, 59–71), while in 1992 Oaxaca, an astounding 48 percent of the 116 decrees issued addressed composition of new municipal governments (Oaxaca State Legislature Decree Record Book, passim). The mention of a governor "wasting" his first year in a six-year administration on postelectoral conflicts comes from Oaxaca, where State Electoral Institute President Cipriano Flóres Cruz (interview) said he was hired to channel conflicts so the sitting governor would not lose the first year of his term to the mediation of postelectoral conflicts.

THE THREE OBJECTIVES OF THIS BOOK

With regard to the first objective, by documenting the gap between the construction of "parchment" formal institutions and their acquisition of credibility, I offer an important rejoinder to theories of institutional design that often take actor consent for granted, especially in the literature on democratic transitions. I argue that formal institutions cannot replace informal ones (the bargaining tables); that is the "training wheels" cannot come off, freeing institutions to perform as their designers intended, until a critical mass of relevant political actors decide to comply with these institutions. The central tenet of this book, that even well-designed formal institutions may actually be subverted by actors' political discretion until unconditional actor consent is granted to them, is illustrated through the novel method of simultaneously considering legal and extralegal focal points – the informal and formal institutions – for resolving postelectoral disputes. I argue that fortifying Mexico's electoral institutions alone was necessary but far from sufficient for guaranteeing acceptance of election results, both by a PRI-state that prized discretion over hand-tying legal institutions and by the opposition, which often benefited, at least in the short term, from PRI-state discretion in postelectoral deal making, and that refused to vest their electoral fates with paper tigers. In pitting ill-studied informal institutions against better-documented formal ones, this work joins a growing body of literature seeking to apply tenets of the new institutionalism to less codified but empirically verifiable patterns of behavior (Carey 2000, Ellickson 1991, Helmke 2002), and to integrating structure- and agency-driven explanations of institutional development (Jones Luong 2000, Knight 1992, Knill and Lenschow 2001).

The key to empirically specifying the gap between the creation of institutions and their acquisition of credibility is to suspend the assumption, pervasive in much of the literature on democratic transitions, that actors automatically comply with governing institutions once overarching pacts have been reached on the new regime's rules. Rigorous inquiry of when institutions do not work, rather than just considering when they do, conduces to new interpretations of microinstitution building, even in circumstances of great uncertainty, such as Mexico's regime transition. A statistical model of the causes of local postelectoral conflicts presented in Chapter 5 underscores a derivative finding, that actor consent is granted to electoral institutions as a function of broader political strategies. My analysis shows that while the PAN follows the logic of a disciplined party amenable to short-term, patronage-seeking arrangements with the

PRI-state, the PRD adheres to no such logic. Rather, local PRD activists act mostly on their own, with postelectoral conflicts resulting as much from a general community-wide recent history of broader social conflicts as from specific concerns about election fraud. Contrary to the pragmatic PAN seeking to maximize elected offices through whatever combination of legal and extralegal tactics appears most effective, the more rural and less educated *PRDístas* tended to mobilize first and ask legal questions later, if at all.

Identification of such differences in party strategies over their acceptance of Mexico's new institutions of electoral justice leads to the second objective of this book, specifying the incentives of individual opposition parties in determining compliance with the authoritarians' legal order. In establishing patterns of opposition party/PRI-state relations, I categorize PRD postelectoral behavior as varying between "antiregime" and "transition-seeking," while the PAN's varies between "patronage-seeking" and "transition-seeking." Among the *PRDístas*, I found severe and even lethal postelectoral conflicts common, yielding few concessions from the authoritarians, while PAN supporters staged few postelectoral conflicts, over major cities only, and nearly always directed by national headquarters. The PAN's national leadership traded support for PRI-state federal legislative initiatives and received interim mayorships and governorships. The PAN's tactic was so pervasive in the early and mid-1990s that it comprised the basic frame of reference for a generation of Mexico's most powerful politicians from President Vicente Fox (2000–6) on down.[3] And as this book argues based on extensive qualitative evidence, the PRI-state's eagerness to trade posts for PAN cooperation, and local PRI electoral activists' poor reactions to being "sold out" by their national leaders, was the biggest catalyst of the rupture between the PRI and the Mexican state, culminating in electoral defeat.

This strategy of "dueling focal points" – concurrent bargaining in formal and informal institutions to resolve postelectoral conflicts – was most

---

[3] Fox lost the Guanajuato 1991 governor's race but fellow *PANísta* Carlos Medina Plascencia (who later headed the PAN Chamber of Deputies faction) was named interim governor when the PRI's victor mysteriously resigned. Fox Interior Secretary Santiago Creel was a citizen councilor of the Federal Electoral Institute (IFE) in 1994 when now-Mayor Andrés Manuel López Obrador of Mexico City, then the PRD's candidate to Tabasco's governorship, was denied his apparent victory in favor of former PRI governor and current PRI national party president Roberto Madrazo. Current PAN Senate Caucus Chair Diego Fernández de Cevallos was his party's "clutch" negotiator with the PRI-state during much of the early 1990s.

evident in gubernatorial and mayoral races, where it was not uncommon for local ruling PRI winners to abruptly resign under pressure from the national PRI-state. Compromise candidates, plural councils, and even opposition interim mayors and governors were named, in a logic of perverse federalism by which PAN activists decried federal intervention in local elections and then complained directly to federal authorities upon losing a race. Before returning to the plan of this book for explaining the microlevel "gap" between when electoral courts were created and when they were infused with credibility, I turn briefly to the macrolevel objective of this book, exposing distinctive patterns in how the authoritarian incumbents and their opponents incrementally negotiate opening using the electoral arena.

AN EDDY IN THE THIRD WAVE: CONTEXTUALIZING MEXICO'S
PROTRACTED TRANSITION

Most work on democratization has addressed the internal division of the hardliners from the soft-liners in the authoritarian coalition, but without systematically considering the role of the opposition or the international community. Furthermore, earlier studies have not focused extensively on self-binding through electoral reforms to enable the soft-liners to control the retrograde hard-liners, who in the Mexican case continued to view the commission of electoral fraud as their patriotic duty, even into the 1990s.[4] Prior to the mid-1990s, the PRI-state behaved ambivalently toward the new electoral institutions the three constituencies had forced the regime to construct. When possible, the federal executive bypassed electoral institutions, choosing instead to negotiate extralegal resolutions to conflicts at informal bargaining tables, even though exorbitant sums have been spent since the early 1990s to give the regime the appearance of clean elections. In fact, measured as cost per registered voter, Mexico's 2000 Federal Electoral Commission budget – some $15 per voter – was among the highest of any large country in the world.[5] In 2000, and every year

---

[4] The idea of "patriotic fraud," thought to have been coined by leaders of the PRI's corporatist bases, is affirmed by former national PRI leader José Francisco Ruiz Masseiu who acknowledged in 1994 that: "In most states we are living in the Stone Age. Patriotic fraud is seen as an honorable practice (Oppenheimer 1996, 193)."

[5] The 2000 elections cost well over a billion dollars. These costs per registered voter are as much as ten times the per capita cost of elections in established democracies like the United States, Germany, the Netherlands, and Sweden. In fact, among López-Pintor's (2000) estimates in forty-nine countries during the 1990s, only two were more expensive

since 1991 (including non electoral years!), the federal government has
spent more on electoral institutions than on the entire legislative branch,
and in election years, electoral institutions receive more than the legislative and judicial branches *combined*, or well over 1 percent of the federal
government's programmable budget (Treasury Secretariat). Why would
the PRI-state spend so much on these institutions only to disregard them
at critical moments? The answer is that the authoritarians sought, quite
reasonably, to placate the three constituencies by building the institutions
but without planning to actually use them.

Constraining notorious electoral fraud by the most retrograde elements of the PRI-state was indeed more readily possible if electoral
reforms bound everyone's hands within the authoritarian coalition. However, fulfillment of such commitments produced the unintended consequence of dividing ruling party interests and those of the governing bureaucracies in long-reigning electoral authoritarian states such as Brazil
(1964–88), Mexico (1929–2000), South Korea (1972–87), and Taiwan
(1949–2000).[6] Such schisms occur because authoritarian elites loyal to
the party continue seeking to maximize electoral victories, while those
loyal to the government favor regime stability over party electoral victories, even if they must placate opposition leaders by conceding elections.
Such separation between state and party in one-party (or military rule
through political party) systems is a necessary but not sufficient condition of democratization. In other words, as the interests of local machine bosses and those of federal technocrats diverge, the discipline of the
party-state unravels, and the strength of the opposition parties' positions
increases.

In the Mexican case, PRI-state officials wished to open electoral competition in a selective and partial manner only, to update information about
opposition strength and placate international critics. Opposition parties
"scared" the regime into granting more concessions (i.e., making the

---

per eligible voter than Mexico 1997 (which was slightly less expensive than 2000): Angola
1992 ($22 per eligible voter) and Cambodia 1993 ($45 per eligible voter). These were
small countries undertaking postconflict elections with extensive international support.
While figures for Angola's later elections are not included, López-Pintor documents a
reduction in Cambodia's 1998 election, to $4.7 per eligible voter (López-Pintor 2000,
73–6).

[6] There are acknowledged classification trade-offs in considering these regimes "one-party"
systems. For example, Brazil and South Korea may be considered military regimes consolidated through a party, while the other two were civilian one-party systems. At the state
and local levels, direct elections were not held in Taiwan during much of the "one-party"
periods. Nonetheless, these regimes share more similarities than differences.

regime's hitherto unfulfilled commitments more credible) through strong shows of coalition strength within their limited openings, and by colluding with international actors pressing for domestic liberalization. Whether opposition forces the party-state to completely and uniformly bind its own hands determines whether electoral liberalization proceeds to full-scale democratization. Where such credible commitments are not made by the state, opposition parties continue resorting to extralegal means (i.e., bargaining outside of formal electoral institutions) in order to resolve postelectoral conflicts, rather than recurring to the institutions created by the authoritarians, presumably to tie their own hands. This process is much more evident in protracted transitions like Mexico's than in the abrupt transitions that characterized most of Eastern Europe and South America in the late 1980s. In stylized characterizations of those pacted transition cases, antiregime social and political movements brought down the *ancien régime* in a single collapse, allowing new elites to replace the old, and to set terms of participation in the new regime in one major negotiation. Protracted transitions like Mexico's differ in that the PRI-state did not collapse, but rather withered away slowly, and through a series of postelectoral bargaining episodes in which the authoritarians underestimated opposition persistence and resourcefulness.

What of the opposition forces that manage to overcome internal factionalism, resource constraints, and collective action problems to "outlast" the authoritarians and "decompress" the incumbents right out of office? Recent scholarship has managed to shift the focus of "transitology" (Przeworski's 1996 term) from intraelite bargaining back to the negotiations between authoritarian elites and their opponents, at least in part. Bermeo, in debunking the "myth of moderation" (that extreme opposition demonstrations and strikes do not produce enduring transitions), argues that in various Third Wave transitions – namely Peru, the Philippines, Portugal, South Korea, and Spain – violence and mobilization were conducive to durable transitions. However, Bermeo reached these conclusions by filtering their effects through the perspectives of pivotal elites (those whose actions directly affected the transition). Whether these pivotal elites would accept democracy depended on whether they predicted extremist or moderate opposition forces would gain control of the transition (Bermeo 1997, 315–18). Outside of the social movements literature, all research on democratic transitions seems to emphasize the role of elites, even if indirectly, as in Bermeo.

Some democratization scholars have considered the importance of the opposition in transitions. For example, Huntington (1991, 113), Share and

Mainwaring (1986, 177–9), and Munck and Skalnik Leff (1999, 195–210) considered authoritarian/opposition bargaining dynamics in constructing typologies of transitions. The issue has even been cleverly phrased in terms of opposition incentives by Przeworski (1991, 18): "If one accepts, as I do, that not all conflicts can be resolved by deliberation and that therefore democracy generates winners and losers, can one ever expect the losers to comply with the verdict of democratically processed conflicts?" However, the particular mechanisms of obtaining loser compliance have been underspecified, except in the most dramatic Eastern European and South American cases where authoritarian walls literally fell, Round Table Talks were launched, and militaries were sent back to the barracks. Protracted democratizations like those in Mexico and Taiwan largely passed undetected until 2000 power alternations in each country sent analysts looking for clues.[7]

Current tendencies to filter the effects of pretransition oppositions through authoritarian elite perceptions extends back at least to Dahl's classic formulation that the likelihood of a government's toleration of opposition varied inversely with the costs of toleration and directly with the costs of suppression (Dahl 1971, 16). Certainly these elite formulations are crucial in deciding whether to allow elections in authoritarian regimes. If an independent regime opposition exists, its course of action will obviously be constrained by incumbent authoritarian decision making. But the opposition's actions will also be shaped by its own interests. And while opposition parties do not become relevant actors in regime transitions until authoritarians grant some role to elections, these parties have by that time usually consolidated themselves for years or decades. While their identities and fates are inexorably intertwined with the decisions of pivotal authoritarian elites, the interests of these parties must be considered apart from those of the incumbents, as they are a significant part of the explanation of regime transition. Transition is not just an insiders' quarrel between the hardliners and the moderates in the authoritarian coalition. There are also hard-line (radical) and moderate oppositions, and they must be more fully modeled, because without them, there is no transition either.

---

[7] In a separate project, McFaul (1999) discusses Russia's "protracted transition" as a stalemate among actors in which electoral democracy has been reached, but entrenched interests preclude the consolidation of liberal democracy. Contrary to the success of Mexico's actors in using electoral democracy to launch "social" or "liberal" democracy, McFaul questions the linear advance of Russia's path, as does Malley (2000) in his study of Indonesia.

Even in protracted transitions, where overarching agreements like Spain's celebrated Moncloa Pact are not reached among a nascent democracy's critical sectors, democratization can proceed in the shadows before it is given the spotlight in founding elections. Whatever the conservative inclinations of voters, their lack of faith in the political system, and constraints posed by political culture, agents must still mobilize these otherwise-disaggregated forces and turn them against the authoritarians. Frequently, opposition parties must make do with incremental concessions from the cautious authoritarian coalition, struggling to overcome internal resource constraints as well as hostility and even repression. In such protracted transitions, nonpublic arenas of struggle are often sought, but they usually fail, as economic and social conditions are not sufficiently adverse to the populace as to make them stake their lives on democracy, such as through the launching of civil wars or *guerrilla* movements. The main protagonists in protracted transitions are opposition parties, which tend toward the center of the political spectrum, where they can more readily turn elections into anti-authoritarian plebiscites.

Parting from the conventional wisdom of the O'Donnell-Schmitter (1986) tradition that the road to democratization is paved with political pacts among authoritarian elites, Geddes notes that such insights have been inductively derived. There has been little grand theorizing about democratization, at least since the Third Wave's commencement with Portugal in 1974. Hence, a selection bias exists, according to Geddes, in considering only unambiguously successful liberalizations, and also in considering cases that have not yet concluded and about which there is no final verdict (1994, 6–7). While democratization theory's exercises of inductive theory building have been powerful heuristics and artfully used by the Third Wave's theorists, such approaches have favored dramatic cases of immediate and thorough democratization (such as the Philippines and Chile in the late 1980s) over slower and more partial transitions (such as those of Mexico and Taiwan).

This work addresses Geddes's critique, seeking to append the "elite pacts" tradition in the democratization literature by more fully specifying an active and crucial role for regime opposition in cases where such overarching pacts are not achieved. In much of the literature, the struggle is depicted as one between factions within the authoritarian incumbents, and the opposition tends to be painted as passive actors whose interests are only factored into democratization when constitutions are drawn up or when posttransition, "founding elections" are held. Constructing a new ideal type of democratization – protracted transitions – entails breaking the bigger issue into several related questions. While the bulk of this work is necessarily addressed to closely documenting the Mexican case, the applicability of the protracted transition ideal type may extend much more broadly, as suggested in Eisenstadt (2000). Filling in the protracted transition ideal type requires the empirical precision of a case-study monograph, which I offer in the pages that follow. Chapter 2 establishes the PRI-state's reasons for establishing institutions to adjudicate postelectoral conflicts. Chapter 3 assesses the regime's overall success in establishing courts to adjudicate these disputes by the mid-1990s, while Chapter 4 compares this relative success with the PRI-state's miserable failure to establish such bodies at the subnational level.

Upon establishing the authoritarians' incentives for binding their hands at the national level even as their subordinates rejected such limitations in Mexico's states, I embark on the second major contribution of this book, confirming that in transitional regimes such as Mexico, where democratic institutions have yet to be consolidated, the behavior of political actors, such as opposition parties, is shaped more at the subnational level by environmental and structural factors than by the limits of formal institutions. This assertion is presented in Chapter 5 as a statistical model to explain the causes of postelectoral mobilizations in Mexico's local races. I find that, contrary to the constitution-based "new institutionalist" hypothesis constructed in Chapter 5, opposition parties mobilize rather than just follow legal channels of postelectoral discontent in municipalities where the victory margin was slim and party-specific conditions are met. While allowing that the mere existence of institutions may condition actors' perceived choices, I argue that the strength of the institutions[8] has little impact on mobilization.

Analysis of my postelectoral conflict model led to the third significant finding of this work, that preferences of opposition parties in relations with the authoritarian incumbents vary widely, and that these preferences can be informally specified. As a complement to the quantitative analysis, Chapters 6 and 7 develop case studies of PAN and PRD postelectoral bargaining and generalize these parties' preferences for interacting with the PRI-state. The reaction of local PRI factions and the federal PRI-state are presented in Chapter 8, and Chapter 9 assesses relations between national and local factions in protracted transitions. A more specific outline follows. Before outlining the organization of my argument

---

[8] For an explanation of how formal institutional strength in ten categories was coded from analysis of the electoral laws, see Appendix B.

in greater detail I briefly explain the importance of the elections as the arena of authoritarian-opposition contention, and then depict the independent variables tested in Chapter 5 as causes of my dependent variable, postelectoral conflicts.

ELECTORAL INSTITUTIONS: OPTIMAL ARENA FOR GAUGING PROTRACTED TRANSITIONS

Despite their decisive impact on protracted transitions, electoral institutions have been grossly understudied, due to the transitions literature bias toward pacted transitions, where new electoral institutions are created from scratch, rather than being repeatedly altered in minor increments. According to Pastor (1999b, 76), "When people think of electoral systems, they do not think of the conduct of elections but rather of constitutional questions – e.g., a presidential or parliamentary system – or of election procedures or practices – e.g., campaign finance...." Pastor attributes this bias to the fact that developed country electoral institutions are taken for granted, while in studies of developing countries, scholars are much more interested in bigger questions of designing democratic institutions, than in whether these nations possess the administrative capacity to implement even basic institutions of governance (Pastor 1999a, 4–5). But these scholars are overlooking important empirical evidence that can be bolstered in broader arguments.

Electoral fraud has existed as long as elections themselves, and history books are full of anecdotal discussions of such fraud, from Napoleon III to the Tammany Hall operators. While irregularities in longstanding democracies such as France and the United States have only recently reopened taken-for-granted election procedures to scrutiny, electoral administration in ethnically divided and administratively underprivileged nations like India and South Africa continuously generates extensive debate. For example, in India hundreds of lives are lost in ethnic/religious conflicts arising with each national election (Wilkinson 1998). The democratization literature has, for all its emphasis on process, largely considered pacts within the authoritarian elites (both formal and informal) as the primary cause of democratization, addressing party formation, public opinion, and the turning of votes into seats only after democracy has been ushered in.

Pastor (1999a, 2) writes that dubious elections can preempt transitions and identifies eighty-one flawed elections between 1988 and 1999 (1999a, 19–25), dozens of which may indeed have hindered democratization processes. I argue that the rigging of elections does matter obviously, but is not decisive in protracted transitions. My main conclusion is that opposition party access to the forum is the most important element for ascertaining whether a protracted transition is possible. Some sort of platform for public debate must exist, and moderate regime opponents must exist[9] and possess a strategy for reforming electoral laws as part of their broader objective of inducing a transition. But independent electoral authorities and level playing fields are not prerequisites for democratic transitions. Protracted transition agents, such as Mexico's PAN and Taiwan's Democratic Progressive Party, may rally for the creation of such institutions to engage the regime in dialogue and build public support while biding time.

Even in dubious rather than model democratizers, electoral institutions are crucial to political opening, as they are often the only arena where opposition parties may legally contest anything at all. Electoral institutions, however rigged, may become the single crucial arena for opposition bargaining, especially in cases where fissures within the authoritarian coalition are insufficient to provide opposition footholds. Even if they seldom or never win concessions, the opposition parties that participate in elections must have some sort of institutional means of challenging authoritarian electoral rules. And even the weakest such institutional fora still offer a platform to the opposition, for without so much as a place to be heard, regime opponents would have little incentive to channel dissent through a party.[10]

Little existing work explicitly questions compliance with regime decisions; in democracies this is taken for granted, and in nondemocracies, it tends to be ignored as an insignificant sideshow to where transitions are conventionally thought to originate, as divisions within the authoritarian coalition. Furthermore, few existing studies quantify degrees of consent by election losers with winners' policies in democratic polities. One work, by Nadeau and Blais (1993), finds that the greater the level of electoral participation, the more likely the losers to accept winners' platforms (in this case Canadians' 1988 endorsement of free trade with the United States). However, this outcome is measured in public attitudes

---

[9] This requirement of a moderate opposition tends to be associated with middle and lower middle income countries, but not with the most impoverished where more polarized oppositions tend to form antiregime *guerrilla* insurgents, as in several of Africa's cases. See Barkan (2000) for the obstacles particular to Africa's protracted transitions.

[10] Threats not to participate, such as Solidarity's threat to depart from Poland's 1989 roundtable talks or the Mexican PAN's decision not to participate in the 1976 presidential election, often exert a greater cost to the regime in terms of domestic and/or international credibility, than a few small concessions that could be granted in exchange for continued opposition participation.

rather than in postelectoral conflicts, and participation in postelectoral conflicts demonstrates a much greater intensity of preferences than merely answering a survey. Nadeau and Blais do reconsider the basic assumption of loser consent, just as I do as a cornerstone of this work, but they pose the issue as one of regime legitimacy. Rather than seeking to measure the more nebulous concept of regime legitimacy, I seek merely to assess whether the relevant actors – opposition party losers – comply with the dictates of the winner-established rules, or challenge these rules when the authoritarians obstruct opposition party efforts to participate in political opening. While "legitimacy" is arguably a more important concept, "compliance" is a more empirically tractable one.

Postelectoral mobilization is only a tentative proxy for actor non-compliance, as instances occur where an opposition party wishes to stage postelectoral conflicts rather than comply with formal institutions for adjudicating electoral disputes, but it may lack mobilizational capacity. Frivolous assessment of such cases puts the analyst at risk of succumbing to an observational fallacy. The answer, for purposes of this study, is to define "compliance" more broadly. I equate lack of mobilization to compliance, as it signifies either a lack of will to mobilize on the part of the opposition, or the inability of the opposition to overcome collective action barriers. As with all political behavior measured in the realm of action, it is impossible to distinguish intent. In other words, silence is not compliance, but the result is the same, and while this "compliance" indicator (opposition respect for laws) is not ideal, it is the best empirical measure available and does provide considerable insight into individual party strategies and how these fit into broader processes of democratization.

CAUSES OF POSTELECTORAL CONFLICTS: POLITICAL TENSIONS VS. WEAK INSTITUTIONS IN FLUX PERIODS

Using this dependent variable of postelectoral conflicts (or not), the central empirical contribution of this work is to test the strength of microinstitutions against other causes of postelectoral mobilization using the negative of opposition party postelectoral conflicts as a proxy for compliance with formal PRI-state institutions. In addition to measuring postelectoral conflict mobilizations, I assess the strength of formal electoral institutions (constructing an index that measures the autonomy of these state electoral institutions from the executive branch of government), in order to test the institutional hypothesis that as electoral institutions grow more autonomous, fewer postelectoral conflicts occur. A concrete measure of electoral institution strength has not been used elsewhere, as transitions have usually been studied in more macro terms. Furthermore, the constant flux of transitions is not conducive to studying subtle institutional changes, even in Mexico's protracted transition, as state electoral codes were reformed before every election. But beyond providing a taxonomy of electoral laws, my research demonstrates that under unstable settings (low institutional stability and high uncertainty about future institutional composition), the strength of institutions alone does *not* explain whether actors (in this case the opposition parties) will obey them. In fact, counter to intuition, the PRD stages more postelectoral conflicts precisely where electoral institutions are more autonomous of the PRI-state's local agents.

Institutions do not determine compliance. Rather, opposition compliance is shaped by the precedent of extralegal institutional channels. In other words, where opposition parties have succeeded at informal authoritarian/opposition bargaining tables, they will want to use them again. Rational regime opponents weigh past interactions more heavily than the fairness of formal institutions in deciding whether to abide by the law or mobilize outside it. The finding is significant for the study of political actors in periods of flux generally, and opposition parties in democratic transitions more specifically, as it demonstrates the primacy of established patterns of bargaining (informal institutions) over formal new institutions, at least until opposition cost/benefit calculations show that vesting themselves in the formal institutions is worthwhile, a conclusion that can take years or even decades to reach.

While the logic behind the conceptual hypotheses and operationalization of the independent variables tested is fully discussed in Chapter 5, I introduce the four hypotheses here. Debunking the assumption implicit in the democratization literature that formal institutions tend to be obeyed once they are pacted into existence, I consider explanations for why opposition parties might defy these formal institutions. Brief descriptions follow:

1. Contrary to the "processes and pacts" democratization tradition, a negotiated institutions explanation would imply a significant role for regime opponents in constructing institutions. An **electoral institution strength** hypothesis states that postelectoral conflicts are more prevalent where formal electoral institutions are less autonomous, thereby prompting the opposition to resort to informal bargaining.

2. The more polarized the local environment is as a result of authoritarian excesses by regional machine bosses, the more likely the PAN and PRD will rebel against adverse elections. Hence, the greater the number of **localized social conflicts** (such as human-rights abuses, agrarian conflicts, etc.), the more likely are postelectoral conflicts.

3. PAN and PRD supporters are more likely to mobilize after closely contested elections than after noncompetitive races. In other words, the opposition party's **perceived electoral competition** with the electoral winner is a rough proxy for opposition party postelectoral bargaining strength.

4. Opposition-party compliance with formal electoral rules is more likely under greater **urban concentration**: that is, in smaller, more rural, and more isolated municipalities collective-action problems predominate. Postelectoral conflicts are thus more likely in larger, more urban, and less remote municipalities, where activists suffer from poor resource distribution but possess more than the minimum threshold of resources required to make collective action more likely.

Additional control variables are introduced in Chapter 5.

Not surprisingly, Hypotheses 3 and 4 were mostly confirmed for both the PAN and the PRD. However, novel results were obtained from my multinomial logit models, reported in Chapter 5, regarding Hypotheses 1 and 2. The most important empirical finding of the whole study was that both PRD and PAN behaviors disconfirmed Hypothesis 1, that strong electoral institutions encourage postelectoral compliance. For the PRD in particular, the opposite relationship held; party activists were more likely to mobilize after elections in states with electoral institutions that – on paper at least – were more autonomous of the executive branch, than in states with weak formal institutions. Hypothesis 2 generated another finding, that localized social conflicts were significant as a cause of PRD postelectoral mobilization (responsible for nearly 60 percent of the 1,300 postelectoral conflicts coded between 1989 and 2000), but not as a cause of the much less frequent PAN postelectoral conflicts. This difference between the conditions of opposition parties' recourse to postelectoral mobilizations is indicative of much more extensive strategic differences between them, discussed extensively in Chapters 6 and 7. In broad terms, the PRD viewed postelectoral confrontations as episodes of greater social conflicts, while the PAN saw them as an informal and partial corrective to the PRI-state's stilted and corrupt formal electoral institutions.

As an extension of my statistical analysis, Chapters 6 and 7 demonstrate, through qualitative case studies, that the two opposition parties conducted postelectoral conflicts quite differently, and in response to different causes. The PRD, which staged hundreds of postelectoral conflicts annually while the PAN averaged fewer than a dozen, decisively protested electoral results partly to contest broader political inequities at the local level. Contrarily, the disciplined PAN took decisions at the national level and enacted them locally. In contrast to the unconsolidated PRD, which alternately displayed antiregime and transition-seeking behavior, the consolidated and pragmatic PAN was more consistently open to patronage-seeking negotiations with the PRI-state. PRD activists lost their lives while PAN activists gained extra proportional-representation seats on city councils.

In discussing the PRD in particular, I apply social movements frameworks that offer theoretical "bridges" between movements and their social/political contexts. I address a lacuna in the party systems literature, which tends to address party or electoral systems or internal party behavior, but without considering interactions between these disparate units. The "new social movements" literature emphasizes such an intersection between actors and the "dimensions of political systems which structure collective action (McAdam et al., 1996, 10)." Contrary to prior approaches stressing the social identities of movement members at the expense of movement accomplishments, these new theorists are informed by economistic thinking. Their movement activists may be motivated by endogenous identities, but they are also shrewdly rational, compensating for their lack of conventional resources (money, training, influence with elites) through appeals designed to construct identities and "frame" urgent messages on the regime's frayed edges (McAdam et al., 14).

By this logic, successful movement leaders convey such a desperate need for collective action that they justify departing from the authoritarians' rule of law through memorable, deviant, and even violent acts. In the case of Mexico's postelectoral conflicts, activists' "framing" of ongoing social tensions (such as the thousands of unresolved agrarian conflicts stemming from the 1930s) and precedents of informal bargaining supersede formal electoral institutions, at least until PRD activists are shown that they have sufficient stakes in the new institutions to comply with their dictates. Consistent with the literature on democratic transitions, Tarrow (1998, 71) writes that contention "increases when they are threatened with costs they cannot bear or which outrage their sense of justice. When institutional access opens, rifts appear within elites, allies become available, and state capacity for repression declines, challengers find opportunities to advance their claims." This is a narrative, then, about how different groups reacted to increasingly desperate and outrageous acts of electoral fraud, as they acquired means of redress and as pressures mounted against their authoritarian perpetrators.

ORGANIZATION OF THE BOOK

This book is organized into nine chapters. The remainder of Chapter 1 specifies my research methods; clarifies my dependent variable, postelectoral conflicts; and considers the understudied mechanism driving the iterated bargaining in protracted transitions, a convergence of expectations about the fairness of electoral institutions between the authoritarians and their opponents. Chapter 2 addresses the question of why the authoritarian incumbents would bind their own hands and allow electoral reforms giving the opposition parties opportunities to contend. Chapter 3 traces the increasing role of the opposition at the federal level in Mexico's electoral courts, and demonstrates that real electoral justice has become possible, even in a semiauthoritarian regime, by analyzing the evolution of Mexico's federal electoral courts from powerless executive-branch rubber stamps into mostly autonomous institutions. In contrast to Mexico's federal electoral justice success story, Chapter 4 evaluates the many failures of electoral courts in adjudicating gubernatorial races extending back decades, and argues for a disaggregation of the unit analysis in succeeding chapters to electoral institutions operating at the most local levels, rather than leaving the analysis at the state and national levels, as in prior studies. The chapter also considers the Mexican oppositions' gambit of "electoral federalism," opening from the localities to the center, and why this has been at best a partial success.

Chapter 5 commences the four-chapter empirical core of the work. Based on over 200 interviews and archival research in the electoral courts of a dozen states, it establishes the prevalent post-1970s patterns of informal bargaining to resolve local postelectoral conflicts, even where electoral courts existed. The chapter sets up Chapter 6 by discussing coding of postelectoral conflicts and analyzing causes of these conflicts at the descriptive level. I use an unbiased data set of over 1,800 local elections in ten of Mexico's thirty-one states from 1989–98 to estimate two multinomial logit models of postelectoral conflicts. Taken together, the statistical models mostly disconfirm the "conventional wisdom" formal institutional-strength hypothesis and suggest the potential explanatory

power of the remaining hypotheses. The overall conclusion is that opposition party negotiating strategies are a more crucial determinant of
whether a regime opponent will launch postelectoral conflicts than the
electoral laws themselves.

Chapters 6 and 7 propose actor-centered explanations to substitute for
the institution-centered hypothesis disconfirmed in Chapter 5. Based on
qualitative case studies of local postelectoral bargaining, I develop ideal
types of opposition postelectoral mobilizations and describe how these
patterns of bargaining between the opposition parties and the PRI-state
actually yield different forms of electoral court failure (and postelectoral
bargaining success). Chapter 6 outlines the sixty-year evolution of the
PAN and its struggle for recognition of electoral victories. I argue that
the most significant internal division within the PAN through its first four
decades was whether to participate in electoral contests and legitimize the
authoritarian incumbents' claims of political pluralism or abstain at the
risk of stalling the party's development and role in any national opening. I develop an ideal type of PAN "defense of the vote" tactics, and
present case studies of this rightist, legalistic, and alternately patronage-
and transition-seeking party's pattern of controversial postelectoral
concertacesión agreements (Mexican slang term combining "agreement"
and "concession") with the PRI-state. The central thesis is that the PAN
successfully linked favorable postelectoral dispute resolution to cooperation with the PRI at the national level, benefiting both parties in the short
term, but damaging the PRI's long-term credibility.

Chapter 7 contrasts the PAN's strategy with that of the PRD. Unlike the national PAN's disciplined, hierarchical, and orderly protests
of electoral fraud and concrete goal-oriented bargaining with the PRI-
state, the PRD was decentralized, disorganized, and divided between
the "party" activists and the "movement" side. Rather than harnessing
legal expertise and mobilizing largely as a complement to filing postelectoral complaints, the PRD, frequently led by local activists rather
than by the national directorate, pursued extra-legal solutions over legal ones and was frequently repressed by the PRI-state, which usually refused to negotiate with the PRD until 1995. Like Chapter 6,
this chapter is structured as a longitudinal discussion of the party's
short post-1988 existence, followed by case studies in PRD-PRI postelectoral conflict resolution (dubbed the "*segunda vuelta*" or "second time
around" for the party's propensity for pressuring the party-state by staging
governability-challenging postelectoral mobilizations after losing decisively at the ballot box).

Chapter 8 addresses the PRI-state's reaction to competition from the PAN and the PRD, identifies schisms in the ruling party between local activists and national leaders, and explains how these splits were amplified through national party leadership concessions to the opposition at the expense of local activists who strove to win competitive elections after more than a half century of uncontested rule. The chapter also examines the split between the PRI and the government, exemplified by the channeling of local postelectoral conflicts through a national appeals electoral court of proven autonomy, which has ruled against the PRI in several critical cases since 2000.

In Chapter 9 I conclude that electoral opening in Mexico has been mostly successful and suggest implications for democratization theory of protracted transitions, a previously unexplored category of political liberalization. I describe the rupture between the PRI and the government apparatus and both actors' adjustments to the new reality of electoral competition and transparent institutions. However, the unevenness of democratization and the continuance of local enclaves of authoritarianism are also mentioned as a caveat that electoral administration must be resolved nationwide before electoral fraud is supplanted by more immediate public-policy priorities. I close my specific reference to the Mexican case by reinforcing the novelty of my approach to assessing judicial institution failure and suggest that this method (comparisons against a status quo "working court" baseline) may be useful in other instances of judicial decision making under uncertainty.

Having "cut" the question of institutional development in regime transitions into component smaller parts, and particularly into assessments of electoral institutions at the federal and local levels and into valuations of opposition party strategies, I conclude Chapter 9 by reconstructing general lessons from the contrast between electoral court failures and the success of parallel but informal institutions of postelectoral bargaining. The generalizable conclusion is a call to temper the agency ascribed to formal or "imposed" institutions as causes of political change, at least during moments of regime transition.

RESEARCH DESIGN: CASE SELECTION AND METHODS

Among protracted transitions from electoral authoritarian regimes – enumerated in Chapter 2 – Mexico is uniquely suited for studying the convergence of state-opposition relations around electoral institutions for several reasons. First, it was governed by the longest-reigning (and arguably the most effective) electoral authoritarian regime in the world, with the PRI controlling governance for seventy-one years before the watershed July 2000 alternation. Second, it has featured both "loyal" coalition parties and "antiregime" blackmail potential opposition parties (Sartori 1976, 123–4), a tribute to the success of the PRI's strategy of dividing the opposition and to the perseverance of the antiregime (at least from 1989–95) PRD and the regime-loyal PAN. Third, it is characterized by great regional variations in levels of electoral competition, administrative efficiency, and social and economic welfare and hence allows for meaningful comparisons within one country. Fourth, with the possible exception of Brazil, Mexico has experienced more thorough federal electoral reforms (five over the last decade) than other members of its protracted transition cohort. This section considers how I utilize these characteristics of the Mexican case to construct general hypotheses of state-opposition bargaining over electoral institutions tested in Chapter 5 by assessing performance of electoral institutions in recent local elections in ten of Mexico's thirty-one states. The twofold research design submits my hypotheses to three chapters of qualitative case studies of the same dependent variable after the statistical tests in Chapter 5.

In summary, the empirical puzzle of this work is to explain how, at least during the early years of Mexico's transition, formal institutions created to adjudicate postelectoral disputes failed so miserably (at least in resolving postelectoral conflicts), while informal institutions established for the same purpose fared so well. In more general terms, the question is what causes institutions to succeed, or from the actors' perspective, what prompts their compliance with some institutions but not with others?

Sticklers for formal evidence of institutional inefficiency might seek, instead of measuring behavioral compliance by actors external to the institutions, to more directly measure institutional performance. In other words, they would seek a means of directly measuring the institutional "slack" available, or with reference to the specific institutions under consideration, the quantity of electoral fraud committed even under Mexico's reformed electoral system. While direct evidence of electoral fraud is cited throughout this work, it is easier to cite isolated incidents of fraud than to aggregate them into any coherent measure of its effects on final vote tallies. Suspicious electoral trends (such as a 100 percent PRI vote in districts where there are three candidates), blatant incidents of crooked election-day ballot tallying or, to use a less charged term, "irregularities" such as the stuffing of ballot boxes or campaign spending at fifty times

legal limits, are analyzed, and testimonials from participants in negotiations to subvert electoral results to prenegotiated outcomes are cited.
However, as also found by other researchers seeking to quantify electoral
fraud (Choe 1997, Lehoucq 1997, Sadek 1995), it is easy to suspect, and
difficult to prove. One solution, the one undertaken here, is to accept that
institutional failure may be measured by a less direct but more accurate
indicator – actor compliance with the institutions. The result may be less
microanalytically rigorous than a hypothetical direct measure of institutional inefficiency (in the form of electoral fraud), but it is a much more
tractable research strategy.

Using this particular definition of electoral institution failure, I briefly
summarize the trade-offs in case selection, answering these questions;
Why study preliberalization electoral authoritarianism? Why the electoral institution issue area? Why comparisons within one country? Why
should that country be Mexico? The gap between theories about institutional origins (i.e., institutions as dependent variable) and institutional
production (i.e., institutions as independent variable) is attributable, at
least partly, to a shortage of cases in which stages of institutional origins
and institutional evolution are clearly differentiated. The key to distinguishing between these phases of an institution's evolution is observation over a sufficiently long period. The accelerated and even discon-
tinuous change associated with pacted democratization processes is not
conducive to discerning more subtle changes in an institution's development. However, consideration of the ontologically prior conceptual moment, when predemocratization changes within the authoritarian regime
redirected institutional development prior to the authoritarians' demise,
does allow identification of discrete changes in the course of institutional
development.

Considering a cross section of authoritarian regimes renders the conclusion that lines of delegation in such regimes are not transparent. Those authoritarian regimes that do allow opposition parties a degree of electoral
expression are the ones offering greater external indicators of the ruling
coalition's composition and its reaction to the opposition. As elaborated
in the next chapter, the Lamounier (1984) "opening through elections"
typology describes the importance of electoral authoritarianism further
down the path toward democratization.[11] It is the "setting up" of the

---

[11] Inspired by the Brazilian opening (1974–88), this label covers cases in which the opposition surprises the authoritarian incumbent through electoral performance exceeding
expectations. The opposition leverages popular support into legal demands on the setting

surprise opposition strength, that is, the opposition-induced leveling of
the playing field, which allows the opposition to extricate the electoral
apparatus from the authoritarian incumbents' control. This process tran-
spires behind the curtain before democracy's opening act, and is thus not
visible to observers focusing instead on democratization's debut. Indeed,
it is at this precurtain moment of incumbent-opposition bargaining that
the opposition tries to "hijack" the state-created electoral institutions,
while the authoritarian state seeks to mediate within its ruling coalition
between soft-liner proponents of slow liberalization at the national level
and hard-liner machine bosses seeking to retreat back to authoritarian
practices more favorable to their particular political domains.

The most logical unit of analysis of pretransition bargaining, then, is
electoral institutions, which are among the more transparent institutions
in electoral authoritarian regimes, as information about their evolution
must by definition be available to opposition parties. Electoral institutions
are frequently the major legal arena of power struggles in the opening of
such regimes, and preliberalization opposition gains can lead to regime-
toppling changes in power configurations. In cases where opposition gains
in electoral institution configuration *do not* lead to full-blown pacted democratization, it is worth noting how the incumbent authoritarians manage to recapture the institutions, or at least guide them away from unfa-
vorable liberalization, and how long the regime can endure the political
and social strain of the authoritarians' reigning in of liberalization.

Within the set of electoral institutions, electoral courts are a worthy
focus in the Mexican case, as opposition party decisions to use them represent their last opportunity in the electoral contestation cycle to undermine
the entire process. From the perspective of opposition party strategy, using
the electoral courts to resolve *ex post* electoral conflicts is tantamount to
accepting the regime's decisions leading up to that moment. More than a
decision about whether to use the electoral court, it is a strategic decision
about whether to accept the entire bundle of procedures and outcomes
the election represents. A decision to appeal to the electoral courts implies tacit acceptance of their credibility (although it is tempered if the

of government policy (such as participation in electoral administration). The authoritarians responded in Brazil through the imposition of "*cassuismos*" (arbitrary electoral laws
limiting opposition access to power), even though this partial reversion of political opening came too late for the authoritarians to stop the momentum of democratization. When
the electoral snowball had started rolling, the authoritarians tried to control the opening through a "calculus of decompression," and at this point, the Brazilian case became
exemplary of the tightly controlled "opening from above" (Lamounier 1989, 51–69).

opposition party rejects the court's verdict and subsequently tries to discredit the institution to bolster its own position through extralegal mobilization). Rejecting the electoral court and/or the electoral process outright forces the opposition to adopt antiregime behavior without even recurring to legal paths of contestation. Given my research design, compliance with the electoral courts (i.e., the channeling of all complaints through them without recurring to mobilization) will be the null hypothesis for actor noncompliance with the rule of law. Hence the resort to political mobilizations instead of or in addition to the use of electoral courts is the dependent variable.

While studying electoral justice in Mexico has until now been the purview of lawyers rather than social scientists, electoral court performance has been addressed for other countries by political scientists. In Brazil, the electoral court was said to have played a critical role in guaranteeing the authoritarian incumbents' credible commitment to electoral opening (Sadek 1995, 41). In Costa Rica, the construction of electoral courts similarly constrained authoritarian incumbents, averting postelectoral conflicts that nearly escalated to all-out civil war (Lehoucq 1995, 29). While qualifying postelectoral conflicts as a regular feature of electoral authoritarian regimes, Choe (1997, 228) notes in his study of South Korea and the long-standing democracies of Sweden and Great Britain that even in the latter that without routinized judicial proceedings and full execution of verdicts, "the legitimacy and trustworthiness of the election itself can be called into serious question." Furthermore, in notorious cases of authoritarian efforts to disregard contrary electoral outcomes (e.g., Panama 1989) it is only after they deplete legal procedures that the intentions of democracy's opponents are stripped bare.[12] These cases illustrate the specific importance of electoral courts, the principal unit of analysis of this work, but do not rule out comparisons to other electoral institutions.

The "comparisons within one country" research design is viable where variance exists in the dependent variable even inside one national unit. The advantage of this design is that it permits researchers to control for

---

[12] Indeed, it was at the moment that the Panamanian Electoral Tribunal was asked to adjudicate General Manuel Noriega's fraud on behalf of his candidate that domestic and international observers denounced the sham elections. The tribunal, accused of direct complicity with Noriega, annulled the election (National Democratic Institute 1989, 116). Postelectoral mobilizations in this case were fortified by resounding international support, prompting Organization of American States (OAS) intervention and the eventual withdrawal of Noriega's cronies from power, but only after extensive bargaining.

variables constant within that unit, ranging from cultural legacies to positions within the international economy. The drawback is that this methodology often cannot provide sufficient observations for statistical significance. However, in the Mexican case, considering longitudinal as well as cross-sectional comparisons of electoral institutions at the sub-national level allows sufficient variance to achieve statistical significance (Chapter 5).

The ordering of authoritarian preferences follows a logic consistent with Roeder's (1993) observation that even in authoritarian regimes, constituencies can be specified, and Knight's (1992) insight that institution building as a problem of distributing "raw" power. However, unlike most efforts to specify the preferences of authoritarian incumbents in electoral authoritarian regimes (such as in Hermet et al. 1978, Lamounier 1989, Liu 1991), I model authoritarian "precurtain" decisions to hold elections and modify electoral institutions as the result both of shifts in support within the authoritarian's internal coalition and of pressure by actors outside this authoritarian coalition. Unlike most previous studies, I emphasize opposition-authoritarian bargaining and the electoral arena, arguing in Chapter 2 that this is a defining characteristic of protracted transitions.

BEYOND "THE OPPOSITION" AS UNITARY ACTORS: PARTIES, MOVEMENTS, AND PARTY-MOVEMENTS

For most Third Wave transitions, particularly those where regimes toppled decisively and were replaced with comparable drama, bargaining between state and opposition political parties was a secondary mechanism. However, in the Third Wave's backwaters, where transitions are protracted and authoritarians unsinkable, incremental bargaining is the path of choice for patient and persistent opposition parties. But it is in such cases where the paradoxes of "permanent oppositions" become highly evident. Party leaders must constantly face the trade-off between short-term particularistic gains (government sinecures) to placate supporters with spoils, and long-term public goods (a democratic rule of law). Indeed, based on a party's level of ideological commitment (public-good seeking) and immediate willingness to collude with the authoritarian incumbents (private-good seeking) three types of opposition parties may be considered in slow-liberalizing authoritarian regimes:

1. *Transition seeking*: Parties willing to legitimize the system by participating in institutions agreed upon by the authoritarians, but only to the end of reforming them from within.

2. *Patronage seeking*: Opposition parties willing to play by authoritarian rules, with the eventual but distant objective of liberalizing the electoral system, in the meantime obtaining offices, public financing, and other resources in exchange for loyally "fronting" opposition candidates to make the regime look competitive.
3. *Antiregime*: Hard-line opposition that refuses to even participate in authoritarian institutions and seeks instead to undermine them, usually through protest mobilizations.

Several caveats are in order about accepting such broad generalizations.[13] First of all, unlike multiparty power-sharing systems, where interparty parliamentary coalitions give even small parties tremendous policy-making power at strategic moments, the authoritarian incumbents are the only source of patronage and grant it sparingly only to loyal (i.e., lapdog) oppositions. Second, unlike democracies, there is no voter accountability, no one to throw the rascals out. As long as the authoritarian incumbents stay in power, there are no other providers of public-sector resources or jobs. Hence, whether or not to deal with the authoritarians is the decisive cleavage in *all* opposition parties/movements. Rather than being only a function of pacting within the authoritarian alliance, democratization is also very much a result of opposition intransigence vis-à-vis the incumbent and a result of opposition internal unity. Authoritarian failure to selectively co-opt or repress opposition prompts decisive regime topplings and pacted transitions. When the authoritarians manage to co-opt or repress at least part of the regime opposition, thereby weakening the forces arrayed against them, they tend to perpetuate their reigns for decades.

Patronage-seeking, antiregime, and transition-seeking parties have different incentives for compliance with a rule of law, whether imposed by the regime or arrived at through iterated bargaining between state and opposition. In the Mexican case, the PAN is not a pure patronage seeker, and the PRD is not a pure antiregime party, but for the sake of argument, let us assume such purity of preferences. The optimal resolution for the regime, and indeed the resolution adopted in the Mexican case,

[13] These characterizations are less true since the mid-1990s. A national leadership change in the PRD toward a more pragmatic position and a new electoral competitiveness (especially in Mexico City, where the PRD won the most important governorship ever disputed in July 1997) prompted greater PRD cooperation. The PAN, which had a tacit pact of cooperation during Carlos Salinas's presidential administration (1988–94) has not benefited as directly from its coalition with the PRI-regime on legislative matters since then.

is to divide and conquer the opposition. Electoral institution reforms are a prime source of patronage the regime can use to entice an opponent it seeks to co-opt. Of course, complications arise if the patronage-seeking party continues to grow under the regime's tutelage, demanding more and more concessions and receiving at least some of them, until the patronage seeker has become strong enough to convert itself into a transition seeker with higher probabilities of success (partially applicable to the Mexican case). Why continue to receive pittance patronage, when opposition party leaders can actually have a chance to win it all?

The scarcity of rewards available to opposition parties/movements in protracted transitions force regime opponents to deal with authoritarian incumbents. Regime opponents either accept low payoffs with high probabilities in the form of the concentrated patronage the incumbents offer in exchange for reforming themselves into lapdog oppositions, or they reject authoritarians' offers and "go it alone" offering high payoffs with very low probabilities (in the event that they actually overthrow the incumbents). In the short term (as long as the authoritarian incumbents continue in power), the transition seekers' offerings to group members are incentives discussed by the movements literature: the forging of collective identities and the framing of causes through appeals to unconventional and extrainstitutional collective action, often including violence.

The antiregime party/movement, the repressed PRD in the Mexican case, is smaller and more desperate, although it too may be co-opted as a patronage seeker if repression becomes too costly for the regime, such as in the face of extensive international scrutiny about domestic democratization. The most genuine threat to authoritarian control of political opening is an opposition coalition, which may be prevented by a wily regime that plays oppositions against each other. This may be particularly effective, as in the Mexican case, if there exists formidable dispersion of potentially antiregime critics along the policy spectrum on both sides of the authoritarian incumbent's policy position. When the array of opposition forces is highly disproportionate, and/or the authoritarian incumbents commit such atrocious acts that patronage seekers become transition seekers or even antiregime actors (the Philippines 1986, Argentina 1983, Romania 1990), then the regime's perpetuation in power becomes dubious, and democratization may begin, either as a quick pact or as a protracted series of bargaining agreements over power configurations of microinstitutions, including those governing elections.

When such authoritarian-provoked atrocities do not occur, at least not of a magnitude adding momentum to opposition parties' contestation, transitions may be quite extended but require the consent of opposition parties (inasmuch as these parties decide to participate in the electoral transition by fielding candidates and promoting the vote). Opposition participation in the face of a tilted playing field and imminent loss requires intense preferences on the part of the opposition (either to receive side payments from the regime or to democratize the nation) and a minimum of organizational structure to make its declarations credible.

In summary, three essential conditions differentiate protracted transitions from other transitions to democracy. First, the authoritarian incumbents must tolerate elections, however stilted the playing field initially, at regular intervals and at most levels of government. Second, a policy space dispersion must exist in which a "catchall" authoritarian incumbent party occupies the center, flanked on both the right and left by opposition parties (whether patronage-seeking or transition-seeking or antisystem) with sufficient differences in platforms and strategies so that there is little chance they will unite, as such a coalition could transform a protracted transition into united opposition pacted transition. Third, an established pattern of patron-client relations must exist by which the authoritarian incumbent rewards followers both inside its ranks (career ladders based on loyalty more than on other factors such as merit) and in the opposition (co-optation). For the Mexican case, Chapter 8 affirms that the PRI-state continued to base rewards and punishments on clientalist incentives even after there was no patronage left to distribute.

FITTING INFORMAL MICROINSTITUTIONS INTO FORMAL AND MACROLEVEL PROCESSES

Contrary to standard elite-driven models of pacted transitions, I propose, in the following chapters, to reorient the debate over democratization, at least in protracted transitions, as an extended bargaining process between party-state and opposition. Within the democratization literature context, I seek to more carefully consider informal "new institutions" in fixed contexts as the arena of these negotiations. The severe conflicts between the coercive authoritarian state and its political enemies often turned violent, resulting in more than 150 slayings of PRD activists over the last decade. However, even the most oppressed of these dissenters acted within expectations about a set of available choices and a range of possible consequences. The difficulty for actors and their observers alike is in reconciling informal expectations with formal rules set out in electoral codes and electoral court case law. The convergence of informal practices with formal procedures required nothing less than the creation of a neutral arbiter by the very authoritarian incumbents standing to lose from its dictates.

Beyond merely broadening opposition strategy choice sets, these informal practices – generations old – established norms of compliance, at least for the decentralized PRD and its predecessor leftist parties whose activists mobilized the discontented in numbers sufficient to force the regime into postelectoral bargaining, rather than having to hire attorneys, document irregularities, and take offenders to court. As long as the PRI-state tolerated these "default" informal practices, local PRD activists, by far the worst perpetrators of postelectoral conflicts, substituted assessments of the vote share they felt they deserved for vote tallies they did not trust, or at least could credibly argue that they did not trust. Local PRD activists did make strategic choices, rather than just rebelling spontaneously. However, unlike the centralized PAN, the PRD's decentralized chapters based calculations on local, rather than national, political contexts.

In conclusion, the story to be told is one of the separation of an independent third-party arbiter from a one-party state. The task was onerous but possible, at least at the national level, as I demonstrate in Chapters 2 and 3. Courting democracy was doomed as long as institutional failures were routine and expected. But when working electoral courts increasingly replaced these failures, to the point that "wolf-crying" claims of electoral fraud were no longer credible, "free and fair elections" ceased to be an obstacle to democratization. Unlike the "partial insulation" constructed by authoritarians in other issue areas, such as central bank autonomy (Boylan 2001, 5), the authoritarian incumbents, buckling to international pressure as well as demands from domestic constituencies, did construct "fully insulated" or autonomous federal electoral institutions, which they never expected would be used. As intractable local conflicts reverberated upward to national negotiating tables, and as the politically savvy and increasingly vital PAN extracted costs for joining coalitions with the PRI, the authoritarians faced increasing constraints on choice. The PAN called their window-dressing electoral institution "bluff." Either the PRI-state would have to take its chances by adhering to decisions by autonomous electoral commissions and courts and at least receive the comfort of a like-minded and often patronage-seeking coalition partner on economic policy, or they would have to go it alone and risk losing to the most antiregime tendencies of the PRD. The PRI consciously chose the former in 1989, and the choice was questioned by a few far-sighted partisans even three years before the 2000 electoral watershed.

While the PRI-state in its heyday tightly regulated the rise and fall of *PRIísta* factions in the states, this discipline did start to fall apart at the subnational level due to structural factors as well as to contingencies of choice. Structurally, the patronage routinely available to reinforce the loyalty of regional machine bosses diminished with the economic crisis and state-shrinking neo-liberalism of the 1980s. Subnational authoritarian throwbacks persisted even after the federal alternation of power in 2000, and as seen in Chapters 4 and 8. They even thrived under the tutelage of so-called PRI "dinosaur" governors – machine bosses who refused to accept multiparty competition. These local bosses' ultimately unsuccessful attempts to manipulate electoral courts, which started as devious in the 1990s and grew desperate after 2000, are extensively chronicled. But I now consider these institutions at the federal level, where electoral justice has become much more than an oxymoron. At the federal level, the costs of adjudicating postelectoral disputes have been externalized to a third party, the PRI-extricated state, despite the deep-seated and often visceral nature of Mexico's postelectoral conflicts. The next two chapters, at least, tell a success story.[14]

---

[14] Sartori (1976) has distinguished between regime-tolerant *loyal opposition* parties and *systemic opposition* parties, which advocate a change in regimes. This distinction, like that between *transition-* and *patronage-seeking* parties, is based on relations of opposition with the incumbents. The difference is that Sartori's definition refers to relations over policy making in consolidated party systems (such as parliamentary democracies). He explains the interest of fringe parties in consistently opposing the dominant legislative coalition. Consistent with Sartori, one can imagine that if a party is small and powerless enough, it would have little to lose from constantly antagonizing the regime, while it would gain extensive publicity and exclusive dominion of its extreme space on the policy spectrum. Systemic oppositions in unconsolidated party systems are placing their bets on regime transition, as the available alternatives are not conducive to the long-term continuance of these opposition parties/movements. In these cases, Machiavellian authoritarians must co-opt some regime opponents and repress the rest in order to deactivate potential challenges, particularly in authoritarian regimes with legitimizing elections (Hermet et al. 1978, Lamounier 1984). From the authoritarian's perspective, once a sizable segment of the transition-seeking opposition (i.e., one important party) has been given the "carrot," it is unlikely that the regime will pay the considerable costs of co-opting another segment of that opposition. Rather, the rest of the opposition will likely get the repressive "stick," as it is materially cheaper and more consistent with authoritarian strategies for dividing and conquering opponents.

2

Ties That Bind and Even Constrict:
Why Authoritarians Tolerate Electoral Reforms

> ...but you must bind me hard and fast,
> so that I cannot stir from the spot where you will stand me...
> and if I beg you to release me, you must tighten and add to my bonds.
>> Ulysses on how to restrain his reaction to the sirens' song in
>> *The Odyssey*[1]

The underdog National Action Party (PAN) unseated Mexico's long-reigning authoritarian incumbents in the 2000 presidential election, but only after preparing decades for the race. The electoral demise of the Party of the Institutional Revolution (PRI) after seventy-one years, ending the longest period of one-party rule in the world, was actually the culmination of a protracted transition to democracy spanning at least twenty-three years. Especially over the last decade, the PAN pushed the authoritarian incumbents to make Mexican elections credible, begging the question of why authoritarians would permit electoral reforms that reduced their capacity for rigging elections, introduced genuine uncertainty into electoral contests, and ultimately, led to the PAN's presidential victory in July 2000.

Clearly, authoritarian incumbents have little interest in political liberalization and undertake such policies only when they perceive that they have little other choice to channel social movement opposition into political parties (such as the Brazilian military dictatorship's consciously taken "decompression" starting in the mid-1970s), gather information about regime and opposition support under rapidly changing circumstances (such as the Polish elections of 1990), mollify international critics (such

---

[1] Cited in Elster (1990, 36).

32

as the People's Republic of China in the 1990s), or use the electoral arena as a means to manipulate the opposition (as in Mexico and Taiwan in the early 1990s and South Korea in the early 1980s). This chapter considers how authoritarian elites can bind themselves right out of power while trying to channel opposition parties/movements on both the right and the left, check their enemies within the authoritarian elite, and placate international opinion.

Miscalculation is said to be the means through which mere "decompression" from above evolves into full-blown democratization. Indeed, only gross miscalculation would allow authoritarians to conduct mostly fair elections in countries like Panama in 1989 and Burma in 1990, only to refuse to transfer power to opposition victors. Authoritarian leaders· such as Chile's Augusto Pinochet, Poland's Weijciech Jaruzelski, and the Philippines' Ferdinand Marcos did not seem to fully comprehend the "hand-binding" implications of inviting international election monitors. Rather, they allowed such observers largely because they perceived absolutely no chance of losing. How could they be so wrong?[2]

However, "sheer miscalculation" overemphasizes the role of elections at the expense of social and political context building before the actual elections. Furthermore, dismissing these rulers' acceptance of elections as simple miscalculations underestimates not only the craftiness of many authoritarian incumbents, but also the roles of the opposition. Wily opposition leaders seize upon slight weaknesses in the authoritarians' credibility and widen them into gaping vulnerabilities using the authoritarians' laws against them. They further complement institutional assaults with extralegal organizing and mobilization, requiring every bit of "calculation, wisdom, courage, imagination, and vision" that Liu (1991) attributes to the rational authoritarian incumbents carefully "selecting the optimal degree of decompression during transition" (56).

Like his fellow analysts of democratization, Liu (1991) correctly distinguishes protracted transitions from the O'Donnell-Schmitter (1986) pacted cases, but his emphasis entirely on the agency of the authoritarian incumbent in causing the transition is at least partially overstated. To begin with, the "optimal degree of decompression" to the authoritarian incumbent is none. Authoritarians only decide to liberalize because of perceived threats. And where those threats are external (such as war or drastic geo-political change, such as implied by *glastnost*) or economic (such

---

[2] For a discussion of the dilemmas of authoritarians in protracted transitions, see also Eisenstadt (2000).

as severe depression), the authoritarians have no time for incremental responses and decompression. As the Argentine, Bolivian, Romanian, Peruvian,[3] Philippine, and East German cases illustrate most vividly, external and/or economic threats tended to prompt decisive ruptures with the past, rather than gradual, top-down changes (Haggard and Kaufman 1995, 45–68).[4] Where such drastic occurrences do not intervene, protracted transitions can be a war of attrition between the regime's ability to placate the opposition with short-term co-optation and the opposition's ability to cut short-term deals with the regime to ensure their survival while maintaining focus on the long-term objective of regime change.

Assessing the background of these short-term deals – Mexico's five transition-era electoral reforms and scores of postelectoral *concertacesiones* – requires seeking the causes of authoritarian hand binding in perceived benefits relating to the "three constituencies": domestic regime opposition, intraauthoritarian elite adversaries, and international critics. In an analysis based on PRI-state relations with these interest groups, I introduce brief case studies of the 1977, 1986, 1990, 1993–4, and 1996 reforms with a nutshell history of state-opposition relations, to be amplified at length in the chapters to follow. Upon establishing the agency of interest groups and political parties in prompting national-level electoral reforms in Mexico, I address a contrary argument common in the literature on Mexico's protracted transition, that structural economic change, rather than the agency of individual actors, caused electoral opening. In a preliminary assessment confirmed through statistical analysis in Chapter 5, I argue that the economic crisis did create conditions propitious to the electoral rebellion starting in the early 1980s. However, these structural conditions alone could not determine the direction of change; rather, individual agency in the form of opposition activist strategies determined how the economic crisis shaped electoral outcomes. Finally, I establish a mechanism of courting democracy in Mexico – emerging in the mid-1980s and enduring to the mid-1990s – as bargaining between the national PRI-state and the national representatives of local PAN strongholds over whether to accept strong PAN electoral outcomes.

I conclude with a discussion of the clinching argument of why authoritarians liberalize. The process of transition was certainly reversible

---

[3] While Peru appeared to be back on a democratic track after 2001, the case may warrant reconsideration after Fujimori's apparent stealing of the 2000 presidential election there.

[4] It should be clarified that authoritarian withdrawals only occurred during economic crises in one subset of Haggard and Kaufman's (1995) cases.

at least through the late 1980s or early 1990s, except that the techno-cratic *PRIístas* setting executive-branch policy vastly underestimated the control their traditionalist colleagues exercised over the party. Hence, the technocratic *PRIístas* modernized the rules of campaigning, expecting to continue to win through their tremendous advantages, but even while sacrificing local elections to ideologically kindred *PANístas* in cases where national legislative alliances were needed (increasingly after 1988). As demonstrated extensively in Chapter 8, the PRI-state's regional machine bosses wanted nothing to do with grueling electoral competition, nor with *concertacesiones,* no matter how noble the economic cause championed by technocrats in Mexico City.

Aside from the few local luminaries whose candidates made it big na-tionally, the mid-level machine bosses' career advancement was based on getting out the PRI vote. Especially during the presidencies of Salinas and Ernesto Zedillo (1994–2000), the national PRI's willingness to sacrifice local machines in favor of locally unpopular (but nationally sustainable) policies of economic opening to placate the PAN and ensure that party's cooperation divided the policy maximizers in Mexico City and the vote maximizers in the regions. As the "magnanimous" national PRI leader-ship in the federal executive branch "threw" local races to the PAN, that party constructed administrative records and electoral competitiveness, to the point that they no longer needed the PRI-state's charitable discretion. Local PRI activists grew increasingly disdainful of the national PRI-state, which in fact split over this issue. The PRI consisted of vote-maximizing regional bosses and their national sympathizers, who recognized the threat of strong, ambitious, and politically starved PAN candidates encroaching on their vote margins while simultaneously forcing reforms of the electoral playing field. Divorced from the party, the state, headed by the national executive, steered economically to the right in a bid to recruit interna-tional investment and promote Mexican exports, implementing policies diametrically opposed to those of the original PRI-state's "revolutionary family," which had always banked on clientelism and leftist populism. Hence, by the late 1990s, when the national PRI finally considered insti-tuting gubernatorial and mayoral primaries to improve candidate quality, the party's legendary internal discipline had already broken down.

WHY LIBERALIZE? THE LOGIC OF AUTHORITARIAN HAND BINDING

Authoritarian incumbents stand to gain several benefits in relations with regime opponents by permitting electoral reforms. First, the authoritarian incumbent can, through multiple iterations of graduated reforms, acquire information about incumbent and opposition popularity across segments of the population. In regimes where elections cannot be "referenda" on a president's policies, leaders may want to routinely meet with the corporatist bases or open up less-risky electoral contests (local elections, legislative branch races, etc.) to create a "sounding board" representative of public opinion. These authoritarian-constituent interactions may take the form of intensive "give and take" bargaining sessions (the Hungarian and Polish round-table talks), or, more likely, the constant reform of electoral laws (in Brazil and Mexico) or the gradual opening of new offices to direct election (in South Korea and Taiwan).

Second, the authoritarian incumbent may divide and conquer the opposition through such reforms. This may be accomplished by supporting artificial "window dressing" opposition parties, such as Taiwan's China Youth Party and Social Democratic Party or Mexico's parties of the "parastatal" left,[5] or it may be achieved by leveraging opposition parties against each other, as Roh Tae Woo did so effectively in South Korea in the late 1980s, helping split the "three Kims" into separate opposition parties, which enabled the liberalizing military dictatorship to win the 1988 direct election for president without anywhere close to a majority of the votes, and then fusing two of these opposition parties into his coalition when he passed power on in 1992. Similarly, the greatest single failure of the Brazilian political liberalization was to limit the opposition to one regime-constructed party, the MDB (Brazilian Democratic Movement) party, which, as a "catchall" opposition of the right and the left, forced each election from 1973 until 1985 to assume the form of a bivariate choice by voters – a referendum on the military dictatorship that the incumbent authoritarians could not win (Lamounier 1989). For even if the authoritarian incumbents "won," their percentage of the vote would never be as high as they would like, given that the opposition received not only votes of support, but also antiincumbent votes.

Third, the channeling of opposition into the electoral arena served the authoritarian incumbent by deactivating strikers, students, and other potentially disruptive troublemakers by forcing them out of the unpredictable realm of street demonstrations and picket lines and into highly regulated campaigns and elections. Such electoral channeling also helped restore credibility to the authoritarian incumbent domestically (such as

---

[5] This term refers to parties at least partially sponsored by the regime to give the appearance of political competition.

in the cases of the Brazilian and South Korean military rulers) and internationally (such as in the "international opinion"–sensitive cases of North American Free Trade Agreement (NAFTA)–negotiating Mexico and United Nations–expelled Taiwan).

Mexico's PRI seems to have liberalized its electoral laws for these three reasons, but also for a fourth: to bind the hardliners within the authoritarian coalition. The party's technocratic leaders, especially in the 1990s, increasingly discounted political bosses' abilities to "get out the vote" as a skill valued by the party. In fact, President Salinas repeatedly undermined the traditional machine bosses by negotiating away their electoral victories at postelectoral bargaining tables with the PAN. Salinas drove a wedge into the party starting in 1989 by placing a much higher premium on getting along with the PAN in federal parliamentary chambers than on getting along with his own party's traditional vote-getting activists. He has been widely blamed for weakening the PRI to the point that *PRIístas* proposed his expulsion from the party. Zedillo continued a more moderate version of Salinas's policy, for the first time consciously divorcing himself from party affairs in his controversial pronouncement of the need for *sana distancia* or "sane distance." Even if economic managers started to hedge their bets by reforming the central bank in a manner that would keep them in power even if they lost national elections (Boylan 2001, 19–20), the PRI's electoral activists did not even begin to conceive that defeat was possible until after the 1996 electoral reforms, the very reforms giving electoral institutions the independence needed to preside unflinchingly over an eventual PRI defeat. While focusing here on the formal institution precedents for the divorce between the PRI and the Mexican state, and the demise of the PRI's electoral system between 1977 and 2000, a few introductory comments about the PRI-state's consolidation are warranted, although they are addressed more extensively in Chapter 4, as are informal institution precedents of postelectoral bargaining tables.

Most analyses of PRI-state consolidation extend back to the Mexican Revolution of 1910–17, in which hundreds of thousands of lives were lost partly over the principle of "effective suffrage and no re-election," after the dictator Porfirio Díaz had his three-decade reign renewed through elections until his enemies took up arms. Mexico's postrevolutionary elite settlement consolidated the PRI party-state by the late 1930s. The 1920s and 1930s set precedents for later regime disrespect for elections as tyrannical leaders ignored gubernatorial races and imposed subordinates to consolidate their political machines. As explored extensively in Chapter 4 with regard to consolidation of local PRI bosses under presidential control, the 1930s were particularly tumultuous, as populist general-turned-president Lázaro Cárdenas squelched political opposition and won popular support for his social programs, including extensive agrarian reform. As the PRI consolidated itself through presidentially "imposed" governors (usually – but not always – ratified through popular election), Mexico's forty-year economic boom from the 1940s to the 1980s reinforced the party's authority and ushered in the high period of PRI hegemony. Through six presidential administrations, the national PRI, having finally conquered the last bastions of postrevolutionary opposition, freely imposed its will (and its candidates) on the states.

In rebellion against Cárdenas's policies, a group of conservative lawyers and business leaders created the PAN in 1939 divided over whether the party should serve as a debating forum of symbolic opposition or as the feisty rebels who bore the brunt of political liberalization (from within the regime) for fifty years. The PAN won its first tiny mayorship in 1946 in Michoacán state and its first federal congressional representation in 1946. But, disillusioned by the PRI-state's intolerance of their strong electoral performance that year, the doctrine side dominated the activists, and from the late 1940s until the late 1970s, the genteel PAN was denied access to all but the most symbolic of positions. General assemblies during the first several decades of PAN existence were punctuated by frequent debates about whether to participate in elections (and accept losing even rigged elections), or abstain and "punish" the PRI by unmasking the regime's elections as uncompetitive shams. The 1976 presidential election was preceded by a particularly fierce internal debate, and the divided party failed to nominate a candidate. Not surprisingly, the PRI won, but not without discrediting the regime, as even unopposed, the ruling party only garnered 82 percent of the vote. In 1977, the PRI-state conducted a nonthreatening electoral reform, designed to increase the presence of the fledgling oppositions, at least to the point of making the authoritarian regime look more democratic. The outlawed communist party (that had not fielded a presidential candidate since 1934) was legalized, as were other small leftist parties, and additional proportional representation seats were created in the lower chamber of the Congress to encourage a leftist presence to counterbalance the PAN.

MINOR REFORMS, BUT CATALYSTS OF A PROTRACTED TRANSITION

In an exhaustive account of the 1977 reforms, Klesner (1988, 391) explains that the PRI realized it had to offer the opposition parties an incentive to field candidates, especially after the PAN's abandonment of the presidential election just a year earlier. The regime's public relations crisis provoked by the PAN's 1976 abstention was addressed using both positive and negative incentives. On the "carrot" side, the regime legalized outlaw leftist parties and encouraged their participation by lowering the threshold of political support needed for parties to conserve their national registries from 3 percent of the vote to 1.5 percent of the vote, and allowing them to obtain "temporary registries" before qualifying for "permanent registries." The regime gestured toward electoral fairness by tightening rules on electoral transparency and guaranteeing the safety of opposition party poll watchers (by not making leftist fugitives reveal their identities), although the federal electoral commission remained under direct Federal Interior Secretary control, and hence under PRI-state dominion. On the "stick" side, directed at the PAN, the regime implemented a law that any party not participating in a federal election would immediately lose its registry (Klesner 1988, 485).

More important than dividing and conquering opposition parties, the 1977 electoral reform was the regime's best hope for shepherding antiregime forces back into the system. It sought to channel *guerrillas* and independent worker and peasant movements, but also to institutionalize dissent against President Luís Echeverría (1970–6). Business groups had grown increasingly estranged from Echeverría's populist policies, and independent labor and peasant movements also gained footing during the early 1970s, adding to the regime's perceived imperative of co-opting these groups back into the PRI's "revolutionary family." The administration's policies of economic growth were based on international borrowing, poorly received measures to reduce tax evasion, extensive land reform (the largest redistribution since Cárdenas), and bloating an inefficient public sector through nationalizations of steel, sugar, and dozens of other industries. Big business resistance to Echeverría, particularly by Mexico's second-largest industrial complex, the maverick Monterrey Group, led to unprecedented capital flight, resistance to his taxation schemes, and at a 1973 Monterrey funeral, unprecedented public defiance.[6] These business elites did not entirely abandon the PRI-state in the 1970s (as they would in the 1980s), but their lack of enthusiasm for government policies was a grave concern to the incoming José López Portillo administration

---

[6] The funeral was for Eugenio Garza Sada, who had been assassinated by *guerrillas*, provoking 1977 electoral reforms seeking to encourage such insurgents to put down their guns in favor of legal channels of political participation.

TABLE 2.1 *Presidential Vote by Year and Party*

Year	PRI Votes	PAN Votes	Proregime Left	Authentic Left	Other	Null Votes
1976	87.8	0.0	5.7	no candidate	0.0	6.5
1982	68.4	15.7	2.6	6.7	2.0	4.6
1988	50.7	16.8	0.0	31.0	1.0	0.5
1994	48.8	25.9	3.8	17.5	0.9	3.8
2000	36.1	42.5	1.0	18.2	10.0	2.1

Sources: Molinar (1991, 45); Gómez Tagle (1997, 42); www.ife.org.mx, with classifications by author. For classification of left parties, see p. 118.

(1976–82), and one which they hoped to at least partially address through electoral reforms (Klesner 1988, 292).

The labor pillar of the PRI's corporatist power structure[7] roundly opposed the 1977 reforms that labor leaders argued would jeopardize their access to elected posts (Middlebrook 1986, 132), and their ability to recruit candidates if victories were less certain. The other most retrograde group within the PRI, the state governors and regional machine bosses, also vehemently resented what they considered the inevitable encroachment of federal reforms on politics in their zones of influence. Doctrinal purists in the PAN and in the newly legalized left also objected, anticipating the additional risk of co-optation that would undoubtedly accompany any increase in electoral spoils (Middlebrook 1986, 135).

The immediate effect of the federal reform was precisely what the PRI-state wanted. In the short term, it improved authoritarian relations with domestic opponents by yielding increased symbolic opposition participation in the federal Congress, which was a rubber stamp for presidential decrees more than a legislative body anyway, without significantly decreasing PRI votes (see Table 2.1). In legalizing leftist parties and channeling them into electoral competition (and out of *guerrilla* movements), the PRI-state placated domestic opponents. Secondarily, it controlled adversaries within the ruling elite by allowing the reformists to bring PRI regional populist/cronies into line. Also, the reform silenced critics on the

---

[7] Corporatism, as described in works on Mexico such as that by Reyna and Weinert (1977, 161), is a means of political control emphasizing mobilization of unions requiring official membership. In Mexico's "exclusionary corporatism," official mobilization was utilized by the PRI-state to replace class conflicts based on redistributive demands with innocuous populist and nationalist appeals. Exclusionary corporatism for social control contrasts markedly with Europe's inclusionary corporatist system (whereby unions were granted partnership in negotiating economic policy) as described by Schmitter (1992).

right, temporarily keeping business elites from turning to the PAN. But the effect of the 1977 reforms would look much different a decade hence, as economic crisis culled anti-PRI protest votes and weakened the party's discipline in anticipation of the sharp division that would follow in the late 1990s.

As evidenced in Table 2.1, the 1977 reforms launched an era of electoral competition that eroded the PRI's hegemony, even despite all the electoral fraud perpetrated by the ruling party during those years. López Portillo failed to restore Mexico's post–World War II double-digit economic growth despite aggressively pumping huge oil revenues into the current account. In fact, for all his visions of a petroleum-driven recovery, López Portillo led Mexico to negative gross domestic product (GDP) growth, deteriorated wages, triple-digit inflation, and the 1982 foreign-debt crisis. The Monterrey Group and other private-sector leaders did intensify their opposition when López Portillo nationalized Mexico's banks to constrain capital flight and disinvestment. The move provoked outrage by traditionally independent business peak associations – the Central Business Chamber (CCE), the Employers' Confederation of the Mexican Republic (COPARMEX), and the National Confederation of Chambers of Commerce (CONCANACO) – which shrewdly incorporated student movements and civic groups promoting democratization and neo-liberal economic policies into their protests (Escobar 1987, 84). Big business was eventually recruited back into the PRI-state's fold, but small and medium businesses, also threatened by Echeverría's and López Portillo's policies, remained uncommitted, and in fact, some even joined the PAN, where they constructed a pragmatic electoralist movement generating a powerful "bottom up" demand for more extensive reforms.

López Portillo's successor, Miguel de la Madrid (1982–8), promised "moral renovation," including the acceptance of electoral competition, and hence recognition of opposition victories. Also, as a state-level follow-up to the 1977 federal reforms, de la Madrid reformed Article 115 of the constitution in 1983, codifying municipal entitlements to federal and state tax revenues (although local taxation powers remained weak) and increasing proportional representation in local administrations to ameliorate postelectoral conflicts. However, the continuing economic downturn (exacerbated by the 1982 debt crisis and López Portillo's peso devaluation) and the introduction of more proportional representation seats for opposition parties led to increases in both electoral and postelectoral competition. De la Madrid recognized over a dozen PAN victories in the disgruntled northlands in 1983 and 1984, but drew the line in the

1986 Chihuahua governor's race, where he personally weighed in on the side of the PRI in the electoral certification of a close and controversial race.[8]

It was the PRI hard-liners who continued to oppose de la Madrid's electoral opening and ultimately forced the president to back down. To the *PRIísta* "dinosaurs," winning at any cost was the only way to ensure political survival. In fact, these operatives committed fraud even when the party won, "to be able to show absolute dominance, and also to continue the internal competition within the PRI hierarchy, within the PRI delegation in Congress, and in the sectoral organizations..." (Cornelius 1986, 135). Resistance within the official workers' unions to electoral reform and political opening also grew, as the PRI-state's corporatist union feared competition from the new leftist parties and their genuine prolabor positions, a deemphasis on "smoke-filled room" influence in favor of votes and elections, and the new importance of technocratic administrative skills (Middlebrook in Cornelius, Gentleman, and Smith, eds. 1989, 299). In short, the Chihuahua governor's race became a showdown within the PRI as well as a contest between the PAN and the PRI. While de la Madrid put his foot down in Chihuahua, he diffused criticism from moderate quarters by simultaneously launching another federal electoral reform. An electoral court of limited authority was also constructed after the federal government was embarrassed by a 1985 PAN complaint to the Organization of American States (OAS) questioning the Nuevo León electoral law's compliance with international human-rights accords after a controversial governor's race there (Ojesto 2001 interview).[9]

All told, the contents of the 1987 reform were mostly regressive. Its most important component was the notorious Chamber of Deputies governability clause ensuring the winning party (even if it won fewer than 251 seats in the 500-seat Chamber of Deputies) a majority of the

---

[8] De la Madrid (interview) clarified that he only declared the PRI's victory after the local electoral institutions had spoken.

[9] While the OAS profoundly embarrassed the Mexican government, there was little less-direct pressure on Mexico from more powerful international actors, like the United States. Mazza reports that despite perception that the United States supported the PAN's new electoral clout in Mexico's northlands, there was very little official mention of electoral fraud suspicions prior to 1986, when Senator Jesse Helms's "Mexico-bashing" hearings included unflattering references to the state of Mexican democracy (Mazza 2001, 36–46).

seats through a combination uninominal and proportional representation formula heavily skewed toward the majority party (Molinar 1991, 82–4). The electoral code also eliminated the status of "conditional party" that had been accorded to the post-1977 new parties not immediately meeting criteria for registration, and increased the Interior Secretary's direct control over the naming of even the most local electoral officials (Molinar 1991, 85–7). The only progressive element of the reform was enhancement of political parties' abilities to audit the electoral list, although the reforms did not specify how these investigations would be conducted (Molinar 1991, 86). In short, despite the initial promise, the reforms offered little to the opposition parties. They were the PRI-state's attempt to roll back 1977, and it might have worked had the PRI not needed an alliance with the PAN after 1988.

Perhaps one of the most significant elements of the 1987 electoral reforms had been to reduce the importance of the Authentic Party of the Mexican Revolution (PARM) and other so-called "parastatal" parties that had always been loyal to the PRI. Prior to the 1987 reforms, Federal Electoral Commission policy was set by a council consisting of the Secretary of the Interior (who doubled as electoral commission director), a notary public, a representative from Congress, and one representative from each of nine political parties (the PRI, the PAN, several leftist parties, a rightist party, the PARM, and the Popular Socialist Party or PPS). The PRI had to negotiate support from the parastatal parties to acquire needed majorities. The reform changed the assignation of electoral council seats, allocating them by proportional representation based on a party's vote share in the prior federal election. The change, quite regressive in terms of opposition party representation, gave the PRI its majority without even having to recruit votes.

Hence, the PARM and PPS, "cut off" from prior perks received from the PRI-state in exchange for their electoral commission votes, stood to lose their party registries unless they miraculously acquired 1.5 percent of the vote in the 1988 elections. They had nothing to lose and were thus free to throw in with Cárdenas, whom no one expected to come close to winning but who these tiny parties reasoned was certain to garner the threshold of votes needed to maintain their registries based on the legacy of Cuauhtémoc Cárdenas's father, President Lázaro Cárdenas, even if the son did not run a successful campaign. No one anticipated that the younger Cárdenas would threaten the PRI-state's hegemony, and even the regime itself, by almost managing to unite a grand coalition of opponents, when the PAN's candidate and Cárdenas briefly considered a postelectoral alliance.

THE 1988 TURNING POINT: PAN AND PRI COHABITATE THE TRANSITION

The reform of 1987 was directed against the PAN, which the PRI-state – and most of Mexico – perceived as the regime's most likely threat in 1988. No one could have predicted that the real challenge to the regime would come from the left. In fact, the little-used electoral law provision that allowed the construction of coalitions between parties, which had been on the books for decades, was used by Cárdenas to register his party with the tiny PARM and PPS, catching the PRI-state by surprise. In terms of its political survival, the PRI-state may have miscalculated by allowing Cárdenas's celebrated defection from the PRI and not repressing his emerging social movement. But the incident served notice to the authoritarian incumbents, who were still firmly in control, and ensured that they would never again underestimate the leftist threat.

Most significant for courting democracy in Mexico, Cárdenas launched months of postelectoral mobilizations that barely stopped short of violence. For a few days in July 1988, the future of the regime seemed to hang in the balance. The PRI-state's concern only deepened when the PAN's presidential candidate – the third place finisher – briefly joined forces with the runner-up Cárdenas to contest blatant irregularities. As elaborated in Chapter 6, the PAN leadership, realizing that they shared the PRI-state's fear of a genuine leftist government and willing to ally with the PRI-state to prevent such an outcome, undermined their presidential candidate's effort to support Cárdenas's probable victory.

The PRI-state failed to anticipate the election's outcome and demonstrated that it was out of touch with the electorate. Salinas, who had barely won 50 percent of the vote even by the official count, had to legitimize the institutions that had elected him. While the consummate technocrat Salinas was initially able to cushion himself from retrograde elements within his coalition, he was susceptible to opposition constituencies and international critics. The new president sought to diffuse the left's challenge by allying with the PAN against Cárdenas's PRD, and he sought to bolster Mexico's international image as a way of obtaining foreign capital inflows to restore the economic vitality that had fallen away during the "Lost Decade" of the 1980s.

A logical means of proving his democratic mettle to international critics[10] and rewarding the PAN for dissociating from the actions of its maverick candidate was through yet another electoral reform. In fact, the stage was set for such a reform by Salinas's promise to the PAN that in exchange for tacitly accepting Salinas's presidency and not endorsing Cárdenas's efforts to destabilize the federal government he would support a pro-PAN electoral reform. *PRIísta* complicity with PAN electoral reform proposals promised by Salinas was revealed by the PAN in a "letter of intent" signed by Salinas (Alemán Alemán 1989), which *PANísta* leaders then released to the public in early 1990 when the PRI congressional delegation refused to honor the president's agreement.

The most critical autonomous institution for mediating the "levelness" of the electoral playing field, the Federal Electoral Institute (IFE), was created in the 1989–90 reform. The previous institution for monitoring elections, the highly controversial Federal Electoral Commission, had been run directly by the Interior Secretary as part of the executive branch. Largely unchanged since its creation in 1946, this institution was notorious for directing elections toward expected outcomes, rather than for its accountability to voters. The Federal Electoral Tribunal (TFE) was also created in 1989 as an autonomous body capable of challenging IFE decisions. An antecedent institution, the Tribunal of Electoral Contention (TRICOEL), had been inaugurated for the 1988 federal elections, but its decisions were widely ignored and largely irrelevant. The next chapter documents how – amidst Mexico's most severe constitutional crisis in decades – the TRICOEL spent 1988 inconclusively debating the technicalities of a few lesser races without access even to the votes or electoral acts, while the PRI-state "bought" congressional certification of Salinas's dubious presidency by granting a half-dozen congressional seats in the Chamber of Deputies to candidates who had not won them.

While serious reforms to the electoral court would wait until 1994 and particularly 1996, the electoral commission was granted greater autonomy in the 1989–90 reform. The 1990 IFE was still dependent on the Interior Secretary, but less directly than before. Like its director, the policy-setting body of the IFE was selected through executive nomination. The powers of the IFE were limited, as there were no strict limits

[10] As in the early 1980s, the United States in 1988 failed to assume a critical position toward the PRI and its alleged electoral fraud. High-ranking U.S. officials strongly suspected that Cárdenas may have won but closed ranks around Salinas because they did not trust Cárdenas's anti-U.S. rhetoric and because "the one we wanted to win, won" (Mazza 2001, 54).

TABLE 2.2 *Percentage of Seats Per Party in Mexico's Lower House (Chamber of Deputies)*

Party	1976	1979	1982	1985	1988	1991	1994	1997	2000
PRI	82.5	74.0	74.8	72.3	52.0	64.0	60.2	47.8	42.2
PAN	8.5	10.8	12.8	10.3	20.2	17.8	23.8	24.2	44.6
Authentic left	0.0	7.0	7.1	9.0	27.8	3.6	14.0	25.0	13.2
Proregime left	8.9	5.8	2.5	5.6	0.0^2	5.4	2.0	1.4	0.0
Other	0.0	2.5	3.0	3.0	0.0	0.0	0.0	1.6	0.0

Sources: Craig and Cornelius (1995, 286); Gómez Tagle (1997, 67–72); IFE 1997 results; www.ife.org.mx, with classification by author, explained on p. 118.

on party finance, allowing the PRI to continue grossly outspending rivals on the traditionally stilted media coverage favoring "the house" and on deployment of bloated state bureaucracies for the PRI-state's partisan cause. Still, the legislation limited PRI overrepresentation in the lower house of the Mexican Congress, provided for a new electoral registry to minimize ballot stuffing, and created a lottery system for selecting and training poll workers (rather than allowing officials to select poll workers sympathetic to the governing party). Allegations of fraud by the PAN and the PRD were still commonplace, centered mostly on irregularities in the electoral registry, but the 1991 mid-term elections generated nothing close to the conflicts of 1988. The PRI, when combined with its parastatal left parties, recovered its absolute congressional majority by a wide margin, without any threats to process legitimacy (see Table 2.2).

During the early years of his term Salinas subordinated the regional political operatives in the PRI-state, stacking his cabinet with "apolitical" technocrats.[11] He seemed to approve of selective political opening, but only if it did not interfere with his real priority, economic liberalization. While recognizing PAN gubernatorial victories for the first time ever starting in 1989, the Salinas administration actively repressed apparent PRD victories. In the words of Centeno (1994, 227): "The message was clear to those who would listen: the government would prefer to negotiate than to repress, but it was prepared to repress in order to negotiate."

---

[11] Some 85 percent of Salinas's initial cabinet secretaries had never held elected office or worked in the PRI (Hernández 1994, 198), whereas a quarter of de la Madrid's cabinet ministers had been active in party politics, which was a drop-off from the 1970s, when at least half the president's ministers entered the cabinet with a substantial record of party activism (Centeno 1994, 139).

Democratization was seen, at least by the reformers among the Salinas inner circle, as a necessary step. However, the president also seemed to view political opening as at best an inconvenience and as at worst an obstacle to enacting economic reforms, which required the kind of strong, centralized leadership that had characterized authoritarian postrevolutionary Mexico.

The voice of international critics also grew increasingly raucous, as the mostly United States–educated Salinas cabinet was acutely attuned to international opinion and desperately sought foreign capital to revitalize Mexico's economy. The late 1980s had not been generous to Mexico's image in the United States. As drug trafficking and corruption scandals in Mexico precipitated unflattering depictions of Mexican politics in U.S. congressional hearings, the U.S. press started to openly decry Mexico's rigged elections, and U.S. officials began favoring the PAN in local elections. While the Reagan and Bush administrations had given Salinas a "bye" on election fraud in 1988, the United States–based international press began, with the Mexico State elections of 1990, to report election irregularities as a main theme of Mexico coverage during the early 1990s (Mazza 2001, 74). Despite international pressures for democratization, which would only increase in the years ahead, the real impetus for the 1990 reforms came from Salinas's need to legitimize electoral institutions, rather than any actual outside pressures. By Salinas's second electoral reforms, in 1993 and 1994, international critics had begun to advocate more directly by funneling money and influence to growing Mexican electoral observation organizations, which, in tandem with international critics, clamored to hold the regime accountable.

Negotiation of NAFTA between 1990 and 1993 might have been an opportunity for the U.S. government and interest groups to assert leverage in Mexico's political opening. However, it was an opportunity not taken, as Bush negotiators lauded Mexico's stability and insisted that imposing "political conditions would be counterproductive, a red flag..." (Mazza 2001, 75). Criticism of Mexico in U.S. circles did arise by 1991, but mostly in relation to lax regulation of environmental problems and worker rights. Salinas acted preemptively to placate the international media before they could jeopardize NAFTA, which was emerging as the centerpiece of Salinas's economic policies. In an unusually transparent bid to curry positive publicity, Salinas "removed" two governors in the *concertacesiones* of Guanajuato and San Luis Potosí in 1991, but only after meeting with foreign press representatives to tell them what was about to happen (Mazza 2001, 84). While such grand gestures deferred international inquiries into Mexican democratization, the 1993 final debate over NAFTA approval, and the early 1994 eruption of armed insurrection in Chiapas, did bring out open discussion of Mexico's democracy deficit (Mazza 2001, 98–105).

With stepped up international scrutiny and increasingly demanding internal critics, Salinas sponsored the 1993 and 1994 electoral reforms, implemented at the height of PAN-PRI cooperation. The reforms, implemented for the 1994 presidential election, extended the autonomy and jurisdiction of the IFE, further scaled back PRI overrepresentation – this time in both houses of the national Congress – and codified a role for electoral observers. No longer nominated by the president, the IFE's policy-making body was now composed of representatives from the political parties, the legislative branch, and nonpartisan citizen "ombudsmen" nominated and approved by the Congress. Exorbitant albeit concrete limits were placed on party campaign spending and election-related media coverage, and electoral registry reforms continued with the introduction of a voter photo-ID card. The TFE was granted broader discretion in identifying and proving the existence of election fraud, and the Electoral College created to certify federal elections was eliminated in all but the presidential race. The 1994 electoral process was deemed transparent by most observers, despite persistent complaints – largely by the PRD – about subtle forms of manipulation by electoral authorities of the electoral registry and gerrymandering the congressional districts.

The PRI-state tread cautiously with the opposition as a result of the destabilizing events of early 1994, which included the launching of the Zapatista guerrilla insurgency in Chiapas and the slaying of the PRI's original 1994 presidential candidate, Luis Donaldo Colosio. While it turned to be unfounded, the Salinas administration seemed to fear an alliance between the PRD and the Zapatista rebels to delegitimize the government. This concern prompted the authoritarian incumbents to offer the PRD what they actually called a Mexican "Pact of Moncloa" – an imaginative but ambiguous promise of greater PRD participation – in exchange for not undermining the 1994 election (Alcocer 1995, 204). Rhetoric aside, the offer was really only a negotiating ploy, but it did moderate PRI-state policies vis-à-vis the opposition and forced the regime to negotiate preelection reforms (Alcocer 1995, 205). It is widely believed that Colosio wanted to overhaul electoral institutions to bind the PRI dinosaurs Ulysses-style and to put his probable presidential victory beyond question. But the international community and its nongovernment organization (NGO) interlocutors also played a crucial role in opening up the electoral process.

Salinas, always concerned with maintaining a democratic image in international eyes, was even more concerned about the January 1994 implementation of NAFTA, especially given that the Zapatista uprising in Chiapas was launched on the same day that NAFTA went into effect. Mexico's four-year negotiation of NAFTA and the country's reliance on the United States for a short-term economic bailout in 1995 forced Mexican elites to accept international norms of democracy as a matter of course by the fall of 1993, when the U.S. Congress approved the trade agreement after a series of congressional floor speeches criticizing Mexico's democracy and human-rights deficit. While U.S.-Mexico bashers recognized historical U.S. encroachments on Mexican sovereignty, they still argued that they could, as of 1994, justify harsh criticism of Mexico's internal governance based on "the responsibility for the interests of our investors and indeed of our larger national concerns to inquire about the political stability of our new partner" (Mazza 2001, 103). Empowered by a new imperative to monitor Mexico, some fifteen U.S. congressional members sponsored a resolution in the spring of 1994 calling on the reticent Mexican government to allow electoral observers and to overcome decades of "rigged elections and entrenched political corruption" (Mazza 2001, 112).

Despite all the controversy over election observation, there was ultimately little of note to observe in 1994. Unlike in 1988, Cárdenas's second presidential candidacy created little stir, as he placed a distant third to the PRI and the PAN after running a poor campaign (see Table 2.1). Moreover, the federal electoral institutions seemed to function autonomously for the first time, as several conflictive PRI congressional victories were stripped from that party by the electoral court and handed to the PAN and PRD. Reviews remained mixed, as Alianza Cívica criticized the inequity of preelectoral conditions, while the Carter Center lauded the advent of improved voter registration lists and voter ID cards but found that the large volume of complaints to the TFE signaled a lack of faith in the process, particularly by the PRD. Indeed, problems remained in the equity of electoral administration, but they had much more to do with the need for tighter regulation of campaign spending than with the active perpetration of election-day fraud.

THE PRI LOSES CONTROL: THE ELECTORAL REFORM OF 1996 AND THE RUN-UP TO 2000

Even more of a technocrat and less of a politician than Salinas, President Zedillo, the unlikely presidential "fill in" for the martyred Colosio, failed to advocate for the electorally powerful but retrograde machine bosses and instead further fortified the technocrats' position. Zedillo's unwillingness in most cases to intercede on behalf of the regional bosses cost his party electorally and sealed the end of PRI monopoly. The PRD and especially the PAN pushed their electoral reform agendas with the help of the truly neutral electoral authorities created in the 1994 reforms, managing to seize the agenda from the PRI, which in 1994 again lost its qualified majority in the Chamber of Deputies, and in 1997 and 2000 lost even its simple majority. Zedillo remained largely aloof of electoral politics, focusing instead on economic policy. A rebellion escalated inside the PRI, pitting the technocrats against the "dinosaur" traditionalists, whose folkloric ways embarrassed the professional federal policy managers, but who were dutifully called back to manage every election.

The 1996 reforms (in anticipation of the 1997 mid-term elections) resulted from a different interparty bargaining dynamic than the pre-1991 and pre-1994 reforms. Having been elected without much of his party's support, Zedillo needed to forge consensus on both the right and left, so his administration sponsored dialogues for reforming government, in which PRD and PAN demands were taken seriously. After Zedillo sponsored eighteen months of negotiations for his administration's "definitive" electoral reform, the PRI reneged on the president's plan to pass the most consensual electoral reform yet. At the last minute, a legislative revolt by PRI congressional members sympathetic to the electoral machines altered sixteen of the points in Zedillo's package by raising the campaign-spending ceiling for private donations dramatically; limiting parties' maneuvering room in the creation of cross-party electoral coalitions, partially restoring "governability clause"–type overrepresentation of the largest party in the Chamber of Deputies; and lessening government regulation of parties' media access (Camacho Guzmán and Pérez Silva 1996).

The result was a watered-down version of Zedillo's reform package, which had proven unpalatable to the PRI's traditionalists. However, the PRI revolt came only in the enabling legislation; the landmark constitutional reforms altering the structure of the IFE and the electoral court had been passed three months earlier by overwhelming congressional majorities from all three major parties. The approved package was still a hard-hitting set of electoral reforms[12] that further distanced the IFE from

---

[12] Indeed these reforms proved so potent that many PRI congressional members, in an unprecedented lack of party discipline, voted against them, even though they had been previously endorsed by the party's leadership.

the executive and legislative branches by allowing the collegial body of ombudsmen to select its own director (rather than submitting to executive nomination), and by giving these citizen counselors (who now set policy without counting the votes of political parties or legislators) the ability to make personnel changes and monitor their own affairs. In the most significant reform to the electoral court, in 1996 it was placed directly under the jurisdiction of the Supreme Court, with magistrates nominated by the judicature rather than by the executive (still subject to legislative confirmation). Perhaps of even greater significance, the electoral court was granted jurisdiction over election-related constitutional conflicts arising at the local level, where great disparities still existed between the ideal of electoral justice and its practice. The other significant changes prior to the 1997 mid-term elections included the first congressional redistricting in twenty years and the tightening of IFE control over public funds used by political parties.

The 1977 reforms are credited with commencing Mexico's electoral opening, but the real overhaul of Mexico's electoral institutions commenced in 1989–90, building on the momentum of 1977. The real mystery then, is how the PRI-state miscalculated so as to let the reform process continue through to 1989, gaining momentum in the 1985–6 reform. The PRI commenced a liberalization process "snowball" it would later prove unable to impede, as demonstrated explicitly in 1996. Before considering the construction of electoral courts and their analogue informal bargaining tables, two other preliminary issues must be addressed in this chapter. First, the role of exogenous shocks – such as the economic crisis that rendered the 1980s as The Lost Decade in Mexico – must be considered as a catalyst of Mexico's transition. Second, a model must be specified of center-periphery relations that will allow explicit linking of these two realms. I address both these issues in turn.

STRUCTURE VS. CHOICE: THE ROLE OF ECONOMIC FACTORS IN MEXICO'S TRANSITION

A high rate of abstentionism was indeed a long-standing characteristic of the Mexican electoral system. Klesner convincingly demonstrates the correlation in the prereform early 1970s among higher levels of turnout and rural districts, less-educated voters, and indigenous communities. As argued by Klesner (1988, 346), industrialization and urbanization were, by the late 1960s, starting to erode the PRI's capacity to get out the vote, as community pressures and outright bribes grew more difficult in more transient and urban settings. The political competition fostered by the 1977 reform exacerbated these trends, apparently relegating the PRI's "strategic reserve" of suspiciously high turnouts, and occasional blatant fraud, further into the rural hinterlands (Klesner 1988, 359). Gómez (1991, 196) notes the paradox in the postreform 1970s of increased electoral competition and decreased voter turnouts, attributable to the ease with which rural *caciques* had previously manipulated vote counts. However, the PRI-state's calculated risk proved to have been well taken, at first. The party-state's reduced margin of maneuvering did not adversely affect PRI congressional majorities or governorships, at least not initially.

The increased abstention was due to the loosening clientalist grip of the PRI combined with the lack of a compelling alternative. In the 1990s, citizens would develop rationales for their votes typical of democratic societies, spawning a generation of important studies on Mexican voter behavior (Buendía 1988, Dominguez and McCann 1996, Magaloni 1996). But getting these citizens back to the polls to choose among real options required a credible opposition, and the rise of the PAN to occupy this crucial role was only possible when the economic hardships of the 1980s prompted collective action by newly identifying *PANístas*. Significantly, these "loose cannon" professionals and businesspeople, mostly from Baja California, Chihuahua, Nuevo León, and other states in Mexico's north, commanded sufficient resources to overcome collective action problems. Unlike the destitute peasants of the south, whose poverty undermined their opportunities to protagonize the breakup of the PRI's political monopoly, the *PANístas* commanded sufficient resources to mobilize without jeopardizing basic human needs, possessed networks of professional and business associations, and had two other advantages over the regime's left-leaning opponents. Unlike the center and the south, which were deeply beholden to Mexico City, Mexico's north was economically linked to the United States more than to the rest of Mexico, even in the 1980s. Finally (and perhaps most importantly), they had bargaining leverage brought by the credible threat of exporting capital and savings that the PRI-state needed to access in order to capitalize its economic policies.

The negative growth of the early 1980s prompted spiraling inflation of close to 100 percent annually, an erosion of real wages, and a rate of capital flight thought to have increased more than tenfold between 1974 and 1982.[13] President López Portillo was furious at the "anti-patriotic"

---

[13] Capital flight in 1974 was estimated at $1.3 billion, whereas by 1982 it had reached $14.4 billion before tapering off to below $9 billion in 1983 and 1984 (Barkin 1990,

capital flight and nationalized the banks in August 1982 in response to a rumor that $300 million had been withdrawn from national accounts in a single day. The decision was downplayed by de la Madrid, who took office early in 1983, but many business leaders, irked by López Portillo's sweeping, capricious, and antibusiness gesture, left the PRI anyway. In fact, by 1985, former *PRIísta* gubernatorial candidates ran well on the PAN ticket, especially in Chihuahua, where a history of PRI-state electoral fraud combined with a powerful civil society strongly supported by the church and a strong neo-*PANísta* candidate.

The PRI-state sought to reign in business defectors, and with some success. Soon-to-be-president Ernesto Zedillo was dispatched as head of the Federal Trust for Covering Exchange Risks (FICORCA) to bail out Monterrey business conglomerates, and prospective *PANístas* found co-optation back into the PRI was not without its rewards.[14] But the snowball had been set in motion, and there was only so much the PRI-state could do. Maxfield (1990) identified political opposition to what she called "the Cárdenista coalition" of state-supported industries, consolidated beginning way back in the 1930s. However, in the early 1980s, Mexico's northlands were undergoing an export-led economic transformation even as the rest of the economy faltered. The number of export-producing *maquiladora* assembly plants in U.S. border towns tripled between 1982 and 1987 (Velasco Arregui 1989, 249–53), and the percentage of Mexico's industrial workers residing in the northern states increased more than tenfold over the 1980s until they comprised over 30 percent of the nationwide industrial workforce by 1991 (Velasco Arregui 1993, 165–8).

The PAN was ideally positioned to benefit from disenchantment with the PRI. Driven by events in the north, where Mexico's first *PANísta* governors-to-be networked while organizing local business-association mobilizations, national membership in the PAN increased dramatically. This was sparked by several early 1980s mayoral election victories including a postelectoral mobilization in 1985 Chihuahua that united intellectuals, civic groups, and the church against PRI-state electoral fraud. Vacillating business and professional groups also realized that even if they were not originally planning to abandon the PRI indefinitely, having another credible option for political participation dramatically

109). In relative terms, the capital flight of 1982 represented almost one-third of total private sector investment (Cypher 1990, 161).
[14] For example, the Chihuahua bank president Eloy Vallina announced his support for the PRI in 1985 in exchange for a favorable government indemnity to his bank, in a strategy that came to be known as the *vallinazo*.

increased their political bidding power, with both the PRI-state and with the opposition.

Many politically moderate PAN leaders understood that factors were coalescing to favor their protagonism of Mexico's protracted transition, although, as will be seen in Chapter 6, they faced resistance from the party's comfortable old-timers, who had not achieved lasting social change over the party's early decades but who had achieved a pulpit for their conservative doctrines. Conditions were ripe for change, but the PAN's more politicized factions, the neo-*PANístas*, battled against the party's conservatives for strategic primacy, costing the party unity and forcing it to reconcile internal factions during the 1970s and 1980s, before finally being united by 1992. The *PANístas* who won Mexico's presidency in 2000 had been in ascendancy within the party since Chihuahua's provocative gubernatorial election in 1986 and had won hegemony upon expelling the doctrinaire conservatives in 1992. The pragmatist neo-*PANístas* had won the mantle of leadership because they proposed a far greater role for the disgruntled northerners in Mexico's political development than the status quo conservatives, because the external threat from Cárdenas and the PRD was deemed more important than internal squabbles, and because as the neo-*PANístas* began to win even a sprinkling of mayoral elections, this was judged – by comparison with past electoral performance – as a resounding success by bandwagoning voters.

THE PAN'S "CENTRIPETAL" DEMOCRATIZATION BY DEFAULT

The PAN's strong showings led to efforts by the PRI to nominate candidates who fit the PAN profile – successful business executives who favored economic liberalization over traditional Mexican statism. In Sonora and Nuevo León, 1985 gubernatorial races were heavily contested and rife with fraud, but the PRI prevailed. It was the 1986 Chihuahua governor's race that ushered in the era of contemporary postelectoral mobilization in Mexico, as the PRI did not triumph so handily and the PAN raised the domestic and international public relations costs of PRI-state electoral fraud to a new level. When Chihuahua PAN incumbent Mayor Luis H. Álvarez lost the governor's race, he launched a hunger strike and a march hundreds of miles long in the PAN's first nationally publicized utilization of mass mobilization tactics. Álvarez's example impacted opposition party strategies more broadly, as political and intellectual leaders of varied ideological stripes joined the postelectoral mobilization that included what have become trademark PAN tactics – mass-based, cross-class contestation; civil disobedience; and international appeals (Chand 2001, 116–29).

While Álvarez confirmed academic accounts of a late 1980s neo-PAN surge due to involvement of "loose cannon" entrepreneurs from Mexico's "barbarous North" (Álvarez interview, Chand 2001, Mizrahi 1994), the party's model for postelectoral conflicts had been taking shape since the 1950s (see Chapter 6). Initially, the northern cities (and Mérida, Yucatán) were the sites of PAN effervescence as the only locales where a critical mass of *PANistas* coexisted with a level of affluence sufficient to allow citizens the resources needed to contest elections. However, as the PAN's postelectoral movements went national by the end of the 1980s, the number of these mobilizations based in northern cities decreased precipitously from 72 percent between 1939 and 1976 to 25 percent between 1988 and 1996. The north's decline in the party's postelectoral visibility was increasingly evident after passage of the 1987 law authorizing substantial dispersions of public funding to political parties for the first time. The northern entrepreneurs would continue to be crucial to the party's membership (and the source of the PAN's first elected governors), but the affluent north's financial resources were no longer essential with the increased flow of funding from Mexico City (Loaeza 1999, 433–8).

The extension of the "Chihuahua Model" to national PAN political strategy was personified by Álvarez, who parlayed his newfound notoriety in 1987 into the national party presidency (Chand 2001, 129–34). As discussed at length in Chapter 6, electoral success replaced doctrinal purity as the PAN's primary objective, and while the party ran a close race in the presidential balloting of 1988, it could not compete with Cárdenas's name nor with Salinas's political machine. The party would have to settle for a "centripetal strategy" (Mizrahi 1997) toward governance, based on building incrementally on local victory after local victory. A fear shared with the PRI of the *cardenistas*' redistributive economic policies prompted the PAN and the PRI into a tacit alliance – also detailed in Chapter 6 – whereby Salinas would recognize PAN mayoral victories and even a few governorships, provided *PANista* parliamentarians closed ranks with the PRI-state in legislative chambers.

Salinas's strategy backfired, however, hastening an end to what was starting to appear like an endless transition. Starting in 1989 with the PRI-state's tolerance of Ernesto Ruffo's Baja California victory in the first PAN governorship permitted ever, local PRI leaders in "victimized" areas blamed the PAN and the national PRI leadership for forcing them to grant *concertacesiones* in a series of cases. The story of the PRI's unraveling by the hands of its own national leadership is told in Chapter 8. The PAN would have preferred a centrifugal strategy of democratization, but the PRI-state was not willing to cooperate in such an immediate challenge to its power base. But it would tolerate *PANístas* encroaching gradually on the power base from the periphery, as the authoritarian incumbents considered the stakes to be sufficiently low that they could afford to give the PAN busywork – improving their own reputations as democrats who sometimes "allowed" the *PANístas* to win – while they ran the country.

While the PAN was no doubt driven by improvisation more than foresight, at least initially, its apparently disjointed strategies of consistently advocating federal electoral reforms in legislative chambers while simultaneously undertaking civil disobedience and postelectoral mobilizations converged dramatically in the 1990s. The party was able to exploit the newly leveled electoral playing field and its standing party organizations built during the post-Chihuahua decade of conflictive elections, inflicting defeat after defeat on the downsized and uncompetitive PRI-state, until finally their bottom-up "centripetal" strategy gained them the presidency in 2000. Economic structural conditions in the mid-1980s dictated that the PAN's electoral path to power would start in Mexico's north. The agency of individual actors like Carlos Salinas and interest groups like the PAN leadership and its growing network of allies determined the southerly direction of change, through Guanajuato en route to Mexico City. As considered in Chapter 7, PRD actors also greatly influenced the direction of Mexico's transition and its duration, both by conditioning the PAN and the PRI, and through their own "centripetal" mobilizations, which were seldom successful but were often severe.

Whatever the democratizing consequences of the opposition's subnational strategies during the 1980s and 1990s, which comprise the central argument of this book, it is still illogical to conclude that the centripetal strategy innately favors democratization. Even before the subnational antidemocratic *PRIísta* backlashes in Tabasco and Yucatán in the wake of the PAN's ascent to the presidency, Cornelius anticipated that "during the present phase of the country's political evolution, the subnational political arena will be the principal source of inertia and resistance to democratization, rather than the prime breeding ground for democratic advances" (Cornelius 1999, 11). Cornelius attributes his prediction in part to a revisionist "Swiss cheese" view of the Mexican center's domination of the periphery (prominently expounded by authors such as Knight [1992] and Rubin [1997]) in which local PRI *caciques* (political chieftains) maintain their dominions free from tinkering by the center, and to diminishing control by the national PRI over local bosses well before 2000. With hindsight, the protagonists of the PRI's antidemocratic movements understand that all those years of allowing PAN centripetal gains helped doom them. In desperate gestures to recover the glory days of local PRI domination, in 2001 Tabasco and Yucatán *caciques* challenged the *PANísta* center, which has, by all accounts, been slow in squelching regional challenges to its authority. The *PRIísta* presidency was considerably weakened under Zedillo, whose policy of *sana distancia* (keeping a "sane distance" from the PRI) resulted from his inability to control regional bosses and his disdain for the sort of visceral and informal logrolling that his predecessor Salinas popularized, even as he allowed the formalization of independent electoral institutions.

CENTER-PERIPHERY FEEDBACK AS UNINTENDED CONSEQUENCE AND AS INTENDED STRATEGY

The electoral reforms of the last decade in Mexico have been extremely dramatic, bringing an electoral system designed to provide legal "cover" of authoritarianism to the doorstep of democracy and with sufficient legal safeguards to carry Mexican democratization as far as the new electoral competition will lead. Refinements may still be made in federal electoral laws, but the focal point of democratization has shifted in Mexico to redefining executive-legislative relations and to the placement of new limits on Mexico's excessive presidentialism. PAN protagonism of Mexico's electoral opening was made possible by the formal liberalization of laws governing elections. But as also evidenced, especially during the crucial 1980s, *PANísta* agents caused these reforms after an exogenous economic crisis atomized many within the PRI-state who had previously been supporters of the authoritarian regime or at least complicit beneficiaries of the regime's successful postwar record of economic development.

This chapter has argued against the primacy of economic variables alone in explaining Mexico's protracted transition. While economic explanations define constraints on actors, they do not explain individual agency. I have described the 1980s economic crisis as a necessary but not sufficient condition for *PANísta* agency in wedging open Mexico's electoral system, town by town, state by state. While the PRD helped push the PAN to action, the left's natural constituencies – the masses of impoverished *campesinos* (peasants) in Mexico's south who did enter the postelectoral fray in the late 1980s and early 1990s but without anything close to the PAN's impact – were often burdened by extreme poverty.

Another structural economic explanation, modernization theory, is useful in placing Mexico among the company of middle income countries more likely to democratize. However, a country's level of "modernization" (often defined merely as GNP) may prescribe limits on the range of options available to actors, but it does not specify which path they will choose (Przeworski et al. 2000, 84–98). The relative immunity of the latent *PANístas* to economic crisis due to the mobility of their capital and their economic ties beyond Mexico City is a direct consequence of economic conditions. But as elaborated in Chapter 6, decisions by disenchanted northern business elites to join the PAN and use it as a vehicle to actively oppose the PRI through a series of local challenges owed more to political choices than to economic circumstances.

Once the neo-*PANístas* focused on subnational elections as the means for pressuring the PRI-state and seeking a "trickle up" effect on nationwide democratization, a sort of feedback loop was created. By exploiting local strengths and forcing national PRI-state decisions about whether to accept local (and later gubernatorial) electoral outcomes, the new activists ensured a national impact for their local victories. Furthermore, they forced the new PRD, hoping for similar electoral and postelectoral victories, into the same dynamic. But with prominent exceptions like Michoacán in the early 1990s, where PRD-led social movements were violently repressed, the PRD did not have sufficient local followings to command attention from Mexico City. While the PRD was still getting its party platform bearings, the PAN was overcoming internal feuds and establishing a two-pronged strategy in escalating Mexico's transition.

Even as the neo-*PANísta* electoralists were striving to win local elections, the party's remaining traditionalists (and later a new generation of parliamentarians) were pushing national electoral reforms that eventually backed the PRI-state into leveling the electoral playing field. The successful evolution of autonomous electoral institutions at Mexico's federal level – surveyed in the next chapter – is largely the result of opposition party compliance with the electoral rules, after decades (in the case of the PAN and the tiny but determined pre-PRD left) of contesting electoral institutions and their results through postelectoral conflicts. The regime was forced to concede a series of electoral reforms leading to this point for a combination of reasons: the weakening of the electoral power of the PRI and internal divisions within the party, the rise of the opposition, and the influence of the international community. But the single most important event in establishing the imperative for electoral reforms was clearly the 1988 federal election and Salinas's subsequent efforts to rectify his credibility gap by complicity with PAN postelectoral mobilization, provided it stayed local and helped promote the PRI-state's national policy agenda.

With the hindsight of 2000, it is evident that the PRI's slippage really commenced in the early 1990s, when Salinas destroyed the party faithfuls' long-standing incentive structure by rewarding local PAN postelectoral mobilizers and their national bosses at the expense of local PRI bases after the *PRIístas* won elections. The post-2000 regional rebellions, described in Chapter 8, are still being directed against this Salinas legacy in states like Yucatán, where 1990 and 1993 PRI mayoral victories in the capital Mérida were traded away to the PAN. While PRI hard-liners such as former governor Victor Cervera Pacheco of Yucatán and former governors Manuel Bartlett of Puebla and Roberto Madrazo of Tabasco ostensibly refuted Fox's federal electoral courts in siding with "home rule" by the Yucatán autocrats, the Fox administration, also well aware of the excesses of the past, refused to squander political capital on *concertacesiones*. The extreme caution of Fox's team in refusing to inflame anti–Mexico City sentiment has rendered the PAN's arrival in power anticlimatic. The PRI hard-liners' hopes that they can goad the new administration into giving them a scapegoat for their electoral misfortunes are dwindling. They have been forced to turn the spotlight of their ire on a previously innocuous institution, the Electoral Tribunal of the Judicial Power of the Federation (TEPJF), subject of the following chapter.

3

Mexico's National Electoral Justice Success: From Oxymoron to Legal Norm in Just over a Decade

> It is my conviction that the president of the republic should not exercise any
> powers other than those explicitly conferred on him by the Constitution and
> the law. . . .
>
> Ernesto Zedillo (Mexican president, 1994–2000)[1]

It was by all accounts another day at the office for one of authoritarian Mexico's more modest parties seeking to contest yet another Party of
the Institutional Revolution (PRI)–state victory in the summer of 1988.
The tiny Authentic Party of the Mexican Revolution (PARM – usually
a satellite of the PRI) had decided to contest extreme electoral fraud in
congressional district 7 in the state of Guerrero. The PARM submitted
its copies of the vote tallies to the new federal electoral court, with poll
officials' signatures at odds with those on certified copies submitted by the
Guerrero electoral commission. Blatant and extensive alteration of official
results was acknowledged but then ignored in the verdict of the magistrates, who argued in the decision that while tampering was evident, the
complaint was unfounded for failing to properly state the allegations, and
that because the electoral court "facing the judicial impossibility of ac-
cessing the electoral packets which should be in the Chamber of Deputies,
confronted a technical and legal impediment to determining which copy of
the results is the real one" (Tribunal of Electoral Contention or TRICOEL
RQ-007 resolution, 4). The verdict was the judicial equivalent of "hand
washing"; leaving the complainant his/her right to petition the opening
of the "official" vote tallies locked in the Chamber of Deputies, but

---

[1] Cited in Rodríguez 1997, 141.

60

with no mechanism for guaranteeing that "right." It was the story of 1988.

Former Electoral Tribunal of the Judicial Power of the Federation (TEPJF) President José Luis de la Peza, also a member of TRICOEL, recalled that the Guerrero Electoral Commission's justification of its crooked vote count was indeed an embarrassment. He characterized the authorities' vote tally manipulation as "absurd," as were the commission's decisions to not consider various polling station (or voting booth) tallies because of "apparent evidence of tampering." According to de la Peza:

The electoral authorities had absolutely no right to exclude balloting stations from the final tally because of suspicions that votes were altered, especially since any alteration of the tally sheets could have only occurred in the offices of the state commission. As I recall, it was a very dirty election. (interview)

De la Peza drafted the resolution, disregarding the electoral commission's official sums and instead analyzing patterns in disparities between precinct-by-precinct PARM and electoral commission tallies. De la Peza's proposed resolution was rejected by the electoral court (by a bare majority, four-to-three vote), rendering it a mere dissent. However, the magistrate's argument and its substantiation merit further consideration as they are instructive of the fraud common in Mexican elections prior to the 1990s and of the electoral court's inability to properly sanction it.

Of the 222 polling stations installed on election day, the Guerrero Electoral Commission tallied results from 184 (arguing that 16 "were misplaced" and 22 were not counted due to "tampering"). Of those 184, the electoral institution's official results corresponded with those of the PARM in 111 cases.[2] In these 111 tallies where the electoral authority and the PARM agreed (representing 50 percent of the total voting stations, and

---

[2] Federal electoral law requires that after the polls close, the lottery-selected poll workers count votes and report them on an official form with carbon copies for the official representative of each political party with a witness present. Each party is entitled to one witness present from the opening of polls to their closure, and that witness is asked to sign the official results, thereby "certifying" that he/she is either in agreement with the tally or at least not barred from observing the process and filing protest writings (*escritos de protesta*) regarding any violations. Prior to 1998, the protest writings from all polls were gathered together by party lawyers, who use them as the basis for filing full-blown electoral court complaints, which must be filed within three days after the election. However, most recently, following a law passed by the state of Queretaro that made the protest writings merely optional, the federal electoral court followed suit in TEPJF Jurisprudence 6/99.

61 percent of those with tallied results), the PARM received 72 percent of the votes, and the PRI received 28 percent. Suspiciously, that trend was inverted when the electoral commission's versions of the disputed tally sheets were summed. In those tallies, the PRI received 83 percent of the votes, the PARM 17 percent (de la Peza dissent in TRICOEL RQ-007, 4). Given the unlikely possibility that the PRI could have won by such a wide margin only in the contested tally sheets, and that the PRI margin of victory on these sheets was just large enough to overcome such a large vote deficit on the rest of the sheets, de la Peza argued that "those of the complainant should be considered valid, rather than those referred to the tribunal by the electoral commission." Because no law existed allowing for consideration of the complainant's word over that of the authority, the formal technical justification for such a decision had to be found elsewhere.[3]

De la Peza's justification for ruling in favor of the PARM was twofold. First, the consensus tallies all carried signatures of party representatives and poll workers, as per the law, while the electoral commission's disputed tallies did not carry such signatures. Second, some of the documents offered by the electoral commission were photocopies, as required, but some were the originals that were supposed to have been remitted to the "official" packet in the Chamber of Deputies. The majority of the electoral court magistrates were not willing to disqualify the electoral commission despite the irregularities acknowledged in its verdict, and de la Peza's resolution was instead relegated to the status of dissenting opinion. Another dissent, by Krieger, was even more searing:

> It is our obligation to resolve complaints that are submitted, when they comply with the submission requirements, and this obligation cannot be subsumed or evaded under the pretext that the Tribunal does not have sufficient proof to resolve them, and thus passes to the Electoral College that responsibility.... If this Tribunal is going to declare itself incapable of resolving complaints in a systematic way, and is going to remit all questionable calls to the Electoral College, then where is the diminishing jurisdictional function of the Tribunal headed? (Krieger opinion on TRICOEL RQ007, 3)

Krieger resigned from the court after writing this opinion, and the Mexican government was compelled to remove the electoral court's

---

[3] The logic here is of forcing lesser laws to serve greater purposes, much like that invoked by the U.S. federal government when it sent Al Capone to jail for tax evasion prior to the strengthening of racketeering laws.

temptation to "pass the buck" to the Electoral College by eliminating the Electoral College.[4]

The ultimate irony of RQ007 is that even after their battle to declare it unfounded, the electoral court's resolution was summarily overturned by the Electoral College. Without so much as mentioning issues raised by the magistrates, in their floor debate the legislators-elect mentioned only the electoral court's requisite "leaving to discretion" of the Electoral College, not the court's verdict in favor of the PRI. The Electoral College declared the PARM victorious, despite this pro-PRI judicial ruling, verifying that indeed, the magistrates' deliberations mattered little (Chamber of Deputies, August 27, 1988, 521).

The electoral court's 1988 initiation did not channel postelectoral dispute adjudication from informal institutions to formal ones. The legal decision makers were completely ignored by the political decision makers, who held all the real clout. Unable to explore case facts, electoral magistrates could not even subpoena or open ballot packets. Thus they had to water down verdicts by "leaving to discretion" the defendant party's right to appeal to the Electoral College to open and recount the votes in well over a dozen cases. Helpless before the horse-trading legislators-elect and their prearranged partisan deals (that dealt multiple congressional seats to losing parties), the judges watched legislators summarily ignore all their decisions, with no recourse but to render dissenting opinions, which were also ignored. The institution needed to be either scrapped to stop drawing attention to the legislators' arbitrary actions, or greatly fortified and allowed to actually work.

And so it went in 1988. The PRI-state established electoral courts and independent electoral commissions to legitimize Mexico's historically fraudulent elections, remove from the agenda opposition-party complaints about the tilted electoral playing field, and placate international critics. However, Mexico's authoritarians never expected these electoral courts to be taken seriously. It was one thing for the authoritarian government, monopolized by the PRI for seventy-one years, to construct benign "window dressing" electoral institutions. It was another matter entirely when the electoral court started annulling PRI congressional victories and granting them to the Party of the Democratic Revolution (PRD). I demonstrate in this chapter how the PRI-state adopted the National Action Party's (PAN) long-standing proposals to create an electoral court

---

[4] An important clarification is that the Electoral College remained for the presidential race in 1994, but was eliminated for 2000.

and fortify its powers between 1986 and 1994, and then how, when the autonomous electoral court annulled four PRI victories in a bold show of true autonomy,[5] the PRI-state sought to rein the electoral court back into the executive's purview, even though it may have been too late. Chapter 8 considers PRI reactions to its loss of the 2000 presidential elections and subsequent efforts to curb electoral institution authority when the TEPJF annulled the PRI-won 2000 Tabasco governor's race and halted efforts by a traditionalist PRI governor to rig the electoral commission prior to the Yucatán 2001 gubernatorial election.

Perhaps even more important than tracing one of democratization's most important electoral-institution success stories of the last decade, this chapter seeks to establish a distinction critical to the argument of the next several chapters. Parallel to considering the evolution of electoral court structures and case law, I also evaluate the evolution of political party compliance with these institutions. Because the PAN has always maintained a disciplined legalism (even if often complemented by social mobilization), the greater change is evidenced in the PRD's behavior. Through its electoral court dealings, it is possible to trace the PRD's evolution from ill-trained antiregime provocateurs through 1994, to transition-seeking legal eagles in 2000 and especially in the post-2000 state-level challenges in Tabasco and Yucatán protagonized by PRD lawyers. This chapter depicts a drastic improvement in case presentation and the efficiency of all parties in deciding which elections to contest, paralleled by incremental improvements in magistrate autonomy and authority. Overall, the ultimate tribute to the contemporary prevalence of electoral justice at Mexico's federal level is the reduction in complaints filed since 1994, when ten times as many cases were filed as in 2000.

Electoral justice, and the credibility of electoral institutions more broadly, benefited most in the 2000 federal election from events that did not transpire. This chapter traces the gradual reintegration of judicial institutions and electoral matters after grave conflicts in the nineteenth century. After briefly describing the nineteenth century debate prompting the separation of judicial decision makers from electoral concerns, I consider Mexico's contemporary electoral courts and their dispute adjudication records in the 1988, 1994, and 2000 federal elections, assessing both institutional reforms and political parties' reactions. Finally, I

---

[5] This out of a total of 300 single-district plurality seats in dispute. The Chamber of Deputies' other 200 seats were determined by a representation formula translating each party's total votes into seats.

consider the particularly dramatic change in PRD complaint-filing strategies, which are most demonstrative of the evolution toward rule of law acceptance. In contrast to the state and local failures presented in Chapter 4, electoral justice at the federal level did evolve from oxymoron to legal norm in a scant twelve years. But as the federal electoral courts were separating themselves from the PRI-state, the PRI-state also underwent a dramatic transformation, but in reverse. The PRI's abrupt change from rule of law champions prior to 2000 to electoral justice foot draggers after 2000 is chronicled in Chapter 8.

THE LAWLESS DISPENSATION OF ELECTORAL JUSTICE PRIOR TO MEXICO'S ELECTORAL COURTS

Debates over the proper role for electoral courts can be traced back to the controversy between José María Iglesias and Ignacio Vallarta in the 1870s.[6] The argument centered on whether individual rights (Iglesias) or a strictly neutral Supreme Court (Vallarta) was more important. To Iglesias, the Supreme Court was competent to issue an *amparo* judgment against any act or authority that violated an individual's rights, regardless of whether the violating authority was federal, state, or local. The sovereignty of any authority (federal on down) was less important than the uncompromised protection of every citizen. Vallarta, on the other hand, viewed Iglesias's tenet of "the incompetence of origin" [*incompetencia de origen*][7] as an influence conducive to anarchy, or at least instability. He believed that while citizens had the right to challenge unjust authorities, filing *amparo* lawsuits was not the proper means. According to Vallarta, the only proper way to challenge the legitimacy of elected authorities was through the Electoral College, which considered election results and took "political" decisions about who should govern (Moctezuma Barragán 1994, 258–65).

---

[6] Vallarta's 1874 brief was written to counter a Supreme Court decision by José María Iglesias, the 1872 Amparo of Morelos, which established that if authorities were "illegitimate from their origins" (that is, not properly elected) then any decisions they made were subject to judicial intervention. While it conveyed a noble ideal, the Iglesias decision was in practice used to selectively undermine state and local authorities in the brutal factional struggles of the era (Ballard Perry 1978, 284–7).

[7] This hypothesis, quickly adopted by 1870s Supreme Court President Iglesias, argued that the federation possessed the legal authority to determine the legitimacy of state authorities and, by extension, the legitimacy of authorities elected by those who were illegitimate (Moctezuma Barragán 1994, 72–6).

While Iglesias may have been the more humanistic of these two legal pioneers, Vallarta was the more powerful. His position reigned during Mexico's *Porfiriato* dictatorship (1876–1910) and was more consistent with the legislative self-certification practiced under every Mexican federal constitution with two exceptions: the short-lived Constitution of 1836, under which the two legislative chambers certified each other's elections, and the equally short-lived Law of Organizations, Parties, and Electoral Procedures (LOPPE) from 1977 to 1986, which was the only "checks and balances" system under which the judicial branch certified the legislative. However, the authority granted the Supreme Court to rule on election-related violations specified in the LOPPE was quite limited. The Supreme Court could only "file a report" on irregularities to the Electoral College of the Chamber of Deputies, which could act on it or ignore it (Galván 1995, 9–11). Judicial activism in electoral certification, then, has been the exception rather than the rule. Political party jurists have long argued that Mexican constitutional law does not preclude electoral *amparos*,[8] but none have been successfully executed in practice. The limits of electoral certification by an independent tribunal without constitutional *amparo* authority were reached with the 1994 Federal Electoral Tribunal (TFE), prompting the government to adopt a sort of informal, de facto electoral *amparo* as of 1997. To understand this shift back to the Iglesias position, one must consider the institutional reversion of Mexico's electoral courts back to Iglesias's side after straddling the Iglesias and Vallarta positions prior to 1996.

The constitutional reform of 1986 created the TRICOEL, which had only administrative powers, notoriously "recommending" resolutions like RQ007 to the Electoral College. The judicature, consisting of seven magistrates and two alternates (judge instructors, who "clerked" and admitted cases), was nominated by political parties and approved by the Chamber of Deputies to serve four-year terms. Magistrates had to be thirty years old and hold a legal degree, and they could never have been clergy members, office holders, or political party directors (Editorial Porrúa 1988, 146–9). Detractors, such as legal scholar Ignacio Burgoa and TRICOEL judge-turned-critic Emilio Krieger, praised the judicial wisdom and inscrutable ethics of the individuals who served on the TRICOEL (Burgoa 1988, 41–3, Krieger 1994, 129) but reviled a strong bias in magistrate selection and a

---

[8] See, for example, Pérez Noriega, who argues in particular that filing of an *amparo* against the TRICOEL did not violate federal electoral law, especially in cases where the electoral court rejected the complaint from full consideration (1989, 12–14).

preposterous institutional dependence on the Electoral College. The parties did propose magistrates, but only to the president of the Chamber of Deputies, where, Burgoa reasoned, "the individuals charged with making decisions were largely PRI affiliates, and thus the designations of magistrates in their majority also pertained to this political institution and not to the opposition" (Burgoa 1988, 34).

Had Mexico's electoral laws been similar to those in other branches of public law (or even private law), there would have existed a writ of *amparo* appeal to the Supreme Court as a corrective to the TRICOEL's jurisdictional weakness and the Electoral College's political motivations (see Vázquez Gómez 1996). However, no such writ existed, and a compelling 1873 precedent forbidding federal judicial jurisdiction over electoral controversies eliminated the Supreme Court as a political actor.[9] And while the *amparo* is a very limited form of judicial review (applying only to the case at hand, with little explicit weight of precedent in future deliberations), such singular treatment is conducive to electoral dispute resolution, in which singular circumstances are the norm. As noted by Galván, the TRICOEL may have been "ephemeral" and "inefficient," but it was still the "first stone" in an electoral justice regime redirecting dispute adjudication away from Mexico's historical tendencies of auto-certification (Galván 1995, 41). A quick summary of the salient features of the 1989–90, 1993–4, and 1996 reforms contextualizes the extensive differences in data presentation between electoral court cases in 1988 and 2000.

Under the 1989–90 reform, the TFE was granted some real judicial (as opposed to mere administrative) authority, distancing it at least nominally from the Electoral College, although the Electoral College could override the TFE with a two-thirds vote. While the Electoral College could still presumably conduct discovery investigations of the electoral packets and other evidence in its possession, the TFE magistrates could not open these packets. However, the Electoral College did respect TFE rulings in all cases in 1991. The court was split into five regional chambers, with the four decentralized electoral courts each composed of three magistrates, while five magistrates sat on the central Mexico City electoral court bench. The regional chambers heard cases only during and immediately after the

---

[9] Periodic "tests" of judiciary jurisdiction over elections were submitted. After the 1988 elections, for example, PAN leader Jesús González Schmal contested Federal District senate races through the filing of an *amparo* with federal courts. The case was rejected from consideration on grounds that no federal court is qualified to hear electoral *amparo* cases.

electoral process, while the central chamber adjudicated disputes related to the preparation of elections (such as conflicts over party registrations, the voter list, campaign spending limits, etc.) as well as complaints generated during the election.

While the overall autonomy of the electoral court from the legislative and executive branches was higher, the selection of individual judges was more compromised. Instead of being nominated by the parties, the magistrates as of 1991 were nominated by the president directly, subject to congressional approval. Despite the continuance of the 1988 party-nominated electoral law experts on the post-1990 federal electoral courts, the change in nomination procedures represented a loss in autonomy, allowing the executive to effectively "stack" the TFE. The eligibility criteria for magistrates was tightened, however, with candidates required to meet the standards of Supreme Court ministers in legal training and nonpartisanship (Federal Secretary of the Interior 1990, 461–7).

The 1993–4 reforms more directly answered critics by eliminating the Electoral College altogether (except in certification of the presidential election, abolished in 1996). Appeals from the TFE were allowed, for the first time, and heard by a congressionally appointed appeals court for each electoral process, with judges named from a list submitted by the Supreme Court president. Congressional appointments to the "primary" court were still made from a list of presidential nominations, but now such nominations could also come from the Supreme Court (subject to the president's discretion). Strict regulations governing conflict of interest by magistrates were codified, as were procedures for dismissing judges. TFE authority was extended at the microlevel in several areas, including case preparation, the range of evidence acceptable, and the tools of magistrate discretion (Federal Electoral Institute 1993, 211–20). As documented in the following case analysis, discovery "subpoena" powers were formalized and augmented, allowing magistrates to open electoral packets (under special circumstances). The range of acceptable evidence was broadened to include technical documents such as video and audiocassettes, and limited but real discretion was granted judges in supplementing case complaints.

If the 1994 appeals chamber was partially integrated into the federal judiciary, the 1997 version of the electoral court, the TEPJF, was entirely subsumed under the judicial branch, with nominations made entirely by the Supreme Court and ratified by the PRI-dominated Senate rather than the more plural Chamber of Deputies. While further refinements were made in magistrate discretion, the main change in 1997 was to extend court jurisdiction to state and local races, which could be heard by the appeals chamber when dissatisfied complainants filed them to the TEPJF. Indeed, as Chapter 8 illustrates, this new power is what made the federal electoral court the true guardian of Mexico's electoral justice by 2000. Personnel changes were also made at this time that did not entirely augur autonomy from the executive branch, demonstrating that the path to electoral court autonomy was not entirely linear. The magistrate who had presided over the TFE in 1991 and 1994 left to assume a position at the PRI-state's core, as Sub-Secretary of the Interior. His successors in 1996 and 2000 were among the original generation of electoral experts nominated by opposition parties, but whose hands seem to have been at least partially tied by integration of their court into the formalistic judicial branch.[10]

THE RISE OF ELECTORAL JUSTICE CASE LAW IN THE EARLY 1990s

Despite the electoral court's improved legal standing in 1991, the Electoral College still considered "altering" election outcomes based on political grounds, but the authoritarian incumbents who won handily in mid-term congressional elections defended the electoral court's honor this time. Negotiated "triumphs" of justice over the law were proposed by the PAN in six Mexico City congressional districts (2, 25, 27, 36, 37, and 39), but the increasingly PRI-dominated Electoral College refused to allow this horse trading. Congressional party leaders conveyed diverging views of the Electoral College's proper role but seemed to acknowledge that the institution's days were numbered. The PRI, in the form of Federal Deputy César Augusto Santiago, argued for the preservation of a "political logic" of election certification, but by preagreed norms. The PAN's Diego Fernández de Cevallos spoke out against auto-certification, and the PRD's Rosalbina Garavito argued that the Electoral College was the only vehicle left through which the dirty elections could be "cleaned" because the electoral court had failed. The PRI refused to cede as it had in 1988, however, and the PAN's hopes of negotiating electoral outcomes favorable to some of its highest leaders who had lost close races were again dashed.

---

[10] The first president, José Fernando Franco González Salas, was known as "tough but fair," in managing an overly centralized electoral court in which he made even the most minor of decisions, but tried to minimize outside political pressures on magistrate decision making. Franco had been nominated to the federal electoral bench in 1987 by the PRI (Chamber of Deputies 1987, 21, 27).

Fernández de Cevallos refused to participate in the futile debates, and insisted that his party would remain in chambers only to "bear witness" to the biased proceedings (Ramírez Bernal and Culebro Bahena 1993, 527–34).

The electoral court may have been empowered in institutional terms, but it received no such boost procedurally. The range of evidence acceptable remained very narrow – public documents only – that is, those filed by official agencies in the normal course of fulfilling their duties (i.e., electoral rolls, polling station opening and closing reports, and polling station vote tally sheets, district commission tally sheets, electoral commission reports, and individual testimonials only when notarized). No private testimonials (witness statements without notarization) or "technical" evidence (videos, photos, cassettes, etc.) were acceptable. In fact, only part of the "public" evidence available to the electoral court could be considered, prompting persistent magistrate Javier Patiño Camarena to dissent nine times over the narrowness of the law given ample evidence of electoral fraud. His contention, legislated into the 1993 reform, was that magistrates should rule as irregular any *casilla* (or polling station) vote tally where the number of votes extracted from the urn plus those not used or disqualified did not add up to the number of blank ballots received at the polling station's opening nor total the number of names crossed off the electoral roll. Even this apparently obvious evidence – by 2000 included in most magistrate resolutions as a Microsoft Word for Windows "cut-and-paste" standard chart – was disqualified from consideration.

Contrary to 1988 and 1991, when magistrates could not open electoral packets, and to 1991, when not all vote accounting information could be used as evidence, the electoral court magistrates in 1994 utilized the discretion granted them to compare preelectoral and postelectoral ballot tallies and order the opening of electoral packets to annul two races outright and change the outcome of two others. This magistrate discretion was wielded in cases such as the Puebla District IV congressional race declared for the PRI but refuted by the PRD in case number SC-I-RIN-94/1994. The case presented perhaps the best example of electoral court personnel actually journeying to Puebla to audit the state electoral commission, finding irregularities in well over 20 percent of the ballot stations[11] and annulling the race outright. Such aggressive action was unprecedented.

---

[11] In fact, there were so many ballot-station irregularities that the electoral court did not even quantify them but proceeded directly to annul the race.

The Puebla allegations were familiar, mainly that the vote totals were different from the number of votes cast and that the poll workers deviated excessively from the "random" list of individuals chosen by lottery. The PRI, in its third-party legal response to the PRD filing, argued that the complainant had neglected to specify particular violations and had instead offered only a general umbrella of causes for annulment followed by concrete complaints but without linking the two (SC-I-RIN-199/94 resolution, 29). Resolution drafter de la Peza agreed that the PRD complaint was disjointed, but decided that even if the abstract causes of annulment had to be matched to case facts through "supplementing the complaint," the electoral court's jurisprudence, that magistrates exhaust all evidence sources within the case file, required the magistrates to restate the argument and fully consider it. The complaint, he stated, "should be understood as a whole, and none of its grievances or infractions may be overlooked" (SC-I-RIN-199/94 resolution, 29).

The magistrates entered their analysis of complaints through the ballot box "causes of annulment" (Table 3.1). Annulment of 20 percent of the ballot boxes (considered by some to be an unreasonably high number) resulted in annulment of the election, as occurred in some dozen municipalities, and in 2000 in the Tabasco governor's race. The magistrates considered whether the complaint was founded (and hence produced ballot box annulment) or unfounded only after the complaint survived the possibility of rejection. The most incomplete cases were dismissed from consideration before even becoming part of a magistrate's case load. Legal and institutional impediments to investigating certain claims (even when they were codified as law) weakened the hands of magistrates early on. Notably in 1988, several of the causes, such as "vote counted out of place," "restriction of party representatives," and "use of violence or pressure tactics," were alleged dozens of times but never ruled as founded by the magistrates. The founded rate of these hard-to-prove allegations improved in 1994 and 2000, as magistrates acquired more discretion to investigate complainant claims. The "use of violence or pressure tactics" cause of annulment was particularly notorious, as proving it seemingly required technical evidence such as videotapes, which were not permitted, or at the very least, the statement of a notary public eyewitness who just happened to be present at the moment of the infraction, which was also highly unlikely.

The TFE magistrates were vested in 1993 with authority to issue orders of extended discovery or even order unprecedented inspections of electoral packets and other evidence, assuring that authorities could no

TABLE 3.1 *Causes of Annulment Invoked by Complainant Parties in "Founded" Complaints*
N = All founded or partially founded "election day" complaints (of inconformity) only

		1988		N = 54	1994		N = 272	2000		N = 60
Cause	Description	Alleged	Founded	Rate (%)	Alleged	Founded	Rate (%)	Alleged	Founded	Rate (%)
1	Install poll outside rules	28	12	43	89	37	42	32	4	13
2	Violate turn-in of votes	11	4	36	3	5	167	4	1	25
3	Vote count out of place	1	0	0	19	2	11	11	0	0
4	Turn-in vote count late	10	0	0	96	6	6	16	3	19
5	Unauthorized poll workers	20	2	10	160	112	70	41	15	37
6a	Precinct vote tallying error	96	24	25	526	223	42	49	15	31
6b	District vote tallying error	73	2	3	124	2	2	4	1	25
7	Vote without ID or registration	54	12	22	149	25	17	16	3	19
8	Restrict party representatives	18	0	0	87	6	7	10	1	10
9	Use of violence or pressure tactics	26	0	0	210	16	8	22	2	9
10	Nonviolent impeding of vote	4	0	0	52	0	0	9	0	0
	Other (ineligible candidate, etc.)	9	0	0	167	0	0	0	0	0
	"Generic cause" (1994)				0	1	n/a	3	2	66
	Overwhelming irregularities (1997)							35	3	9
	TOTAL CLAIMS	350	56	16	1682	437	26	252	50	20

Note: In the 1994 case where there is greater than a 100 percent "founded rate" (underlined) this is due to additional allegations made by magistrates who as of 1994 could supplement the complaints if they found new evidence covered by complainant allegations in the course of reviewing case files. The complainants usually invoke many more than just one "cause of annulment."

Source: Author-directed review of case files with law student research assistants.

longer fail to cooperate with impunity. Such orders of discovery inves- tigation occurred 8 percent of the time in 1994 and only 2 percent of the time in 1997, but this was mostly due to procedural changes in com- plaint processing.[12] Two such inspections led to the discovery of proce- dural irregularities sufficient to annul elections.[13] The TFE dispatched judicial clerks to supervise the recounting of ballots and the recalculat- ing of polling station acts, "second guessing" the work of polling station workers and local electoral officials in Puebla Congressional District IV and in Veracruz Congressional District XXII. At least a half dozen such special inspections were ordered in 1994, although magistrates stressed that this was still an exceptional act, invoked only "when there was great suspicion of the documentation submitted" (García Moreno interview).

The issuance of such orders of extended discovery was one of two prin- cipal tools of judicial activism available to magistrates as of 1994. The other such limited but important authority granted them was the abil- ity to "supplement the complaint," codified in 1994, after the dissenter Patiño Camarena argued that the magistrates should be able to compare the number of ballots counted before the polls opened to the sum of those "voted" and "unused" at poll's close.[14] By 1994, three forms of magistrate discretion by "supplementing the complaint" became routine: considering the initial protest writing as well as the formal complaint in cases where the latter was incomplete and could be complemented by the former, reformulating complainants' alleged violations to better "fit" evidence offered, and in more extreme cases, "adding" charges to the com- plainant's case when, during inspection of the evidence, the magistrates discovered other irregularities. Jurisprudence 39/98 obliged the TFE to "consider all the documents of the complainant" thereby depleting "the principle of exhaustiveness" in reaching verdicts. However, when such

---

[12] Judge instructors, who subpoenaed and prepared the case for the presiding magistrate's consideration from 1988 through 1994, were eliminated in the 1996 reform. Hence magistrates got control over cases earlier and could subpoena documents in the first instance, rather than having the judge instructors subpoena them and then requiring the magistrates to request them again when the initial subpoena went unanswered (Rebollo Fernández interview).

[13] The cases are SX-264/94 and SC-199/94, in which more than 20 percent of the ballot boxes were annulled due in part to the orders of inspection, which allowed the magistrates to gather sufficient evidence to prompt annulments of the elections.

[14] Among cases in my sample, the dissenting vote was submitted with SC-047/91, SC- 071/91, SC-111/91, and SC-117/91. In 1994, this criteria was adopted as jurisprudence when applied by Magistrate José Luis de la Peza to case SC-180/94. By 2000, this infor- mation was part of most complaints.

judicial exhaustiveness resulted in the annulment of more ballot boxes than the complainant had requested, the annulment could also be adverse to the complainant.

Overall, the 1997 electoral dispute adjudication process moderated the magistrates' hard-fought gains of 1994 by limiting magistrate authority to "supplement the complaint" through a regressive jurisprudence declaring, in contradiction to 1994 policy, that "blank spaces" on official tallies were in themselves insufficient cause to annul votes (Jurisprudence 8/97, Third Period, TEPJF 1997a, 138). Appeals chamber activism, largely limited in 1994 to rubber stamping of lower-court decisions, also took a regressive turn in 1997, although with increasing judicial branch independence in time for the electoral court's incorporation into this branch, appeals chamber conservatism became less of an issue by the 2000 election. The increasing autonomy of the judicial branch mitigated against any innate conservatism of the judicial branch (as compared to the electoral court's prior ombudsman model).

Also by the 1990s, compliance by electoral authorities with electoral court subpoenas of information improved greatly (Table 3.2). In 1988, the TRICOEL issued subpoenas for evidence in the possession of authorities in twenty-four of the sample cases, and only seven of these were affirmatively answered (in four cases the authority did not respond, and in twelve it is impossible to tell as the documentation in the case file was incomplete). As candidly explained by 2000–3 TEPJF President Ojesto, who was also a member of the earlier courts, "In many cases the law was ambiguous and the electoral authorities sent no documentation, and we would subpoena evidence but then realize that the local electoral authority had closed down shop, that its officials had gone home, sending

TABLE 3.2 *Subpoenas by Magistrates and Actor Compliance*
N = *sample of 25 percent of all election day complaints filed*

Year	Authority Compliance (Pct.)	N	Complainant Compliance (Pct.)	N	Compliance by Third Parties (Pct.)	N
1988	34	8/24	N/A	N/A	N/A	N/A
1991	82	31/38	13	3/24	100	1/1
1994	94	61/65	54	81/150	100	2/2
1997	100	23/23	30	3/15	100	2/2
2000	94	32/34	50	1/2	100	2/2

Source: Author-directed review of case files with law-student research assistants. The total number of cases considered was 143 in 1988, 305 in 1994, and 26 in 2000.

the electoral packets to the Electoral College, as specified in the law, but leaving us no way to obtain any documents" (1995 interview).

Federal electoral authorities in the states and municipalities lacked incentives to comply with these summons, as there was no penalty for not complying, and in fact, by failing to comply, authorities could often sabotage the opposition-party complainant's chance of building a case against the PRI-state. And if electoral authorities had no incentive to comply, the Electoral College had a disincentive. The electoral court judges were forced to work at cross purposes with the political motivations of the prospective members of Congress, who were overwhelmingly inclined to certify their own elections without excessive concern for legal formalities. Even in 52 percent (twenty-eight out of fifty-four) of the ballot box–annulling verdicts, the TRICOEL cited the lack of access to electoral packets as a cause of remaining uncertainty. The Electoral College did not once respond to pleas by the magistrates for the Electoral College to open electoral packets and verify allegations. In fact, not only did the Electoral College ignore the electoral court's legal reasoning; they actively imposed political resolutions in violation of the spirit of the law in thirteen cases by postponing certification of the elections to make room for postelectoral "horse trading" that resulted in the granting of Electoral College "victories" to five second-place finishers (Gómez Tagle 1994, 93).

By 2000, PRI-state compliance with electoral court requests was the norm, as well over 90 percent of the electoral court subpoenas to electoral authorities were obeyed, up from 34 percent in 1988. However, compliance by the complainant parties remained low (50 percent in 2000), demonstrating that these parties' strategies were still to submit complaints whenever there was any doubt of electoral fairness and follow up with the proof later, if such proof became available. Their strategy was to justify postelectoral marches over the paper trails left by unsubstantiated (and thus unfounded) electoral court complaints. In other words, in the legal realm, the ill-prepared opposition, especially the PRD, frequently resorted to "crying wolf," and electoral authority nonresponse only added to their justifications, even if their complaints were groundless.

CORRESPONDING IMPROVEMENTS IN QUALITY OF MOST PARTIES' COMPLAINTS

As magistrate discretion increased, so did party compliance with the procedural requirements of filing complaints. In 1988, rejected complaints were more poorly prepared than those in later processes. For example, more than half of the dozen 1988 cases filed by an unauthorized complainant were signed by the losing candidate him- or herself, rather than by the designated party representative, whereas by 2000, that mistake was committed in only one case. Although outright rejection of cases was uncommon in 1988, a disproportionate number of cases filed in 1988 lacked judicial "form," were filed outside the time frame permitted, or failed to specify the election being challenged (TRICOEL 1988, 357). In fact, 37 percent of the 1988 complaints did not even specify the election contested. By 1997 and especially by 2000, complainants' mistakes were more subtle; complainants failed to submit the proper "protest writing," or they alleged election irregularities outside the jurisdiction of election-day complaints (such as electoral-list name "shaving" or irregularities in the number of ballots printed, etc.) or that were not specified as causes of annulment. In 2000, for the first time, complainants cited thousands of electoral court jurisprudence statements in their complaints, illustrating great advances both in party training and in acceptance of electoral law as a legitimate discipline.

Even among the "founded" cases, all ballot boxes alleged in a complaint were rarely annulled. Even in 2000, when close to 60 percent of the complaints annulled ballot boxes, only an average of 3 percent of the claims – among the dozens and even hundreds often alleged – were ruled as "founded."[15] The percentage of complaints lacking judicial form, filed outside the proper time frame, or wanting for complainant signatures dropped considerably, and the percentage of "founded" cases increased with each electoral process. Indeed, the percentage of complaints in which at least one ballot box received a "founded" verdict increased from approximately 10 percent in 1988 to over 50 percent in 1997 and 2000. Measured in polling station ballot boxes, the percentage of those challenged that were annulled jumped threefold from less than 1 percent in 1991 to 3 percent by 2000.

Broken down by party, the verdicts rendered process by process were even more revealing. The PAN and the PRD filed the vast majority of the complaints before 1997, with the two parties combined accounting for over 85 percent of the complaints filed in both 1991 and 1994. However,

---

[15] It should be noted that even the annulment of 11 percent of the ballot boxes challenged only represented 1.2 percent of the total vote (Federal Electoral Tribunal 1997[a], 22). The 11 percent annulment rate is more a sign of greatly improved targeting of complaints by the political parties than any "softening" on the part of the electoral courts.

in 1997, the PRI replaced the PRD as the most frequent filer, submitting some 43 percent of the complaints, while the PRD filed 41 percent and the PAN 13 percent. Also notable is that the PAN, the party of lawyers and "rule-of-law" proponents for almost 60 years, attained a much higher rate of founded verdicts (with at least one ballot box annulment in 83 percent of its 1997 filings) than the PRI (55 percent in 1997) or the PRD (37 percent in 1997). Prior to the 1997 turning point, the PRI filed few complaints, and among the two opposition parties, the PAN had a consistently higher rate of founded cases than the PRD.

Another compelling trend has been toward a broader distribution of allegations among all the causes of annulment. In 1988 only five causes of annulment occurred a dozen or more times in the fifty-four "founded" or "partially founded" cases: the installation of polling stations in unspecified places, vote-tallying error at the polling station level, and voting without ID or without being on the registration list. By 1991, more causes of annulment were stipulated in the law, but two of them had still never been proven to the magistrates' satisfaction, despite dozens of allegations: the use of violence or pressure tactics, and delayed submission of vote counts by precinct authorities. A powerful addition to the causes of ballot box annulment, known as the "generic cause" of annulment, was made in the 1993 electoral reforms. This cause allowed magistrates to annul entire races without regard for individual polling stations (or ballot boxes) but rather when "generalized violations" compromised the integrity of the process.[16] The "generic cause" was invoked several times in 1994 and even had a decisive role in annulling one election (Veracruz Congressional District XXII). In 1997, this potentially powerful tool for "blanket annulment" (annulling ballot boxes without a specific cause) was also used to annul Chiapas Congressional District III, but that verdict was overturned by the appeals chamber.[17] The generic cause of annulment was never applied as the sole cause until ST-21/2000 in 2000, when two slayings next to the *casilla* closed the polls in Zihuatenejo, Guerrero state. All causes

---

[16] Actually, yet another cause of annulment was added in the 1996 reforms, the cause of "overwhelming irregularities," which is similar to the 1994 "generic cause" except that it is less powerful because it may be used to annul only ballot boxes, rather than entire elections.

[17] The PRD's original complaint alleged the stealing and burning of ballot boxes, the failure to install polling stations, and hence the failure to receive balloting. The complaint was ruled as founded, but the Appeals Circuit overturned the decision, arguing that while 16 percent of the citizens were unable to vote, 84 percent were able to vote, and the three-to-one margin of the PRI victory meant that the voters who were unable to cast their votes would not have made a difference.

of annulment were founded in at least one case by 1994. Prior to that election, it was nearly impossible, given the narrow range of evidence acceptable, to "prove" acts such as proselytism at the polling stations or threats against voters, without the presence of a notary public bearing witness to such events.[18]

Wolf crying was evident in complainant parties' repeated failures to submit protest writings or to document the authority of representatives elaborating complaints. These oversights indicated that the parties desisted when they knew they would not have a solid case, preferring rejection to compliance with subpoenas for a case that would be ruled as unfounded. Such rejection roused antiauthority sentiment more than a case's acceptance, which allowed electoral authorities to "steal the thunder" of postelectoral protesters, at least until the complaint was ruled unfounded. Thus the brunt of noncompliance with magistrate requests clearly shifted from the authorities in 1988 to the complainants after 1990. Sanctions for noncompliance with such subpoenas were legislated in 1993 but tend to go unenforced in election day complaints.[19]

The *PANistas* – who had championed stronger electoral institutions since 1946 (Chapter 6) – pushed in 1996 to have the federal electoral court subsumed under the Supreme Court and to make it an appeals circuit for conflictive state cases, as state courts were not always bias free (see discussion of Huejotzingo, Puebla in Chapter 6).[20] The PAN was satisfied with the reforms, and leaders summarized shortcomings of post-1996 electoral justice as "a problem not of institutions but of the people who staff them."[21] But the PAN also benefited from amicable relations with the PRI-state and a postelection "defense of the vote" staff of electoral lawyers known as "the parachutists," who would in the early

---

[18] Notary public (and former electoral magistrate) Schleske Tiburcio (interview), said legal lacunas have allowed notaries to avoid serving as witnesses of electoral fraud. Among these are loosely interpreted rules allowing notaries to avoid any request that will physically endanger them and requirements that considerable notary charges be paid in full before they serve as witnesses.

[19] Fines were imposed by the TFE on political parties that exceeded campaign spending rules for the 1994 federal elections (the first such fines ever imposed by the TFE). These were not part of the "complaints of unconformity" but rather were covered in other complaints.

[20] Federal Electoral Tribunal President Fernando Ojesto in a 2001 interview attributed the entire impetus of the 1996 reform to the Huejotzingo conflict.

[21] This is a paraphrase of a statement by former congressional member Fernando Pérez Noriega, who said that with the 1996 reforms, the PAN was satisfied that the electoral playing field was level (Pérez Noriega interview).

1990s "drop in" anywhere to train local attorneys and supervise post-electoral complaint filings. And when all else failed, the PAN at that time had crack *concertacesión* negotiators who could be counted on to maintain close contact with the Interior Secretary, federal PRI headquarters, and even the president, and who were known for extracting concessions (be they interim governorships or plural mayoral councils including *PANista* participation) at the extralegal bargaining table following the pattern developed in Chapters 5 and 6.[22]

THE GRADUAL EVOLUTION OF PRD COMPLIANCE WITH ELECTORAL COURTS

Activists from the PRD, a more mass-based party comprised of laborers and peasants rather than formally educated professionals, expressed misgivings about incorporating the TFE into the Supreme Court prior to 1996, arguing that the most popularly accessible judicature to which the TFE could be jurisdictionally "attached" would be the federal circuit courts, which specialized in simplifying laws and were accessible to every major city (del Villar interview). PRD officials raised numerous valid reservations about the procedural excesses of the TFE. Among these, PRD faithful argued that the existence of only five chambers made justice physically as well as formally inaccessible, and that the three-day deadline for filing postelection complaints and the immediate deadline for filing "protest writings" (filed on election day by party representatives at the polling station) placed extreme demands on the few judicially trained *PRDístas* available. Furthermore, they argued, complainants had no opportunity to counter evidence presented by authorities or defendants (the winning political party whose victory is being challenged) once a case was opened (i.e., there was no means for them to refute counterallegations). However, post-1996 PRD strategists complied with the federal electoral courts, acknowledging that the burden was on them to ensure party activists possessed the resources and training to file credible complaints. In 1994, the party did not assume this responsibility and was accused, by electoral court authorities and dissenters within their party, of subverting

---

[22] The main negotiator, Diego Fernández de Cevallos, was named the PAN's 1994 presidential candidate, but not merely for his negotiating skills. Besides serving effectively as the PAN's *concertacesión* "closer," "El Jefe" Fernández de Cevallos was a charismatic leader and a brilliant parliamentary orator but seemed to lack the "common touch" needed to be president.

Mexico's formal electoral institutions' credibility (Romero, Tuñon, del Villar interviews).

At the nadir of the party's strategy favoring informal over formal institutions during the period of direct competition between electoral courts and postelectoral bargaining tables (Chapter 4), the 1994 PRD sought to undermine the entire electoral process by submitting some 500 versions of a photocopied "knock-off" master complaint challenging electoral list credibility.[23] The TFE magistrates balked at repeatedly answering hundreds of pages of allegations that had already been addressed in due course through a preelectoral complaint appealing a Federal Electoral Institute (IFE) General Council decision on the matter. The PRD strategists insisted they were not trying to sabotage the judicial process by "jamming" the court with the bulky preelaborated format, which in most cases was devoid of evidence beyond that already presented in the preelectoral case. Rather, they argued that the "list-shaving" complaint had been sent by the national party to local chapters as a mere guide to filing postelectoral complaints (Tuñon interview). If this was the case, it was a poor guide, as only two out of eighty of the nearly identical "list-shaving" format complaints in my sample were ruled "founded" for any ballot boxes at all, and in both cases the copy master was invalid but contained "founded" evidence attached to the prefabricated format. In addition to the list-shaving "boilerplate" there were at least four other PRD stock prefabricated complaints in 1994 that were filed at least a dozen times each, bringing the PRD "prefabrication" rate (as a percentage of total complaints filed) to a whopping 72 percent (Table 3.3). The PAN had experimented with "knock-off" generic presentations in 1991, largely abandoned the practice in 1994, and filed no such prefabricated complaints in 1997 nor in 2000 (a partial explanation for that party's high rate of "founded" cases). The PRD also presented few "knock-offs" by 2000 and targeted allegations more specifically than the 1994 prefabricated complaints that sometimes covered thousands of ballot boxes at a

---

[23] The complaint charged the IFE with "shaving" the names of PRD supporters off the electoral list and finding means to allow PRI supporters to vote multiple times (by granting them multiple voter IDs, creating several names for the same person, etc.). The complaint charged that the creation of this list was biased and that its external audit was also compromised. The TFE judges ruled the photocopied presentations "unfounded" in cases where they were not complemented by case-specific allegations of election-day fraud. Magistrates argued in their resolutions that the PRD's "list shaving" charge had been fully considered and answered in the appropriate venue, an appeal complaint from the IFE (complaint RA-400/94).

TABLE 3.3 *Photocopy "Knock-Off" Complaints by Party and Year*
N = Sample of 25 percent of all "election day" complaints filed

Complainant	1988	14%	1994	64%	2000	19%
	Copy Cases/ Party Total	Percentage of Party Cases	Copy Cases/ Party Total	Percentage of Party Cases	Copy Cases/ Party Total	Percentage of Party Cases
PAN	2/46	4	6/35	17	0	0
PRD (FDN coalition)	15/68	22	163/225	72	1/12	8
PRI	2/21	10	2/4	50	0	0
Other	1/8	13	25/41	61	4/5	80

Note: While it was obviously impossible to recognize a particular "knock-off" complaint format the first time it was encountered, upon coming across the second example of a new format, the researcher notified the rest of the group about the characteristics of the format so that the rest could identify it. In 1994, a half-dozen frequent "knock-off" formats were identified, while in the other processes, only two or three common formats were identified. Once two identical complaints occurred in the sample, all occurrences of that format were classified as "knock-offs."

Source: Author-directed review of case files with law-student research assistants. The total number of cases considered was 143 in 1988, 305 in 1994, and 26 in 2000.

time. Correspondingly, annulment rates improved in these later elections, and the number of frivolous complaints decreased.

This deluge of "knock-off" complaints artificially boosted the total number of complaints submitted in 1994 and, hence, the electoral court workload and exorbitant taxpayer expenditure. The surge in filings in 1994 is evidenced in the sixfold reduction in the total number of complaints of inconformity filed – from 1,232 complaints in 1994 to 194 in 1997.[24] All told, some 64 percent of the postelectoral complaints filed in 1994 (by all parties) contained prefabricated "knock-offs." The majority consisted of nothing more than the preelaborated format, sometimes with a "fill in the blank" space for individual complainants. Hundreds of others featured checklists for the complainant to select from among a menu of electoral law articles violated or "causes of annulment" invoked, and some even offered extended space for the construction of "customized" allegations. Magistrates continued to maintain that the purpose of the protest writing was precisely to keep parties from filing "frivolous" claims justified on political, rather than judicial, grounds. The argument for fining frivolous complaint filers resonated through electoral court chambers after 1994 (de la Peza interview).

The PRD jurists insisted they did not file the hundreds of "list-shaving" formats (and hundreds more of their other "knock-offs") merely as a prelude to street demonstrations, marches, the taking of public buildings, and other postelectoral pressure tactics (interviews with Romero, Tuñon, del Villar). They acknowledged that such party behavior was contrary to the intended function of the protest writings and other procedural formalities that sought to raise the costs of frivolous complaints. However, they argued that the removal of such barriers was the only way to liberalize access to electoral justice and reduce paperwork for political parties and electoral authorities alike. Tuñon stated that even in the most conflictive localities, PRD strategists took proper judicial challenges to electoral results seriously. While he explained that national PRD Executive Committee policy was "never to storm a municipal building before receiving a judicial resolution," impatient local activists often disobeyed, perceiving electoral courts as crowd control mechanisms that served largely to diffuse mass mobilizations. By this reasoning, courts deliberated until tempers cooled and they could announce their inevitably unpopular decisions.

---

[24] Since 1997 was not a presidential election year, there was less overall interest. But this fact does not explain the entire difference. In 1991, also a midterm election, there were 465 election-day complaints filed.

The PRD's 1994 electoral court subterfuge can be best understood as the swan song of the radical, antiregime faction of the PRD, led by Cárdenas and his judicial advisor Samuel del Villar. Cárdenas's team sought in 1994 to retroactively "charge" the PRI-state for its sins in 1988. In the electoral reform run-up to 1994, Cárdenas tellingly refused to endorse electoral reforms approved by the PRD's moderate wing (which headed the party's legislative caucus), on the grounds that "this would betray my convictions in tying our hands and leaving us without the possibility of denouncing fraudulent results, which could result from a tainted election" (Aguilar Zinzer 1995, 276). The angry populist in 1994 called for his followers to fill the *zocalo* (Mexico City's colonial square) as a repeat of 1988, when popular support could be directly translated into postelectoral mobilizations, even if electoral fraud precluded its translation into official electoral results.

In addition to ending the indiscriminate submission of 800-page "knock-offs," which electoral court magistrates privately equated to a PRD effort to undermine the entire election, the PRD – and the PAN – have dramatically increased their rate of vote annulments. The PRI has not made such progress. But while the PAN and the PRD have refined their case preparation, they have also targeted their complaints more strategically over time. The percentage of congressional districts challenged by both opposition parties has dropped from the 60 and 70 percent range in 1988 to the 20 and 30 percent range in 2000. Moreover, inspection of close congressional races[25] (Table 3.4) reveals that while only 5 to 10 percent of the PRD's complaints in 1988 and 1994 were filed in races where their margin of loss was fewer than 10,000 votes (between 5 and 30 percent of the votes cast), 70 percent of their 2000 filings were in close races. The PAN, which has always been a fairly effective complaint filer, shows a less drastic but still significant increase in its percentage of cases filed in tight races, from 31 percent in 1988 to 77 percent in 2000. The PRI has experienced a reverse trend, perhaps due to its postelectoral desperation in 2000, characteristic of the PRD in the 1980s and early 1990s. Complaint filings in tight races, where the complainant is far more likely to overturn the election, may be the best

---

[25] The PRD legal advisor, Hector Romero, (interview) said party strategists considered a close congressional race to be one in which the margin of victory was fewer than 3,000 votes, where a substantiated complaint could hope to gain the party 70 to 100 votes per *casilla* (ballot box) over several dozen *casillas*. In gubernatorial and senate races, the margin was more like 10,000 votes. Unlike in past elections, the closeness of the official results was the PRD lawyers' first consideration.

TABLE 3.4 *Elections Contested and Close Races Contested by Party Chamber of Deputies Majoritarian Districts Only in Presidential Election Years Close races are defined as those where fewer than 10,000 votes separate the winner and runner-up*

Party and Year	Number of Court-Contested Races by Party	Party Filings % of Total Contested	Number of Court-Contested Districts in Close Races	Close Race Filings as % of Total Filings
PAN 1988	137/213	64	43/137	31
PRD 1988	166/213	78	17/166	10
PRI 1988	59/213	28	42/59	71
Other 1988	1/213	0	0	0
PAN 1994	61/208	29	23/61	38
PRD 1994	180/208	87	9/180	5
PRI 1994	6/208	3	6/6	100
Other 1994	15/208	7	0	0
PAN 2000	13/61	21	10/13	77
PRD 2000	20/61	33	14/20	70
PRI 2000	29/61	48	16/29	55
Other 2000	15/61	25	0	0

Sources: Official electoral results and federal electoral court records.

indicator of the increasingly rational distribution of parties' postelectoral efforts.

The 2000 presidential election was acknowledged by both the PRD and the PRI as beyond the margin of electoral court contention, and in its single most important demonstration to date of its acceptance of the rules of the game, the PRD announced days after the election that it would not file presidential race complaints. As if to reconfirm the lack of discipline that defined that party, three local PRD activist groups filed complaints anyway, but they were readily dismissed by electoral court judges and party faithful alike. The PRI was also forced to immediately accept adverse results by President Zedillo's election day concession, viewed by traditional *PRIístas* as nothing less than all-out treason (see Chapter 8). The PAN, which had been conditioning public expectations for postelectoral mobilizations for months before the race, ultimately had nothing to complain about.[26]

---

[26] Presidential candidate Vicente Fox, in a meeting with Carter Center representatives, contributed to expectations of fraud, arguing that some 3 percent of the votes could still be altered, and that while he would be prudent, he would also seek "moral authority" as well as legal recourse after the election (author participation in group interview led by Robert Pastor).

As of the summer of 2000, all three parties had finally vested themselves in Mexico's credible electoral institutions, routinizing formal institution legal challenges as a legal recourse rather than as a mere prerequisite to the informal institutions of street demonstrations and bargaining tables. The journey to institutionalization was by far the longest for the PRD, although subnational PRI leaders in early 2001 threatened to deinstitutionalize its participation in electoral justice institutions (Chapter 8). In national elections, the PRI did learn to appeal close losses, in an uncomfortable turnabout, and the PAN adjusted to its new incumbent status. As each party grew increasingly strategic in defending votes through postelectoral legal campaigns, they started challenging elections they had actually won in 2000 as a defensive strategy to protect victory margins against poaching from vote annulments in cases filed by runner-up parties. Jurisprudence 29/99, cited in several 2000 cases, codified winning parties' rights to file complaints as a defensive strategy.

CONCLUSION: ACTOR COMPLIANCE AND INSTITUTIONAL EVOLUTION

The 1994 judicial activism represented the "high-water mark" of autonomy of the ombudsman-model electoral court, as incorporation into the federal judicial branch in 1996 introduced a new set of incentives for federal electoral magistrate career advancement, which had not existed when the "stand-alone" electoral court was autonomous of the judiciary.[27] These pressures were evident in the appeals chamber's reversal of all significant lower-court verdicts in 1997 and its repeal of the most important jurisprudence of 1994, effectively revoking prior magistrate discretion. The ascent of two federal court careerists to the Supreme Court straight out of the electoral court's appeals chamber in 1995 may have distorted magistrates' career expectations, according to this line of reasoning.[28]

---

[27] This argument is further elaborated in Eisenstadt (1999).

[28] That two out of eleven Supreme Court justices named in 1995 came from the four careerist federal judges on the appeals circuit seems to have given prominence to the electoral court as a spring board. However, former electoral court magistrates stated confidentially that they felt this was a unique circumstance, that the electoral court gave a public platform to these magistrates at a moment when the Supreme Court was being reformed (and nine new members selected), but that they were both highly qualified for Supreme Court nomination well before assuming electoral court duties. Nonetheless, the perception that loyal service to the federal court might be rewarded by rapid career advancement may have subtly altered the electoral court's tendencies.

The reactive TEPJF appeals chamber in 1997 overturned all three cases affecting electoral outcomes. Complaints SX-28/97 (PAN) and SX-29/97 (PRD) challenging the PRI victory in Chiapas District III were overturned, as the appeals chamber found that the lower court had interpreted the "generic cause" of annulling elections too liberally and that irregularities (noninstallation of polling stations in 19 percent of the district) were not decisive due to the extensive margin of PRI victory and the irregularities' failure to reach the 20 percent threshold for annulling elections. This ruling was quite controversial, however, due to the 75 percent abstention rate thought to have been caused by widespread fear throughout the district, the center of the Zapatista *guerrilla* movement's activities.[29] By the drafter of the majority opinion's own admission, the verdict was influenced by a compelling but political interest in punishing the masked saboteurs who disrupted the election, rather than encouraging future election obstructers by "rewarding" fraud perpetrators with ballot box annulments (Orozco Henríquez interview).

Another appeals chamber decision overturned the Guadalajara circuit's revocation of a PRD victory in favor of the PRI (SG-29/97) and restored victory to the PRD in District XIV (SG-15/97), on the grounds that the Guadalajara chamber had overstepped its discretion. The Guadalajara circuit had annulled the PRD votes decisive in reversing the election outcome by supplementing the PRI's complaint and annulling some ten polling stations (out of the total of twenty-three annulled in a district containing thirty-four polling stations) based on the existence of unacceptable

---

[29] Both PRD and PAN activists pointed out dangers in extrapolating voting patterns as the Appeals Circuit did in ruling that even if the additional polling stations had been installed and all votes had been for the opposition, the PRI still would have won. Namely, they said that reasoning differently would have yielded the conclusion that had even a minority of the "scared off" abstainers voted for the PRD, the outcome would have changed. This election, marred by tremendous pressures for its postponement, was highly controversial from the beginning. The opposition parties felt it was the only pressure-induced electoral court verdict in an otherwise "clean" dispute adjudication process (Martínez Valero, Vargas Manríquez, Villavicencio 1998 interviews). The Appeals Circuit split five to two, and the majority decision's author, Orozco Henríquez (1998 interview), acknowledged that the court needed to send the political message that individuals outside the legal regime (i.e., the masked vandals who burned and stole the ballot boxes besides parties' and other recognized formal institutions' actors) could not get away with sabotaging elections for their own gain. Orozco Henríquez said that in addition to weighing the insufficient legal evidence, the court considered the poor precedent that would have been set by annulling the election, giving a possible "green light" to future saboteurs.

blank spaces on the district vote tallies. The third and final appeals chamber revocation reversed another Guadalajara circuit decision, overturning a PAN victory in favor of the PRI on the grounds that the lower court had exercised too much discretion in taking the PAN's "defendant" argument as "fact" and neglecting decisive vote-counting errors. The appeals chamber reverted the PAN's 133-vote victory to a 17-vote PRI win.

Some electoral law experts (particularly in the opposition parties) were concerned that lower circuit magistrate use of new discretion grew excessive in 1997. But overall, the apparent imperative to "curb" lower circuit magistrate activism from the judiciary-stacked appeals chamber (expressed in the revocation of so many decisions) did not seem to apply to the 1994 liberalization of rules regarding the admission of evidence. The 1994 reforms permitted nonpublic evidence (exhibits beyond documents produced by officials in the conduct of their jobs), such as technical evidence (image and sound reproductions, etc.), for the first time, but subject to magistrate discretion.[30] Technical proof was admissible, if presented to complement more "directly admissible" forms of evidence (García Alvarez 1994, 6), a category still limited to public documents (those filed by public officials or notarized).[31] But while presentation and consideration of technical evidence grew increasingly routine, it has not been found decisive in a federal election case since 1994.[32] The formalities required to present technical evidence appeared to impede complainant case preparation. In particular, obstacles to invoking technical evidence included the requirement that all nonpublic documents be notarized and the electoral court's unwillingness to accept testimonials or "private" evidence from any source, even from polling station officials or party representatives if

[30] More specifically, only "public" proof was admissible in 1988 and 1991. In 1994 and 1997, "presumptive" proof and "instrumental" proof were acceptable, but this was merely based on magistrate interpretation of public documents. In 1997, "private" proof (any nonpublic documents offered by the complainant, including expert witness testimony, actor testimonials, confessions, etc.) was accepted for the first time, but it was very rarely accepted in practice.

[31] Technical evidence was offered by complainant parties prior to the 1993 reforms but was not supposed to be considered. None of the seven exhibits of technical evidence offered in 1991 was considered in the resolution, but one of the two exhibits presented in 1988 was mentioned in the verdict. There was no discernible bias in acceptance of this form of evidence, except perhaps in 1988, when PRI-presented photos were considered by the magistrates.

[32] Examples of extensive consideration of technical proof include cases SG-39/94 and SG-42/94.

the testimony went beyond documentation generated in the routine performance of their jobs.[33]

The increasing autonomy of the Supreme Court from the executive
branch starting in 1998 and the resounding liberation of judicial agents
from their PRI-state nominators after 2000 seem to have bolstered the
independence of the federal electoral court.[34] The relative quiet after the
2000 presidential election storm did not afford the federal electoral court
magistrates the opportunity to exercise their discretion, but landmark decisions mere months later overturning the Tabasco gubernatorial election
and conditioning preelectoral conditions in Yucatán (Chapter 8) did allow
these judges to assume the mantle of electoral justice without all the earlier
caveats.[35] What did this evolution say about the acquisition of electoral
institution credibility, and could it be repeated at the subnational level?

Clearly, in 1997 Mexico's "judicialized" federal electoral court was less
autonomous at both the macro level of institutional design and the mi-
cro level of case analysis than in 1994 when the institution controlled its
budget and was beyond any other PRI-state bureaucratic jurisdiction. By
2000, however, the political parties did not seem to care about this formal
loss of autonomy, as they had fully vested their fates in the formal institution's rulings. While compliance by the PAN and the PRI was hardly surprising because they were the parties with the highest stakes in Mexico's
electoral institutions, PRD behavior has been more enigmatic. The previously belligerent PRD's compliance with the less autonomous court in
1997 and 2000 suggests that factors besides institutional autonomy are
decisive, at least during the moments of extreme flux that characterize
democratic transitions. While the importance of actor compliance will be
considered at length in the chapters that follow, the PRD's acceptance of
a Supreme Court–co-opted electoral court (rather than an independent
ombudsman electoral court) implied that increases in PRD acceptance
of formal institutions were greater than any decreases in electoral court

---

[33] In 2000, there was one exception, complaint 5/2000 in the Mexico City circuit, which
deposed several citizens on whether they had replaced previously named polling-station
authorities and then considered this evidence in the founded complaint.

[34] Ojesto Martínez Porcayo (2001 interview) questioned (but did not categorically deny)
the effect of the 2000 election in making judges more willing to cast anti-PRI verdicts.
He argued that the magistrates' new powers were a direct result of improved complaint
filing by the political parties.

[35] Anticipating a need to publicize and fortify their credibility for a contentious postelectoral period after 2000 presidential balloting, the TEPJF had advertisements placed into
citizens' phone bills in the months ahead of the election, asserting that the electoral court
was "politically independent, professional and impartial."

independence. The effect of how changes in stakes altered strategies is evident from the contrast between the party's patent unwillingness to undermine the 1997 elections, in which the party fared relatively well, and its extensive 1994 postelectoral campaign to undermine the presidency, which was a lost cause. In 2000, the PRD seemed unwilling to renege on its 1997 compliance with formal institutions, and under the party's more pragmatic leadership – since the important 1995 leadership shift from the radicals to the pragmatists (Chapter 7) – the emphasis has been on legal rather than extralegal challenges.

But the PRD's tactical change was due more to exogenous factors than to activists' opinions of the federal electoral courts. They may have shifted strategies upon realizing that jamming the courts with "knock-offs" did not help their dim prospects in 1994 but rather cost them goodwill with federal electoral officials. However, it is more likely that the PRD complied with electoral courts because they had no reason not to do so. By winning more seats than they expected in 1997, the *PRDístas* became defenders of the postelectoral status quo, in whose interests most judiciaries tend to act. Indeed, skeptics may wonder whether the PRD's tactics have changed whether the PRD merely accepted the electoral court verdicts, as the majority benefited them, without concern about adverse precedents for the future. But such criticism would entail an assumption of naive PRD strategists, who in actuality no doubt considered long-term benefits and liabilities of judicializing the electoral court in opting to defend formal electoral institutions after a decade of undermining them.

The PRD electoral reform negotiators initially accepted the 1996 judicial takeover of electoral courts provided ratification was by the more plural Chamber of Deputies rather than by the Senate and nomination was by parties' congressional caucuses rather than by Supreme Court ministers.[36] The PRD legal strategists disavowed their 1994 mistakes, which favored neither their legal image nor their hopeless extralegal cause. Furthermore, they insisted that given the context of the party's postelectoral recriminations, criticizing the electoral courts' flaws after 1997 would have undermined the credibility of institutions that dignified *their* victories (not to mention that one of the appeals chamber cases reverted a PRI victory granted in the lower chamber back to them).

---

[36] According to negotiator Villavicencio, the PRD struck these demands in exchange for concessions on the right of the absentee vote for Mexicans abroad. The possibility of capturing the votes of the millions of PRD-sympathetic Mexican citizens living in the United States was the party's primary reform objective (1996 interview).

The construction of autonomous electoral courts may be explained as credible commitments between the PRI-state and opposition, but such bargaining only explains the nature of the two-actor bargaining. However, such microanalytical games of cooperation are deficient, failing to address the context of negotiations or, in this case, to place negotiations into the broader regime transition. Consistent with researchers asking not just how democratization occurs, but also how deep it runs (O'Donnell 1997, Przeworski 1996), we may question the value of autonomous "ombudsman" electoral courts when elections themselves are "clean," if their results are subject to extensive parallel negotiations based on opposition parties' extralegal shows of strength to attain postelectoral "justice" on the PRI-state's otherwise tilted playing field. The autonomy of the courts is less important than opposition parties' willingness to vest their futures in them. While certainly a degree of autonomy from the executive is necessary to induce opposition compliance, autonomy alone is not enough.

In practical "institutional engineering" terms, whether to construct autonomous ombudsman institutions or more government-dependent judicial institutions depends on whether the institution builders seek short-term or long-term payoffs. In the short term, independent ombudsmen can certainly provide much greater autonomy over very discrete and limited jurisdictions. The drawback, in addition to the dangers of generalizing from narrow jurisdictions, is that such ombudsmen commissions sap vital resources that may be needed to bolster a weak judiciary. More than to budgets and buildings, I refer to prestige resources, a regime's inscrutable public servants whose names are needed to lend credibility. Signals of a regime's serious intentions such as naming high prestige officials to direct institutions with sensitive mandates – like human-rights commissions, electoral courts, or special prosecutions – may hardly be understated. In the Mexican case, the Federal Electoral Commission was headless for over a year after the 1996 reforms as the parties labored to find an inscrutable but nonpartisan leader. Likewise, the battle over naming the 1994 attorney general's special prosecutor for electoral crimes was more contentious than any cases brought by his office.[37] Reserving domains for the rule of law offered immediate relief in epic problems (such as pervasive

---

[37] There were several rounds of voting before the government and the parties could agree on a candidate (Alcocer 1995, 51–2). Part of the problem in selecting legal authorities was that no national bar association existed to offer professional assessments of candidates (Cossío Díaz 1996, 31–2).

human-rights abuses or chronic electoral fraud), and removed these issues from the realm of the negotiable in otherwise ongoing bargaining between PRI-state and opposition.

In democratization, judicial reformers must continuously extend courts' prerogatives to countermand corruption and insulate judges so that they may arrive at purely judicially based verdicts. However, the more prerogatives judges are granted, the more vested become their interests in preserving the status quo, and the less impartial they become in dealing with the regime's adversaries. The Mexican reformers' initial answer, parceling areas of greatest authoritarian abuse among ombudsman beacons of autonomy, was only partially successful. In the case of the electoral courts, such measures effectively established safeguards within their limited areas of jurisdiction, but they could not force actor compliance. Furthermore, such institutions are costly, expending reputations of credible individuals, whose endorsements were needed elsewhere, and scarce resources. As framed by the thoughtful reformer Victor García Moreno (interview), "How many islands of accountability can we create if impunity still fills the rest of the horizon?"

Ombudsman institutions may best be considered stopgaps. As in the 1980s Chilean and Argentine truth commissions, motivated task forces could shine light on small areas and remove subjects from the realm of the negotiable, but their efforts could not be sustained. Long-run institutional development required full investment in the judicial branch despite initial lapses in autonomy such as those experienced in the 1997 electoral court. Most importantly, the vesting of actors – like Mexico's PRD – could offset any losses in institutional autonomy. The Mexican bet – fortified greatly by the separation of the PRI from the state in 2000 – is that the federal judiciary, even with all its remaining PRI-state nominees, will overcome inherent weaknesses to dispense the electoral justice opposition parties have come to expect. Future research could more directly test internal means of establishing magistrate accountability.

Contrary to static ideal typical autonomous courts, the tension inherent in building courts during transitions is whether to favor actors' short-term interests or the broader long-term interest of judicial autonomy. Preliminary evidence indicates that transitional regime realists have tended to favor the former, while idealistic advocates of courting democracy continue to hope for the latter. Both groups have sought, with only limited success, to construct beacons of a democratic rule of law on unsteady ground, before fully draining the swamps of authoritarianism. In Mexico, the enterprise of constructing federal electoral courts was resoundingly successful, especially from the post-2000 vantage point. This accomplishment at the federal level is especially impressive considering the historical starting point, addressed in the next chapter, of Mexico's battle for electoral justice against the governors, traditionally the most powerful regional machine bosses.

4

Mexico's Local Electoral Justice Failures: Gubernatorial (S)Election Beyond the Shadows of the Law

> Contracts...have a major drawback: the transaction costs of arranging and enforcing them. Because of these costs, members of a group may find it more welfare maximizing to honor the default rules that third parties have set.
>
> Legal theorist Robert C. Ellickson[1]

Among the most important discretionary powers of the president has been the naming and removal of governors, the president's premier agents in their respective states. The relationship between the president and the governors has been a peculiar one, defying the system of electoral justice successfully imposed at the federal level and routinely violating the federal pact. This chapter details the president's "hiring" and "firing" of the governors, and the governors' "hiring" and "firing" of the mayors, throughout the twentieth century, demonstrating the strong and arbitrary tradition of presidential imposition (whether "papered over" by elections or not), which was only recently cast aside by President Vicente Fox for a new standard of more gentle executive-branch intervention. I argue through discussion of the aggregate cases of presidential appointment and dismissal, as well as through three case studies from the early 1990s, that if the federal electoral courts discussed in the last chapter offered electoral justice success stories, gubernatorial races epitomized institutional failure during the crucial decades of Mexico's protracted transition. Given this broad pre-2000 range in outcomes of the institutions of electoral justice (ranging from institutional accountability at the federal

---

[1] Quotation from Ellickson (1991, 246).

level to widespread failure at the gubernatorial level), I argue that mayoral races occupy the middle of this spectrum between successful and failed electoral justice outcomes. Indeed, local races provide the proper level of analysis for microlevel considerations of incumbent-opposition bargaining, as these elections offer variation in the configuration of both formal and informal dispute-adjudicating institutions, as demonstrated at length in Chapters 5 through 8.

The best way to assert the primacy of the local electoral arena for closer study is to first briefly consider elections at the state level, explaining the significance of these races for political opening but also showing that electoral courts have not been determinantal to date in assessing the outcome of gubernatorial races. Gubernatorial races are important in their own right. During the Party of the Institutional Revolution (PRI)–state's heyday, they served as the linchpins of presidential imposition in the regions. Analysts have also argued that the power of the governors has reverberated down to the most local levels, as patterns of presidential-gubernatorial relations are replicated by the governors in their relations with the mayors. Furthermore, given the pre-2000 importance of "same party" governors to amicable federal and state public administration[2] and the extreme executive discretion in federal allocations, the proximity of relations between the governor and president may dramatically affect social spending in even the tiniest of villages (Mizrahi 1997, Rodriguez 1997). In Mexico's hierarchical and centralized regime, where local taxation authority was almost nonexistent and federal inflows accounted for well over 90 percent of most municipal budgets, presidential control was nearly complete.

The overall thesis of the chapter is that the arbitrary practices of gubernatorial selection (the *dedazo* or "fingering" by the president in consultation with the national PRI), a mainstay of Mexican politics from the 1917 constitution through the late 1990s, also set the standard for mayoral selection, until increasingly defiant opposition parties challenged them, albeit informally, starting in the 1970s and 1980s. I illustrate the

---

[2] Prior to political competition, the biggest rift between presidents and governors occurred when a new president started his six-year term "inheriting" some two-thirds of the last president's governors, who, like the president, were elected to six-year terms, but with elections staggered every two years. The previous president's governors were usually "lame duck" caretakers until the sitting president replaced them and augmented federal cash flows to credit the incoming president's allies. This federal electoral business cycle was broken even before 2000, as PRI victories were no longer assured, and because states rescheduled gubernatorial races to coincide with presidential elections.

federal PRI-state's lock on gubernatorial (s)election through the early 1990s by considering three critical gubernatorial races. I argue that by 1995 the failure of the PRI-state to discipline breakaway local PRI factions in the landmark postelectoral mobilization in Tabasco signaled the end of the unlimited federal PRI-state monopoly over its local chapters. While these gubernatorial races illustrate the increasing might of opposition parties at postelectoral bargaining tables and the increasing rifts between the formerly monolithic PRI-state and its increasingly independent local affiliates, they offer no evidence whatsoever that electoral courts, the purported dispensers of electoral justice, had any role in local postelectoral deliberations.

WELL-OILED POLITICAL MACHINES: TRADITIONAL GOVERNOR IMPUNITY IN MEXICAN POLITICS

The postrevolutionary elite settlement in the 1920s and 1930s set the tenor for the arbitrariness of future gubernatorial (s)election. The strongest of the postrevolutionary *caudillos* (political/military bosses), Plutarco Elias Calles, governed behind the throne nine years after leaving the presidency (1921–30) in what has come to be known as the "Maximato period." Calles routinely replaced enemies with his own military/civilian subordinates, a practice Cárdenas perfected while wearing the presidential sash (1934–40) in an effort to undo Calles's influence in Mexico's regions (Table 4.1). The 1917 constitution, in addition to providing politically progressive safeguards to muzzle the Mexican Revolution's battle cries,[3] also contains provisions fortifying central authority over the states. The legal backbone of this anti–states' rights regime was Article 76, granting the federal Senate broad authorities of intervention to preserve the constitutional order, dissolving state governments, and imposing presidentially nominated (and Senate-ratified) interim governors (González Oropeza 1987, 107). Furthermore, Article 122 permitted federal intervention in the states at the behest of the state executive or legislature (presumably in cases of insurrection or internal disturbance) and Article 89 granted the president the right to raise troops in defense of the federal patrimony

---

[3] The constitution has been widely interpreted as "not only a political constitution, but also a social constitution" (Aguilar Camín and Meyer 1993, 63) intended to bolster the disadvantaged through clauses such as Article 27 mandating widespread land reform, and Article 123, liberalizing labor standards, hailed as "the most advanced labor code in the world" (Hansen 1974, 90).

TABLE 4.1 *Number of Governors Per Year Not Completing Their Terms in Given Periods*

Characterization of Period	Years	Governors "Retired"	Governors/ Year
Revolutionary Aftermath	1928–34 (6)	21	3.50
Emilio Portéz Gil	1928–30 (2)	7	3.5
Pascual Ortíz Rubio	1930–2 (2)	9	4.5
Abelardo L. Rodríguez	1932–4 (2)	5	2.5
National PRI Consolidation	1934–52 (18)	41	2.28
Lázaro Cárdenas	1934–40 (6)	19	3.17
Manuel Avila Camacho	1940–6 (6)	11	1.83
Miguel Alemán	1946–52 (6)	16	2.67
PRI Hegemony over Regions	1952–88 (36)	35	0.97
Adolfo Ruíz Cortines	1952–8 (6)	9	1.5
Adolfo López Mateos	1958–64 (6)	3	0.50
Gustavo Díaz Ordaz	1964–70 (6)	2	0.33
Luis Echeverria	1970–6 (6)	9	1.5
José López Portillo	1976–82 (6)	6	1.0
Miguel de la Madrid	1982–8 (6)	6	1.0
Violation of Federal-State Pact	1988–94 (6)	17	2.83
Carlos Salinas de Gortari	1988–94 (6)	17	2.83
"New" Federalism/Pluralism	1994–2000 (6)	4	0.67
Ernesto Zedillo	1994–2000 (6)	4	0.67
Era of Opposition Alternation	2000–???	???	???
Vicente Fox	2000–6	???	???

Sources: Amezcua and Pardinas (1997, 24–7), Hernández Rodríguez (1994, 204–16), Anderson (1971, 345–6), González Oropeza (1987, 155–233), and Vázquez (1993).

(Anderson 1971, 33).[4] The net effect of these laws was to codify the president's long-standing supreme political authority over the governors, and to provide some criminal impunity to wayward governors.[5] In other words, governors can be "fired," but only by the president and only under the aegis of the strong and disciplined PRI, which could ruin political

---

[4] A more recent constitutional reform to Article 110 offered some protection to the governors against federal prosecution by determining that governors could be held responsible – but to the state legislatures they controlled – even if they violated federal laws (González Oropeza 1996, 67).

[5] This gubernatorial impunity was most blatantly flaunted after the massacre of seventeen opposition sympathizers in Aguas Blancas, Guerrero in July 1995 (Cornelius 2000, 124). The peasants were killed by police, apparently under state government orders. The governor was forced to resign, but criminal investigations recommended by the National Human Rights Commission and Interamerican Human Rights Commission were ignored (Camargo 1998c).

careers instantly. The governors are largely immune from criminal prosecution, and since there is no reelection, they cannot be punished by the electorate.

During the postrevolutionary consolidation of power, generals revolted in ten states, prompting Calles to settle for coexistence with local bosses he was unable to tame. In Michoacán, San Luis Potosí, Chihuahua, Coahuila, Guanajuato, Queretaro, Sonora, Tabasco, Veracruz, and Zacatecas, Calles acceded but sought to bring local *caciques* into the fold by creating a national political party from which he could monitor them. Hence the PRI was born (dubbed the National Revolutionary Party or PNR until decades after its 1929 founding), emphasizing individual party membership over that of corporatist groups, which would later dominate the PRI (Anderson 1971, 44). Barely a decade after the twentieth century's first bloody social revolution, ideological commitment had been jettisoned in favor of the "catchall" pragmatism of the PNR/PRI, created largely so that Calles could tame the regions. Calles's inability to fully control the regional governors and agrarian and labor leaders forced him to select a more moderate successor, Lázaro Cárdenas, also a former revolutionary general and governor of Michoacán. Cárdenas first tapped the mobilization potential of the highly organized and monopolistic mass political party created by his predecessor.

Cárdenas did not enjoy strong relations with his predecessor, however, and Calles openly challenged Cárdenas's reformist policies. Cárdenas was able to chase Calles's supporters from federal and state offices, and "through rigged elections, the use of Article 76, and with the aid of federal troops, Cárdenas had his agents [instated] in twenty-two of the twenty-eight states and territories" (Anderson 1971, 51). The extent of Cárdenas's federal interventionism can hardly be exaggerated. The general who had fought a revolution for "effective suffrage and no re-election" imposed nineteen unelected governors on Mexico's twenty-eight states, trampling the federal pact (Amezcua and Pardinas 1997, 24–7; González Oropeza 1987, 219–24). Cárdenas's interventionism (Table 4.1) institutionalized the definitive central authority and consolidated postrevolutionary control, unrivaled for forty more years until Salinas exceeded Cárdenas's penchant for violating states' rights.

Cárdenas countermanded the regional *caciques* through interlocking corporatist interests and responsive state agencies that became the backbone of the hegemonic PRI.[6] Cárdenas replaced the negative incentive

---

[6] The party's name was formally changed from the PNR to the PRI in 1946.

of violence with the positive incentive of patronage by creating peasant, urban worker, and "popular" sectors (comprised mostly of teachers and government employees) through which grievances could be channeled, decisions taken, and government largesse allocated. Avila Camacho (1940–6) and Alemán (1946–52), like Cárdenas, further consolidated both the party and the executive branch, by breaking down independent political machines in the states and installing governors loyal to them. The construction of perhaps the world's longest-reigning inclusionary corporatist regime carried risks, however, as granting the three "popular sectors" authority to nominate candidates (or at least to formalize the president's nominations) also produced a backlash in the 1940s, which reached its nadir in the most notorious postelectoral conflict on record, the 1946 slaying of twenty-seven conservative regime opponents in León and the injuring of some sixty more (Rionda 1995, 6). The lack of primary elections, especially in states where the local PRI machine was only loosely connected to (and not controlled by) the national PRI, provoked further conflict. In 1946, reforms within the party broadened the "consultation of the bases" in candidate selection, although the adoption of primaries was resisted, ostensibly because the PRI still had not consolidated complete control over several states. The consolidated PRI ran roughshod over opponents, inaugurating six presidential administrations of PRI high hegemony (see Table 4.1), using presidentially imposed governors to increase presidential powers in the periphery.

The PAN, founded in 1939, did evolve into an electoral presence, but not until the late 1950s. From 1941 to 1959, fewer than half of the gubernatorial races were contested by any opposition candidate at all, while by the late 1970s, at least three parties fielded candidates in every election.[7] The PRI candidate selection continued to be undemocratic, responding to the party's sectoral demands to run cronies rather than to the unheeded popular candidate endorsements. By 1958, PRI local party leaders started to internally condemn excessive centralism, and local activists rebelled (albeit unsuccessfully) against federal imposition of gubernatorial

---

[7] According to Anderson, 41 percent of the gubernatorial races between 1941 and 1959 were contested (44 percent in the 1940s, 39 percent in the 1950s), while between 1960 and 1964, 53 percent of the races had an opposition candidate (see Anderson 1971, 77, 91, 97, 112). Between 1979 and 1985, after electoral reforms to encourage opposition, PPS candidates were fielded in every race; PAN and PST candidates in 94 percent; PSUM candidates in 90 percent; Mexican Democratic Party (PDM) and PARM candidates in 81 percent; and Revolutionary Workers' Party (PRT) candidates in 16 percent of the gubernatorial elections (author compilation from electoral data).

candidates in Morelos. In San Luis Potosí, Tabasco, and Chiapas, the local PRI was able to overthrow inferior candidates who had been imposed over popular local leaders. In response, Adolfo López Mateos (1958–64) promised, as part of his presidential campaign, to limit federal imposition of gubernatorial candidates (the *dedazo* "fingering"), and in 1960 minor changes were made in national party statutes, instituting party primaries in a few trial states and granting state PRI chairs and governors automatic membership on the party's National Council for the first time to guarantee regional – as well as sectoral – channels to federal party headquarters. These primaries were largely discontinued, however, when local PRI favorites used them to defeat nationally imposed but locally unpopular candidates, such as in Sonora 1961 (Anderson 1971, 100–13).

The regime in the 1960s accepted a few token opposition mayoral victories but would not permit gubernatorial victories by regime opponents. It seemed to have made strides toward greater tolerance of opponents, especially in comparison to the country's first postelectoral bloodletting in 1946 León, where the president preferred sacrificing his governor to permitting a rightist opposition mayor to take office. However, these local victories seemed to have little impact on national policy, except to renew futile efforts by moderates within the PRI to reform candidate selection procedures (Bezdek 1973, 182–3). With the rise to dominance of the PRI's "hard-line" in the late 1960s, these opposition victories were again forbidden, such as in Tijuana 1968, Mérida 1969, and Garza García 1969, where probable PAN victories were denied. In fact, the PRI-state went so far in Tijuana as to commit outright fraud on election day and then annul the elections on the basis of "irregularities" they had provoked, naming an interim mayor... from the PRI (Anderson 1971, 102).

The PRI national president Carlos A. Madrazo sought in the mid-1960s to reform the PRI, shaking up the governors and "sector" leaders, who selected local candidates through the authoritarian *dedazo* (selection by pointing of the president's or governor's finger). He introduced intraparty primaries and "straw polls" to select the most popular candidates (rather than those most vested in local machines), and introduced these vital reforms in several local races before an autocratic governor "blocked" his efforts in Sinaloa by running "his candidates" as independents (and making sure they won) when Madrazo's system yielded PRI candidates popular with voters but not with the governor. Madrazo quit the national PRI presidency after his reforms mostly failed (Bailey 1987, 72–4), and the party's retrograde candidate-selection procedures survived several more reform efforts, notably by Jesús Reyes Heroles in the 1970s and by

Luis Donaldo Colosio in the early 1990s. The party remained largely un-changed even into the late 1990s, when once again, party primaries were introduced sporadically and with great resistance before they were more consistently adopted – at least in much of Mexico – in the late 1990s and after 2000.

PERFECTING POSTELECTORAL POKER: THE OPPOSITION DEALS THEMSELVES IN

Throughout the 1960s and 1970s, the federal government rarely resorted to the removal of governors to consolidate national party bases, and def-initely not at its pre-1950s rate (Table 4.1).[8] Small opposition inroads were again allowed by the 1970s, and even encouraged after the PRI's embarrassing unopposed campaign for the presidency in 1976, but the party-state's tolerance was yet again exhausted in 1983 after the 1982 economic crisis produced a series of PAN victories in Mexico's north-ern states. The half-dozen newly legalized parties of the left, unable to coordinate joint candidacies or coalitions, commenced the modern strat-egy of "*la segunda vuelta*" soon after their 1977 legalizations. Seeking to minimize municipal conflicts over elections and budget allocations, the federal government approved a 1983 reform to Article 115 (reinforcing the administrative autonomy of the municipality) that routinized the designation of localities' shares of the federal budget, which had pre-viously been allocated without any guidelines (Chavarría 1994, 133). The reform also guaranteed each municipality a quota of "proportional repre-sentation city council members" that, contrary to the law's stated intent, actually increased the frequency of postelectoral conflicts, as extra propor-tional representation (PR) council seats were negotiated as "consolation prizes" for mobilized opposition parties who accepted losses without es-calating conflicts. The new law did diminish the severity of postelectoral conflicts by creating "chips" for which the postelectoral protestors could play and hence incentives for them not to outbid PRI-state tolerance.

The historical record of municipal governance prior to the 1980s is ex-tremely sporadic. But even so, evidence exists of the correlation between increased opposition proportional representation and an increase in the frequency of postelectoral conflicts in states like Oaxaca. According to Díaz Montes (1992, 74), the number of the state's 570 municipalities "in

---

[8] Constitutional reforms in 1978 made this difficult to do through the dissolution of powers.

conflict"[9] increased from ten in 1971, to fifty in 1980 (the election after the 1977 federal electoral reform), to seventy-one in 1986 (the election after the 1983–4 federal municipal reform). Compelling but nonsystematic evidence from other case studies confirms these trends, as violent postelectoral conflicts by electoral losers on the antiregime left (Party of United Mexican Socialists [PSUM], Socialist Workers' Party [PST], Communist Party [PCM]) and transition-seeking center (Popular Socialist Party [PPS], Authentic Party of the Mexican Revolution [PARM], Party of the Cardenista Front for National Reconstruction [PFCRN]) occurred in Chiapas (Guillén 1998, 195–9), Guerrero, Hidalgo, México State, Michoacán, Tabasco, Tlaxcala, and Veracruz (Alonso 1985, 357; Calderón Mólgora 1994, 62). State governments responded to postelectoral conflicts by constructing more plural municipal councils in the late 1980s and early 1990s. These makeshift compromise "plural councils," designated by state legislatures' rubberstamping of governors' decrees, allowed opposition parties representation on local administrations, even if the most important posts – like mayor and treasurer – were nearly always left in the hands of the PRI. The creation of plural councils obeyed local political circumstances and the governor's whim more than any more formal logic. But they proliferated in the early 1980s as office-starved opposition parties realized that gaining a foothold in local governance – however small – required little more than rounding up protesters after an election to clog streets, obstruct commerce, and perhaps occupy city hall for a few days. In Oaxaca, for example, only one municipal election was annulled and two municipal councils created by the state legislature in 1971. By 1980, thirteen elections were annulled in Oaxaca and seventeen municipal councils were created. In 1986, thirteen elections were also annulled, but twenty-nine municipal councils were constructed (Díaz Montes 1992, 74).

Even in the late 1970s and early 1980s, great differences existed in the postelectoral tactics used by the newly legalized left and those of the established National Action Party (PAN). While the decentralized parties of the left protested willy-nilly without broader resonance, the PAN captivated national attention through its postelectoral antics, setting a precedent for the landmark federal postelectoral mobilization of 1988. Chihuahua state, which was embroiled in early 1980s postelectoral conflicts during the de la Madrid presidency, drew widespread attention to PRI-state

---

[9] Díaz Montes's (1992) definition of municipalities "in conflict" is more inclusive than the one I adopt in my analysis in the next chapter, but the study is important as possibly the only one that quantifies the creation of plural councils back to the 1970s.

repression of an "unacceptable" PAN victory for the first time and set the tenor for the 1988 postelectoral imbroglio. Indeed, no discussion of post-electoral conflicts is complete without mention of the PAN's 1986 post-electoral stand in this arid border state where *concertacesión* failed but civil disobedience raised the ire of Mexico's Catholic Church hierarchy, hundreds of medium- and large-scale business owners, scores of famous intellectuals, dozens of civil society groups, the increasingly independent national media, the international community, and millions of Mexican citizens. These elections have been studied extensively (see Chand 2001, Lau 1989, Martínez Assad 1988, and Mizrahi 1994), but are addressed here as context for the decade of postelectoral mobilizations to follow, which I assert in the remaining chapters were the principal mechanism of courting democracy in Mexico.

While the PAN had counted mobilization among its postelectoral re-sponses to grotesquely unfair electoral rules and PRI-committed electoral fraud since the 1950s, Chihuahua escalated the pitch of *PANista* nation-wide calls for legality and electoral justice by an order of magnitude as the first-ever sustained civil disobedience after a gubernatorial race and as the first to snowball from the rugged desert to the president's pine-lined estate in Mexico City. The PRI-state's declaration of victory by President de la Madrid, backtracking on his 1983 commitment to "moral renovation" by recognizing opposition victories, was met with open defiance, rather than with the PAN's usual perfunctory demonstrations and verbal reprimands at the parliamentary podium. This time, work stoppages, international bridge blockades, and hunger strikes were capped by a march hundreds of miles long from Chihuahua to Queretaro by Chihuahua City's *PANista* mayor and national "moral" leader, Luis H. Álvarez. The PAN's success in captivating Mexico in this 1986 postelectoral drama also confirmed the utility of civil disobedience in galvanizing public support, if not in gaining leverage for *concertacesiones* (which did not function in 1986 de-spite serious efforts by the PAN). Protagonists of civil disobedience in the Philippines' democratization taught the *PANistas* in Mexico City, and Gene Sharp's *The Politics of Non-violent Action* was read in PAN seminars throughout the nation (Gómez 1991, 373–5).

The *PANistas* formally made Active and Peaceful Civil Disobedience (dubbed "RECAP") an integral part of their strategy for 1988. Perhaps more importantly, they demonstrated the success of these tactics to op-position leaders across the spectrum, including the left's most important figure, Heberto Castillo, head of Mexican Socialist Party (PMS), who paid a "solidarity" visit to Chihuahua and called for an unprecedented grand coalition of the regime's opponents. Castillo, who possessed even more moral capital than Alvarez after having been tortured and jailed as a leader of Mexico's 1968 student protests, advocated defiance of the government, thus forcing the PRI-state to choose: "either it respects the popular will or else we engage in violence. I am ready to die" (Gómez 1991, 372). Castillo's selfless renunciation of his 1988 presidential candidacy in favor of Cárdenas gave further credence to his calls for sacrifice.

SALINAS AND THE RENEWED PRESIDENTIAL DISCRETION IN CENTER-PERIPHERY RELATIONS

Although it underscored the PRI-state's unwillingness – as of yet – to grant concessions to the PAN, Chihuahua 1986 radicalized the opposition on both sides of the spectrum, honing a new postelectoral weapon for national PAN party strategists and also sparking the determination of leaders on the left. At the local level, however, postelectoral conflicts by the tiny precursor parties of the Party of the Democratic Revolution (PRD) continued as isolated and spontaneous uprisings, largely uncoordinated with national developments springing from Chihuahua. It was the *PANístas* who planted the seeds of democratization from the periphery toward the center in the mid-1980s, even if it was the leftist Cardenista Front (FDN) coalition that harvested them in 1988.

By the late 1980s, the *PANístas* would come to warm a regular seat at the PRI-state's nascent postelectoral bargaining tables, but only to adjudicate mayoral election disputes. Even with enhanced competition by the PAN, opposition gubernatorial victories were off the table, especially after Chihuahua, until the Salinas administration sought to "legitimize" Mexican democracy, albeit selectively. It took recognition of PAN gubernatorial victories – starting in Baja California in 1989 – to fully understand the role of the governors in the matrix of Mexico's strong presidentialism. That first opposition governor, the feisty Ernesto Ruffo Appel, filled Mexico's newspapers with accusations of fiscal arbitrariness by central government bureaucrats and launched an acrimonious debate about "the new federalism" (Guillén López 1992, Rodriguez and Ward 1995). The long-standing subservience of the states to federal budgetary discretion was suddenly a national issue, as was the federal government's sudden interest, when the PAN started winning governorships, in targeting federal social spending to areas of PRI vulnerability (Molinar and Weldon 1994).

TABLE 4.2 *Comparison of Causes for Removal of Governors*
Alemán (1946–52) and Salinas (1988–94) Administrations

Cause	Alemán	Salinas
Ingovernability – opposition party postelectoral mobilizing	0	7
Ingovernability – unpopular policy choices	2	4
Federal appointment (unrelated to governor performance)	2	4
Disputes within the PRI	3	1
Municipal imposition	3	0
Personal reasons (poor health)	3	0
Succession conflicts with federal government or legislature	2	0
Governor faces strong suspicion of graft	0	1
Governor faces criminal charges (or strong suspicion)	1	0
TOTAL	16	17

Source: Anderson (1971, 345–6) for Alemán period and media accounts for Salinas period, coded by author.

In the early 1990s, Salinas revived the despotic practice of removing governors to consolidate his own authority against the backdrop of diminishing PRI hegemony, effectively co-opting the PAN by bringing them to the postelectoral bargaining table, which generated several local and statewide postelectoral conflicts for each *concertacesión* actually granted. Salinas removed seventeen governors during his administration (Table 4.2); since the era of Cárdenas and his successor Alemán, no previous president had forced the resignation of more governors. When compared to governor removals by Alemán, who, unlike Salinas, faced municipal and regional challenges to his authority, the Salinas record was quite arbitrary indeed. That is, while Salinas imposed governors based on a proactive center-to-periphery negotiating logic, his distant predecessors in the era of PRI-state consolidation imposed governors largely as a *post hoc* response to regional disturbances, in a "periphery-to-center" pattern of negotiations. Of his seventeen dismissals, Salinas removed the largest number of governors (seven) by acceding to postelectoral demands by the opposition for their removal. Alemán removed *no* governors due to postelectoral disturbances, but instead forced the resignation of the greatest number, three, attributable to disputes within the PRI, and three more due to candidate impositions by municipalities (Anderson 1971). While no systematic pre-Alemán data exists, anecdotal evidence indicates that the Alemán administration, coming at the end of PRI-state consolidation, required considerably less imposition over the regions than his own predecessors in the 1920s and 1930s.

A crucial difference between the PRI periods of consolidation and hegemony was that in the 1920s and 1930s the president's own allies might be sacrificed to co-opt regional machine bosses. Such sacrifices were not required during the 1960s and 1970s, when the PRI-state's hegemony was at its peak. During the 1920s and 1930s, these maverick machine bosses or *caciques* could be isolated, placated, and kept at arm's length, all within what the PRI-state's ideologues had come to call "the revolutionary family." By the late 1980s and especially the 1990s, these special interests were national opposition parties intent on turning the PRI-state's bargaining disposition against their political enemies. Because the new opposition parties were decreasingly geographically based, they could not as easily be isolated. While the PAN held no more than a few pockets of support, for example, these pockets ran from the U.S.-Mexico border states, through Mexico's Central Valley, and to the southern border at Yucatán. Increasing activist mobility and growing media penetration rendered untenable the Cárdenas-Alemán strategy of cordoning off *caciques*. But Salinas, the ambitious economic reformer, did not realize this. Like his consolidation-era predecessors, Salinas sought to selectively reward and punish those threatening his national policies. Unlike Cárdenas and Alemán, Salinas thought he could broker informal deals with opponents, without irking PRI insiders.

The first public dissents in nearly forty years between PRI state chapters and the party's federal headquarters arose over Salinas's arbitrary designation of governors. This dissolution of PRI unity, which "spilled over" into legislative affairs, commenced at the Guanajuato State Legislature in 1991 and escalated in Mexico's federal congressional chambers[10] and on the streets of Villahermosa, Tabasco in early 1995, before peaking in a 2001 confrontation in Mérida, Yucatán between the federal electoral authorities and one of the old PRI's most notorious governors. I evaluate these gubernatorial postelectoral negotiations in three case studies: Salinas's quintessential "*concertacesión*" to the PAN in 1991 Guanajuato, the failed 1992 effort by the PRD in Michoacán to receive similar treatment from Salinas, and the so-called "rebellion of the PRI" over the 1994 Tabasco governor's race signaling the end of this postelectoral negotiation

---

[10] While the 2000 elections eliminated most vestiges of PRI discipline, the opposition's 1997 inroads in the Chamber of Deputies had already cracked this fabled partisanship across a range of issues, from budget agreements to Chiapas peace plans to electoral reforms. The first outright disobedience of PRI leadership by "back bencher" legislators since before World War II was the executive branch's 1996 electoral reform, opposed by a large majority of PRI legislators.

norm. After highlighting the effects of presidential discretion on the gradual erosion of PRI discipline over the last decade of Mexico's protracted transition here, Chapter 8 addresses the abrupt change in PRI strategies exemplified by former Yucatán Governor Victor Cervera Pacheco's 2001 defiance of federal legal mandates. That case, in which a PRI regional machine boss directly defied a clear legal verdict, represents a dramatic shift from extralegal arbitrariness by Mexico's president under Salinas (and Zedillo to a lesser extent) to illegal arbitrariness by several unbridled PRI traditionalist governors – led by Cervera Pacheco – under Fox. If the 2000 election was the climax of Mexico's democratic transition, the Cervera standoff in Yucatán was its *dénouement*.

Of the three pre-2000 cases presented here, Tabasco represents Zedillo's unambiguous break with the Salinas line, albeit not without nearly succumbing to the PRD and traditional forces in the national PRI. Because Zedillo reneged on his removal of PRI governor-elect Roberto Madrazo in January 1995, there have been relatively few postelectoral conflicts, at least at the gubernatorial level. Tabasco was the critical case for establishing a less arbitrary and interventionist pattern of center-periphery relations, one that Zedillo apparently established out of weakness and that Fox has followed. The *PANista* president's firsthand experience with the *concertacesión*'s erosion of both the rule of law and party discipline conditioned his own insistence on resolving center-periphery crises through legal rather than political channels. The common denominator of these three cases is that the legal route to resolving conflicts, exemplified by state electoral courts established well before the conflictive elections, was largely irrelevant.

GUANAJUATO AS THE PAN'S MODEL FOR SALINAS-ERA POSTELECTORAL CONFLICTS

Guanajuato was the exemplar case of PAN-PRI postelectoral negotiations. The rules of PAN-PRI engagement were similar to those in place since Salinas signed his 1989 letter of intent to cooperate with the PAN (Chapter 2), but rather than merely achieving replacement of one PRI candidate with another less objectionable to the PAN as in a half dozen other cases, the PAN finessed the naming of a *PANista* interim governor, over the vehement protests of Guanajuato's local PRI. Furthermore, by emphasizing the arbitrary abuse of authority through which a *PANista* other than candidate Vicente Fox was named, the PAN's original candidate, Fox, capitalized on the injustice of the process to reinforce his reformer credentials. Despite the extensive publicity of this case, coming five years after the Chihuahua precedent for postelectoral conflicts, rule by an unelected governor was nothing new in Guanajuato, which had been governed to date by more interim, provisional, and substitute governors than by elected authorities (Rionda 1995, 2).

For a potential *concertacesión*, the initial vote gap between the PAN and the PRI was not promising for the PAN. The official electoral results in 1991 disappointed the PAN, granting Fox some 417,000 votes, second to PRI insider Ramon Aguirre's 622,000 (with then-PRD parliamentarian and cofounder Porfirio Muñoz Ledo claiming third place with 100,000 votes). Upon receiving no satisfaction at the electoral court, Fox consulted with PAN headquarters in Mexico City and launched demonstrations all over the state. The national PAN's decision to advance to full mobilization was taken after the judicial route failed, but knowing that the *PANístas* did not have conclusive evidence of overwhelming electoral fraud (Alemán Alemán 1993, 103, 117–18). Postelectoral demonstrations were largely symbolic in Guanajuato; the real pressures were applied by the national PAN to the Secretary of the Interior and to Salinas himself.

Mexico City PRI-PAN postelectoral negotiations were fruitful for two reasons even as mobilizations trickled off in Guanajuato. First, the PRI was counting on PAN congressional support of two Salinas initiatives, and, second, the poor international press on the "fraud of Guanajuato" worried the federal government, which was vigorously promoting foreign trade and investment. The national PRI had conducted its "cost-benefit" assessment and decided to "sacrifice Guanajuato in order to maintain its alliance with the PAN" (Nuñez interview) in the Chamber of Deputies, to attain the qualified majority needed to pass Salinas's proposed constitutional reforms of Church-state relations (Article 27), and to end Mexico's post-Cárdenas agrarian reform (Article 130). Other sources found causes of PRI tolerance in unsparing editorials in the *Wall Street Journal* and *New York Times*, which made the Guanajuato elections a source of conversation at the North American Free Trade Agreement (NAFTA) Secretarial meetings in Seattle, to the consternation of the PRI-state (Alemán Alemán 93; Rionda 1996, 11).[11]

Like most of the PAN's contemporary *concertacesiónes*, the deal was consummated between PAN Federal Deputy (and 1994 presidential

---

[11] The *New York Times* August 26 editorial placed Mexico in the unflattering company of Cuba, Guyana, and Surinam as the Western Hemisphere's last authoritarian regimes. See Puig (1991).

candidate) Diego Fernández de Cevallos and the then-Interior Secretary, PRI traditionalist Fernando Gutiérrez Barrios (Alemán Alemán 1993, 62, 86, 125). Prior to its rulings, Fernández de Cevallos insisted that the election "be cleaned through the electoral court" (Alemán Alemán 1993, 93) but when his problem was not "solved" there he settled for a "decorous way out," which was to name an interim governor, but from the PAN (121–2). In a discussion between PAN leaders and Salinas, Fernández de Cevallos invoked the threat of 1976, when his party did not field a presidential candidate, warning that his party would not participate in the 1994 presidential elections if there was no commitment to a democratic transition. He added that without a favorable electoral environment, he doubted the successful negotiation of NAFTA (Alemán Alemán 1993, 124). The "decorous way out" was for the Mexico City PRI to circulate copies of Aguirre's resignation speech even before the governor-elect had been ratified by the Guanajuato Electoral College (Alemán Alemán 1993, 127). The Electoral College, or rather the minimum quorum of fifteen out of twenty-eight, met after the outgoing legislature "took" the capital building to prevent the incoming legislators from ratifying a *PANista* governor (Rionda 1995, 12). Sub-Secretary of the Interior Arturo Núñez was charged with persuading the minimum number of incoming *PRIista* legislators to sign the agreement, arguing that "between violence and *concertacesión*, the lesser evil is *concertacesión*" (Núñez interview).

The PAN's interim governor, Carlos Medina Plascencia, took office with the stated objective of winning passage of an electoral reform that would create propitious conditions for electing his replacement. The interim governor's hands were tied in the *concertacesión* by the mandatory inclusion of a state Interior Secretary from the PRI, who was to monitor the federal government's interest in Guanajuato's affairs. Medina Plascencia (interview) said he held several meetings with Salinas over the electoral reform, which was finally approved in a progressive form, but only after the federal Interior Secretary pressed the national PRI leadership, which in turn pressured the Guanajuato local PRI to accept the reforms. The *concertacesión*, giving the PAN three years of administrative experience before winning reelection in 1994, forced electoral reforms to level future state election playing fields and destroyed PRI unity. It was heralded for years as the ultimate postelectoral victory. Fox proved the big winner, as he claimed the public relations mantle of the underdog victim without tarnishing himself with the mundane but constant disputes between the PAN's interim governor, the *PRIista* State Interior Secretary, and the national PRI, even as Fox's allies readied Guanajuato's electoral laws for his second gubernatorial bid, which he won handily (and officially) in 1997. If judged by its impact on furthering his national legislative agenda and on conditioning international opinion, Salinas's experiment in center-forced power sharing in the periphery was a success in the short term, although it would prove within a decade to be the PRI-state's undoing. But if postelectoral conflicts and interim governorships exemplified PAN success, they never worked for the PRD, as the 1992 Michoacán governor's race demonstrates.

MICHOACÁN AND THE PRD'S MODEL FOR SALINAS-ERA POSTELECTORAL CONFLICTS

Michoacán represented a failed effort by the PRD to cash in on PAN postelectoral strategies. It provided the clearest example of the unwillingness of Salinas's PRI-state to extend the same "courtesies" to the PRD as it did to the PAN. The governor's race followed an egregiously fraudulent state legislative race in 1989 and conflictive local races that same year in which dozens of PRD activists were slain in postelectoral violence culminating in the army's forced removal of hundreds of protesters obstructing several city halls (see Chapter 7). A state electoral reform had been approved by the Michoacán legislature in 1992, but had been negotiated directly between the local PRD and the federal Interior Secretariat in Mexico City (without any national PRD "honest broker" as most of the PRD's national leadership at the time was the Michoacán chapter). Threatening uncontrollable postelectoral mobilizations if there was no PRI-state acquiescence, PRD candidate Cristóbal Arias met with Interior Secretary Fernando Gutiérrez Barrios to level the state's preelectoral playing field, hoping the PRI and PRD could agree on "a pact of civility" to monitor electoral institutions and invite outside observers. Negotiations broke down, however, and Arias was not granted any deals. The PRD's gubernatorial aspirant was not helped in his negotiations by the ubiquitous Cuauhtémoc Cárdenas, who decried the illegitimacy of the Salinas government even as Arias tried to negotiate with Salinas. Arias's advisers said they repeatedly sought appointments with Salinas to clarify their transition-seeking position and distance themselves from Cárdenas's antiregime bromides, but to no avail (Rivera Velázquez interview). Instead, the preelectoral environment grew acrimonious. The PRI candidate Eduardo Villaseñor, disturbed by rumors that the election was being negotiated, *à la* Guanajuato, insisted at press conference after press conference that "Michoacán will not be negotiated!" and threatened that a PRD administration would govern through violence and intimidation (Beltrán del Río 1993, 237, 248).

Well before the election results were tallied, Salinas congratulated Villaseñor, and the national PRI contacted the PRD, ostensibly to compare results using each party's official copy of the results, broken down by precinct.[12] However, when Arias met with the PRI negotiator in Mexico City, he learned that the real agenda was to find "alternatives to conflict." These negotiations did not prosper (and in retrospect appear to have been a stalling tactic by the PRI to cool PRD tempers), and electoral authorities in Michoacán, such as Electoral Tribunal President Hilda Navarro, proclaimed that any action taken outside the electoral court, where all of the PRD's twenty-eight complaints were summarily rejected, "was juridically senseless" (Beltrán del Río 1993, 285). To avoid possible PRD mobilizations, the pro-PRI quorum of the Electoral College met clandestinely at a cultural center rather than in their State Capitol legislative chambers, hastily certifying the election without bothering to notify PRD legislators of the "special session." The act prompted two months of civil disobedience of a severity reminiscent of Chihuahua but unknown in Guanajuato.

From August 8 until October 5, 1992, throngs of PRD activists from all over Michoacán converged on the capital city, launching a march of pigs and other farm animals bearing PRI logos, the occupation of state buildings such as the state Supreme Court, and several hunger strikes. Without any known contact between the Interior Secretariat or the national PRI, and with relatively little contact with Cárdenas or the PRD national headquarters, thousands of Michoacán PRD activists sustained a civil disobedience campaign, even as Villaseñor took office (and Arias was sworn in during a "parallel" ceremony).

The costs were high: four PRD activists were shot dead, Arias's campaign headquarters was set on fire, and two other PRD activists, including a legislator-elect, were fired upon. The PRD's pressure was unrelenting, as Villaseñor was blockaded out of the state capitol by a constant PRD mobilization there, and PRD hecklers ambushed him repeatedly during

---

[12] The PRD gathered 3,462 out of 3,632 acts, meaning that party representatives had actively witnessed 95 percent of the voting and vote tallying. The PRD attorney, Samuel del Villar, said the party had failed to get all the acts (needed to judge the outcome) because party representatives had been expelled from polling booths or simply "treasoned" the party. Seeking to maximize evidence he did have, del Villar discounted results from voting booths not corroborated by PRD act copies and subtracted an average number of "false votes" from PRI totals, yielding a resounding Arias victory. However, electoral authorities did not concur with del Villar's tallying methods (Beltrán del Río 1993, 277).

his first weeks in office. The federal government intervened, not by dispatching negotiators from the Secretary of the Interior, but rather by convoking the Secretary of Defense to announce the launching of "Operation Michoacán Clean-Up," to put an end to the state's "delinquency." Unlike 1990, when soldiers violently removed PRD activists from municipal buildings in some thirty towns and cities after a year of postelectoral conflicts, the military threat this time was a bluff, although local police forces became increasingly belligerent in restoring order. Finally, under presidential order (Beltrán del Río 1993, 325–8), the national PRI negotiated Villaseñor's resignation. He was replaced by another PRI hardliner, two-time Michoacán Interior Secretary Aucensio Chávez, granting Arias and the PRD a symbolic triumph, but seeming to promise further repression in the longer term. Contrary to the PAN's performance in Guanajuato, which made Fox's national reputation, there was no reprieve for Arias, who became a pawn in the antagonism between Cárdenas and Salinas.

ZEDILLO'S POSITIONING AT TABASCO: *SANA DISTANCIA* AND NONNEGOTIATION OF GOVERNORSHIPS

Salinas's incursions into state affairs were discontinued by his successor, despite Zedillo's best intentions to negotiate a Salinas-style pact over the 1994 Tabasco governor's race. Zedillo's Interior Secretary and the national PRI engaged the Tabasco PRD's losing gubernatorial candidate, Andrés Manuel López Obrador, in bargaining an end to two months of PRD oil-field blockages, street protests, and work stoppages but reneged on their deal when the local PRI refused to cooperate. The Tabasco PRI had violated campaign spending limitations fiftyfold and with impunity;[13] had jammed the state's electoral apparatus with biased officials who committed flagrant election-day "engineering" including a mysterious blackout of the vote-tallying computer, which turned back on with 4 percent fewer votes cast; and had done the usual "get out the vote" promotions and petty ballot stuffing (see Eisenstadt 1999). The official

---

[13] The PRD's López Obrador came into possession of remarkable evidence, certified by a probe by the *PANista* federal Attorney General, that Madrazo spent over $50 million on his campaign, or eighty times more than he declared, and well over the legal spending limits. The Supreme Court in 1996 ruled that the federal investigation violated the federal pact and delegated further inquiries back to state authorities, who complacently served at the discretion of the alleged violator. The investigation of Madrazo died quietly, and heralded by the PRI's hard-liners, Madrazo was elected president of the national PRI in 2002.

results, a 56 percent (PRI)–37 percent (PRD) split, were contested in fifty-three complaints to the state electoral court, which summarily rejected all of them. The PRD did not expect electoral justice, but López Obrador, who moved on to become Mexico City's mayor between 2000 and 2003, explained that "Whatever we do, it will be construed as acting outside the law, so we must proceed through strict legal channels [in addition to extralegal channels] to avoid these criticisms. We must follow this legal course, even as we mobilize citizens, knowing that it [the law] does not work" (interview).

One of the PRD's only successful negotiators with the federal Interior Secretariat to date (and now Mexico City's popular mayor and an oft-mentioned 2006 presidential candidate) López Obrador was unable to renegotiate state electoral laws like his counterparts did in Guanajuato and Michoacán. He refused the terms imposed on Arias's failed bid to conduct a bipartisan electoral act tally – precommitment to the official outcome of the election without any reversion to postelectoral tactics. However, what he lost in negotiations with the Interior Secretariat before the election, López Obrador seemed to win back afterward, until the local PRI in Tabasco turned the PRD's own "*segunda vuelta*" strategy against its creators.

The Tabasco PRD marched to Mexico City and occupied the city's central square, threatening to interrupt Zedillo's swearing in as president. While this negative inducement to cooperation was less appealing to the PRI-state than the *PANístas'* positive-inducement promises of legislative coalitions, Zedillo Interior Secretary designate Esteban Moctezuma agreed to serve as a sort of extralegal solomonic counsel, disposed to annul the Tabasco state elections (for governor and mayor) if the PRD could satisfactorily demonstrate irregularities in 20 percent of the ballot boxes – the threshold of annulment established in the Tabasco electoral law (López Obrador 1996, 170). But first the Tabasco demonstrators had to evacuate the Mexico City site of Zedillo's imminent inauguration. The PRD demonstrators did relocate to another plaza, and the meetings to assess electoral irregularities commenced, but then dragged on, appearing increasingly like just another stalling tactic by the PRI-state to diffuse tensions and "outlast" the PRD's mobilization.

Fortunately for the PRD, however, Zedillo requested PRD (and PAN) support for a consensus electoral reform he hoped his administration could negotiate, thereby ending opposition cries of electoral fraud once and for all. As dialogue over Tabasco lagged in January 1995, the PRD forced the PRI-state to agree to at least "reconsider" 1994 postelectoral controversies in Chiapas, Veracruz, and Tabasco in exchange for PRD participation in reform talks. However, when word of this possible *concertacesión* reached Tabasco, local PRI leaders preempted the PRD by taking to the streets themselves. The Tabasco legislature's Speaker of the House said the local party felt abandoned by Mexico City, agreeing among themselves to refuse any resignation tendered by the governor-elect, and that furthermore, they would adopt PRD mobilizational tactics to get Mexico City's attention. The national PRI did respond positively. The forced resignation of Governor-elect Roberto Madrazo had been negotiated, and Madrazo was negotiating a federal post that would allow him to save face, when the "Rebellion of the PRI" provoked injuries and ingovernability in Tabasco and forced President Zedillo and his operatives to rescind the forced resignation (Eisenstadt 1999). Zedillo, lacking the authority and/or will to commit such strong-armed violations of the federal pact, quickly distanced himself from the PRD's *segunda vuelta* gone sour and reaffirmed his campaign's staunch "rule of law" advocacy (which had framed his candidacy in opposition to Salinas). The PRD's failure here, combined with a generalized reorientation from antiregime activism to transition-seeking advocacy at the party's decisive 1995 Oaxtepec conference (Chapter 7), prompted a reduction in postelectoral mobilizations at all levels, to the point that by the late 1990s they became the exception rather than the rule.

GENERALIZING FROM THE GOVERNOR'S SHELL GAME: INSTITUTIONAL FAILURE AND PRESIDENTIAL DISCRETION

The crux of these three cases is that proof of electoral fraud had little to do with the success of postelectoral mobilizations in gubernatorial races. Instead, success in achieving an opposition interim governor (Guanajuato), or as a second-best solution, a new PRI interim governor and promises (even empty ones) of reconciliation and electoral reform (Michoacán), depended more on the intensity and endurance of postelectoral campaigns, the disposition of the president and federal government toward the opposition party at a given moment, and the strength and willingness of the federal executive to impose his will on local PRI critics. High-ranking PAN officials acknowledged that they did not have sufficient evidence to overturn the PRI victory in Guanajuato, and thus had to pursue a low-road strategy of postelectoral mobilization, rather than the high-road strategy of judicial complaint filing (Hernández Rodríguez 1994, 203). It worked. The PRD in Michoacán also lacked convincing evidence to prove victory

(Beltrán del Río 1993, 277–9; Rivera Velázquez interview). But the PRD, whose leaders could not realistically hope for the PAN's postelectoral success, acknowledged that short of *interinatos* (interim governors and mayors), they aspired to what would come to be referred to as a "technical tie" (*empate técnico*) – deposing Villaseñor, in exchange for an interim governor from the PRI, but perhaps one more acceptable to the PRD (Solorzano interview). This reasonable-expectation second-best strategy worked, but at the high cost of maintaining mobilizations throughout Michoacán for several months, and risking activists' lives.

In Chihuahua 1986, the precursor of these postelectoral conflicts, savvy postelectoral positioning by the PAN sounded a call to civil society nationwide and offered opposition parties a glimpse of the potential of postelectoral mobilization to articulate demands at moments of PRI-state weakness. But even this potent mobilization did not win the governorship for the PAN's candidate, Francisco Barrio, although like Fox, he gained a celebrity status that propelled him to the governorship in 1992 and then to a prominent post-2000 post as Fox's cabinet-level anticorruption czar. In Tabasco, where the PRD amassed compelling evidence of PRI gross campaign overspending, the new federal executive tried to intervene but was unable to dislodge the local PRI. Here the local PRI adopted the "*segunda vuelta*" strategy, disregarding the legal norms of electoral transparency promoted so fervently, at least in word, by President Zedillo, who was also the PRI's national leader. As acknowledged by López Obrador, the formal procedures of electoral justice were just one more rung upon which the opposition parties could rest before climbing to the next extralegal step. In 1995, the tradition of federal trampling on the governors was too deeply entrenched to be easily subordinated to an abstraction as ephemeral as the law.

Given Salinas's excesses and the historical precedent against free and fair gubernatorial elections, it is possible to understand the miserable failures of establishing electoral justice at the state level, compared with the overall federal success of institutionalizing electoral justice. As seen in Chapter 3, the federal electoral court rapidly developed an elaborate set of autonomous institutions for resolving postelectoral conflicts, which since the early 1990s have mostly succeeded. Prior to 1996, however, federal law did not apply to the states, and what opposition parties could not win at the ballot boxes, they sought to win in the streets. Guanajuato was clearly on the minds of opposition party activists who reasoned that while it was physically impossible to prove irregularities in the requisite 20 percent of the polling stations to judicially overturn an election, it was possible to converge on the state capital for several weeks, paralyze traffic, obstruct entry to government buildings, and garner international news coverage. However, for the PAN these mobilizations were mostly "shell game" distractions to buy time and credibility where the decisions were taken, in Mexico City. But where the PAN's partisans spilled ink staging postelectoral mobilizations, the PRD's activists spilled blood. Their protests were usually spontaneous, sometimes violent, and occasionally fatal.

To their bargaining detriment, the PRD lacked PRI-state interlocutors who would allow them to test the PAN's postelectoral mantra that "all politics is national." The new party learned quickly that the Salinas administration would not cede governorships to his former presidential rival and the PRD. Their electoral and postelectoral struggle was thus confined to a smaller scale, and the PRD had to stake postelectoral futures on city halls rather than on state capitols. Indeed, it had always been at the local level that the bitterest postelectoral battles had been fought (at least as of the late 1970s). And at the local level, the federal government did not care as much about conserving power (especially in the PRD's usually small and rural enclaves).[14] Moreover, the scale of the mobilization required to destabilize a town was much smaller than that required to destabilize an entire state. The PRD could readily control any municipality until negotiations could be concluded and protesters sent home. This was usually not the case at the state level.

Since 1988, there have been no enduring postelectoral mobilizations in defiance of federal electoral results and only a handful of conflicts over governors' races (all resolved effectively from Mexico City since Alemán squelched the last regional rebellions in the 1940s). Between 1989 and 2000, I coded nearly 1,300 postelectoral conflicts over mayoral races, and while these conflicts tended to be severe, localized, and even violent, the gubernatorial conflicts tended to be diffuse and fleeting by comparison. While precise postelectoral conflict data is scant for the 1980s (my database starts in 1989 and covers local election conflicts only), a rough index of the intensity of postelectoral contestation in mayoral, gubernatorial, and state legislative races may be gleaned by comparing the number of electoral court cases submitted to contest each type of race. Indeed, for

[14] De la Madrid (interview) acknowledged "playing a role" as the senior *PRIísta* in the designation and approval of gubernatorial candidates, but insisted that his government – except for the Monterrey mayoral race in 1985 – delegated mayoral candidate selection to his governors.

a sample of seventeen elections in twelve states during the 1990s, there
were three times as many mayoral challenges as legislative challenges,
and four times as many complaints filed in local races as in gubernatorial
contests.[15]

Where gubernatorial races were subject to federal executive intervention (either through the Interior Secretary or the president himself, acting
for the national PRI), intervention in mayoral races came from the federal executive at the beckoning of the PRI, but more often from the state
governor or other subnational actors. While the dynamics of local-level
postelectoral negotiations are discussed in Chapters 6, 7, and 8 and the
causes of such postelectoral conflicts are tested in Chapter 5, the last section of this chapter addresses the development of opposition-party competitiveness at the local level, demonstrating that widespread competition
is a phenomenon of the last decade only, and that electoral competition
increased postelectoral competition. I conclude by tracing the dual existence of extralegal postelectoral mobilizing strategies and legal electoral
courts to the late 1980s and early 1990s, thereby justifying the reduction
of the Chapter 5 quantitative analysis scope to local postelectoral conflicts
since 1988. Like the aforementioned opposition to gubernatorial *dedazos*
dating to 1986 Chihuahua, the 1990s contestation of local postelectoral
conflicts also stemmed back to the 1980s. But the legal structures of extreme discretion in the hiring and firing of Mexico's mayors was built into
the rules decades earlier.

MAXIMATO TO *MAXIMINO*: MUNICIPAL ELECTIONS
AND PRI-STATE REPRESSION

The revolutionary ideal of municipal sovereignty, enshrined in Article
115 of the 1917 Constitution, was trampled upon by *cacique* governors,

---

[15] Most, but not all, of the seventeen mayoral and legislative elections were concurrent.
There were only five gubernatorial races in the sample, which was limited by acces-
sibility of state electoral court data. Appeals filings were not counted in the sample,
only cases filed in the first circuit. The dominant patterns held in every election except
Campeche 1997 where there were more gubernatorial filings (sixteen) and more legislative race filings (eleven) than local election filings (six). The elections in the sample
were as follows (concurrent mayoral and legislative races unless otherwise indicated):
Coahuila 1990 (local), Coahuila 1991 (legislative), Mexico 1990, Mexico 1990 (gubernatorial), Guanajuato 1991, Coahuila 1993 (local), Coahuila 1994 (legislative), Mexico
1993, Guanajuato 1994, Guanajuato 1995 (gubernatorial), Jalisco 1994, Nuevo León
1994, Sonora 1994, Veracruz 1994 (local), Baja California 1995, Sinaloa 1995, Sinaloa
1995 (gubernatorial), Chiapas 1995, Michoacán 1995, Michoacán 1995 (gubernatorial),
Veracruz 1995 (legislative), Zacatecas 1995, Mexico 1996, Mexico 1996 (gubernatorial),
Campeche 1997, and Campeche 1997 (gubernatorial).

just as that mythical juridical figure, state autonomy, was regularly violated by Machiavellian presidents from Calles to Salinas. In fact, the federal legal procedure for undermining municipal authority was similar to the legal power plays described by González Oropeza (1987) in the usurpation of states' rights by the president. The governor-controlled state legislature dissolved municipal administrations on grounds of "ingovernability," replacing them with interim municipal councils, usually the governor's cronies, especially in large or geo-strategically important cities. Any governor worthy of the president he served followed this judicially inscrutable but politically expedient formula perfected, perhaps, by Puebla's ruthless Maximino Avila Camacho (1937–41), who served under President Cárdenas, and his brother, President Manuel Avila Camacho (1940–6):

The intervention of the *maximinista* administration in local elections assured that most of the municipalities would be composed of allies sympathetic to the "political line" of the governor, who spread his influence throughout the state, fortifying alliances even with power brokers in the far corners of Puebla.... To ensure his plan of regional domination, the governor thoroughly exercised his constitutional rights, dissolving municipalities that remained outside his yolk, and naming, in their place, municipal council governments.... (Valencia Castrejón 1996, 106–7)

Through his skillful combination of legal maneuvering and extralegal power grabs, Maximino managed to indefinitely postpone local elections in Puebla's capital and three other large cities, attributing the postponement to divisions within PRI union leadership that threatened the state's "internal order" (Valencia Castrejón 1996, 108).

The 1977 legalization of leftist parties and the 1983 mandate of proportional-representation city council seats provoked a rapid increase in electoral and postelectoral conflicts between the left and the authoritarian regime in Mexico's impoverished southern states, complemented by the PAN's persistent local electoral inroads, mainly in Mexico's northern states, Central Valley (the Bajio), and Yucatán. The 1980s brought a handful of PRI-state-recognized victories by the newly legalized left in towns like Alcozauca, Guerrero (population 15,500), Altamirano, Chiapas (21,100), and Magdalena Ocotlán, Oaxaca (population 1,000), the largest of which, Juchitán, Oaxaca (population 76,000), stretched the limits of the authoritarians' tolerance (Tables 4.3 and 4.4). Mostly, recognition of local party competition just meant that the regime had to conceive of new "legal" forms of repression or just give up on appearances. Indeed, rather than looking to the conciliatory speeches of national PRI reformers to understand the ruling party's prevailing mood,

TABLE 4.3 *Municipal Races Won by Opposition Parties*

Party	1978–80	1981–3	1984–6	1987–9	1990–2	1993–5	1996–8
PAN	16	28	17	30	86	235	256
Left/PRD	3	5	4	72	63	164	211
PMT	0	0	0	0	0	0	0
PCM	2	3	1	0	0	0	0
PRT	0	0	0	0	0	1	1
PSUM	1	2	3	0	0	0	0
Proregime Left	14	10	9	35	21	25	31
PST/PFCRN	1	3	1	11	10	9	0
PPS	9	6	4	15	3	5	1
PARM	4	1	4	9	7	1	0
PT	0	0	0	0	1	10	21
PVEM	0	0	0	0	0	1	9
PDM	1	5	4	0	0	2	1
Regional parties	0	0	0	0	0	0	1

Source: Author calculations based on official results from each of the thirty-one states (excluding the Federal District). Underlined party name signifies an antiregime or transition-seeking "authentic left" party, while italicized party name signifies that the party is part of the patronage-seeking "proregime left." The category "Left/PRD" encompasses "authentic left" and "PRD." "Proregime left" encompasses all the parties elsewhere referred to as "parastatal left."

TABLE 4.4 *Percentage of Population by Municipality Governed by Each Party*

Party	1978–80	1981–3	1984–6	1987–9	1990–2	1993–5	1996–8
PRI	99.1	93.9	98.1	91.3	86.9	67.3	52.7
PAN	0.2	5.2	1.2	4.5	11.1	27.0	27.3
Left/PRD	0.0	0.0	0.0	2.6	1.1	4.5	19.2[a]
Proregime Left	0.7	0.6	0.5	1.6	0.9	1.1	0.8
PDM	0.0	0.3	0.2	0.0	0.0	0.1	0.0

[a] Approximately half of this figure is attributable to the 8,483,600 residents of Mexico City, which the PRD won in 1997.

Source: All municipal populations are given according to the INEGI's 1995 estimates, and divided into the estimated national population of 91,120,400 (all figures rounded to the nearest hundred). PRI data are derived as the remainder when all other party population percentages are subtracted.

the views of local PRI leaders on the front lines of Mexico's ever-so-limited 1980s experiment with political pluralism might be more instructive. For example, in reply to allegations by the PSUM (Unified Socialist Party of Mexico) that *PRIístas* were killing their supporters in Xochiapa, Guerrero in 1983, PRI activist Héctor de Jesús Hernández argued that the PRI was extracting "an eye for an eye" and that "all of a year's work organizing the indigenous groups in the mountains was ruined by the communists in four hours.... We are no longer willing to allow ourselves to be mistreated by these reds" (Arreola Ayala 1985, 336, fn. 15). Anecdotes abound of extralegal persecution of opposition party leaders, although no systematic records document such abuses until the late 1980s, when the National Human Rights Commission and several nongovernmental organizations began cataloging abuses against the "old left's" more moderate successor, the PRD.

With some exceptions, violence by local *caciques* against opposition leaders was spontaneous and not directly linkable to government officials, who usually maintained plausible deniability. Prior to the advent of state electoral courts in the early 1990s, there was no direct legal institutional response to postelectoral conflicts to compete with extralegal sanctions against the opposition (electoral fraud and repression). However, at least two intermediary, semilegal processes did exist, manipulable by *Maximino*-inspired governors into indirect means of quelling local tensions. The first was the creation of plural municipal councils, inevitably led by a PRI mayor, but containing opposition party representation. The second, "whitewashing" electoral results through electoral institutions, such as PRI-state-controlled state electoral commissions and electoral courts, grew shamelessly obvious by the mid-1990s, as the authoritarians lashed out for legal cover to protect their weakening hegemony. In several states, behind-the-scenes manipulation of elections and "autonomous electoral institutions" by powerful governors was constantly claimed by the opposition (and a well-founded concern in states like Chiapas, Michoacán, Nuevo León, Puebla, Sonora, Tabasco, and Yucatán, as documented in Chapters 6, 7, and 8). Overall, however, these institutions were forced to "go public" through the legislatively mandated replacement of PRI cronies with formally educated, reputable, and politically neutral citizens ("ombudsman" types who more often than not were university professors without partisan antecedents),[16] who were held accountable through close scrutiny by increasingly powerful nongovernment organizations and an increasingly adversarial media.[17]

---

[16] In some states, the electoral commission ombudsmen and electoral court magistrates were nominated by parties (subject to approval by the other parties), while in others they were nominated by the state legislature, the state supreme court, or directly by representatives of "civil society," that is, state bar associations or law school faculties.

[17] Liberalization of the print media traced back to 1976, when President Luis Echeverría purged critical editors from Mexico's newspaper of record, *Excelsior*. These editors founded a weekly news magazine, *Proceso*, critical of the regime, and gradually pluralized

Struggles internal to the PRI prompted most of the untold hundreds of municipal councils formed from *Maximino's* era through the 1980s, but the persistence of the PAN and the hard left instigated new patterns of legal electoral manipulation in the 1980s and early 1990s. While much of the historical record has been lost, it is known that in the early 1980s, municipal councils served as the governors' legal solution of choice for postelectoral conflicts, just as in the 1940s. Between 1978 and 1981, for example, some twenty-five plural municipal councils were formed after controversial local elections; this for a period when only forty-one opposition victories were allowed nationwide by the authoritarian incumbents (Assad and Ziccardi 1988, 41), for a ratio of almost two municipal councils for every three opposition victories. By comparison, during the three-year period between 1990 and 1992, there were fifty-seven municipal councils formed, but with 202 opposition victories recorded (a ratio of approximately four victories to one municipal council), and between 1993 and 1995, only nineteen municipal councils were created, compared to 557 opposition local electoral victories (a ratio approaching twenty-nine to one).[18]

A USER'S GUIDE TO POSTELECTORAL CONFLICTS AND THEIR SPOILS

Anecdotal accounts and interviews reveal that by the mid-1980s, postelectoral conflicts had supplanted internal PRI disputes as the main cause of forming municipal councils. By the early 1990s, the earliest available internal Secretary of the Interior records of municipal council creation show that postelectoral conflicts were responsible for almost 70 percent of the municipal councils, while internal conflicts in the PRI provoked 10 percent of the municipal councils, and other causes (corruption scandals,

---

the news media in the early 1980s with the rise of liberal opposition newspapers such as *Uno Más Uno* and *La Jornada*, and, in the early 1990s, with a harder-hitting conservative newspaper, *Reforma*. Television was pluralized in the early 1990s with the rise of TV Azteca to compete with the notoriously biased, state-allied monopoly, Televisa.

[18] See description of database constructed for all mayoral races in Mexico's thirty-one states between 1989 and 2000, based on coding of national and local print media (discussed in Chapter 5 and Appendix B). The numbers cited refer only to municipal councils formed specifically to alleviate postelectoral conflicts. Those created after corruption-related mayoral resignations, to govern new municipalities constituted between electoral cycles, etc., were not counted.

the formation of new municipalities, etc.) yielded 20 percent of the municipal councils.[19]

The creation of a municipal council was often not the end of the conflict. *PANísta* leaders reported that their proportional-representation city council members were expelled from city council meetings or denied paychecks by *PRIísta* mayors, particularly in rural areas during municipalities' first experiences with plural administration (Rivera Pérez interview). The PRD activists alleged even more dire violations: that proportional-representation city council members were obstructed from doing their jobs, denied access to meetings, kidnapped, threatened, extorted, or expelled from towns in Michoacán (PRD 1994, 190), Mexico State (PRD 1994, 146, 147, 148, 150), and Zacatecas (PRD 1994, 313) during the early years of their participation. In at least one case, Guerrero after the 1993 elections, the state government refused to recognize PRD city councilors until the party vacated buildings its activists had occupied (Benítez 1994). Such violations of democratic norms of representation were unfortunate, but these were mild compared to the PRD's most severe allegations, that four of their proportional-representation city council members were slain over political disputes in Atizapán de Zaragoza, Mexico State (PRD 1994, 139); Meztitlán, Hidalgo (PRD 1994, 130); Zitácuaro, Michoacán (PRD 1994, 190); and Tezoatlán, Oaxaca (PRD 1994, 236). Two of these charges were fully corroborated by the federal government's National Human Rights Commission.[20]

Violence against the left was poorly documented until the PRD's internal attempts at documentation were complemented by a federal

---

[19] These federal documents were incomplete, accounting for only 103 municipal councils in fifteen of Mexico's thirty-one states, between 1989 and 1996. Furthermore, the reasons for each municipal council creation were given in only sixty of these cases (Federal Interior Secretary 1996, passim). Hence the percentages given are based on a sample size of sixty. Researching municipal councils formed only in postelectoral conflicts between 1988 and 1996, I identified approximately 100 when the sample was extended to include all thirty-one states, while these internal government documents attributed only forty-two of the sixty to postelectoral conflicts.

[20] The Meztitlán charges were substantiated by National Human Rights Commission findings (Recommendation 199/92) against four municipal police officers who killed the *PRDísta* council member in 1991, possibly under direct orders of the *PRIísta* mayor, and then disappeared (National Human Rights Commission 1994, 236–7). The National Human Rights Commission also issued findings in 1993 (Recommendation 221/93) to support the PRD allegations in the 1989 Tezoatlán case, where arrest orders were issued for two town police officers who had slain a PRD town-council leader "for no apparent reason," but arrest warrants were never served (National Human Rights Commission 1994, 422–4).

governmental initiative to punish human rights abuses in Mexico's most violent regions by "freelancing" *caciques*, and groups like Amnesty International and Americas Watch shined international light on Mexico's human-rights abuses. The PRD, in a thoroughly documented but only partially corroborated study by its parliamentary group, alleged 250 politically motivated slayings during Salinas's "*sexenio* of political violence (1989–94)," claiming that 112 of these (45 percent) were directly linked to elections (PRD 1994, 339). My own tally of party documents, corroborated by news accounts and/or government reports, totals 125 PRD deaths between 1989 and 1994 as the direct result of local postelectoral conflicts, and an additional 27 between 1995 and 2000.

Before analyzing causes of a representative sample of postelectoral conflicts in Chapter 5, I assess the two means of resolving postelectoral conflicts. Only by understanding authorities' reactions to the conflicts is it possible to understand these parties' incentives for staging postelectoral mobilizations. The focus here is on the postelectoral conflicts by the PAN and the PRD, which staged 203 and 742 postelectoral conflicts respectively, throughout the country, between 1989 and 2000. I also collected data on PRI postelectoral conflicts, which totaled 186 throughout the country between 1989 and 2000, and those by "third parties" (non-PAN, non-PRD opposition parties), which staged 136 postelectoral conflicts in the national sample period. But prior to Tabasco 1995, which split the party faithful, PRI postelectoral conflicts were always staged against national party wishes, and third parties had little luck in winning side payments from the regime in exchange for discontinuing postelectoral antics. Clearly, the PAN and the PRD staged many more postelectoral conflicts, and received greater concessions from the regime in exchange. Between these two parties, the PRD staged some four times as many postelectoral conflicts, with ten times as many casualties and almost all of the more severe conflicts.

How were the postelectoral mobilizations launched and subsequent bargains struck? The losing party staged mass demonstrations, blocked freeways, burned ballots and electoral material, took over public buildings, declared "parallel municipal governments" to sabotage public works by the winning party, and initiated mob brawls when demonstrations were dissipated by local authorities or challenged by PRI counterdemonstrations. As vividly demonstrated through postelectoral negotiation ethnographies presented in Chapters 6 and 7, PRD demonstrations tended to be isolated, enduring, and threatening to local governability, while PAN mobilizations tended to be centrally orchestrated, theatrical, and nonthreatening. The PRD launched more severe postelectoral conflicts, but usually settled for minor PRI-state concessions. The PAN usually conducted minor postelectoral conflicts merely to complement "smoke-filled room" bargaining with the PRI-state, and received cogovernance arrangements, or even the replacement of PRI mayors elect with their own losing candidates. Such agreements tended to be struck in the legislative branch.

Postelectoral bargaining tables between the PRI-state's Secretary of the Interior and state PRI and PRD representatives were sometimes set up to mediate contentious cases, such as Michoacán 1992 and Chiapas 1995 (Chapter 7). The resulting agreements, discreetly and informally reached by officials embarrassed to be negotiating voters' choices, nevertheless turned heads when city council members from the losing ticket took office over the election winner, or "co-city managers" were named, and from the electoral loser. Minor changes in local cabinets were so common that in states like Guerrero, Oaxaca, and Veracruz, hundreds of last-minute "accommodations" were made with the opposition after each local election. In Veracruz, the practice was institutionalized in the *gazetazo*, so named because of the last-minute change in the incoming administration as published in the official government record or *gazeta*. In 1991, over eighty last-minute *gazetazo* changes were made in local administrations, including forty-four postprinting corrections (see Figure 4.1). In all, such changes were made in 18 percent of Veracruz's 207 municipalities (Rodriguez 1992). In 1994 Tlaxcala reached new levels of accommodation by resolving a bitter PRI-PRD dispute by naming two mayors of Amaxac de Guerrero (CESEM 17038); in Huautla de Jiménez, Oaxaca, three interim mayors were named in 1992, as the PRD, the PPS, and the PRI all contested power (Moreno Alcántara interview); and in Guerrero 1993, new extremes of informality were reached when new plural city council members spontaneously "appeared" to take office even after months of postelectoral bargaining had considerably altered the list of office takers (Díaz and Zamarripa 1993, 33).

Third-party oppositions like the PPS and PARM, which rarely won mayorships but retained electoral strongholds in Veracruz during the 1990s, assured spoils to activists through postelectoral conflicts waged entirely over proportional-representation city council seats, and admitted that while they had not won elections, "we deserve at least 100 proportional representation seats [upon being assigned only 60]" (Rodriguez 1991). Tacitly acknowledging the party's instrumentalism, one earnest PRD leader stated, "We will accept extra proportional representation sinecures, but where we really won, we want the mayor's seat"

Decreto Número 203

Artículo Unico.— Son legales y en consecuencia válidas, las elecciones efectuadas el día 10 de noviembre del año en curso para la renovación del Ayuntamiento de

Tlaltetela, Ver.

Que confirma la resolución emitida, por la Comisión Municipal Electoral, la que expidió las Constancias de Mayoría correspondientes.

Se declaran ciudadanos electos para el Período Constitucional 1992-1994, con la obligación de ocupar sus respectivos cargos, previa protesta de Ley, el día Primero de Enero de 1992, como integrantes del Ayuntamiento.

Cargo	Propietarios	Suplentes
Presidente	ENRIQUE HERNANDEZ RUIZ	JUAN YAÑEZ GUTIERREZ
Síndico Unico	JUVENAL CADENA ROSALES	BASILIO QUEZADA MUÑOZ
Regidor 1°	MARIA DE JESUS GARCIA VAZQUEZ	EUSTACIA MORALES PRADO
Regidor 2°	ROBERTO YAÑEZ GONZALEZ	OCATAVIANO ROSALES TORRES

TRANSITORIO

Artículo Unico.— El presente decreto surtirá sus efectos legales al día siguiente de su publicación en la Gaceta Oficial, órgano del Gobierno del Estado.

Dado en el salón de sesiones de la H. Legislatura del Estado, en la ciudad de Xalapa-Enríquez, Veracruz, a los dieciocho días del mes de diciembre de mil novecientos noventa y uno.

Ing: Abel Ruiz Lopart
Diputado Presidente

C. Rosa Evelia Jiménez Cruz
Diputada Secretaria

FIGURE 4.1 Decree Number 203 – "*Gazetazo*" Recomposition of Tlaltetela, Veracruz Town Council. Larger type indicates postproduction changes in town council composition. *Source:* Veracruz State Government (1991).

(Rueda 1990). These arrangements were made wholesale, especially in states where they had become the postelectoral norm. In Chiapas 1995, even librarian's assistant and part-time city driver positions were negotiated by the PRI-state to placate losers (see Chapter 7). The deals were rarely recorded, but they seem to have occurred in 20 or 30 percent of the municipalities in Mexico's most conflictive states. Whenever a bargaining table was set up, the opposition knew they were going to win something, whatever the election's official results.

In summary, the precise magnitude is indiscernible, but extralegal means of resolving postelectoral conflicts predominated, and opposition parties' awareness of this fact compounded their incentives to continue blocking freeways and storming city halls. Electoral courts, which had debuted uneventfully at the federal level in 1988, were fortified and extended to the states, based mostly on PAN pressures for electoral reforms, and also by international actors. But the result was not an immediate fortification of the rule of law. Rather, the initial result was an extra tool at the disposal of the opposition parties in their battle against the PRI-state, a complement to their extralegal tactics but not a substitute for them.

The prevalence of informal bargaining tables summoned by opposition demands provided self-reinforcing incentives for the opposition to repeatedly recur to these means, which at the very least left them with local administrative posts, albeit at the cost of property damage, injuries, and deaths. While the side-payments offered in these arrangements tended to be extra proportional representation seats on the municipal administration, they did vary widely – from material benefits such as the bulldozer offered to discontented *PRIístas* in Coahuila 1990 in exchange for their vacating city hall in Parras where they had lost to the PAN (Cobos 1991), to the naming of "co-mayors" from the losing parties, creating the hydralike three-mayor town in Oaxaca. As in the gubernatorial postelectoral sweepstakes, the PRI-state's need for a national legislative partner rendered the PAN's local postelectoral gains as PRD losses. But whatever meager patronage they could receive from the PRI-state, PRD sympathizers in repressed rural enclaves perceived they had little to lose by launching postelectoral mobilizations. However, the party leadership realized they could not continue risking activists' lives through postelectoral confrontations. Even if leaders from the transition-seeking side of the PRD preferred the decent odds of winning scraps from the postelectoral bargaining table to the long odds of winning through formalistic electoral court complaints, they took notice of the potential – at least in the abstract – for a legal cover of electoral justice to protect them. However, the institutions envisioned by the PRD strategists were much different from those established by the regime.

Imaginative opposition leaders, eager to appropriate claims to legality from the PRI-state's arsenal, established propaganda "people's courts" to highlight differences between their positions and those of the PRI-state. By framing electoral justice using alternative assumptions to those of the regime, opponents demonstrated that their unabashedly biased courts were no worse than those constructed by the official arbiters. Starting in Chihuahua 1986, a "People's Jury" of local notables was formed by critical (pro-*PANísta* but allegedly nonpartisan) opposition civic groups, to monitor elections and issue the predictable conclusion that the election warranted annulment due to its "great number of irregularities and vices" (Lau 1989, 87).[21] Another similar "People's Electoral Court" was formed in Michoacán 1989, which declared, contrary to the state electoral commission, that the PRD had won a vast majority of the state legislative races (Zamarripa 1989).

Perhaps the most comprehensive effort to publicize the lack of electoral justice, constructed on extralegal but somewhat credible bases, was the "Electoral Defender of the People of Chiapas" and the "Electoral Tribunal of the People of Chiapas," which this time consisted of local and national notables convened through nongovernmental channels to rule on electoral fraud in the 1994 governor's race (Vargas Manríquez and Moreno Corzo 1994). The publicity-seeking intentions of this body, headed by an actress rather than a jurist, were more transparent than its administration of justice. However, based on the premise that no judicial certification of the election would be possible anyway (as the electoral court still possessed only administrative power to recommend verdicts to the legislature), this righteous group took on the responsibility and, not surprisingly, pressured for recognition of a PRD victory.

These nongovernmental "judges and juries" benefited from international electoral observers, who were welcomed in Mexico by the growing network of in-country nongovernment organizations starting in the late

---

[21] An earlier "People's Tribunal" was actually established as part of the PAN's Puebla 1983 postelectoral mobilization (Alvarez de Vicencio 1995, 142), but it did not seem to have much transcendence.

1980s (Dezalay and Garth 1996). International election observers and charitable foundations were decisive in helping professionalize a wave of Mexican election-monitoring nongovernment organizations,[22] but PRI-state nationalism relegated these eager international democratizers to the subordinate role of helping fund Mexican colleagues. Under Salinas's compulsion to respond to international democratization pressures during NAFTA negotiations, the PRI-state formally accepted international observers for the 1994 federal elections, but not without one of the most contentious intraelite debates of Salinas's term.

Concurrent with broad "civil society" opposition pressures on the regime using condemnation of electoral fraud from parallel informal electoral-institution platforms, the opposition parties began seeking to "legalize" extralegal bargaining through requests to compare their electoral result tallies with those of the PRI, on the premise that disparities could be "cleansed" directly through intraparty bargaining, rather than withstanding negotiations with the PRI-state's stilted electoral institutions. Righteous but pragmatic PAN negotiators even constructed a legal argument for their constant circumvention of legal channels, referring to their patronage seeking as "partial restitution" of electoral injustices (Alcántara interview). The PRD also invoked legal justifications, at least on occasion. Party leaders signaled their postelectoral poker face by declaring the existence of the "technical tie" (Solís and Sotelo 1995) despite the fact that there was always an "arithmetic" winner, and in every technical tie declared by the PRD, this winner was the PRI.[23]

Both the PAN and the PRD sought to project legality onto their extralegal postelectoral confrontations by grafting electoral code rules onto negotiations that from the inception clearly violated legal procedures. Throughout this legal limbo period of dueling focal points, after the extralegal route had gained opposition credibility but before the legal route had, the opposition parties partially "vested" themselves in the regime's illusion of legality by insisting that they would not call for election

---

[22] These effective nongovernment organizations included, for example, the Civic Alliance (Alianza Cívica), the National Accord for Democracy (ACUDE), the Mexican Human Rights Commission (not the federal government agency), and the Mexican Human Rights Academy.

[23] There were a few literal "technical ties" in local elections – where two parties actually did receive the exact same number of votes – such as in 1994 Suaqui Grande, Sonora (population 1,300), and 1996 Ayapango, Mexico State (population 4,900), but neither of them resulted in postelectoral negotiations. Predictably, these genuine "technical ties" occurred in very small towns, which were not of urgent interest to political parties.

annulment unless they could prove irregularities in 20 percent of the polling booths, the threshold mandated by federal and state electoral laws. In state and local races such as Puebla 1989 (PAN), Baja California 1992 (PAN), Durango 1992 (PAN), and Michoacán 1992 (PRD), proposals were made by second-place finishers to compare their vote tallies with those of the PRI, which stood only to lose by granting such postelectoral negotiating space at the threshold of *concertacesión*. The increase in op- position party votes after the 1980s economic crisis, combined with this blurring of lines between legal and extralegal bargaining, which made out- comes less certain than exclusive recourse to the legal or extralegal routes, prompted the PAN to increasingly work within reformed legal channels only. The very parallel existence of competing formal and informal arenas of dispute adjudication forced a need for change.

CONCLUSIONS: DUELING FOCAL POINTS AND A WEAK
RULE OF LAW

The first objective of this chapter was to illustrate the traditional power of Mexico's presidents and governors as (s)electors of lower officehold- ers. Linchpins in the geo-politics of presidential control and monitor- ing in the regions, the governors in particular were bolstered first by the perverse federal municipal reform of 1983, and second by the increased premium on territorial "bases" in post-1990 power struggles within the PRI (see Chapter 8). As Rodríguez 1997 (116) points out, "decentraliza- tion" mostly brought paradoxical increases in gubernatorial authority. Hence, the election of these crucial presidential agents was an unlikely place to seek the birth of electoral justice. Case study after case study showed that governor selection was tightly controlled through the mid- 1990s (not to mention that electoral fraud remained difficult to prove in statewide races). Presidential *dedazos* of the governors and the long tradi- tion of electoral fraud in accompanying cosmetic elections extended back to the founding of PRI dominance. Postelectoral bargaining over mayoral races had a shorter tradition, as before the late 1980s the PRI-state did not even bother. Also, while in mayoral dispute settlements the PAN was much more successful than the PRD, the PRD also resorted to postelec- toral mobilization, hoping to win in the *segunda vuelta*, or second round, what they lost on election day. And while the stakes were low, PRD ac- tivists able to wreck havoc were usually rewarded with at least a symbolic town council position, if not a lesser job or two.

The late 1980s and early 1990s witnessed two separate and divergent focal points of actor behavior. The first, that of the opposition parties, was based on expectations of what they could extract from the regime by mobilizing, and contrarily, what demands the PRI-state could credibly meet, thereby minimizing opposition party fatigue from mobilizations without jeopardizing the regime-controlled electoral opening. The second was the convergence of expectations around the regime's nascent but utterly biased state electoral institutions. The regime sought to channel postelectoral contestation through biased electoral institutions, which were, in the most blatant cases, intended primarily to diffuse tempers and adhere to the PRI-state's script, whether written and produced by the governor or by the federal Interior Secretary (see Eisenstadt 2002).

As acknowledged in interviews cited extensively in Chapters 6 and 7, opposition activists felt compelled to at least pay "lip service" to formal institutions, as postelectoral protocol for negotiating with the PRI-state required the opposition to have exhausted formal institutional routes first. Similarly, PRI-state officials claimed that they had no choice but to grant postelectoral concessions to keep heightened opposition expectations at bay. How could this dual cycle of high expectations from extralegal bargaining and low expectations from legal proceedings be broken? The legal and extralegal routes to postelectoral conflict resolution converged in the mid-1990s, but only after Mexico's weak rule of law endured several years of direct competition between these two convergence points of actor expectations.

5

The Gap Between Law and Practice: Institutional Failure and Opposition Success in Postelectoral Conflicts, 1989–2000

> In Berlin the wall fell, in Chile Pinochet departed, in Nicaragua the Sandinistas accepted their defeat, and here in Mexico we still can't resolve a local election. We are definitely arriving late to the 21st Century.
>
> Political analyst Federico Reyes Heroles[1]

Given that the PAN's 2000 victory required that the National Action Party (PAN) garner the most votes and that the Party of the Institutional Revolution (PRI) allow the *PANístas* to count them, the precise moment when these dual transformations became inevitable is difficult to specify, even in retrospect, although several 1990s indicators emerged that courting democracy in Mexico would soon give way to democratic consolidation. Scholars of subnational politics (Chand 2001, Cornelius 2000, Mizrahi, Rionda 1995, Rodriguez and Ward 1995) noted that especially since 1989, Mexico's protracted transition was proceeding from the periphery to the center. Observers of the PRI (González Compeán 2000, Hernández 1994, Langston 2000a) tracked that party's gradual decomposition starting in 1990. Institutionalists paid increasing attention, as of the 1990s but especially after 1997, to the evolving power of PAN and Party of the Democratic Revolution (PRD) congressional delegations and their increasing balance against the PRI (Lujambio 1995, Ugalde 2000, Weldon 1997). Finally, public-opinion specialists documented the general public's increasing willingness to risk voting for the opposition (Buendía 1998, Domínguez and McCann 1996, Magaloni 1996) and the new importance of the independent media in framing campaigns and elections

---

[1] Quoted in Amezcua and Pardinas (1997, 57).

(Lawson 2002, Moreno 1999). However, politicians and analysts alike were at a loss to anticipate precisely when the PRI-state would lose control of the transition.

Underlying these specific trends was the broader and more structural realignment of winners and losers underway since the abrupt economic changes in the 1970s and 1980s, credited with dramatically altering state-society relations and hence the power structure of Mexican politics. This study adds a compelling "party organization against *concertacesiones*" explanation to reconcile the elite-driven transitions literature and reinforces the "centripetal democratization" argument gaining cache among scholars of Mexico. While recognizing the constraints posed by economic forces on each individual's range of actions, my unit of analysis is individual party agents rather than structural forces. Rather than applying top-down *kremlinology* to trace changes in Mexico's authoritarian incumbent coalition and positing political opening mostly as the outcome of technocrat-dinosaur battles within the PRI with or without a pact, I systematically project the importance of local political struggles in national postelectoral bargaining about how to court democracy in Mexico. By recognizing the *ad hoc* grassroots decision making of local PRD supporters in particular, I identify patterns of democratic opening outside the elite battles in Mexico City.

The national elite battles (treated exhaustively by authors such as Centeno [1994], Maxfield [1990], and Williams [2002]) do explain much of the PRI's rise and hegemonic period, as documented in Chapter 4. However, I argue in this chapter that powerful complementary movements were arising in the poor, rural, elite-less regions, long taken for granted by PRI electoral operatives as the "green vote" for its rural source and as Mexico's nonpetroleum "strategic reserve" of votes. Indeed, these predominantly southern regions, where authoritarian *caciques* held tight grips, were characterized by a level of destitution that rendered local activists – whose constituents often needed calories more than democracy – unlikely transition seekers. But parallel to the important structural coalition shifts brought by radical economic change, the PRI's agents of change in the center were gradually losing their reserve domain in the periphery. The authoritarian moderates who had always taken rural voters for granted were the most surprised in 2000,[2] when the rural poor took their clientalist offerings and

---

[2] For 1988, Aziz and Molinar identify polling stations where 100 percent of votes were tallied to the PRI, and find that many of these states – such as Chiapas, Guerrero, Oaxaca, and Veracruz – are also the poor, rural states that generated the most postelectoral complaints

then voted for the opposition. Over two decades of protracted transition, the transition seekers in the countryside had gradually come to believe in the power of the vote; they had embarked on the transition from "clients to citizens" (Fox 1994).

So as a rejoinder to the partial but incomplete elite-based explanations of Mexico's transition, I offer in this chapter the first comprehensive assessment of local causes of Mexico's postelectoral conflicts. Once I explain causes "on the ground" of these conflicts, I dedicate the next three chapters to the local-national nexus, arguing that the relative success of these conflicts by the PAN – and even by the PRD – dramatically reshaped political party expectations and behaviors, and ultimately tore the PRI apart. For now, I describe how I coded an unbiased sample of mayoral postelectoral conflicts in ten states, including mainstays from the traditional PRI vote reserve and others with historic opposition strongholds. I identify statistically significant causes of postelectoral conflicts, demonstrating that in the case of the PRD, conflicts were highly correlated with long-standing agrarian conflicts and "demand for services" mobilizations, as well as with perceived levels of electoral fraud. Contrary to the local causality of PRD mobilizations, I conclude that even the most local of PAN postelectoral conflicts were driven by national negotiations, partially vindicating elite-based explanations, but across parties, rather than just within the authoritarian coalition. This finding begs a question: if the PAN – the party that ultimately wrested the presidency from the PRI – negotiated all its *concertacesiones* with the national PRI, why bother studying postelectoral mobilizations by the PRD?

The most direct answer relates directly to the PRD, as the *segunda vuelta* was the party's most important strategy until 1995. However, given that the PRD still only governs a handful of towns and Mexico City and was relegated in 2000 to being democracy's bridesmaid, the more important answers may be in terms of how these PRD tactics affected the PRI and the PAN. While the PAN had far greater success turning postelectoral conflicts into seats, the PRD and its predecessor leftist parties pioneered the process and offered the credible prospect (explored in Chapter 6) of challenging the PRI in coalition with the PAN, a challenge implicitly posed by Álvarez and Castillo in Chihuahua 1986 and explicitly posed

---

(Aziz Nassif and Molinar 1990, 166–171). Studies by the Augustín Pro Human Rights Group demonstrate that in local elections such as in Mexico State 1990 and Tabasco 1991, the PRI managed to consistently garner over 100 percent of the votes in many precincts (Augustín Pro 1990 and 1991).

by Cárdenas and Clouthier in 1988. Second, even if the PAN and PRD did not ally, the visceral and lawless uprisings by *PRDístas* made PRI-state administrators cringe, rendering the measured and hierarchical PAN more attractive as a national legislative coalition partner with each PRD building occupation. Salinas's disdain for Cárdenas is said to have driven his policy making as much as positive incentives, and the PAN's critical decision in the heated summer of 1988 not to join the antiregime PRD set a course for alternation between the party's patronage-seeking tendencies and transition-seeking proclivities. The constant upheaval posed by PRD mobilizations and the threat of PAN collusion with them led Salinas and the PRI moderates to repeatedly negotiate *concertacesiones* with the PAN at the expense of their own party. These agreements had the unintended consequence, detailed in Chapter 8, of alienating local PRI machine bosses from national party headquarters, contributing to the erosion of party discipline and, ultimately, to the PRI's inability to retain control over its rural bastions.

The PRD's strategy, inherited from the outlaw protesters in the 1970s and 1980s as much as from the PRI's channels of "institutionalized revolution," also had a direct impact on PAN tactics. In contrast to the *PRDístas*, for whom all politics was local, the PAN started the 1980s as an urban party with a half dozen chapters and no rural penetration.[3] Given that winning free and fair elections was not an option as elections were rigged and the PAN possessed few followers outside state capitals, *concertacesión* was the party's means of acquiring administrative experience and resources and extending its presence. They watched and learned from their erstwhile allies in the PRD. The difference between the two regime opponents, expressed starkly in the statistical analysis to follow, is that while PAN postelectoral conflicts were less prevalent where stronger electoral institutions existed, such institutions actually increased the PRD propensity for mobilization. This fact, perhaps more than any other, reveals the PRD's lack of faith in formal institutions and their ability to use them.

I further address the effects of postelectoral negotiations on the organization of these three parties in the chapters that follow. Here I quantify postelectoral conflict and describe the extent of this phenomenon during the most intense decade of Mexico's protracted transition. I propose

---

[3] The exception is Yucatán, where the PAN has a long history of activism in the capital city Mérida and spread to rural areas as candidates passed over by the PRI looked for a party that would register them as mayoral candidates.

structure- and agency-driven hypotheses to explain Mexico's postelectoral conflicts, discuss their specification, and report results of statistical models, which confirm that rather than deriving directly from the weakness of "paper tiger" electoral institutions in the sample states, PAN postelectoral mobilizations were provoked by high perceptions of electoral fraud, and PRD mobilizations – some four times as frequent as those by the PAN – correlated with broader indices of social upheaval. In other words, PAN postelectoral conflicts were about the fairness of elections, while for the PRD, postelectoral conflicts were another "spillover" of broader underlying social tensions.

I construct two multinomial logit models with data from nearly a thousand municipalities in ten states. A longitudinal model spans a crucial nine-year period (1989–98), while a cross-sectional model assesses the midpoint elections (1992–5) in greater depth. Model 1 (referred to as "ALL T") covers three three-year mayoral elections in hopes of capturing the causes of PAN and PRD postelectoral bargaining at its height (which spans from the mid-1980s – for which data are not available – to the mid-1990s) and during its decline at the end of the 1990s.[4] Selected to coincide with the advent of local electoral courts to adjudicate these disputes, the second of the three electoral cycles is highlighted in Model 2 (referred to as "T2"). T2 confirms that as the electoral institutions in Mexico's states grew more autonomous from the governor, opposition parties used these institutions more and resorted to postelectoral conflicts less. However, contrary to conclusions of most macrolevel studies of democratization, the evidence shows that the progression was not entirely linear. That is, the gap between the reforming of institutions and opposition party compliance with them is empirically evident.

During the formative years of these electoral institutions, other independent variables, such as level of social conflict endemic to a particular municipality, were more important than these institutions at least to the source of most postelectoral conflicts, the PRD. While the bivariate dependent variable, postelectoral conflicts by the PAN and by the PRD, diminishes in the third mayoral period of the sample to the point that no reliable statistical patterns could be found, I argue with less systematic evidence that the dueling focal points in T2 extend forward to T3 and

---

[4] The models cover only elections in municipalities for which demographic and economic variables were available at the beginning of the nine-year period. The new municipalities created in the sample states over the course of the study (given in Appendix A) were not included.

later. Similarly, while unable to collect the data, I argue that the primacy of informal institution negotiating tables, seen in the PRD's T2 and ALL T behavior and shown in the last chapter to extend back to the 1980s and even earlier, also held true for the PRD's leftist predecessors in T1 and T0.

While Model ALL T, in presenting three times as many cases, allows for the testing of more independent variables – particularly state-level variables – without prohibitive covariance, Model T2 is more robust, with a greater fit of expected values to the empirical facts. In snapshot form, it presents the concentrated form of the argument, vividly representing the use of electoral courts as a means to the end of postelectoral conflicts by cutting deals, be they formally or informally negotiated. True to my argument in Chapter 1, protracted transitions may be best observed from the vantage of a microinstitutional "snapshot" of bargaining over institutions and their outputs. I argue below that the direct tension between formal and informal institutions, brought out so clearly in Model T2, actually extends backward to the decades prior to this study, when the formal institutions were Interior Secretary rulings or state legislative decrees rather than electoral courts, but for which little documentation is available even of actual electoral winners.[5] Before reporting and interpreting the estimations of the models, I briefly analyze the postelectoral conflicts dependent variable and how I coded it.

DESCRIPTIVE ANALYSIS OF THE POSTELECTORAL CONFLICT STATE SAMPLE

The ten states incorporated into the sample were selected to assure broad variation in levels of postelectoral conflict. Two states with among the highest number of postelectoral conflicts were selected (Chiapas and Michoacán, where these occurred in as many as 40 percent of the local races during the period studied), as were two states with among the lowest incidence of postelectoral conflicts (Nuevo León and Sonora, with postelectoral conflicts in fewer than 5 percent of the races). Variation was also sought in geographical dispersion, rural-urban mix, and the degree of electoral competition between PRI and opposition. In all cases, this

---

[5] Disparities in reporting of local electoral results between the Interior Secretariat, the Office of the President, the parties, and scholars led one researcher to spend over a year corroborating the most plausible version of pre-1990s results and compiling them into a comprehensive reference (de Remes 2000).

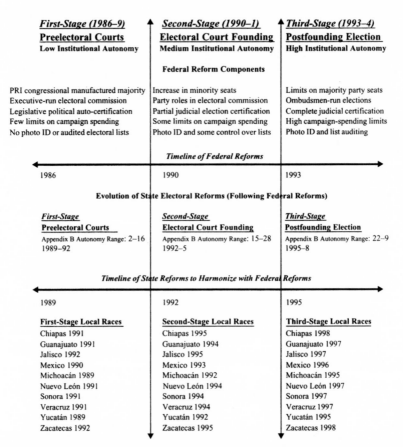

FIGURE 5.1 Classification of State Electoral Codes According to Institutional Evolution. *Source:* Author classification of state electoral codes (see Appendix B, Table B.2, and Bibliography).

competition was measured only between the PAN or PRD and the PRI, as three-way competition (PAN-PRI-PRD or two of these and a smaller opposition party) existed in only a handful of cases during the three-election cycle of the ten-state sample. As demonstrated in Figure 5.1, the three-election cycle was selected so as to anchor T2 as the cycle when state-level reforms introducing autonomous formal institutions of postelectoral conflict resolution were first implemented. T1 was then identified as the election prior to this institutional innovation, and T3 was defined as the race immediately after this change. Figure 5.1 shows that reforms in the states followed major federal electoral reforms, with an average lag of some two to three years behind federal electoral reforms.

The sample of states is fairly representative, identifying PAN or PRD postelectoral conflicts in some 15 percent of the municipalities in T1, 15 percent in T2, and 4 percent in T3. The sample was limited by the cooperation of electoral court judges in providing information on cases they heard.[6] A slight bias exists toward larger states with urban capitals (such as Guanajuato, Jalisco, Mexico State, Nuevo León, and Veracruz), as electoral officials more readily disclosed information in cities with university research traditions (where electoral officials were frequently also law school professors), previous interest had likely been expressed by foreign electoral observers, electoral competition was an accepted fact, and comprehensive newspapers more consistently tracked "citizen demands."[7] I have tried to offset this large state bias by adding more rural states (Chiapas, Yucatán, and Zacatecas), although data limitations were prohibitive. The final sample, consisting of some 30 percent of Mexico's states, possesses over 40 percent of the national population, and is similarly slightly overrepresented in postelectoral conflicts identified.

All processes represent the first local election for which autonomous electoral courts existed, defined as those possessing the ultimate authority over electoral certification of local races (Figure 5.1 and Appendix B).[8] These electoral courts were often not fully independent – as they often relied on the governor for nomination – but at least by the second period of study they could be considered sufficiently independent to be courts, rather than mere administrative agencies. Courts existed in some states during the first period, but with a highly subordinate status. All of the first period courts possessed the authority to suggest resolutions to the Electoral College, but in no case could they impose resolutions with the weight of law.

---

[6] I was summarily denied access to the electoral court dockets in Chiapas, Tabasco, and Yucatán, which were, perhaps not surprisingly, among the most controversial electoral courts. In Tabasco, the presiding magistrate even denied the existence of court records. These information barriers were overcome for Chiapas and Yucatán. In Chiapas, political parties provided photocopies of the docket (corroborated by publication two years later of the court's proceedings), while in Yucatán, competition between the *PANísta* and *PRIísta* dailies prompted unusually serviceable newspaper accounts.

[7] Four states were eliminated from the sample because available local newspapers were too fragmented and/or focused on a few urban areas to carry extensive coverage of rural citizen demands for coding of that variable (Campeche, Chihuahua, and Tamaulipas), or because creation of many new municipalities during the study period caused flux in municipal boundaries, making municipal demographic variables unreliable (Tlaxcala).

[8] In many cases gubernatorial elections were still decided by an electoral college, to which the electoral court could make "recommendations" (as in the case of the 1988 federal elections).

Multiple opposition party mobilizations in one municipality were rare, but when they occurred, in every case I entered only the mobilization by the non-PRI contender (PAN or PRD), as there were not enough PRI or third-opposition-party mobilizations to allow for the model to retain statistical significance when they were included as dependent variable categories. In the dozen or so cases with mobilizations by both the PAN and the PRD, the higher vote-getter among the runner-up parties was credited with the conflict, as I considered that party to be the main postelectoral contender (and usually there was a large margin between second and third place finishers). Just as electoral contention was either PRI-PAN or PRI-PRD but almost never PAN-PRI-PRD (at least not until the late 1990s), postelectoral contention also followed this pattern during the period under study.

The descriptive data averages for my ten-state sample are mostly representative of national averages for frequency and intensity of postelectoral conflicts, and in the demographic characteristics of municipalities with such conflicts (population, standard of living index, etc.). My sample deviates by no more than 5 percent from the national average in most categories.[9] Comparisons are drawn between my sample and the nationwide universe of postelectoral conflicts in Appendix A. Even before specifying my postelectoral conflict model, a preliminary descriptive analysis of all postelectoral conflicts identified in Mexico over 12 years – including those in ALL T – conveys great differences in the demographic and socioeconomic characteristics of the municipalities contested through PAN mobilizations versus those contested through PRD mobilizations (Table 5.1). The nationwide sample described in these tables depicts at least three patterns relating to the prevalence of postelectoral conflicts, their severity, and the profile of municipalities where such mobilizations prospered.

First, the prevalence of postelectoral conflicts, especially between 1989 and 1994, is evidenced in Table 5.1. During that period the PRD staged postelectoral conflicts in one out of every five races where the party fielded candidates. PRD postelectoral conflicts were more than twice as likely as election victories, and for the PAN this figure was only slightly lower. Postelectoral strategies by the PAN tapered off dramatically during the second half of the study period (1995–2000) and electoral strategies prospered, with the PAN winning some 20 percent of the elections in which it fielded

---

[9] This estimate is based on a tally of 1,325 local postelectoral conflicts nationwide in Mexico's 2,400 municipalities during the twelve-year period of my sample, with 1,267 by political parties and the remainder by *usos y costumbres*.

TABLE 5.1 *Comparing Opposition Parties' Electoral and Postelectoral Presence, 1989–2000*

PRD N	PRD pct	Postelectoral Conflicts vs. Electoral Victories	PAN pct	PAN N
2,450	51	Candidates run 1989–94[a]	61	2,429
3,485	87	Candidates run 1995–2000[a]	83	3,342
208	8	Elections won 1989–94	8	189
453	13	Elections won 1995–2000	20	670
4.801 million	3	Population governed 1989–94	12	19.630 million
17.776[b] million	11	Population governed 1995–2000	39	63.768 million
487	19	Postelectoral conflicts 1989–94[c]	6	157
255	7	Postelectoral conflicts 1995–2000[c]	2	46

Note: Total population, based on 1995 estimates, is 82.369 million. Since the "population governed" number covers six years or two local election cycles, it must be halved and then divided by the total population to get the percentages given. For postelectoral conflict coding, see p. 293.

[a] This is the number of elections running candidates from the opposition parties as a percentage of the total number of mayoral elections held nationwide, estimated at 4,781 for 1989–94 and 4004 for 1995–2000. The main differences is that over 400 municipalities were removed from partisan contention in the Oaxaca 1995 and 1998 local races, with candidates competing through traditional pleibiscites dubbed *usos y costumbres* (see Chapter 7). Appendix A compares the frequency of postelectoral conflicts nationwide to those in the ten-state sample over similar (but not identical) time periods to those considered here.

[b] The PRD's population governed over the last two mayoral election cycles of the sample doubles if the Mexico City regency – won by the PRD in both 1997 and 2000 – is counted, but as in most analyses, I count this as a governorship.

[c] As a percentage of races where the party fielded candidates.

candidates, particularly in large cities, allowing the party's mayors to govern 39 percent of the population. Evidence from the three years since 2000 indicates that the PAN's electoral success rate has only improved in mayoral and gubernatorial elections.

While less attention was paid to postelectoral conflicts by the PRI and by Mexico's small parties, data were gathered on these too, and warrant mention as a further demonstration of the PRD's overwhelming recurrence to these tactics, as compared to all other parties. Between 1989 and 2000, the PRI launched 186 postelectoral conflicts resulting in eighteen deaths; third parties (mainly the leftist Authentic Party of the Mexican Revolution [PARM], Party of the Cardenista Front National Reconstruction [PFCRN], and Popular Socialist Party [PPS] in the early years and the centrist Workers' Party [PT] in the later years) were responsible for

136 conflicts yielding seventeen deaths; and nonpartisan *usos y costumbres* mayoral selection through traditional rather than electoral procedures – legalized before Oaxaca's 1995 elections in hopes of stemming conflicts in that polarized state – provoked several dozen conflicts with several fatalities.[10] The PRD was responsible for all remaining conflicts, or 59 percent of the 1,267 conflicts between 1989 and 2000, and 80 percent of the 200 deaths attributable directly to party-driven postelectoral conflicts. And while PRD postelectoral conflicts averaged above level two in severity level (implying repeated confrontations with authorities), the PAN, the PRI, and the "third parties" (lumped into one residual category) all averaged closer to a level one (a single march or demonstration). The PAN and PRD postelectoral conflicts are slightly overrepresented in the ten-state sample, where they occur in 14 percent of the cases across the three periods (implying a broader rate of postelectoral conflicts including PRI, third party, and *usos y costumbres* conflicts of about 18 percent), whereas nationwide, conflicts by all parties occurred in a mere 15 percent of the local races.

Indeed, PRD conflicts were much more severe than PAN conflicts, producing 152 deaths over the period studied, whereas only 3 deaths were directly attributable to PAN postelectoral conflicts. And while Table 5.2 indicates that about one-third of the conflicts by both *PRDístas* and *PANístas* yielded PRI-state concessions, the degree of concessions differed by magnitudes. In the case of the PAN, the *concertacesiones* gave them governors and mayors of state capitals, while the PRD got proportional-representation city council seats in small towns and second-tier administrative jobs. While the quantitative analysis presented below demonstrates stark differences in PAN and PRD postelectoral conflict frequencies and severities, it does not sufficiently draw the distinction between the strategies behind variance in the modalities of postelectoral conflict and negotiation. Chapters 6 through 8 fill in the patterns sketched out here.

NATIONAL CAUSES OF MEXICO'S LOCAL POSTELECTORAL CONFLICTS: A NULL HYPOTHESIS

Consolidated democracies that adhere to a strong rule of law tend to possess a separation of powers and hence a high level of institutional

---

[10] While I expect that media underreporting of rural postelectoral conflicts has led to a general underrepresentation of postelectoral conflicts, this may be particularly true in Oaxaca. Rather than turning to electoral institute analysis that may overstate conflicts, however, I decided to stick to secondary sources in this case.

TABLE 5.2 *Characteristics of PRD and PAN Postelectoral Conflicts and Victories, 1989–2000*

PRD Victory	PRD Conflict	Descriptive of Municipalities	PAN Conflict	PAN Victory
661	742	N conflicts-victories in all 8,785 elections	203	859
11 percent	13 percent	Conflicts-victories where party candidates ran	4 percent	15 percent
low	moderate	Average Level of Poverty	low	low
34,200	46,800	Average population	110,400	97,100
N/A	79 percent	Share of 945 PAN/PRD conflicts	21 percent	N/A
N/A	2.1	Average severity of conflict	1.4	N/A
N/A	29 percent	PRD N = 212 Severe conflicts PAN N = 23	11 pct.	N/A
N/A	152 deaths	Deaths in severe conflicts	3 deaths	N/A
N/A	30 percent	Severe conflicts yielding regime concessions	30 percent	N/A

Sources: Author postelectoral database, de Remes (2000), INEGI (1997, 2001), CONAPO (1993, 2001). For postelectoral conflict coding, see p. 293. Post-electoral conflict coding is explained in Appendix A (p. 291).

autonomy, including in institutions established to adjudicate postelectoral conflicts, which are often taken for granted. Opposition parties that lose elections nonetheless tend to comply with electoral institutions, filing postelectoral complaints for close races and abiding by verdicts, and by accepting official results without postelectoral appeals in routine cases with wide victory margins.[11] The proximity of the runner-up to the electoral winner largely determines whether electoral complaints are filed, as it is these cases where fraud at the margins can impact electoral outcomes. While mobilizations may occur, they are to influence public opinion and hence pressure judges, albeit indirectly. There exist no postelectoral mobilizations with the intention of directly "winning" (or at least collecting a "consolation prize") through informal bargaining channels outside judicial chambers.

---

[11] The stark differences are highlighted between postelectoral contestation under a consolidated rule of law versus under a regime of uncertain actor compliance, by considering the 2000 U.S. presidential election. While the second-guessing of the Florida vote tallies will continue for years (e.g., see Ceaser and Busch 2001), once Al Gore's challenges to George W. Bush were addressed by the Supreme Court, Gore desisted and there were no more postelectoral mobilizations. The Mexican pattern of postelectoral mobilization is simply not part of the choice set in democracies with loser compliance, like the United States.

Consider the negotiation of postelectoral conflicts in regimes that only weakly adhere to a rule of law. In such cases, the proximity of the runner-up to the first place finisher in a given race is not significant, per se. What matters is the strategy of the authoritarian incumbent and opposition parties more broadly speaking. That is, the incumbents must decide what demands to make on the opposition, and the opposition must decide case by case whether to comply with authoritarian incumbent demands in legal systems where such compliance is not a given (and have the internal discipline to enact these desires).

This assumption of compliance is stated as follows:

1. Consistent with the "processes and pacts" democratization tradition, a **recourse to national formal institutions** explanation implies a complete adherence of opposition forces to the rules of the game, once the pact is signed and these rules agreed upon. This hypothesis implies full cooperation by all opposition with the government. Electoral disputes are settled using established legal institutions only, rather than through extralegal bargaining.

The hypothesis is mundane when applied to actual cases, but at a more abstract level, it is the principal explanation for the pacted transitions to democracy. Disconfirming this hypothesis lays the empirical groundwork for a broader reassessment of pacted rule of law transition theories at the microinstitutional level, which has commenced elsewhere by specialists like Dalpino (2000) trying to understand why the pacting model is not applicable to twenty-first century protracted transitions like those in the People's Republic of China and Iran. The strong form of this hypothesis is that there will be no postelectoral mobilizations once democratization has been pacted nationally and is in local implementation, while a weaker form states that an increasing number of electoral court complaint filings will cause a decreasing number of postelectoral conflicts. In other words, a negative relationship between electoral court filings and postelectoral conflicts is consistent with this hypothesis.

Moving beyond the pacted transitions model, the evidence presented here brings into question a crucial assumption behind that model, namely that regime opponents act with a single voice, or in social science parlance, that they are unified actors. In the protracted Mexican case, the data reveal extensive differences between opposition party strategies and imply further differences within local party organizations (especially within the PRD) and across regions. Such extensive variations are hardly surprising to scholars of party behavior and social movements, generally, and

Mexican politics in particular. Panebianco (1988, 7), for example, notes the crucial effect of agency loss on party organization. Leaders often possess interests different from those of the rank and file, and may not always pursue objectives stated as those of the party. Internal incentive structures for keeping discipline and unity and preventing the breakdown of group objectives into extreme factional rivalries determine overall party effectiveness. If such considerations are important in democracies, where competitive parties can expect to win elections and thus reward loyal activists, they are even more crucial in authoritarian regimes, where opposition parties' rewards expectations are much more modest. It is in considering internal party cohesion that the social movement literature becomes relevant. Movements seem to compensate for a lack of material rewards by psychologically embroiling participants in the "cause" and by shrewdly recognizing societal shortcomings that can serve as "framing" for their pleas.

The decentralization of decision making among PRD party movements allowed for spontaneity, but also for disorganization. If the PAN was excessively centralized, leaving little discretion to local leaders, the PRD tended toward the opposite extreme. The winner, at least along the subnational battle lines where Mexico's initial decades of protracted transition were mostly waged, was the PRI-state. As observed by Cornelius et al. (1999), a pattern was established whereby "in those spaces where, entrenched, hard-line *PRIísta* leaders continue to hold sway, we can anticipate even greater impunity and more rigid authoritarian control, including freer recourse to official violence" (11). Indeed, this pattern has only become more entrenched with the demise in 2000 of the PRI-state's national moderates, leaving their local *cacique* affiliates "on their own" as a loose network of bosses trying to perpetuate a monopoly on the use of coercion that they no longer possess, at least not according to national laws. Subnational explanations are needed, and provide the actual hypotheses tested.

FOUR SUBNATIONALLY DETERMINED CAUSES OF MEXICO'S LOCAL POSTELECTORAL CONFLICTS

If institutions are explicitly considered as an entire range of possible behaviors, rather than as merely "rules of the game," their study may more readily include extralegally constituted and informal arenas of bargaining between actors, as well as the legally constituted, formal arenas. Informal institutions leave few records of their construction or use; hence it is

difficult to precisely measure compliance with them, although interviews
with protagonists convey how these institutions work in particular cases
(see Chapters 6, 7, and 8). Whether formal institutions are significant in
reducing postelectoral conflicts should be a testable proposition, as such
conflicts should be likely where formal electoral institutions are "weaker"
or less autonomous from the authoritarian executive. A first hypothesis
is derived as follows.

1. Contrary to the "processes and pacts" democratization tradition,
   a negotiated institutions explanation would imply a significant
   role for regime opponents in constructing institutions. An **electoral institution strength** hypothesis states that postelectoral conflicts are more prevalent where formal electoral institutions are less
   autonomous, thereby prompting the opposition to resort to informal bargaining.

The "Electoral Institution Strength" hypothesis is operationalized in the
way institutions are typically measured, according to their formal constitutions. I have coded "autonomy from the executive branch" of the
thirty electoral codes in effect in the ten states during periods of my
study (Appendix B). A negative relationship between this conventional
institutional variable and parties' propensities for postelectoral conflicts
provides evidence that institutions are sufficient in prompting opposition
acceptance of electoral institutions.

A second hypothesis considers postelectoral conflicts as a form of social movement. Mexico's postelectoral conflicts are not "cycles of contention" that, according to Tarrow (1998, 144), possess "heightened
conflict, broad sectoral and geographic diffusion, the expansion of the
repertoire of contention, the appearance of new organizations and the
empowerment of old ones, the creation of new 'master frames' linking
the actions of disparate groups to one another, and intensified interaction
between challengers and the state. . . . " Nor may postelectoral conflicts be
considered among the "everyday forms of peasant resistance" identified
by Scott (1985, xvi) as "the ordinary weapons of relatively powerless
groups: foot dragging, dissimulation, desertion, false compliance, pilfer-
ing, feigned ignorance, slander, arson, sabotage, and so on." Postelectoral conflicts fall in the middle of this continuum between heightened
collective action spreading from town to town and individualized resistance deployed by peasants in their daily struggles. They are in most
cases isolated but collective actions revolving loosely around elections.
The remaining question is whether there exist ulterior structural causes

that could be framed by party activists in the context of electoral demands.

The existence of this possibility, that postelectoral conflicts were framed by rational activists to direct antiregime behavior into postelectoral protests, suggests the hypothesis:

2. The more polarized the local environment is as a result of authoritarian excesses by regional machine bosses, the more likely the PAN and PRD will rebel against adverse elections. Hence, the greater the number of **localized social conflicts** (such as human rights abuses, agrarian conflicts, etc.), the more likely are postelectoral conflicts.

This is an actor-driven, rather than structural, hypothesis requiring that actors channel dissent through collective action. Structural indicators of socioeconomic adversity – such as the percentage of households earning fewer than two minimum wages per day (approximately U.S. $3.00) – are also tested, as control variables, but less as a cause for the social unrest than as direct causes of postelectoral conflict in their own right.

Operationalization of Hypothesis II presented the greatest data collection challenges of this study. After unsuccessfully seeking itemization of human rights violations disaggregated to the municipal level, I settled for an index of three indicators: one measuring state-level human-rights abuses, one broadly coding local demands for services, and one directly measuring perhaps the oldest and most pervasive social conflict, agrarian conflict. The index is based partially on what Ekiert and Kubik (1999) describe as "protest event analysis" coded from media sources. I constructed a scale composed of two coded media sources and a third, primary source (explained in greater detail in Appendix B): (1) a statewide indicator of conflictiveness compiled for 1993–5 (and then averaged) based on press reports by two Mexico City nongovernment organizations, the Agustín Pro Juárez Human Rights Center and the "Heriberto Jara" Center for Municipal Services (CESEM), and daily newspaper CD-ROM collections, (2) an index of local conflicts compiled from one local and one national news source for the six months prior to each of the three election cycles studied (spanning from 1989 to 1998), and (3) an index of agrarian conflicts per capita from 1998 government reports of conflicts. The vast majority of these conflicts had persisted since the 1930s without resolution. The federal Attorney General for Agrarian Issues was created in 1992 to identify and resolve these long-standing conflicts. Although authorities resolved some 90 percent of the 89,667 agrarian conflicts in my ten-state sample identified between April 1992 and November 1998, the fifty-year legacies of these divisions still presented a useful proxy for social unrest that could be "framed" by political entrepreneur opposition activists.

To measure more urban, nonagrarian forms of local social contention, I coded "citizen demands" from the local and national newspapers specified in Appendix B for six months prior to each local election. These demands spanned a broad range of issues – from pleas for sewage, running water, and electricity to demonstrations against specific acts of corruption or human rights violations. The severity of the mobilizations was coded (Appendix B) provided they met two conditions: they could not be related to elections (as this would have increased collinearity with the postelectoral conflict dependent variable), and they had to have been precipitated by specific local acts or conditions (rather than be local responses to national provocation). The relative importance of these local conflicts was weighted by aggregating the local news source with a national print media source so that presumably the more significant conflicts would log two mentions (and a higher score) than those only mentioned in the local paper. Continuity of local media across the nine years of the ten-state study was difficult to attain, and its lack forced me to eliminate four states from the sample – Campeche, Chihuahua, Tamaulipas, and Tlaxcala – and to resort to national press coverage in a fifth case – Chiapas – where no reliable local press existed during the early years of the study.

While not formally aggregated into Hypothesis II, a second – more self-evident – variable related Hypotheses II more directly to recent histories of postelectoral conflict. The variable, a simple bivariate or "dummy" variable expressing whether past postelectoral conflicts had been staged in the municipality, relates past postelectoral tensions to those in the current period. While this variable ideally would have extended back several periods, media records of T_0, needed to assess prior postelectoral conflicts in T_1, were limited. Very few records were available before the advent of more independent national newspapers in the mid-1980s, and they were unreliable until the early 1990s, when local media started covering postelectoral conflicts more extensively.

The third overall working hypothesis is much less complex and is generated by literature on U.S. congressional campaigns, which are instructive despite their innumerable differences with local elections in Mexico (particularly before the deepening of political liberalization). The hypothesis adheres to the simple logic, spelled out by Jacobson and Kernell (1981, 34–8), that campaign contributors concentrate resource donations on the candidates they feel are most likely to win. Extrapolating to the Mexican case, where local elections are better endowed with labor than with money, it may be reasoned that even after losing in the official (and frequently rigged) vote count, opposition party activists are more likely to contest elections they came closer to winning and perceive that they actually may have won. The hypothesis, then, is as follows.

3. PAN and PRD supporters are more likely to mobilize after closely contested elections than after noncompetitive races. In other words, the opposition party's level of **perceived electoral competition** with the electoral winner, and perception of whether the election was clean, is a rough proxy for opposition party postelectoral bargaining strength.

This "Perceived Electoral Competition" hypothesis is operationalized through two straightforward indicators. First, perceived parity refers to electoral competition, and this is measured as the proximity of the opposition party's official vote tally to the PRI tally. This is a more informative ratio than drawing a comparison between the election winner (the PRI in over 80 percent of the races during the study) and first runner-up, because as a rule the PAN and the PRD did not contest elections won by parties other than the PRI (and the overwhelming pattern of two-party competition meant that, for example, where the PAN won, there would be no real PRD organization to challenge them in any case). Where the ratio is between 0 and 1 and there are extended postelectoral mobilizations by the runner-up, the hypothesis is confirmed. A positive relationship between this PRD-to-PRI or PAN-to-PRI ratio and the number of postelectoral conflicts would be consistent with this hypothesis.

Because the crux of my argument is that official election results are just the beginning, a second indicator is also required based on party perceptions of the level of electoral fraud involved in reaching the official results. The best proxy for perception of fraud that would prevent a truer reading of vote parity is the number of electoral court cases filed after the election. On those occasions – rare by T2 and T3 – activists launched postelectoral conflicts before their lawyers filed complaints (not uncommon in T1 and earlier in PRD mobilizations). The filings are used (in a scaled manner explained in Appendix B) as the best single indicator of how rigged the opposition parties perceived the elections to be.

This work has sought to accept the challenge of measuring electoral fraud indirectly by insisting that while the "legitimacy" of elections cannot be directly measured, the best proxy for "illegitimacy" is whether they provoke postelectoral mobilizations. In this instance, however, where the dependent variable being modeled is precisely an opposition party's propensity for such conflicts after local elections, it would be tautological to argue that the existence of postelectoral mobilizations is the best proxy for whether such elections were credible. Hence, the filing of electoral court complaints is the proxy for perceived electoral fraud.

The last hypothesis directly tests some of the structural variables that I argue help shape – but do not fully determine – the opportunities of this preceding agency-driven hypothesis. Consistent with theories of "resource deprivation" and "collective action,"[12] the most rural and least integrated of Mexico's citizens will be the least likely to rebel against electoral fraud. While Hypothesis II tests the relationship between postelectoral conflicts and broader manifestations of social unrest, this hypothesis directly considers the effects of community population and geographic isolation on postelectoral mobilizations. Some overlap may exist in that the objective demographic conditions measured here may also be subjective causes of the citizen demands coded as part of the "localized social conflicts" hypothesis. However, results show that these variables are complementary rather than excessively collinear, probably meaning that their relationship exists in an abstraction beyond the empirical indicators tested.

The hypothesis, then, tested by considering several related variables, is as follows.

4. Opposition party compliance with formal electoral rules is more likely under lower levels of **urban concentration**, that is, in smaller, more rural, and more isolated municipalities, where barriers to collective action are higher. Postelectoral conflicts are thus more likely in larger, more urban, and less remote municipalities, where activists may still suffer from poor resource distribution but yet possess more than the minimum threshold of resources required to undertake collective action.

---

[12] This hypothesis combines aspects of Gurr's relative deprivation theory, hypothesizing that mobilization occurs because of frustration caused by an imbalance between "what one gets and what one considers one's due" (Eckstein 1980, 144), and Tilly's collective action theory, whereby mobilization can only occur when there exists a confluence of the shared interests, organization, and opportunity needed to overcome barriers to action (Eckstein 1980, 147). The emphasis here is on material barriers to action, as more isolated individuals will have less information for assessing their "due," and larger groups possess more potentially mobilizable members. The expressly material aspects of these theories – namely that citizens above a threshold of deprivation are more likely to protest – are also considered, but as control variables.

In areas of more concentrated population, with better outside communication and larger communities from which to draw potential protesters, social and economic problems may still be felt (and, in fact, distribution of wealth may be even more skewed than in rural areas). But the existence in urban areas of more information to condition citizens' expectations means that they will be less vulnerable to traditional political machine bosses. Hence, while socioeconomic control variables were also included, the possible demographic cause of postelectoral conflicts was the only one tested directly by Hypothesis IV. The variable was operationalized according to three measures more fully explained in Appendix B, which were all statistically significant in both models as causes of mobilization by at least one of the parties. First, a measure was used of population, taking the natural log of census data. Second, a measure was constructed of the percentage of residents living in the municipal "seat," as opposed to in the surrounding communities also comprising the municipality (analogous in level of aggregation to a U.S. county). Finally, a measure was found of the number of people per square kilometer in each municipality.

Three socioeconomic control variables were also used, not formally part of Hypothesis IV, but no doubt related. First, a reliable measure with great variance from the government's index of economic marginality (see Appendix B)[13] was included, the percentage of households earning fewer than two federally set minimum wages. Second, a measure was created and tested of municipal income per capita. Finally, in recognition of the political and economic disenfranchisement of Mexico's indigenous communities, I added an "indigenousness" control variable – the percentage of each municipality's population (over five years old) speaking primarily languages other than Spanish.

Descriptive data on average populations of postelectoral conflict sites offer a partial and preliminary confirmation of Hypothesis IV. While

---

[13] In previous iterations, I had used the Mexican National Geographic Statistics and Information Institute's (INEGI) standard-of-living index, a composite of nine questions included in Mexico's 1990 and 2000 census including: (1) percent of illiterates, (2) percent of the population more than fifteen years old not having finished primary school, (3) percent residing in home without indoor plumbing, (4) electricity, (5) paved floors, (6) sewage, (7) level of residential overcrowding, (8) percent living in towns of fewer than 5,000 residents, (9) percent earning fewer than two minimum wages (National Council for Population 1993, 26–9). For the model estimations reported here, I chose only indicator nine, as it was among the most direct measures of poverty and because it had a much greater variance than the composite index.

population of the average PRD-won municipality – 34,200 people – is close to the average population for all of Mexico's 2,418 municipalities, the average PRD conflictive municipality (46,800) and the average PAN-won municipality (110,400) and PAN conflictive municipality (97,100) are well above the national average, with the PAN's won and contested municipalities both three times larger than the population of Mexico's average municipality.[14]

In summary, the four hypothesized causes of postelectoral conflicts by the PAN and PRD, along with their indicators and preliminary character-izations of findings, are summarized in Table 5.3. The formal "Electoral Institution Strength" and "Perceived Electoral Competition" hypothe-ses represent standard theories in electoral studies. My argument hinges on at least partially disconfirming them in favor of the "Localized So-cial Conflict" hypothesis and its social movement study complement, the "Urban Concentration" hypothesis. While variations of Hypotheses III and IV are quite common in the social movements literature, their juxta-position with the electoral studies–derived hypotheses is unprecedented. I maintain that great variation exists between the PAN and the PRD with regard to these opposition parties' overall strategies and relations with the regime and, hence, with regard to whether they confirm these four hy-potheses. The operational indicators of these hypotheses described previ-ously and in Appendix B are tested in the multinomial logit models ALL T and T2 in which the dependent variable is postelectoral mobilization and the possible outcomes are no mobilization, PAN mobilization, and PRD mobilization.[15]

---

[14] While formal calculations were not done for PRI-won municipalities, it may be con-cluded, given that the average population of other municipalities won and contested by the opposition party were similar to those of the PRD and because the PRI-contested municipalities had an average population of 92,000, the noncontested municipalities where the PRI won were smaller (and poorer) than the national average. This conclusion is consistent with PRI-state and opposition strategists' characterizations of the rural poor as the key to PRI electoral dominion for all those decades.

[15] ALL T consisted of 3,012 local elections. Some 78 percent of the 423 mobilizations in ALL T were by the PRD and 22 percent were by the PAN. In T2, representing only elections where PAN and PRD values are both between 0 and 1 – meaning that both parties fielded a candidate and that their candidates did not win – conflicts occurred in 105 out of 464 municipal races (the total size of T2 was 1,005). The PRD accounted for 77 percent of these conflicts; the PAN accounted for 23 percent. The PRI and Third Party mobilizations are not considered in the models, which are limited to three values: $y = 0$ is for no mobilization, $y = 1$ represents PRD mobilizations, and $y = 2$ is for PAN mobilizations.

TABLE 5.3 *Postelectoral Conflict Causes*

Hypothesis	Operational Indicator	Summary of Findings	
		For PRD	For PAN
I. Electoral Institution Strength Opposition compliance is less likely under weaker electoral institutions	Index of institutional autonomy based on electoral law indicators	STRONGLY DISCONFIRMED	NEITHER CONFIRMED NOR DISCONFIRMED
II. Localized Social Conflicts Opposition compliance is less likely where social unrest is greater	Number of collective citizen demands coded by municipality or state	STRONGLY CONFIRMED	NEITHER CONFIRMED NOR DISCONFIRMED
III. Perceived Electoral Competition Opposition compliance is less likely in closer and/or fraudulent races	Ratio of opposition-to-PRI votes and index of perceived election fraud	STRONGLY CONFIRMED	STRONGLY CONFIRMED
IV. Urban Concentration Opposition compliance is less likely in larger and more densely populated communities	Population density, population, and percentage of residents living in municipal seat	CONFIRMED	CONFIRMED

REPORTING MULTINOMIAL LOGIT ESTIMATES OF POSTELECTORAL
CONFLICT MODELS

Beyond the variables related to the four hypotheses, three other "control" variables were included. First, using Federal Electoral Institute (IFE) data[16] on the percentage of precincts "covered" by PAN and PRD poll workers on election day of the 1988, 1991, 1994, 1997, and 2000 federal elections, and extrapolating data for the years between these elections (Appendix B), I used these indicators as proxies for state PAN and PRD organization levels. While the variable was not tested in T2, where I had to limit the number of statewide variables or risk excessive collinearity among them, these measures, dubbed "PAN Organization" and "PRD Organization," were used in ALL T. The second control variable was an ordinal scale (from one to four – explained in Appendix B) of each governor's national trajectory prior to assuming the governorship. This indicator was added to control for claims by scholars of subnational governance in Mexico that governors with stronger ties to the national PRI-state were accorded more discretion and hence could be more repressive of social demands including postelectoral mobilizations. The third variable, "Period," was added to ALL T only to control for the particular election cycle (T1, T2, or T3) that pertained to a given election. While "PRD Organization" and "Period" were statistically significant, "PAN Organization" and "Governor National Profile" were not.

The results, reported in Tables 5.4 and 5.5, do at least partially confirm Hypotheses III and IV, the "Perceived Electoral Parity" and "Urban Concentration" hypotheses, for both parties. Predictably, both the "Ratio of PAN-to-PRI Votes" and "Ratio of PRD-to-PRI Votes" were statistically significant in both ALL T and T2, and generated by far the greatest changes in predicted probabilities of either model in T2.[17] The other important indicator within this hypothesis, "Index of Electoral Fraud," was also statistically significant in T2 – the only model where it could be tested – and shown to greatly affect predicted probabilities when its value was set at opposite extremes. Overall, in terms of predicted probabilities,

---

[16] I tried to collect more localized data from the electoral commissions of the ten sample states but quickly found that it was spotty and did not cover the entire time period of the study.

[17] Partial collinearity with "PAN Organization" and "PRD Organization" in ALL T no doubt reduced these variables' effect on predicted probabilities in that model. "PRD Organization" was significant in ALL T, yielding a large change in predicted probability at extreme values, while "PAN Organization" was not statistically significant.

the two vote ratio variables were the most powerful in T2, as when varied between their extremes (while all other variables were held constant at their means), each of these party ratios could alter the probability that postelectoral conflicts would be staged by at least 40 percent. In ALL T, the effect of these dramatic predicted probabilities was no doubt diminished by the related party organization variables, which were not tested in T2 (see fn. 17).

Among the demographic and socioeconomic indicators related to the "Urban Concentration" hypothesis, only the "Percent Earning Subminimum Wage" variable was not significant in either model. Among the demographic variables in ALL T, "Population" and "Pct. Population in Municipal Seat" were significant for both parties and "Municipal Population Density" was significant for the PAN. Of the related socioeconomic control variables, "Indigenous Language Speakers" and "Municipal Income per Capita" were significant for the PRD. These findings and accompanying predicted probabilities (Table 5.5) confirm that both parties tended to launch postelectoral conflicts in larger communities with greater population densities, and while the PAN tended to mobilize in urban areas, the PRD tended to mobilize in communities low on public resources (but with only moderate poverty levels) and with higher concentrations of indigenous language speakers. Fewer of the "Urban Concentration" variables were significant in T2, although "Population" was still significant as a factor in PRD conflict mobilization and "Pct. Population in Municipal Seat" was significant as a cause of PAN conflict mobilization.

However, much less predictably, the "Electoral Institution Strength" argument was strongly disconfirmed for the PRD; that is, the variable was statistically significant in ALL T, but the positive coefficient indicates that – contrary to the hypothesis – *the more autonomous the electoral institutions, the more likely the PRD is to stage postelectoral mobilizations.* This result contradicted the PAN's strategy, denoted by statistical significance in T2 in the predicted negative direction, indicating that greater electoral institution autonomy yields fewer postelectoral conflicts. This compelling result implies that, at least during the "dueling focal points" period of recourse to both formal and informal institutions for adjudicating postelectoral conflicts, the PRD pursued strategies mostly without regard for formal institutions. In fact, choosing to mobilize where institutions are stronger implies a consistent lack of faith by party lawyers and activists in formal institutional channels. This faith in street demonstrations over judicial proceedings, despite their poor success rate on the streets, attests to the limited range of options that PRD activists perceived. "Electoral

TABLE 5.4 *Multinomial Logit Estimates of Postelectoral Conflict Models*
Model ALL T – Longitudinal Model for Ten States, 1989–98

Independent Variable	PRD Mobilize vs. No Mobilization			PAN Mobilize vs. No Mobilization			Range	Mean
	Coeff.	S. error	T-ratio	Coeff.	S. error	T-ratio		
Constant	−7.88456	1.19643	−6.59	−9.11835	2.02333	−4.51		
Social conflicts index	0.74897	0.12174	6.15	0.36148	0.22593	1.60	0.5–4.0	2.00075
Prior electoral conflicts PRD	0.34651	0.83729	4.14	0.80254	0.49055	1.64	0.0–1.0	0.10027
Prior electoral conflicts PAN	−1.96553	0.31404	−6.26	0.54194	0.34526	1.57	0.0–1.0	0.04316
Strength of institutions	1.59227	0.55891	2.85	−0.26437	1.09810	−0.24	0.07–0.97	0.57379
PRD organization (poll watchers)	3.21104	0.38158	8.42	−0.49097	0.68660	−0.72	0.0–0.99	0.61960
PAN organization (poll watchers)	−1.08396	0.57102	−1.90	0.26706	0.98656	0.27	0.1–1.0	0.63588
Ratio of PRD-to-PRI votes	0.34651	0.08373	4.14	−1.27715	0.62639	−2.04	0.00019–0.9980	0.37587
Ratio of PAN-to-PRI votes	−1.96553	0.31404	−6.26	1.52370	0.25824	5.90	0.00021–0.99581	0.38907
Pct. earning subminimum wage	−0.99900	0.74901	−1.33	−0.51459	1.35717	−0.38	0.304–0.951	0.68803
Municipal income per capita	−0.00099	0.00050	−1.99	−0.00021	0.00081	−0.27	17.34–2156.78	264.346
Population (natural log)	0.50811	0.08016	6.34	0.47078	0.11604	4.06	5.728–14.31218	9.6714
Pct. population in municipal seat	1.20882	0.31079	3.89	1.89378	0.54044	3.50	0.0055–1.00	0.47587
Indigenous language speakers	0.86759	0.33128	2.62	0.62858	0.65836	0.95	0.0–0.85986	0.12763
Municipal population density	−0.00874	0.00576	−1.52	−0.03392	0.01463	−2.32	0.00387–200.2366	2.32513
State governor national profile	−0.02326	0.09550	−0.24	0.33920	0.17883	1.90	1.0–4.0	3.19
Period	−1.42552	0.29365	−4.85	−1.10676	0.43882	−2.52	1.0–3.0	2.00

Note: Bold signifies variable is statistically significant at .05 level. Reference category: No mobilization (no mobilization = 0).

Source: Estimation of postelectoral conflict model. Log-likelihood = −1077.2443. Pseudo R² = 0.2453. N = 2986. The total sample of all municipal elections over three cycles in ten states was 3,012, with all data available in 99 percent of the cases.

Model T2 – Cross-Sectional, Reduced Sample Model for Ten States, 1992–5
Elections were only considered in which postelectoral mobilization by the PAN or PRD was plausible. That is where "Ratio of PAN-to-PRI Votes" and "Ratio of PRD-to-PRI Votes" were greater than zero (meaning the party received votes) and less than one (meaning that the party did not beat the PRI).

Independent Variable	PRD Mobilize vs. No Mobilization			PAN Mobilize vs. No Mobilization			Range	Mean
	Coeff.	S. error	T-ratio	Coeff.	S. error	T-ratio		
Constant	−9.18669	3.22946	−2.84	−8.22512	5.23311	−1.57		
Social conflicts index	**1.36297**	0.74745	**3.55**	0.35939	0.51194	0.70	0.5–4.0	2.06588
Prior electoral conflicts PRD	0.49824	0.41650	1.20	0.08507	0.87591	0.10	0.0–1.0	0.28818
Prior electoral conflicts PAN	−1.36064	0.96432	−1.41	−1.21753	0.91907	−1.32	0.0–1.0	0.34013
Strength of institutions	−0.91991	1.81611	−0.51	**−7.61609**	2.93669	**−2.59**	0.04–0.83	0.65592
Index of electoral fraud	**1.55912**	0.59046	**2.64**	**3.55794**	0.92367	**3.85**	0.00–1.67	0.22389
Ratio of PRD-to-PRI votes	**5.20081**	0.71506	**7.27**	−0.59967	1.75780	−0.34	0.00019–0.9980	0.28818
Ratio of PAN-to-PRI votes	0.05987	0.86863	0.07	**6.26944**	1.26146	**4.97**	0.00021–0.99581	0.34013
Pct. earning subminimum wage	−3.20646	2.11625	−1.52	1.14672	3.04235	0.38	0.304–0.951	0.68803
Municipal income per capita	−0.00121	0.00152	−0.79	0.00037	0.00169	0.22	17.34–2156.78	218.22
Population (natural log)	**0.55614**	0.19823	**2.81**	0.08880	0.29982	0.30	7.2807–14.1164	10.13564
Pct. population in municipal seat	0.70792	0.74745	0.95	**3.40700**	1.28571	**2.65**	0.0162–0.9997	0.42892
State governor national profile	−0.37203	0.28509	−1.30	0.39107	0.39244	1.00	1.0–4.0	3.34

Note: **Bold** signifies variable is statistically significant at .05 level. **Reference category:** No mobilization (no mobilization = 0).

Source: Estimation of postelectoral conflict model. Log-likelihood = −164.2316. Pseudo R^2 = 0.4563. N = 460. The total sample of all municipal elections over one cycle in ten states was 1,005, but the sample, split to consider only races with plausible PAN or PRD mobilizations, consisted of 464 municipal elections (the opposition parties failed to field candidates in a majority of cases). However, all data were available in 99 percent of the reduced sample.

TABLE 5.5 *Predicted Probabilities for No Mobilization, PRD, and PAN Mobilizations*

		MODEL ALL T			MODEL T2		
Independent Variable	Value	All No Mobilize	All PRD Mobilize	All PAN Mobilize	T2 No Mobilize	T2 PRD Mobilize	T2 PAN Mobilize
Social conflicts index	High = 4.0	80.40	17.18	2.42	42.11	32.38	25.51
	Low = 0.5	97.65	1.52	0.83	84.83	0.55	14.61
	DIFFERENCE	−17.25	15.66	1.59	−42.72	31.83	10.90
Prior electoral conflicts PRD	High = 1	89.08	8.24	2.68	N/A	N/A	N/A
	Low = 0	94.53	4.20	1.27	N/A	N/A	N/A
	DIFFERENCE	−5.45	4.04	1.41	N/A	N/A	N/A
Prior electoral conflicts PAN	High = 1	92.27	5.47	2.26	N/A	N/A	N/A
	Low = 0	90.43	8.25	1.32	N/A	N/A	N/A
	DIFFERENCE	1.84	−2.78	0.94	N/A	N/A	N/A
Strength of institutions	High = 0.83	94.94	3.68	1.39	74.16	3.42	22.41
	Low = 0.04	90.43	8.25	1.32	71.44	6.82	21.63
	DIFFERENCE	4.51	−4.57	0.07	2.72	−3.40	0.78
Indigenous language speakers	High = 0.85986	89.82	8.11	2.08	N/A	N/A	N/A
	Low = 0	94.67	4.05	1.28	N/A	N/A	N/A
	DIFFERENCE	−4.85	4.06	0.80	N/A	N/A	N/A
Ratio PRD-to-PRI votes	High = 0.998	93.82	5.56	0.62	29.06	65.21	5.73
	Low = 0.0002	93.85	3.94	2.21	72.93	0.91	26.16
	DIFFERENCE	−0.03	1.62	−1.59	−43.87	64.30	−20.43
Ratio PAN-to-PRI votes	High = 0.9958	95.12	1.38	3.50	5.13	0.29	94.58
	Low = 0.0002	90.02	9.24	0.73	91.75	4.95	3.29
	DIFFERENCE	5.10	−7.86	2.77	−86.62	−4.66	91.29

Municipal income per capita	High = 2156.78	98.31	0.72	0.97	N/A	N/A	N/A
	Low = 17.34	92.90	5.67	1.43	N/A	N/A	N/A
	DIFFERENCE	5.41	−4.95	−0.52	N/A	N/A	N/A
Population	High = 14.1164	63.50	29.00	7.51	51.69	26.06	22.25
	Low = 7.2807	98.15	1.39	0.46	80.27	0.90	18.83
	DIFFERENCE	−34.65	27.61	7.05	−28.58	25.16	3.42
Pct. population in municipal seat	High = 0.9997	90.52	8.15	1.32	72.21	5.95	21.83
	Low = 0.0162	95.97	2.63	1.40	74.44	3.06	22.50
	DIFFERENCE	−5.45	5.52	0.08	−2.23	2.89	−1.33
Municipal population density	High = 200.237	99.16	0.84	0.00	N/A	N/A	N/A
	Low = 0.0039	93.93	4.58	1.48	N/A	N/A	N/A
	DIFFERENCE	5.23	−3.74	−1.48	N/A	N/A	N/A
PRD organization (poll watchers)	High = 0.99	85.35	13.40	1.25	N/A	N/A	N/A
	Low = 0.0	97.93	0.64	1.43	N/A	N/A	N/A
	DIFFERENCE	−12.58	12.76	−0.18	N/A	N/A	N/A
Period	High = 3	98.39	1.13	0.48	N/A	N/A	N/A
	Low = 1	80.45	16.00	3.55	N/A	N/A	N/A
	DIFFERENCE	17.94	−14.87	−3.07	N/A	N/A	N/A
Index of electoral fraud	High = 1.67	N/A	N/A	N/A	54.72	28.74	16.54
	Low = 0.00	N/A	N/A	N/A	74.56	2.90	22.54
	DIFFERENCE	N/A	N/A	N/A	−19.84	25.84	−6.00

Institution Strength" was not very elastic in either model; that is, setting this variable's values at their extremes (while leaving all other variables at their means) only altered the predicted probability of postelectoral mobilization by either party by less than 5 percent.

Also notable to this study's ambition of recasting Mexico's electoral opening as a social as well as electoral movement, the "Localized Social Conflicts" hypothesis was strongly confirmed for the loose, social movement PRD, but not confirmed for the hierarchical and centralized PAN. These results unambiguously demonstrate – across both models – that for the leftist opposition, at least, postelectoral conflicts result from local antiregime decisions as well as from conventional explanations such as electoral institution strength. The "Social Conflicts Index" was statistically significant in ALL T and T2, and generated substantial changes in predicted probabilities, meaning that the highest recorded level of social conflict (holding other variable coefficients at their means) increased the PRD's propensity for postelectoral conflicts by 16 percent (ALL T) and 32 percent (T2). The other variables considered under this hypothesis, "Prior Electoral Conflicts PRD" and "Prior Electoral Conflicts PAN," were statistically significant for the PRD only, and in ALL T only. However, the impact of these variables on predicted probabilities of postelectoral conflict was low, demonstrating that a history of nonelectoral social conflicts was a much more powerful cause of postelectoral conflicts than was a record of prior postelectoral conflicts. The implications of these findings are dramatic. To the PRD, postelectoral conflicts were not really about the elections, which partisans conceded that they could not win at the polls or through formal institution channels. Rather, elections were seen as the opportunity to contest broader social ills (such as those measured in the index, such as statewide human rights abuses, local agrarian conflicts, and local citizen demands for services) for remote and disenfranchised citizens with little to lose.

The model estimations suggest several important findings, at least with regards to the PRD. First and perhaps most important as a caveat to "new institutionalist" studies of political development, standard assumptions that institutions will be obeyed may hold for stable institutions in stable regimes, but this automatic recourse to formal institutions does not hold here, at least not for the party causing the vast majority of postelectoral mobilizations. Electoral institution strength is not decisive in predicting compliance, at least not during important moments of flux. Rather, at least with reference to Mexico's postelectoral mobilizations, the decision to undertake collective action is taken by local activists rather than by centralized party hierarchies, and is taken based more on the general level of conflict between the authoritarian incumbents and opposition than on the proximity of their vote share to that of the PRI-state winner.

In summary, the statistical model confirms the legal and electoral rationality of the PAN, disconfirming that these motivations were important causes of PRD postelectoral conflicts. Rather, the PRD breaks down as a national party, obeying a localized social movement logic rather than a national, hierarchical electoral logic of conventional political parties, at least during the peak of dueling focal points – electoral courts and bargaining tables – in the mid-1990s. The multinomial logit estimations confirm that an opposition party's electoral performance is a necessary but not sufficient factor in determining whether that party will abide by the official results. The findings disconfirm the democratization literature's implicit assumption of actor compliance with broad pacts, and instead offer evidence, at least in the case of PRD mobilizations, that the decision to mobilize is taken locally and based on local social conditions as well as on which party got the most votes.

CONCLUSIONS: LOCAL POLITICS SUPERSEDE FORMAL INSTITUTIONS

The gap between formal and informal institutions represented so graphically by T_2 is also representative of T_1 and T_0, for which complete data were not available. Extrapolating backward, I would argue that if T_0 data were available, the gap between the parallel sets of institutions would be even wider, as compliance with formal institutions is the norm by T_3, and the data available during T_3 is insufficient for statistical analysis. Indeed, the frequency of postelectoral conflicts per year dropped fivefold over the period studied, from some 250 partisan postelectoral conflicts nationwide at their 1992 peak, to one-fifth that many by 2000.[18] The statistical models do not offer answers about the precise mechanisms by which opposition parties decide to stop mobilizing after decades and comply with electoral institutions. But small-n analysis explains the motivations of PRD activists for breaking the bizarre patterns documented here in order to stop sacrificing activists' well-being – and even lives – at postelectoral

---

[18] A tally of postelectoral conflicts in 2001 reveals a further decrease in their frequency. That year, only thirty-four postelectoral conflicts were noted (although inclusion of *usos y costumbres* conflicts in Oaxaca's 2001 local power transfers would no doubt boost the total back up to its 2000 level).

protests. Small-n analysis can also clarify the PAN's rational but out-
wardly contradictory policy of respecting electoral institutions but also
staging postelectoral conflicts. And most importantly, it can explain how
this cycle of postelectoral violence and bargaining led to great conflicts
within the PRI and its divorce from the interests of the Mexican state that
led to the demise of the PRI-state in 2000.

While the PRD's behavior has been revealed as internally consistent but
not entirely explicable by conventional electoral studies hypotheses alone,
an apparent contradiction also exists in PAN behavior with respect to its
local organization. On the one hand, local chapters seemingly impose sufficient order as to render statistically significant the electoral institution
strength variable (measured by state) and to ensure the filing of electoral
court cases with greater success than other parties. On the other hand,
postelectoral conflicts seem to overwhelm local party organizations, just
as they do in the case of the less-disciplined PRD. In other words, what
justification would the legalistic PAN have for ever succumbing to *concertacesión*? The PAN's behavior may be readily explained, but not through
variables specified here, although the preceding analysis does depict the
PAN in most states during ALL T as a patchwork of loyal followers in
municipal population centers with little penetration of rural areas. The
explanation is that, given these demographic obstacles and the party's disciplined and hierarchical structure, the PAN's state organizations literally
dictate the party line in most instances from the state or regional capital,
adhering predictably to the rule of law over postelectoral conflicts. However, special interventions, sometimes even counter to state PAN wishes,
were conducted by national headquarters at flash-point moments when
postelectoral stakes were high and when the PAN brought particularly
strong leverage to bear in exchange for postelectoral patronage from the
PRI-state.

The next chapter explains the apparent contradiction between the consistent pattern of state and local PAN behavior and the ruptures in this
pattern brought by postelectoral conflict negotiations staged directly by
the national party leadership with the highest representatives of the PRI-
state. While the national headquarters' strategic negotiations cannot be
measured quantitatively (as there is no reliable measure of national "back
channel" intervention in local elections), especially given the relatively
low number of PAN postelectoral conflicts to begin with, scores of interviews and secondary accounts establish the patterns of national political
(as opposed to judicial) intervention I elaborate in Chapter 6. Chapter 7
extensively depicts the PRD's mode of conducting postelectoral conflicts,

which is quite consistent with findings revealed by the quantitative analysis: the party is driven by local grievances that supersede state and national chapter dictates. That party has been guided during much of ALL T by often spontaneous, transition-seeking political conflicts from the national level on down.

Having demonstrated the critical differences between the PAN and the PRD in their adherence to "Electoral Institution Strength" and "Localized Social Conflicts" hypotheses, I now elaborate, through the case-study method, how these two opposition parties differed in specific postelectoral strategies and, indeed, how their relations with the PRI-state in postelectoral negotiations was, during the formative periods of each opposition party, the most important intraparty obstacle to each party's consolidation. Using an extension of the analysis in Tables 5.1 and 5.2, I evaluate each opposition party's legal and extralegal responses to particular postelectoral challenges and relate these to the parties' overall roles in courting democracy.

6

The National Action Party: Dilemmas of Rightist Oppositions Defined by Authoritarian Collusion

> ...Because all subjects cannot be armed, if those whom you arm are benefited, one can act with more security toward the others. The difference of treatment that they recognize regarding themselves makes them obligated to you....
>
> Niccoló Machiavelli's *The Prince* (83)

The National Action Party's (PAN) creators never really intended for their "party," envisioned as a debating society with a ballot presence, to evolve into a potent electoral force, much less the engine of Mexico's electoral opening. Most of the party's doctrinaire founders wanted a quiet eddy of political discussion in the tumultuous sea of authoritarianism that surrounded them. However, while most of the founders wrote statutes and bylaws as narrow exercises in the citizenship they never expected to broadly practice, founder Manuel Gómez Morín accurately predicted the manipulation of "loyal opposition" parties (such as the fledgling PAN) by authoritarian incumbents. Gómez Morín wrote in 1939 that "electoral participation at this time could very well become an open escape-valve to put an end to public pressures, a means to exhaust the impulse of the citizenry, a path to dissolve – possibly through superficial concessions that would conceal the real issues – the collective impulse..." (von Sauer 1974, 101). Gómez Morín used terms remarkably similar to those of authoritarian Brazil's engineer of "the strategy of opening from above" in the 1970s, Golbery de Cuota e Silva, who, true to the PAN founder's projections, viewed political liberalization, using the same "escape valve" metaphor, as a necessary evil, the only alternative to instability (*Veja* 1980, 6). Clearly the PAN was in a position to benefit from this "escape valve," as the centrist Party of the Institutional Revolution (PRI) had no intention of permitting leftists to share power, since they would have sought to decisively redistribute it.

In addition to the obvious distinguishing feature of conservative parties (that their core constituents are the upper strata of society), these movements rely on cleavages other than class – "horizontal" cleavages that also may be seized upon by the political left – such as religion and regional or national identities (Gibson 1992, 15–20). However, Gibson's description presupposes a democratic polity, one where the conservative party is a regular participant in elections. In the nondemocratic polities considered in this work, electoral participation is far from given. Conservative parties must address a dilemma implied by Gibson of whether to broaden their support base and dilute their message in order to win, accept losing, or abstain. The most ideological of these parties' small upper-strata constituencies resist the sacrifice of essential principles for a broader electoral appeal at the risk of legitimizing authoritarians by participating under regime rules. In contrast to the ideologues and sectoral representatives (from business, the church, etc.), more pragmatic party bureaucrats tend to favor the electoral route as the only gradual path to change. The key then for such parties in ascertaining whether to prioritize electoral viability or doctrinal purity turns on what the authoritarian incumbents are offering for conservative participation and what they are offering if the conservatives abstain.

The main point in Gibson's discussion of conservative party behavior, further stressed by Loaeza (1999), is that however much such parties threaten antisystem behavior, they can very rarely tolerate ruptured change. Indeed, they are true supporters of protracted transitions, preferring status quo authoritarianism to calls for radical change from the left. Unlike ideologically true leftist oppositions, whose transition-seeking activities by definition seek to overthrow the regime, conservative oppositions can be induced to serve as accomplices to the authoritarian incumbents' extended time frame for political liberalization.

If the authoritarian incumbents manage to manipulate the conservative opposition successfully, they may reward ideologically compatible conservative opponents with sinecures, campaign funding, and other forms of patronage, within limits. They may also channel the opposition, co-opting or coercing opponents who "get out of hand" and ensuring that the conservative opposition attains a sufficient following to appear autonomous to outside observers but not so much power as to actually threaten the hegemony of the authoritarian incumbents. In the Mexican case, this paradoxical circumstance of an alternately authoritarian-fostered and authoritarian-hindered regime opposition has been dubbed "liberalization as an alternative to democratization" by Loaeza (1994, 107–8).

Given this paradox, are conservative parties like the PAN net contributors to democratization or net detractors from this cause? The answer appears obvious from the twenty-first century vantage of the Fox administration. But also consistent with my argument in Chapter 2, I contend that the PAN played a decisive role well before 2000 in leveling Mexico's electoral playing field, reform by reform, campaign by campaign. I further claim that the waging of this electoral battle of attrition, lasting fifty years before Mexico even arrived at the brink of democracy in the mid-1990s, was far from a foregone conclusion to the internally divided PAN. This chapter breaks the analysis into three stages in internal PAN development to demonstrate the party leadership's changing answer to the central uncertainty of whether to remain a small upper-class doctrinaire party or to "dilute" its ideological purity in order to champion political opening as its chief cross-class electoral appeal. The nascent PAN was unequivocally doctrinaire and antielectoralist during its formative first stage (1949–76)[1] and unabashedly pragmatic in its third and most recent, consolidation stage (1989–present), with leadership shifting between these two poles during intervening years. This chapter seeks to trace the evolution of the PAN by considering a typology explained in Chapter 1: the party's relations vis-à-vis the regime (the "antiregime opposition–patronage-seeking opposition" continuum). Also, I explain PAN and PRI-state perversions of the rule of law in the electoral realm, illustrating the last chapter's argument with detailed qualitative analysis of three cases of PAN-PRI postelectoral bargaining. Before assessing the empirical record, I outline the PAN's models of electoral and postelectoral activism, emphasizing how these have changed.

The party's evolution from debating society to competitive electoral opposition was characterized by bargaining between the national PAN, the national PRI, and the national PRI's interlocutors in government, mainly the Interior Secretary. Indeed, the *PANístas* may not have behaved differently from strategic candidates in American politics theories

---

[1] Under the tutelage of its first president, Manuel Gómez Morín, the characterization of the party as a "debating society" was not apt. After a disillusioned Gómez Morín stepped down in 1949 after being cheated at the polls by the PRI-state in 1946, the party adopted the more doctrinal, less politically expedient position characterized by the first period.

who decided to run for Congress depending on whether, at the national level, "it promises to be a good or bad year for the party," which in turn hinges on "national economic and political conditions" (Jacobson 1992, 163). However, at least during the early 1990s *concertacesión* years, *PANístas* sought national coattails for postelectoral campaigns as well as in electoral campaigns. As evidenced by the case studies to follow, the national party constantly linked local postelectoral bargaining with the national party's behavior in legislative fora, and in other arenas where the PRI-state could benefit greatly from a complacent loyal opposition.

The PAN experienced extensive defections in 1992 over its increasingly "cozy" relations with the regime, and the PRI lost followers in the states and cities where certified electoral winners were sacrificed for the PAN. What the PAN and the PRI lacked, prior to sufficiently credible electoral courts, was a third actor to externalize the losses from their disputes. The state should have performed as such a third-party arbiter, financing independent investigations of competing claims and rectifying damages by declaring new winners, convoking new elections, etc. This was precisely the function of a working electoral court. But as long as the PRI-state was one entity sanctified and protected by formal institutions entirely of its own creation, the PAN (justifiably) recognized no such third-party arbiter. The PAN did start to recognize state electoral courts as credible third-party arbiters in the mid-1990s. But the party's strategists realized that once they had certified the credibility of these formal institutions, retraction of such profound statements would debase the institutions and their party by making them out as capricious and politically driven. Undecided between recognizing imperfect institutions and accepting imperfect side payments, the PAN vacillated during much of the 1990s and then pursued both options.

PAN STRATEGIES OF ELECTORAL OPENING: EXTRALEGAL MEANS TO LEGAL ENDS

The PAN critics, like former Party of the Democratic Revolution (PRD) electoral affairs director Javier González Garza (interview), acknowledged that unlike the PAN, the PRD never had credible negotiators who could guarantee execution of agreements negotiated with the PRI-state. The PRD could not speak with one voice, as Diego Fernández de Cevallos, the controversial "clutch" postelectoral negotiator and 1994 presidential candidate, did for the PAN.[2] Furthermore, the PRD never benefited from PAN agreements with President Salinas. *PANista* election losers could demonstrate fraud with electoral acts and documentation, then the Salinas administration would accept the results, even if they were adverse to the PRI. The PAN's *quid pro quo* was support for most pillars of Salinas's conservative political and economic reforms.[3] The PRD, then headed by Cárdenas, never publicly cooperated with the administration. Until 1995, the PRD leadership did not even recognize the Salinas or Zedillo governments.

Did the PAN in fact deal with Salinas? While they would not confirm details, ranking PAN leaders referred to a "special relationship" between the PAN and the PRI during Salinas's term giving the PAN privileges as the regime's loyal opposition (Alcántara, Castillo Peraza interviews). National PAN officials also admitted conducting direct communications with the PRI-state's party leadership, Secretary of the Interior, and, in some cases, with the president himself (Castillo Peraza, Fernández de Cevallos, Medina Plascencia, Correa Mena, Manzanera, Coindreau Garcia interviews). Case-study reconstructions of postelectoral negotiations further illuminate differences between PAN and PRD approaches. First, I discuss postelectoral conflict within the context of the PAN's historical rise and overall electoral strategy. I assert that, like other opposition parties in protracted regime transitions, whether to cooperate with the PRI regime or abstain from elections was the singular, defining cleavage within the party from its 1939 founding until its 2000 ascent to power. After establishing the overwhelming importance of this "cooperate-abstain" cleavage in internal conflicts, I consider the PAN's position vis-à-vis regime participation during the post-1988 political liberalization and how this is reflected in its postelectoral strategies. I then elaborate postelectoral negotiation case studies in three of the party's most successful negotiations: Mérida 1993, Monterrey 1994, and Huejotzingo 1996. I conclude this chapter by discerning patterns in these case studies of PAN postelectoral

---

[2] González Garza said that Secretary of the Interior and former Mexico State Governor Emilio Chuayffet expressed little faith in PRD negotiators in 1993, insisting that the national PRD present one credible negotiator with whom all deals could be executed without agency loss. "I want a Diego Fernández de Cevallos in the PRD," Chuayfett is said to have uttered (González Garza interview).

[3] Those are largely considered to be the extensive trade and financial liberalization accelerated between 1989 and the signing of NAFTA in 1993, the 1992 Church reform, and the 1992 *ejido* privatization agrarian reform. The PAN actively supported all these initiatives, while the PRD actively opposed them.

mobilization, mainly that they were always initiated in Mexico City be-tween the national PRI and PAN leadership; that they always involved a respect for established laws and an effort to sidestep them without violat-ing them entirely; and that they usually coincided with moments of high PAN blackmail potential, should the PRI have failed to cooperate. In the next chapter I contrast the PAN's disciplined disobedience with the PRD's disorganized dissent.

The PAN's development and consolidation can be broadly divided into three periods: 1939–76, 1977–88, and 1989–2000. During the first period, culminating in the PAN's 1976 abstention from the presidential election leaving President López Portillo unopposed, the PAN behaved as doctri-naire rather than tactical opposition. That is, the party did not hesitate to challenge the regime rhetorically, but always with the understanding that challenging the regime electorally (at least at the national or state levels) was off limits. In Gibson's terms, the party in this formative period refused to broaden its coalition. The second period, marked by bitter infighting over relations with the regime, represented the PAN's transition from an elite-based, antiregime but doctrinaire party seeking primarily to "edu-cate" Mexicans, to a "loyal opposition" electoral force willing to cut deals with the regime, but only in exchange for collective rewards (guarantees of mayorships, proportional-representation congressional seats, public cam-paign financing, etc.). The party experimented with opening to represent a broader electoral base, and with the use of mobilizations and even violence to counter authoritarian injustices. But it was not until the third period that this pragmatic faction (known as the neo-*PANístas*) took decisive con-trol of the party. They consolidated a loyal opposition, patronage-seeking relationship with the regime and actively pursued the cross-class coalition required to win elections.

Throughout these periods of fundamental change, the PAN has always maintained its characteristic emphasis on electoral transparency, seeking domestic and international witnesses to the frauds that passed for elec-tions in Mexico. The PAN's defense of local and state electoral victories improved drastically, but, as will be seen, the antecedents of its contempo-rary strategy for postelectoral mobilizations were already evident in the 1950s. The PRI-state's capacity to perpetrate fraud against the PAN was also a time-tested fact. The PRI-state's worst pre-1988 electoral fraud episodes included the following heinous offenses against the PAN: the 1968 mayoral races in Mexicali and Tijuana, where the regime annulled elections rather than declare PAN victories; the corrupt 1969 Yucatán governor's race (denied to Mérida's *PANísta* mayor who had been elected in 1967); and the fraudulent 1985 Nuevo León and 1986 Chihuahua gubernatorial races.

THE "PARTICIPATE-ABSTAIN" CLEAVAGE IN PAN'S GENTEEL OPPOSITION YEARS (1939–77)

From its inception, the PAN defined itself in opposition to the PRI-state. Founded in 1939, the party won its first federal legislative seats in 1946, in what then-electoral officials have dubbed "the first *concertacesión*" (Lamadrid interview). The PAN's original objective "was to become a force for the political re-education of Mexico along Catholic social doctrine lines so as to save the Revolution from producing either a socialist-Communist or national bourgeois-liberal capitalist state, both of which were inherently exploitative in the PAN view" (Mabry 1973, 183). While there was talk at the party's founding convention of supporting a non-PRI presidential candidate in 1939,[4] there was no consensus for such a rupture (von Sauer 1974, 102). The PAN did not support any presidential candidate until 1952, when it proposed Efraín González Luna to oppose the PRI-state's designated heir, Adolfo Ruiz Cortines (1952–8). González Luna won a scant 8 percent of the vote, placing second among PRI-state opponents to Cárdenas ally and PRI dissenter Miguel Henríquez Gúzman. In 1958, the PAN's Luis H. Álvarez won close to 10 percent of the vote, capturing second place, which the party held consistently (aside from 1976) until the Cuauhtémoc Cárdenas upset of 1988.

The PAN advocated for electoral reforms as a platform centerpiece from the very beginning, commencing its half-century-long battle for electoral transparency in 1947, when the party first proposed the creation of a federal electoral tribunal (PAN 1990, 11), a proposal iterated five more times, in 1948 (PAN 1990, 15), 1955 (PAN 1990, 27), 1972 (PAN 1990, 70), 1980 (PAN 1990, 94), and 1986 (PAN 1990, 123), during the PAN's prolific but unsuccessful early legislative history. All told, 35 of the party's 321 pre-1988 legislation initiatives were electoral reform proposals (author tally of PAN 1990). But even in its early years, the party made greater gains informally by threatening to blackmail the PRI-state, such as when it threatened to withdraw its federal electoral commission representative in

---

[4] Cárdenas's leftist proclivities prompted great opposition among those who became the PAN, but even their opposition failed to provoke the *PANístas* to break with their moderately "abstentionist" line in favor of antiregime candidate Juan Almazán (Mabry 1973, 37–9).

1960 after particularly unconscionable electoral frauds in Yucatán 1958 and Baja California 1959 gubernatorial races, which persuaded authorities to endorse the electoral reform of 1964 (Prud'homme 1997, 22).

Bitter internal conflicts twice precluded the PAN from fielding national candidates during this initial period. In response to vulgar fraud against the PAN in national legislative races and in the Mérida, Yucatán mayoral race, PAN 1958 presidential candidate Álvarez led the first hostile backlash against the PRI-state, declaring federal elections invalid, demanding that its six federal legislators not assume their seats in Congress,[5] and withdrawing from the Federal Electoral Commission (von Sauer 1974, 127). Disagreement over the appropriateness of these tactics, in a party that many followers still considered more of a Christian philosophical society than an electoral opposition, generated reprisals at the party's 1961 national convention. The 1961 dispute resulted in expulsion from the party of several more doctrinaire leaders and a decline in the party's electoral performance, which had reached about 10 percent in federal races. Nonetheless, the effects of this electoral decline were nominal until the 1964 reform established a handful of proportional-representation congressional seats, principally to induce the PAN back into the game.

Under the pragmatism of Álvarez (1970–6) and other decreasingly doctrinaire leaders, the party began to actively campaign, winning mayoral races in the early 1970s under President Luis Echeverría, who had vowed to "allow" opposition victories to help restore the PRI-state's faltering image as a democracy with competitive elections. However, in 1975 PAN leadership reverted back to the doctrinaire conservatives, who tried to rid the party of excessive interest in elections and of the broadening influence of business elites and rightist interest groups. A showdown transpired over the selection of an opponent to PRI nominee and designated presidential successor José López Portillo. Acrimonious internal debate tipped the party's balance from the conservatives toward the pragmatists, but not before internal dissent precluded the fielding of any 1976 presidential candidate. While winning his unopposed election by a comfortable margin, López Portillo was embarrassed internationally by having no challengers and still only mustering 82 percent of the vote.

In 1976, the PAN did not really choose to abstain, as the party did field legislative candidates; rather, failure to participate electorally was the consequence of grave internal divisions. However, arguments for launching

---

[5] Only two obeyed these commandments; the other four were expelled from the party.

the PAN's most powerful tool against the PRI-state – abstention – had been made at varying moments by both the pragmatists and the doctrinaires. To the pragmatists, such as Álvarez and José Angel Conchello (party president from 1972–5), abstention was the PAN's best (and only) means of "punishing" the PRI-state for its tilted electoral playing field and manipulated outcomes. Regional precedents had existed for this national threat of abstention. For example, the PAN opted in 1973, in violation of national party statutes forcing parties to participate in federal elections, to abstain from Baja California's congressional races in protest of perceived government fraud in the 1971 local elections. In 1970, the party, arguing that Nuevo León's electoral registration lists were too tainted, withdrew its candidates from local races there.

Doctrinaire leaders, like Efraín González Morfín, the party president who resigned from the PAN in 1978, were also proabstention on philosophical grounds; they did not wish for the party to stray from its original doctrine of moral Christian education and place excessive emphasis on electoral posts. When the Hidalgo PAN decided to participate in 1975 state elections there, the González Morfín–led National Executive Committee vetted the decision and disqualified the party's candidates (Boni 1977, 291). However, it is not clear whether the Hidalgo PAN was denied on abstract philosophical grounds, "electoral playing field" issues in the state, or, as is more likely, because the growing party had not resolved its policy about minimum candidate qualifications. The doctrinaire wing's purity extended to candidate selection: they greatly preferred socially conservative, card-carrying *PANístas*, while the pragmatists considered this position to be elitist, especially if there was an available former *PRIísta* with a local following or an organic peasant leader willing to borrow the PAN label and make a run of it. If what Boni terms "the abstentionist debate" (1997, 294–7) divided the PAN through an indirect reference to the PRI-regime during its first several decades, whether to collude with the PRI-state or undermine its authority became the defining explicit cleavage within the PAN by the mid-1980s.

1977–1988 AND CHIHUAHUA 1986: FORAY INTO BIG STAKES POSTELECTORAL CONTENTION

The "abstentionism" conflict was relegated to the background during the early 1980s, when President de la Madrid's "moral renovation" platform included "allowing" the PAN to "keep" electoral victories, at least until around 1983 when the party became threatening. The PAN had managed to remain doctrinally pure but politically impotent until the early 1980s, when its preference for grandstanding without governing gave way to a much more practical position. Suddenly, the oldest, best organized alternative to the PRI found itself the receptacle of wholesale business elite defections from the PRI's unpopular economic policies, which had led to a precipitous peso devaluation and the subsequent debt crisis of 1982. The party's 1988 presidential candidate, pragmatic business entrepreneur Manuel Clouthier, represented this new and modern faction of the party, based on the strategy of postelectoral mobilization to challenge the authoritarian regime.

De la Madrid allowed important 1983 PAN municipal victories to stand in Chihuahua, Nuevo León, Sinaloa, Sonora, and San Luis Potosí, although he retreated to prior authoritarian strategies of nonrecognition after subsequent opposition victories (Bailey 1987, 79–83), forcing the PAN to resort to postelectoral mobilizations in order to "cash in" victories not recognized at the voting booths. Over twenty extensive *PANista* postelectoral mobilizations were staged during de la Madrid's six-year term, as compared to thirty-one during the thirty-six years prior to 1983. Currency controls and a bank nationalization in 1982, followed by negative growth, a contracted domestic market, the debt crisis and an oil price shock in 1985, prompted export-oriented business leaders, particularly in Monterrey, to stray from the PRI. This uncoupling of business groups from the PRI led to the unraveling of Mexico's corporatist foundations.[6] Although some groups, such as Monterrey's biggest conglomerates, were brought back to the progovernment fold through offers of debt bailouts, many small- and medium-sized business leaders who were members of the same increasingly defiant business associations did not receive generous government loyalty "buy back" offers. While the PRI may have been able to "buy back" a few large entrepreneurs, it could not buy back the diffuse middle classes who swelled the PAN, and the PRI's systematic denial of PAN victories in close races only further galvanized the increasingly defiant neo-*PANistas*.

Strong PAN showings prompted *PRIistas* to nominate candidates fitting the PAN profile – successful business executives who favored economic liberalization over traditional Mexican statism. In Sonora and Nuevo León, 1985 gubernatorial races were heavily contested and rife with fraud,

---

[6] Corporatism, as described in the Mexican context by Reyna (1977, 161), is a means of political control emphasizing governmental political mobilization through membership in official unions to demobilize class groups that may otherwise issue redistributive demands.

but the PRI prevailed. It was the 1986 Chihuahua governor's race that ushered in contemporary postelectoral mobilization in Mexico, as the PRI did not triumph so handily and the PAN raised the domestic and international public relations costs of PRI-state electoral fraud to a new level. When Chihuahua mayor Álvarez lost the governor's race, he launched a hunger strike and a march hundreds of miles toward Queretaro,[7] in the PAN's first nationwide appeal to mass mobilization. After decades of internal bickering and widely ignored but original postelectoral mobilizations, the PAN had become the protagonists of Mexico's centripetal, albeit protracted, transition.

Recall from Chapter 4 that the Chihuahua 1986 postelectoral mobilization rapidly mushroomed into a national social movement, replete with work stoppages, international bridge blockades, hunger strikes, petition drives by intellectuals and interest groups such as the church, and Álvarez's famous march. The postelectoral campaign even drew solidarity visits from leftist leaders such as the Mexican Socialist Party President Heberto Castillo, who openly sought an elusive grand alliance with the PAN (Chand 2001, 120) that would have rendered subsequent Cárdenas postelectoral mobilizations true threats to regime stability. This new pattern of "process framing" PAN activism was further reinforced in 1987 and 1988 by Philippine civil disobedience trainers and nationwide Active and Passive Civil Resistance (RECAP) seminars. Another pattern, a much more deep-seated one, of federal intervention in local affairs, was also reinforced in Chihuahua. De la Madrid publicly exhorted the Chihuahua electoral commission to validate the state elections after admitting that the Interior Secretary had reviewed all the fraud documentation presented by the PAN to state authorities, finding insufficient evidence to bring electoral certification into question. As a seeming afterthought, the federal secretariat acknowledged, in word at least, that "the process in question is the jurisdiction of state institutions" (Hiriart 1986b).

The Chihuahua 1986 protest was hardly the PAN's first. The PAN's northern strongholds (and the state of Yucatán) set precedents for the conduct of postelectoral mobilizations. Some dozen petitions were filed by the PAN to the Supreme Court in the 1950s, 1960s, and early 1970s,

---

[7] In symbolism that was not lost on the PRI, Álvarez chose Queretaro because it was the site of the 1917 constitutional convention marking the end of the bloody Mexican Revolution and a return to the rule of law. The PAN has long argued that the crisis in popular representation in Mexico has been brought about not by an undemocratic constitution, but by the failure to obey it. Indeed, Hansen (1974) assessed Mexico's written constitution as one of the most progressive in the world.

denouncing electoral fraud, but with no positive results through the judicial process.[8] National and regional PAN leaders were brought in to "bear witness" to local races as early as the 1950s (starting with the 1952 Durango mayoral race), and the national parliament, always heavily dominated by the PRI, was increasingly utilized by the PAN's token delegations as a platform from which to denounce electoral fraud (starting with the 1956 mayor's race in Ciudad Juárez).

The early PANístas originated the "dueling focal points" strategy combining simultaneous appeals to formal and informal institutions. To complement due process of electoral complaints through the courts, activists appealed to the federal Interior Secretary, or directly to the president in most of the forty-two pre-1986 postelectoral conflicts (Álvarez de Vicencio as cited in Eisenstadt 1998, 227). As somewhat of a last resort, a strategy of RECAP was increasingly used. These movements originated locally in the 1960s and 1970s, involving hunger strikes (such as in the Mexicali mayoral race in 1968); city-hall takeovers (starting with the Tacámbaro municipal election in 1971 and the Compostela mayor's race in 1972); protest caravans and marches (in several Chihuahua 1980 municipal races); "strikes" on payment of utilities or taxes (commencing in the 1975 Ciudad Sabinas mayor's race); and the naming of People's Tribunals to "judge" electoral fraud perpetrators (a strategy first registered starting with the 1983 Puebla mayoral race). Most of the PAN's postelectoral tactics, with the exception of the 1961 electoral commission walkout, were pioneered in local elections, as it was only in these races that the PAN was given any chance of winning prior to the mid-1980s.[9] The PAN itself implicitly realized the futility of "wasting" even creative and well-executed postelectoral tactics on national races (or even gubernatorial contests before the mid-1980s), as such victories were out of reach, whether by outright victory or concertacesión.

Contemporary national PAN activists credit Álvarez with improving the PAN's arsenal to include civil disobedience or RECAP campaigns, which captured national attention for the first time ever. Based on the Chihuahua 1986 model, PAN 1988 presidential candidate Manuel

---

[8] In its most blatant admission of utter weakness, the Supreme Court in 1975 reaffirmed the enfeebling Vallarta Thesis (Chapter 3), claiming that the Puebla City mayor's race, and all election-related complaints, were outside its jurisdiction (Álvarez de Vicencio 1995, 132).

[9] When the PAN did win, as in 1968 Mérida and 1968 Hermosillo, it was frequently due to the fielding of an ex-PRI leader who did not win the official party's internal nomination and thus defected to the PAN (Boni 1977, 308–9).

Clouthier launched postelectoral mobilizations to protest fraud, and in fact launched mobilizations with Cárdenas and the left until the PAN's decision to recognize Salinas went against the left's decision to declare the president illegitimate. Álvarez took the knowledge of RECAP with him to the national PAN presidency from 1987 to 1993, and the strategy, combining legal and extralegal contestation, became commonplace by the PRD in the aftermath of the 1988 election (Alcántara interview).[10] Álvarez said his tactics, based in part on his reading of Gandhi,[11] were based on improvisation. He said he did not anticipate the launching of an entire new approach to challenging the authoritarian regime, but that once it drew attention, he sought to apply it wherever PRI incumbents denied his party electoral justice (Álvarez interview).[12]

Álvarez's tactics were controversial, as they required sacrificing doctrinal purity for electoral salience, a radical turnabout from what the party's elders advocated. The 1986–93 Álvarez PAN presidency was a turning point for the party, as his maverick neo-*PANístas* from the north alienated traditionalists. The southward shift in party strength, as the northerners increasingly isolated themselves from PAN moderates, was first evident in postelectoral mobilizations – 72 percent had been staged in northern cities between 1939 and 1976 compared to a mere 25 percent in the north between 1988 and 1996. The north's decline within the party was also increasingly evident with the PAN's acceptance of public funding after a 1987 law made this possible. Accepting public money was controversial, and the party's National Council rejected the $10 million offered in 1987 before accepting it the next year, on the condition that no more than 25 percent of the party's funding could come from public coffers (Chand 2001, 129–31). The northern entrepreneurs continued to be crucial to the party's membership (and the source of the PAN's first elected

---

[10] The three major opposition candidates (Clouthier, Cárdenas, and Rosario Ibarra of a smaller left party) met in the Chihuahua home of Álvarez to sign a "Call to Legality" to pressure the PRI in defense of the vote.

[11] Longtime PAN leader Jesús González Schmal defined RECAP as an adaptation of philosopher/practitioners from Gandhi to César Chávez to Jesus Christ. However, González Schmal also made clear that, theory aside, the core of RECAP was practical disobedience of electoral authorities combining civil disobedience fasts and marches with publicity campaigns and negotiations with allies to join the sustained campaign to pressure the PRI-state (Pérez Rayón 1988, 37–8).

[12] Álvarez won the national consensus in 1986 when then-party president Emilio Madero wanted to limit national PAN support for the postelectoral struggle in Chihuahua. Álvarez quieted the rebellion against Madero while also maintaining support for his postelectoral mobilizations. See Zamarripa (1992b).

governors), but the affluent north's financial resources were no longer essential, with the flow of funding from Mexico City (Loaeza 1999, 433–8) increasing into the 1990s. The federal money was initially received with great suspicion, as party activists had viscerally distanced themselves from the PRI-state for generations. This would all change after 1988, however, due mostly to the threat posed by Cárdenas to the PRI-state's status quo and to the PAN's economic conservatism.

CHOOSING PATRONAGE OVER TRANSITION AFTER 1988

For a few days in July 1988, the fate of Mexico's ruling party hung in the balance. The fulcrum of this balance – the honest broker between the incensed Cárdenista coalition and the PRI-state's "electoral alchemists" – was the PAN. The zenith of uncertainty for the authoritarian incumbents was reached on election night, as "massive computer tallying failures" blacked out official results, and Cárdenas, Clouthier, and Rosario Ibarra of the tiny radical Revolutionary Workers' Party (PRT) issued a joint statement saying that they would not accept fraudulent results. Clouthier sought out Cárdenas for several days after this declaration, hoping to launch the grand coalition of civil disobedience, but an overwhelming force worked against the pragmatic and spirited Clouthier – his party's national leadership. If there was anyone or anything the PAN disliked more than Salinas and the PRI, it was Cárdenas, his populist coalition, and the threat of abrupt change that would have endangered the neo-liberal economic reforms launched by the PRI-state, with the PAN's blessings, starting in 1985.

The PAN would not tolerate Clouthier's desire to mobilize to Cárdenas's direct benefit. Party President Álvarez and the PAN National Council thanked Clouthier for his service to the party at their July 22–23 meeting and then virtually "dismissed" the disgruntled candidate, whose supporters considered organizing a broad civic resistance outside of the PAN's structure after meeting resistance within it (Loaeza 1999, 461). Meanwhile, upon seating his members in the Chamber of Deputies to certify Salinas as president, Álvarez set the precedent for a *sexenio* of PAN co-optation, declaring that "we have to be capable of negotiating and accepting partial and provisional formulas of transition . . . " (Loaeza 1999, 462).

Hopes of a PAN-Cardenista Front (FDN) coalition were dissolved on July 9, when Cárdenas publicly declared himself winner despite an alleged agreement between the two opposition parties on a joint public position that the elections were too close to call, given the exorbitant electoral fraud. According to Loaeza (1999, 457), the parties had sworn to jointly pursue annulment of the July 6 federal race and call for a new election. Cárdenas, Clouthier, and Ibarra continued to dialogue for a month, but Clouthier insisted on verifying the magnitude of electoral fraud and annulling the race, while Cárdenas wavered in his commitment (Loaeza 1999, 461–5).

Cárdenas certainly had the most to gain from adjusting the vote count rather than scheduling another election. And Clouthier's goodwill aside, it was the PAN's leadership that had the most to lose from watching their greatest political enemy replace them as Mexico's second electoral force. Indeed, the alliance-pursuing Clouthier at several rallies had cried out that "The Philippines is the answer!" but his mantra was not shared by the party's more conservative leaders (Loaeza 1999, 448). As for most conservative parties, the worst scenario for the PAN would have been an extended postelectoral mobilization leading to ingovernability and even regime change. The PAN's patronage-seeking strategy of linking fates with the PRI rather than with the Cárdenas coalition bore fruit immediately, as the PAN was granted plurinominal congressional seats in the "horse-trading" and a promise by Salinas of electoral reform based on PAN proposals.

The uneasy alliance between the PAN and the PRI was sealed by a letter of intent in which Salinas promised to endorse PAN federal electoral reforms (most of which involved enhancing the powers of the Federal Electoral Tribunal [TFE]).[13] While some of the PAN's agenda was incorporated, the PRI-state's reform package fell way short of *PANista* hopes, prompting them in January 1990 to expose their signed agreement with Salinas, which the PRI congressional leadership refused to honor because they had not signed the Salinas-negotiated accord (Alemán Alemán 1989). In an uncharacteristic lapse of discipline, the disillusioned PAN's congressional caucus split their vote, although the leadership delivered the needed complement to the PRI's unanimous support to attain the

---

[13] The PAN sought to grant the electoral court "the last word" on election certification and more powers to investigate fraud allegations (such as opening electoral-commission vote-tally packets). These reforms were included in the PRI's subsequent proposal and approved by the PRI majority Chamber of Deputies. The proposal not incorporated by the PRI called for magistrate nomination and ratification by the Chamber of Deputies. The eventual, watered-down law transferred nomination authority to the executive, with the chamber only ratifying the executive's choices.

qualified majority for passage (the PRD caucus voted against the measure). The PAN's lesson was that negotiating with the regime was going to require more leverage than just a presidential signature. Salinas's lesson appeared to be that controlling the PRI was going to require more than just his signature. Both sides adjusted their expectations.

1988–1992: BUILDING THE JUSTIFICATION FOR *CONCERTACESIÓN* AS "PARTIAL RESTITUTION"

The PAN's internal debate over whether to cooperate with the PRI-state resumed, and the old-timers lost ground in the 330-member National Council and grew increasingly frustrated at the marginalization of that body to the benefit of the National Executive Committee (the party president's fifty-member "kitchen cabinet" with only token members from out-of-power factions). Like their predecessors in the 1970s, the 1990s rebels argued that the party was becoming excessively centralized and corrupted by special interests, conservative business associations, and religious groups, which detracted from its original civic mission. But they also registered a new complaint: the PAN was becoming too complicit with the federal government, and they, as part of the National Executive Committee, wanted to be apprised of all PAN-government negotiations (Reynoso 1993, 141).

The 1990 National Council meeting that reelected Álvarez to a second three-year term as party president alienated prestigious party elders, including former presidential candidate Pablo Emilio Madero and longtime activists Jesús González Schmal and José Angel Conchello. These leaders, accused of "attacking the unity of the party and of advocating for a homespun organization rather than a modern, national party" (Reynoso 1993, 139), created an internal front called the Democratic and Doctrinaire Forum upon exclusion from Álvarez's National Executive Committee. The Forum (or *Foro*), dedicated to updating party principles and improving the party's new federal electoral reform proposal, lasted until 1992, when several National Executive Committee snubs[14] prompted them to form their own splinter party. Although tiny, the prominent *Forista* party carried

---

[14] In 1991, González Schmal and another *Forista* sympathizer were removed from high positions on the proportional-representation congressional seat list, in a direct affront by the National Executive Committee. Álvarez publicly ridiculed the *Foristas*'s world of ideals, "where nothing ever got done," and the *Foristas*'s proposals for party reform were rejected outright by the National Council (Reynoso 1993, 146–7).

sufficient weight to embarrass the PAN upon denouncing the party and endorsing Cárdenas in 1994.[15]

Álvarez's public pronouncements were revealing after the party's first admission of *concertacesión* in accepting an interim 1991 PAN Guanajuato governor to "partially restore" fairness after fraud there cost Vicente Fox the governorship. According to a National Council release: "National Action considered the extreme dichotomy drawn by purists between dialogue and confrontation to be false, simplistic, and sterile; that the party could conduct legitimate negotiations or justified protest movements in defense of Mexicans' human rights without violating party doctrine precepts" (Reynoso 1993, 146). With the *Foristas* vanquished, the compelling question within the PAN seemed to be which public attitude would prevail: shame from its recurrence to *concertacesión*, or justifiable pride in the outcome of these negotiations.

Dissatisfaction with the *concertacesiones* was a leading catalyst of the *Forista* purge. While the PAN had tolerated a few local *concertacesiones* prior to 1991, the one that rankled with the old-time *PANístas* was Guanajuato. According to Loaeza, the bargaining agreement, accepted by the *PANístas* as an "antidote to swallowing the bitter pill of their poor showing in the [concurrent] federal elections" (1999, 503), was unpopular with the *Foristas* who opposed bargaining with the regime, as well as with those who did not oppose bargaining with the PRI-state, but who insisted that Fox be granted the governorship to which he had been elected. By this reasoning, the PAN's willingness to settle for "partial restitution" by granting the governorship to a *PANísta* interim governor, former León, Guanajuato mayor Carlos Medina Plasencia, set a horrible precedent without "cleansing" the crooked election.

This gradualist, patronage-seeking approach was also resented by local *PANístas* who did not happen to grab National Executive Committee attention. In Sonora, one of the few states to date where *PRIísta* "electoral alchemists" were actually prosecuted by the state's attorney after being caught red-handed, *PANístas* complained vehemently that they could not receive partial restitution because Fernández de Cevallos and his negotiators were too busy haggling over the concurrent Guanajuato governor's race. "We prove fraud and they [the PRI candidates] are replaced, but by more of the same," complained the PAN's candidate in the Sonora

---

[15] González Schmal ran for governor of Coahuila in 1993, but as the PRD's candidate. He then served as a high-ranking official in Cárdenas's Mexico City administration briefly in 1997–8.

town of San Luís Rio Colorado, where local *PANístas* overrode national orders to desist from postelectoral conflicts, and negotiated – PRD-like – without any national leverage. "We need for more than just the [PRI] head to fall; we want the entire body," ("Dimite Candidato el PRI," 1991).

With all the post-Guanajuato grumbling, Álvarez sought to limit his party's hemorrhaging by acknowledging that in fact, maybe the dissidents had been right; the PAN had grown subservient to the PRI-state. Upon reiterating the party line that authoritarian regression necessitated "*concertacesión*" despite its adverse consequences for democratization, Álvarez parted from the script with the following announcement at a National Council meeting (italics mine):

Within the party there is a lamentable situation; those who do not achieve recognition of legitimate victories, and *even on occasion, those who cannot even prove their victories*, blame the national leadership, as if their political solutions depended on this leadership. This is a perverse and subtle attack on the party, which I exhort you to consider seriously. (Zamarripa 1992d)

Under rumors of further defections by high-level *PANístas* including Fernández de Cevallos, the Executive Committee moderated its position, forcing the PAN's congressional delegation back to work (it had boycotted legislative labors for a week to protest electoral fraud in Puebla, Sinaloa, and Tamaulipas), and Álvarez persuaded the National Council to impose gubernatorial candidates in cases like San Luis Potosí, when the divided Executive Committee failed to make decisions (Zamarripa 1992a). True to the *Foristas'* admonition, the process of constructing a symbiotic relationship between the PAN and the PRI was by late 1992 already irreversible, benefiting both parties in the short term, but to the long-term detriment of the PRI. In the next sections, I discuss the mechanics of PRI-PAN *concertacesión* and then apply the general model to three notorious cases.

PERFECTING *CONCERTACESIÓN*: MODELING THE PAN'S CIVILIZED DISOBEDIENCE

By the late 1980s, the PAN was sufficiently centralized and disciplined to organize even local RECAP campaigns at the national level, a necessary prerequisite for credible bargaining by the national PAN with the national PRI. Acts of civil disobedience were only undertaken after a vote by the National Executive Committee (Alcántara interview), and while they were commonplace and even "overused" at that time, RECAP tactics have rarely been sanctioned since 1991, as partial cooperation with the PRI regime has usually produced recognition of electoral victories. Besides, such practices "wear down" communities, extracting a cost when freeways are blockaded or taxes not paid, prompting "the people to tire and to not want to resort to these practices, a lesson the PRD has not yet learned" (Alcántara interview). Other PAN leaders, like Carlos Castillo Peraza, Álvarez's successor as national president (1993–6), also accused the PRD of distorting RECAP and the postelectoral bargaining such mobilizations could produce. According to Castillo Peraza:

The PRD thought every PAN victory was a gift from the regime, so that therefore they should also undertake mobilizations. But they usually had no proof [of fraud]. We simultaneously gathered legal evidence of fraud and staged mobilizations.... Metaphorically, the PRI tried to win elections on Saturday [through unfair campaign advantages and vote buying], the PAN on Sunday [election day], and the PRD on Monday by occupying City Hall. (interview)

On the one hand, Castillo Peraza denied the existence of a "standard operating procedures manual" for postelectoral mobilization, but on the other, he acknowledged that several variables were regularly considered by the national leadership in such decisions, including the size of the mobilization site city, composition of the workforce and social groups,[16] and whether the PAN could seize a simultaneous strategic national and/or international political moment (interview).

In this conspicuous absence of Castillo Peraza's "standard operating procedures" manual, it is possible to speculate about its likely contents. However, three characteristics of PAN strategic behavior pervade the following case studies. First, given the PAN's "legalistic" predisposition, it devoted considerable resources to working within the rules. The PAN always sought to "cover" extralegal negotiations with a cloak of legality, or at least with a legalistic rationale. The party's doctrinaire legalism simplified political activism during the party's two historic stages, when it either played by regime-dictated rules and fielded candidates or abstained altogether. By the post-1988 third stage, the PAN had resigned itself, epitomized by Álvarez's "partial restitution" justification as opposed to what he had called "false purity and idealism." However, except where legality utterly failed them (such as in the cases of Mérida 1993 and Huejotzingo

---

[16] Castillo Peraza referred specifically to whether the prospective RECAP site was a "company town," requiring mobilizations after work hours, and whether a significant number of students or homemakers might carry mobilizations during factory hours or during harvests in rural areas (Castillo Peraza interview).

1996 examined in the following text), the PAN always preferred reinter-preting the rules, or obtaining justifiable exceptions, to breaking them outright, even when the rules were unjust. The PAN sought to promote the rule of law by "whitewashing" extralegal negotiations through proper legal channels. Except in the Mérida 1993 *concertacesión*, which was bla-tantly illegal, there was always an Electoral College, an electoral court, or at the very least a PRI mayor's "stealth retirement" followed by an interim mayor from the PAN, to give legal cover to postelectoral bargains.

Second, the party's penchant for working within the system, however distorted, prompted the resolution of prospective postelectoral conflicts through the flawed but existing legal system. The PAN's extensive "de-fense of the vote" efforts often upped the ante for the PRI-regime of deny-ing opposition victories. Tactics deployed as part of this strategy included ensuring that all precincts (and particularly those in rural or fraud-riddled areas) were occupied by a PAN party representative empowered to file election day complaints, confirm ballot tallies, and challenge irregulari-ties before higher authorities. Also, the PAN routinely sent congressional delegations and staff lawyers to observe heavily contested local races and to coordinate legal "defense of the vote" campaigns with local PAN ac-tivists. The party, in contrast to the PRD and its predecessors, also sought always to pool its official vote tallies from each polling station to compare its final partisan tally with that of the electoral authorities. As strategists like Germán Martínez and Ernesto Ruffo made clear (interviews), hav-ing party representatives in each of a municipality's polling stations to file "protest writings" and acquire the all-important party copy of that polling station's results was the single key to defending PAN victories.

With poll-by-poll results, the party had a baseline for detecting ir-regularities in aggregate computer tallies at the district and state levels. By the mid-1990s, members of the national PAN's crack team of elec-toral lawyers[17] could anticipate the votes needed to overturn elections and allocate energies to file cases over irregularities of a tactically useful magnitude. However, as late as the early 1990s, the PAN did not even have candidates to field in many local races, much less polling station representatives to monitor every ballot box (see Table 5.1 to compare percentage of mayoral candidates registered in 1989–94 and 1995–2000

---

[17] Castillo Peraza (interview) referred to the PAN National Executive Committee's dozen roving lawyers as "the parachutists," who landed wherever needed to help local party activists troubleshoot irregularities on election day and prepare postelectoral complaints under tight deadlines.

and see Appendix B for estimates of party polling-station representatives by state and year). From the mid-1980s until about 1994, the National Executive Committee coordinated electoral observer missions and "defense of the vote" campaigns for important local races to the detriment of national party publicity campaigns and platform writing (Alcántara interview). In states where PAN resources were limited, the party concentrated its polling-station representatives in one or two municipalities, but with the assurance that they would reach every polling station, because if they lacked even one precinct vote tally out of hundreds, their legal case collapsed (Pérez Noriega interview). Possessing a much lower threshold for legal flexibility than the PRD, they refused to take liberties such as inferring votes, as the PRD had on several occasions.

The PAN also pressed its cases at the national level, subordinating local mobilizations to national negotiations, which inevitably involved the threat of blackmailing the PRI-state on legislative votes, and/or denunciations at international fora. Before late 1991, when the PRI regained its qualified (two-thirds) majority in the Chamber of Deputies needed to pass constitutional reforms, the PAN threatened to withdraw support for PRI initiatives if electoral victories were not recognized. After late 1991, the PAN was still able to threaten withdrawal from various national dialogues on electoral reforms or electoral certification (such as of the 1994 presidential race). Also available was the international card, which the PAN successfully played using a 1987 complaint, which yielded an Organization of American States (OAS) verdict in 1991 that embarrassed the Mexican government, stating that the existing Nuevo León electoral law did not guarantee individuals' political rights in accordance with the OAS Human Rights Convention Mexico had signed (OAS 1995, 11). This verdict, perhaps the PAN's most important victory of all against the PRI-state, was credited with forcing Mexico to establish a federal electoral court in the late 1980s (Ojesto interview, 2001). While the PAN was never again able to defame the Mexican government's electoral shortcomings as grandiloquently as in this precedent-setting 1991 decision, it has tried repeatedly to do so.[18]

---

[18] Complaints filed contemporary to the Nuevo León decision included the following: PAN versus Chihuahua local elections (case 9768 filed in 1985) and governor's race (case 9828 filed in 1986), PAN versus Durango local elections (case 9780 filed in 1986), and PAN versus the State of Mexico local elections (case 10956 filed in October 1991). While none of these cases resulted in favorable verdicts (OAS 1991 and OAS 1994), the party also sought to achieve propaganda victories, even where judicial wins were improbable. The international appeal strategy dated back to the early 1980s, when the party published

National postelectoral efforts were complemented by grassroots mobilizations, but only at the behest of the national PAN leadership. All RECAP mobilizations, for example, were said to require National Executive Committee approval (Alcántara interview) at one of its twice-monthly Mexico City meetings. The problem, according to other ranking PAN officials, was that the National Council, the 330-member body of the highest-ranking elected officials and PAN administrators that convened at least every three years to elect a party president, was a representative body but was never brought in for microlevel party policy making. Even local postelectoral mobilizations originated at the national level, where "liaisons with the PRI-state" designated by the national PAN president conducted negotiations unbeknownst to the National Council and even, on occasion, to the "kitchen cabinet" National Executive Committee. The discretion granted post-1991 clutch negotiator Diego Fernández de Cevallos to improvise his representation before the national PRI, the Interior Secretary, and even the president was controversial among National Executive Committee members, some of whom felt that it "kept them in the dark" about all-important negotiations (Ruffo interview). Apparently, consistent with its extremely centralized structure in other respects, the PAN bargained with one voice, which answered only to the party's president. While their unity made them the envy of the PRD, their lack of internal democracy raised enduring questions among "out-group" activists. Considering the postelectoral mobilizations of Mérida 1993, Monterrey 1994, and Huejotzingo 1996, I further generalize the form assumed by PAN conflicts and, in Chapter 7, differentiate them from those of the PRD.

MÉRIDA, YUCATÁN 1993: NATIONAL PRI-STATE USURPS A WEAK ELECTORAL COURT

Even before the unprecedented 2001 governor's defiance of a federal electoral court verdict (Chapter 8), Yucatán was the most renegade of Mexico's states. The Mérida 1993 *concertacesión* was the only patently illegal postelectoral settlement in my 1990s case-study sample and the one where the state-federal pact was most clearly violated. The PRI-PAN settlement blatantly contradicted *pro forma* procedures and was possible because of the severity of the political crisis combining a struggle among

---

"How PRI in Mexico Commits Fraud in Elections." English-version pamphlets, including *The Democratic Plea of PAN in Yucatán* (1995) and *The Democratic Reason of the PAN in Huejotzingo* (1996), were widely distributed to international organizations.

the state's *PRIístas* with a growing PAN electoral insurrection temporarily placated by an earlier *concertacesión* in 1990. That deal resulted in the resignation of a PRI governor over pressures to revoke what he had called as a clear PAN victory in the Mérida 1990 mayoral race.[19]

The 1993 postelectoral settlement, characterized as "antidemocratic" and "illegal" by the highest PRI negotiator and the victimized PRI mayoral candidate alike (Rodríguez Lozano and Paredes interviews), resulted from national PAN pressures on the federal PRI-state. The preliminary tally was 107,307 PRI votes to the PAN's 105,761. The PAN's specific complaints included the removal of more votes from ballot boxes than had been cast, disappearance of ballot tallies, failure to properly install voting booths, computer error, and receipt of votes by unauthorized individuals. The PAN's political leverage, after a newly constructed local electoral tribunal rejected all their cases, appears to have been a preelectoral agreement between the national PRI and PAN to grant Mérida to newly nominated PAN presidential candidate Fernández de Cevallos, hoping he would serve as a counterweight to the PRD, which had renominated Cárdenas (Rodríguez interview).[20] By some accounts, Fernández de Cevallos had actually threatened to resign his candidacy if the PAN was not granted Mérida, dangerously leaving Salinas's successor with no credible opponent other than Cárdenas to harvest all the anti-Salinas votes (González Ramos 1996, 191).

The PRI faced a delicate problem when, contrary to national PRI wishes, the local party chapter declared its candidate victorious, prompting the PAN to launch an extensive postelectoral mobilization led by national figures like Fernández de Cevallos and local party elites. Amador Rodríguez Lozano, then national electoral action secretary of the PRI, said (interview) that he irritated Interior Secretary Patrocínio González Garrido by preparing a judicially sound defense of the PRI vote for the Yucatán electoral tribunal (rather than just allowing the court to "whitewash" the election).[21] The Yucatán electoral tribunal magistrates were

---

[19] The PAN victory was certified by the state electoral commission, but the PRI refused to accept this outcome. Governor Victor Manzanilla Schaffer endorsed the PAN victory, but then said undue pressures were exerted on him from Mexico City to declare a PRI victory, so he resigned (Manzanilla Schaffer 1995, 60–5).

[20] While the precise motivation for such agreements may never be fully discerned, such admissions by a high-ranking official *still in office* merit serious consideration. Rodríguez Lozano said the agreement was struck between Salinas's Chief of Staff José Córdoba Montoya and Fernández de Cevallos.

[21] Conflicting with Rodríguez Lozano's proclamations, PRI-stilted media accounts stated that Rodríguez Lozano conceived a judicial "way out" working with *PANista* Federal

flown to national PRI headquarters in Mexico City, where the Interior Secretary proposed judicial loopholes by which they might annul the election.[22] This effort to judicially overturn the PRI victory was said to have been orchestrated by González Garrido at President Salinas's personal request (Rodríguez interview, *¡Por Esto!* 1993a).

The PAN complemented its Mexico City pressures with a local civil disobedience campaign commencing the day after the election, with Fernández de Cevallos vowing not to leave Yucatán until his party's triumph had been recognized. Hundreds of PAN sympathizers stood outside the state legislature, burned a copy of the Yucatán electoral code, and resolved to take their case as far as the United Nations (*Diario de Yucatán* 1993a). Even before the electoral tribunal ruling, Governor Dulce María Sauri, citing "circumstances which preclude me from doing my job," resigned, apparently refusing to "throw" the election for the PAN (*Diario de Yucatán* 1993b). Divisions between the federal and local PRI chapters reverberated for months, as otherwise-popular PRI presidential candidate Luis Donaldo Colosio was greeted in Mérida by rude chants of "no more *concertacesiones!*" (Sánchez 1994).

Despite lobbying from Mexico City and the daily PAN protests in Mérida, it became clear that the electoral court either refused or felt legally unable to overturn the election.[23] Upon making no headway with the electoral court magistrates, the national PRI sent for the party's state legislators, flying them to Mexico City for discussions. Rodríguez said "they spent a tormented 24 hours" being convinced to overturn the mayoral race in the Electoral College. The resulting settlement, an Electoral College vote to designate the "runner-up" *PANista* to fill the term when the PRI victor resigned under protest, clearly violated the Yucatán state constitution.[24]

The official Electoral College statement "selecting" *PANista* Luis Correa Mena to fill in for PRI victor Orlando Paredes Lara acknowledged the political (rather than judicial) nature of its action, lauding Paredes's

Deputy Fernando Gómez Mont, in representation of Fernández de Cevallos (*¡Por Esto!* 1993a).

[22] Copies of the Mexico City–proposed tribunal resolution were not available. In fact, hard-to-reach Yucatán Electoral Tribunal President Melba Angelina Méndez Fernández refused access to any of the electoral court's files in July 1996 and would not furnish any information (interview).

[23] Yucatán electoral tribunal president Méndez Fernández denied having been to Mexico City (interview), although state PRI leaders corroborated reports of the trip.

[24] Article 9 of that document calls for the naming of a temporary replacement, but only until a new election may be convened.

resignation as "an act of the highest civic value, which puts the interests of Mérida and the State of Yucatán ahead of those of any person, interest, or party."[25] Furthermore, the act states that "given this overwhelming circumstance, this Commission considers that to maintain political stability, social harmony and an acknowledgment of the political participation and maturity of Mérida's citizenry, it is necessary to give the triumph to the party which won second place in the election, in this case, the National Action Party" (Yucatán State Legislature, 369). There was no mention of any legal justification for granting the post to the runner-up, nor any legal argument that Correa Mena should have won the election. No mention was made, either, of Correa Mena's interim mayor status or of whether special elections would be convened. Even though the national PRI-state's arm twisting failed to convince local electoral court magistrates to comply, the PRI-state had managed to usurp the court and implement its *concertacesión* with the national PAN through proper electoral procedures and preserve the form, if not the substance, of a legal resolution. Mérida 1993 was the procedural high watermark of *concertacesión* and one of the most embarrassing moments ever for Mexico's rule of law advocates. While its illegality was unsurpassed, its political impact may have been surpassed by *concertacesión* in the PAN bastion most menacing to the PRI-state, Monterrey.

MONTERREY, NUEVO LEÓN 1994: NATIONAL PRI-STATE CONVINCES A WEAK ELECTORAL COURT

Recall that the 1985 gubernatorial race in Mexico's third-largest city had resulted in widespread postelectoral mobilization, defection from the PRI by prominent business elites including PAN gubernatorial candidate (and later governor) Fernando Canales Clariond (Guadarrama 1986, 95–101), and the embarrassment of Mexico by the OAS, which actually ruled in favor of the PAN (OAS 1995 Summary 8/91, García de Madero and Santos de la Garza interviews). The 1994 mayoral race was held concurrently with presidential balloting, giving the PAN leverage in certifying the president's election in the federal Congress without any of 1988's complications, but in exchange for favorable treatment in Monterrey. An implicit threat existed, according to political analysts, that the national PAN might trade its Salinas-era government "coalitional" cooperation for a

---

[25] An embittered Paredes denounced the agreement even in 2001, insisting that he had never resigned (interview).

"blackmail" alliance with the PRD (González Ramos 1996, 190–5). By this scenario, the PAN and PRD would jointly annul 20 percent of the presidential votes nationwide and provoke a certification controversy in the wildcard TFE (González Ramos 1996, 191),[26] where the PRI was not assured of controlling the outcome, at least not without costs to regime legitimacy.

The official vote tally was PRI 237,505 votes and PAN 229,959 votes. The PAN filed complaints in 31 percent of the 1,215 balloting stations, alleging numerous complaints including the following: more citizens voted than had registered, balloting stations were relocated at the last minute, and more ballots were counted than were cast (Nuevo León Electoral Tribunal 1994, 1–74; Nuevo León Electoral Commission 1994, 154–6). The Nuevo León Electoral Tribunal rejected most PAN allegations as unsubstantiated or beyond electoral court jurisdiction. Tribunal president Roberto Flores de la Rosa defended the ruling, denying rumors of external "involvement" in the electoral court's affairs (Flores de la Rosa interview).[27]

Pressure on the Monterrey electoral authorities mounted, as the PAN prepared appeals to newly inaugurated appeals chambers (consistent with the 1993 federal reform model). Mobs gathered outside the electoral appeals court, demonstrating for two weeks before the body ruled in favor of the PAN, allegedly under intense pressure from the national PRI (*El Norte*).[28] In the interim between the first electoral court verdict and the appeal, several protests were organized, including a "Museum of Fraud" exhibit for the Monterrey Fair. The PAN's candidate threatened broad local mobilizations, intervention by "clutch" negotiator Fernández de Cevallos, and presentation of the case before the OAS (Guardiola and Hernández 1994). But as in Mérida, incentives to resolve the conflict seemed to come from Mexico City, with local demonstrations serving as bread and circuses.

---

[26] Former Interior Sub-Secretary Arturo Nuñez said he had not been privy to details of the Monterrey negotiations, but acknowledged that the PAN may have traded peaceful presidential certification for a favorable resolution of the Monterrey conflict (Nuñez interview).

[27] Complaints about electoral commission performance (the substance of many PAN complaints) were outside the scope of the electoral court's jurisdiction, which only covered the content of the electoral commission's rulings. The electoral court's pro-PAN rulings did narrow the PRI's margin of victory from 7,500 votes to just under 4,000, but without changing the outcome.

[28] Roberto González Verduzco, chief magistrate of the appeals court refused to answer questions about the case, except to reiterate that the ruling was legal (interview).

Pressures mounted against the Nuevo León PRI in Mexico City. Then–PAN national Federal Electoral Institute (IFE) representative Antonio Lozano Grácia publicly issued a "lament that on this occasion, again, the law has been manipulated in favor of the Party of the Institutional Revolution, exercising a control over electoral tribunals in a manner which perverts the entire electoral process" (Solís 1994). Nuevo León PAN president José Luis Coindreau García (interview) admitted contacting national PRI leaders in Mexico City prior to the election. He said his communication was with the PRI's then–IFE representative Francisco Ruiz Massieu, conducted through Lozano Grácia. The dialogue between national leaders of Mexico's premier parties was said to have yielded an agreement that "the PRI would leave the Monterrey election alone" that they would not prearrange electoral outcomes with state electoral institutions (Coindreau García interview).

Coindreau García denied postelection contact with the PRI or even with the PAN leadership (Coindreau García interview), and while the PRI's declared victor, Jorge Manjarrez Rivera, said he had been pressured to resign, he refused to elaborate (Manjarrez Rivera interview). By some accounts, there was a Mexico City meeting between national PAN and PRI leaders and the Interior Secretary, where the Monterrey fraud allegations were reviewed, the PAN was accorded victory, and Ruiz Massieu was charged with "convincing" local PRI leaders of the decision (González Ramos 1996, 192). Castillo Peraza was said to have relayed the message to Monterrey, anticipating the pro-PAN appeals verdict in an intercepted cellular phone conversation to PAN mayoral candidate Jesús Hinojosa Tijerina, on the eve of the appeal ruling.[29]

The appeals court did judicially defend its controversial reversion of the victory from the PRI to the PAN. Ten ballot boxes were annulled because the municipal electoral committees erroneously sent their results to the State Electoral Commission rather than to the Local Electoral Commission. The electoral tribunal had ignored the mistake because there was no apparent intent to commit fraud, while the appeals circuit ruled that regardless of intent, the packets were still late, which was sufficient cause for annulment (Nuevo León Electoral Appeals Court, 105). Another twenty-two ballot boxes were annulled due to addition errors, mistakes

---

[29] Castillo Peraza would not discuss details, although he did not deny striking such deals (interview). According to media accounts, the taped cellular phone conversation from Castillo Peraza to PAN candidate Hinojosa Tijerina before the appeal ruling instructed the nervous soon-to-be mayor to organize a party, which he would fly in to attend (González Ramos 1996, 264–5).

made in filling out ballot tallies, etc., which the electoral tribunal had also discounted as careless oversights by ill-trained poll workers. The appeals court upheld the word of the law in these instances too (Nuevo León Electoral Appeals Court 1994, 115, 118). In short, the disparity in conclusions between the electoral tribunal and nonrelated appeals body demonstrate the discretion available in applying the law.

As with other *concertacesiones* between the PRI-state and the PAN such as Mérida, the 1991 Guanajuato governorship, and the Huejotzingo case to follow, the Monterrey deal heavily divided the PRI. The deal favored complicity with the PAN to avoid gridlock in the Congress at the expense of PRI traditional electoral machines, seeking electoral victories at all costs, even if victory meant extended opposition protests. Despite declarations by then-national PRI president Ignacio Pichardo Pagaza accepting the electoral appeal ruling, PRI senator Leónardo Rodríguez Alcaine declared that "The PAN did not win in Monterrey; legal subterfuges have 'let' the PAN win in Monterrey." A high official in the Mexican Workers' Federation (CTM), a centerpiece of the party's clientalist machine, Rodríguez Alcaine suggested that the Monterrey PRI "take to the streets" to defend the vote ("El Norte"). However, the national PRI was still too tightly controlled in 1994 to allow such local expressions of autonomy.[30] Unlike the party after its post-2000 downsizing, there were still spoils to dole out among the PRI faithful who bided their time and waited their turns.

HUEJOTZINGO, PUEBLA 1996: NATIONAL PRI-STATE DISCREDITS A WEAK ELECTORAL COURT

In contrast to the postelectoral conflict in Mexico's third largest city, Huejotzingo (population 41,700) was by far the least important of these cases in geo-strategic terms, but its implications for national PAN-PRI relations were even greater than those of *concertacesiones* in the two metropolitan state capitals. If Mérida represents the boldest informal bargain, Huejotzingo exemplifies the most shameless violation of legal precepts by a formal institution. Indeed, Huejotzingo confirmed the *PANístas'* worst fears about rigged electoral institutions, demonstrated the lengths that local PRI operatives would go to in order to ensure their

---

[30] As noted in Chapter 4, by 1995 defiance of local PRI victims of national PRI *concertacesiones* was open and boisterous, in the Tabasco rebellion of the *PRIístas*. Rodríguez Alcaine's disobedience was a public prelude.

dominion, and offered the PAN a taste of the PRI-state intolerance usually reserved for the PRD. Complaints about Huejotzingo resulted, for close to the first time,[31] in an electoral tribunal's overturning of a PAN victory in favor of the PRI. The ruling reversed a logic whereby electoral courts were strictly for opposition party losers rather than for the PRI-state, which still used its prerogative of backdoor channels of contestation at the Interior Secretariat. Even after the Puebla State electoral tribunal's sloppy ruling to restore the PRI, the PAN mobilized from Mexico City and finessed the *PRIísta* mayor's resignation in favor of a PAN-selected interim mayor. The PAN's national leverage was participation in the informal "political reform" bargaining table established by the Interior Secretariat in 1995 to resolve differences over state and national electoral laws and conflicts. The objective of Interior Sub-Secretary Arturo Núñez (interview b) was to disarm opposition party demands threatening to derail President Zedillo's negotiation of a "definitive" electoral reform and a broader "reform of the state" initiative. But the PAN managed to stall talks by walking out in early 1996 on the principle that no town was too small for free and fair elections (Manzanera interview). Strategically, Huejotzingo was important not only because of PAN leverage from the national talks, but also because it was a clear case of PRI-state manipulation of Puebla's electoral court against the PAN.

The PAN's particular complaint, a rallying cry for extensive RECAP civil disobedience mobilizations,[32] was that the Puebla Electoral Tribunal selectively annulled just enough ballot boxes to attain the 20 percent threshold and overturn the results. Citing last-minute changes in polling station locations and poll officials, the PRI and the tiny Party of the Cardenista Front for National Reconstruction (PFCRN) filed requests for the annulment of thirteen polling stations. The Puebla Electoral Tribunal "accumulated" these complaints [merged them into one] and annulled eleven of the polling stations, shifting the final vote to PRI 3,819 and PAN 3,791. Because no appeal court yet existed in Puebla, its ruling was final. The PRI had won by twenty-eight votes.

---

[31] Actually, state electoral tribunal rulings had previously overturned PAN victories in favor of the PRI in a few earlier cases, such as Guaymas, Sonora in 1994.

[32] Some of the Huejotzingo mobilizations, such as a gathering of *PANísta* women who were forcibly removed from Puebla's state capitol building and the symbolic "burial" of electoral justice by white-faced pallbearers on a march through Huejotzingo, harkened back to the PAN's RECAP days more than demonstrations in Mérida or Monterrey (Rivera Pérez interview). This was probably because, as in the PAN's preconsolidation period, the local mobilizations lasted months rather than merely days, and were led by local *and* national leaders.

Analysis reveals that annulments granting victory to the PRI were indeed arbitrary in several of the eleven polling stations. In two cases, the "official list" name given of a polling station worker varied from that person's signature on the official electoral act. The PAN did in both cases provide reasonable evidence, for example, that C. Pedro Morales Seynos and Pedro Morales Corona were in fact the same person, as were C. Arturo Nuñez Ramirez and C. Gelacio Nuñez R., identifying themselves by one name in formal situations but signing the more informal variant.[33]

The Puebla electoral court's inflexibility in the PRI's allegation contrasts markedly with a similar "false identity" allegation made in another concurrent mayoral race in Huachinango. In that case, the same tribunal reviewed the four different permutations of the name "Maria del Consuelo Vargas Valderrabano" appearing on official documents and concluded that the variants (Maria del Consuelo Vargas Maldonado, Maria del Consuelo Valderrabano, Maria del Consuelo Vargas V., and Maria del Consuelo Vargas) were in fact the same person and that "the only error here was in the filing of the electoral acts" (Puebla Electoral Tribunal 1995c, 9).

What explains the inconsistency? The PAN, in a press release subtitled "The State Electoral Tribunal: A New Type of Election Fraud" (and in dozens of other interviews and flyers), stated that these rulings, annulling just enough votes to switch the first- and second-place finishers, indicated complicity between the electoral court, municipal authorities in Huejotzingo, and the PRI-state. The party argued that other annulments were equally unjust, such as that of an entire ballot box due to a transcription error in a polling station report (the street address "Vicente Guerrero 1105," correctly given on the vote tallies, was listed as "Vicente Guerrero 1150" on the act of polling-station installation), and that private testimonials were accepted as evidence because they were certified by a notary *post hoc*, even though the only legally admissible evidence required the notary himself or herself to witness events (National Action Party 1996c).

Puebla governor Manuel Bartlett, self-proclaimed member of the "syndicate" of traditionalist governors and the federal Interior Secretary overseeing Salinas's election in 1988, declared the Huejotzingo file closed.[34] Reminiscent of Chihuahua 1986 (but with much more political

---

[33] Details of these allegations are presented in PRI complaints IN-9/95 and IN-10/95 (4–5), and the tribunal's resolution, 19–21.

[34] Rumors circulated that Bartlett and some investors wanted Huejotzingo in PRI hands so that party allies could build a new airport and commercial complex in the area (Granados Chapa 1996). In March, national newspapers such as *Reforma* published

leverage), the PAN launched a multifaceted pressure campaign, occupying Huejotzingo's city hall as of February 1996 and organizing sit-ins, highway blockages, and marches throughout the state. Nationally, the PAN made Huejotzingo a litmus test of the Zedillo administration's willingness to "intervene" to correct local injustices. National PAN President Felipe Calderón cried out that "democracy passes through Huejotzingo" at a rally in Puebla's capital attended by most of the PAN National Executive Committee (Calderón 1996). National PAN pressure was exerted by withdrawal from the political reform talks where the PRI-state sought legitimation through participation by all three major parties (Solís 1996), and by denouncing Bartlett and Puebla's electoral institutions at international fora such as the United Nations Human Rights Commission (Vázquez and Kuramura 1996).[35] After months of stalled reform talks with no exit from the stalemate without negotiating Huejotzingo, Zedillo ordered PRI concessions, yet again, to the rancorous disappointment of PRI national president Santiago Oñate and his Puebla allies (Mejía 1996).

More formal than the closed-door lobby sessions in PRI national headquarters over Mérida or the presumably private cellular phone conferencing to resolve Monterrey, the Huejotzingo bargaining table openly involved local and national leaders from the PAN and the PRI. It was as if, after years in the closet, *concertacesión* had been accepted as a public fact of Mexican politics. The PRI's sacrificed Huejotzingo mayor-designate, Miguel Mártinez Escobar, said negotiations were "democratic" in that local leaders were granted input and interim administrators were appointed by both parties (interview). "Normally, the Interior Secretary tells you that the negotiation is over, and who stays," said the declared PRI victor, a former state legislator who had headed the state electoral commission and revealed intimate familiarity with postelectoral bargaining protocol (Martínez Escobar interview). Both parties insisted on symbolically resolving the conflict in Puebla rather than Mexico City, with local actors leading negotiations and, at least on the PRI side, relaying proposals to the national party through the party's regional representatives

Bartlett's manifesto about the PAN's "violent," "perverse," "inflexible," "self-serving," and "unjust" pursuit of the case (Bartlett 1996, 22–7). In May, the Puebla PRI added two more nationally circulated pamphlets to the PAN-led propaganda battle, *The Law and Tolerance for Arbitrariness and Rancor* and simply *Huejotzingo*.

35 The PAN also published a widely circulated pamphlet, *The Democratic Reason of the PAN in Huejotzingo*, in Spanish and English (PAN 1996a). The author noticed copies of this pamphlet and the Puebla PRI's rebuttal in state and party offices from Mexico City to Tuxtla Gutierrez, Chiapas during the spring 1996 controversy.

(oft-ignored liaisons between state and national leaders). Despite the in-vocation of regional symbols, Manzanera traveled from Mexico City to "sit in" on behalf of the national PAN (interview). As in Maximino Avila Camacho's Puebla PRI-machine governorship a half-century earlier, a formal legislative declaration ordering the municipal council creation sealed the deal (Puebla Executive Branch 1996).

CONCLUSION: PAN'S (POST)ELECTORAL INNOCENCE
AS A CASUALTY OF ITS STRUGGLE FOR POWER

The PAN irreversibly chose pragmatic electoral opposition starting in the mid-1980s, after a half-century of strategy swings in which doctrinally pure but nonelectoral tactics trumped pragmatism and patronage seeking. Early experiences with electoral and postelectoral contention accustomed the nonthreatened PRI-state to negotiating with the conservative opposi-tion. These exposures also taught the diligent *PANistas* what was needed to provoke true political opening, so that those demanding democracy could better design incremental reforms. The PAN was invaluable in persuading the incumbent authoritarians to opt for opening rather than repression in the early 1990s. As seen in the following chapter, the PAN soothed the PRI-state by offering an ideological mirror of the PRI's neo-liberal economic policies after the mid-1980s. It offered a sort of alternation without real change but one that guarded outward appearances, while the uncompromising PRD espoused antiregime rhetoric and transition seeking, alienating that party's leaders and winning them nothing, in the postelectoral realm at least, but the authoritarians' contempt.

But if the PRD presented the antiregime threat prompting the PRI-state to side with the alternately transition- and patronage-seeking PAN against the left, the *PANistas* performed the heavy lifting of Mexico's protracted transition. The PAN protagonism of electoral opening came despite the party's willingness to play loosely with official electoral re-sults, bargaining them away when they felt justified in blackmailing the PRI-state into "throwing" a mayorship on the heels of a crooked electoral court ruling or an arm-twisted electoral college session. And legal justi-fication, and sometimes a touch of righteousness, could always be found for serving as an accomplice to the subversion of electoral institutions the *PANistas* had worked so diligently to construct. Interviews with PAN rule-of-law advocates revealed conflicts between their legalistic righteousness and their sense of political entitlement. They appear to have been guided by a slightly self-serving notion that *concertacesión* allowed them to attain the outcomes they would have achieved through formal institutions, had those institutions ruled properly. But this reasoning, articulated so cleverly by Álvarez, allowed the remaining doctrinaire conservatives and the pragmatic neo-*PANístas* to coexist and link their objectives in their unrelenting struggle for a level electoral playing field.

From a normative perspective, the PAN was certainly not to blame for what it could get away with, if party leaders saw this as a means toward the end of democracy, and historically the party was Mexico's most consistent institutional advocate of electoral opening. But only a particular confluence of circumstances explains why the PRI-state only temporarily tamed the PAN's reformist tendencies and failed to control the party once the PRI-state started "allowing" its electoral victories. Part of the answer stems from internal dissent within the PAN. The party waged a legal battle of attrition using the incremental staging of electoral reform demands clause by clause and state by state. However, with the rare exception such as Chihuahua 1986, their gestures were cautious and incremental, despite the occasionally boisterous antiregime bromide at a rally or sit-in. *PANísta* references to the Philippines aside, they were ultimately unwilling to jeopardize the status quo and risk any radical change. Indeed, the fear they shared with the PRI-state of the PRD hard line, directly evidenced in the 1988 federal postelectoral conflict as well as in the Mérida and Monterrey cases presented here, was the basis of their crucial alliance with the PRI.

In addition to its own formidable efforts, the PAN also benefited from a series of serendipitous coincidences. The PRI-state faced its strongest internal dissent ever (the Democratic Current departure in the late 1980s), as the regime's policies shifted to the right, undermining the electorally strong leftist political bosses and replacing them with neo-liberal technocrats out of touch with the Mexican electorate. This internal dissent was complemented by international pressure on the PRI-state to democratize (or at least appear to be democratizing) in time for the 1993 U.S. congressional vote on the North American Free Trade Agreement (NAFTA), and by a fist-waving PRD that made the genteel PAN seem like a mock trial team.

Certainly there were limits to the PAN's postelectoral bargaining success, such as the parliamentary faction's week-long 1992 walkout from the Congress to protest election fraud in Durango, Puebla, and Tamaulipas, which yielded nothing but the realization that without a concrete threat (to vote against PRI-state constitutional reforms, to abstain from electoral certification of the presidency, to actively oppose reforms requiring PAN approval for credibility) the regime viewed them as little more than a nuisance. By the late 1990s, it was evident to the *PANístas* (Huejotzingo excepted), that the postelectoral card had been mostly played out, although desperate and disorganized *PRIístas* increasingly turned to these tactics after 2000, seeking to "cash in" on all the postelectoral bargaining sessions they had tolerated. But as for the PAN, even the usual formula of a corrupt PRI crony as a target, compelling legal evidence of fraud, and catchy national and international leverage and marketing, failed to usurp the designated PRI governor of Yucatán, Victor Cervera Pacheco, in 1995. Even worse, Fernández de Cevallos's overtures for a *concertacesión* in the 1995 local races in Cancún and Cozumel were met with sarcasm rather than counteroffers (Alemán Alemán 1995). The opposition's collective realization after the 1995 Tabasco standoff with the PRD that Zedillo was not playing by Salinas's rules was accompanied by a structural decrease in *PANísta concertacesiones*. Electoral success obviated the need to recur to postelectoral bargaining, which had never been more than a second-best strategy anyway.

As their struggle for postelectoral justice played out, the *PANístas* subverted the norms of courting democracy and representation to case-by-case contingencies, mouthing righteous paeans to ideals of social justice all the while. They managed, by combining philosophical and political justifications into a coherent policy, to have their postelectoral bargaining and their legal precepts too. And probably even to their own surprise, the PRI-state allowed them to get away with it. The PAN constantly insisted that *concertacesión* was "partial restitution," as if to say that in bypassing popular election to name their candidate as interim mayor or governor after not having been declared the winner, the "original sin"[36] of electoral fraud by the regime could be rectified. While this rationale provided legalistic cover, it also forced the PAN to focus citizen attention on the norms of democratization and electoral opening, even if in the breach. That is, in excusing themselves when they violated the high standards they set for democracy and citizen participation, the PAN at least imagined how a more ideal system would look, and in a nation with few national democratic traditions, this was no small feat. In short, they created a baseline of expectations for how proper formal institutions should work.

By the time postelectoral bargaining lost effectiveness in the mid-1990s, the party had figured out how to win elections anyway, and was tackling a

---

[36] PAN luminaries such as Alcántara, Medina Plascencia, and Castillo Peraza (interviews) even placed the issue on an almost biblical plane by using this phrase.

new primary challenge, cultivating transparency and "good government" as the incumbent party, so that they could avert the "throw the rascals out" electoral accountability they had helped propagate (Arce interview, Rodríguez 1997). With the prominent exception of Cervera Pacheco's 2001 defiance of the federal electoral court in Yucatán, discussed in Chapter 8, the few lingering postelectoral conflicts are now resolved at the state and local levels or in the federal electoral appeals court, freeing the resources of the PAN National Executive Committee beyond having to constantly revisit the tedious minutiae of electoral observation and defense of the vote (Alcántara interview).

To be sure, the PAN faces many new challenges as incumbents, even as the party revisits old issues, such as executive-party relations under Fox and the continuing lack of democracy in its own internal structure. Fox has received only mixed reviews in his handling of the Tabasco postelectoral conflict and Yucatán's preelectoral conflagration, as activists have criticized his inaction and willingness to allow Cervera Pacheco and other *caciques* to tread upon the new sanctity of electoral justice that he himself helped promote on the streets of Guanajuato in 1991. And as during the campaign, the PAN hierarchy has felt slighted by the president's maverick Friends of Fox campaign organization that directly collected funds at informal meetings and over the Internet rather than delegating that task to party channels (although investigations of improper campaign fundraising, which surfaced in 2002 and continued to mar the party's image through much of 2003, may have given PAN operatives cause for relief that they were left off of the money trail). Few old-guard *PANistas* were named to Fox's cabinet, and when the party did finally revise its 1965 elitist and exclusionary internal rules (Schlerer Ibarra 2001) in 2002, the reform rendered party membership even less accessible (Germán Martínez, 2002 interview). The PAN's candidate selection procedures remain those of an exclusive debating club, while the platforms it writes reverberate through all walks of Mexico's political life.

As Fox's legislative failures compounded in 2002 (see Chapter 8), the president and reelected PAN national president Luis Felípe Bravo Mena searched for common ground, or, in contrast to Zedillo's "sane distance," a policy of "sane proximity." There was to be no PAN-state, however, just the PAN and the state. Despite persistent rumors (such as that Fox had negotiated the 2001 Tabasco gubernatorial election with Madrazo),[37] the PAN discreetly avoided direct Interior Secretary intervention in local

---

[37] See, for example, Olmos and Guzmán (2001).

politics. The relegation of *concertacesión* to the PAN's own internal "Museum of Fraud" does not detract from the strategy's effectiveness as a way station between authoritarianism and democracy. As the ex-*Foristas* without a party debate the normative virtues of winning through what at its worst may be considered theatrical blackmail, the ascendant neo-*PANístas* bet all their incremental gains on the electoral route and won big, after treading water for the party's first forty years. The PAN in the 1990s accepted the PRI-state's sparse financing, as usual, while waving the conservatives' banner of "transition through order." But to their credit, they overcame Gibson's and Loaeza's dilemmas by forging a broad electoral coalition on an antiregime platform, delicately demanding electoral justice but without falling from the regime's good graces. As demonstrated in Chapter 8, the PRD and PAN rarely joined forces, thereby averting the full-scale antiregime alliance common in pacted transitions. But the PRD's angry intransigence toward the PRI-state offered great, if unintended, consolation to the PAN. While the PAN's patronage-seeking dissent may have been necessary to provoke an orderly, albeit protracted, transition to democracy, I now demonstrate how misplaced PAN and PRI fears were. If the PRI-state underestimated the unsinkable *PANístas*, they repeatedly overestimated the PRD, replaying the 1988 Cárdenas nightmare rather than assessing the *PRDístas* for what they were, a spirited but highly disorganized movement who needed to resolve their own internal problems before they could effectively challenge the regime.

7

The Party of the Democratic Revolution: From Postelectoral Movements to Electoral Competitors

> For my enemies, the law;
> for my friends, whatever they want.
>
> Getulio Vargas (Brazilian president, 1930–45)[1]

The Party of the Democratic Revolution (PRD) also spent its formative years debating whether it was even going to perform the functions of a conventional political party.[2] From the beginning, disagreement existed over whether the "party" prioritized the electoral route to power, or whether ideological purity and moral righteousness demanded that the "party" labor primarily as a social movement above the electoral fray, refusing to legitimize PRI-state elections with their participation. The moderates' lack of defined objectives forced the party to bow to the antiregime "movement side" agenda that routinely called for *segunda vuelta* postelectoral mobilizations as lighting rods for antiregime sentiment. These groups were often at odds, as the "party side" struggled to compete electorally, but without sufficient resources or internal support from the "movement side," which was always more visible and expedient. The consolidation of the party into a (more or less) unified body committed to facilitating Mexico's democratic transition from within the existing electoral system is traceable only to 1995. The miserable failure

---

[1] Quoted in O'Donnell (1997).

[2] By Sartori's definition, a party expresses the opinions of the governed within a pluralistic system. While parties tend to represent a unified ideology or at least a set of governing principles, factions (or constituent social movements) – like those prevalent in the PRD – tend to represent only a part of this platform, or in the extreme, only a single issue or cause (see Sartori 1976, 7–19).

of the party's previous strategy of electoral fatalism, that is, the a priori recognition that the party would receive its electoral merits only through the *segunda vuelta* (and not even through the elections themselves), led to an inevitable reassessment after a string of poor electoral performances in the early 1990s. Like the strategy of the National Action Party (PAN), the PRD's strategy toward postelectoral conflicts, then, has been the single most important change during its consolidation into a key protagonist in Mexico's protracted transition. However, there are more differences than similarities between these two opposition parties' strategies with regard to their willingness to resolve postelectoral disputes through legal channels.

The PRD played a crucial role in facilitating Mexico's democratic transition, but much more for its effect on the other two main actors, the PAN and the Party of the Institutional Revolution (PRI), than for its own antiregime protagonism. This was true at least until 2000, when the party's dominant transition-seeking propensities allowed the party to forge an implicit pact with the PAN to vote out *cacique* governors in Mexico's southern states, like Chiapas and Yucatán. During its first decade, the PRD, which actually waned after 1989 as an electoral force, constantly reminded Mexico's economic conservatives in the PAN and PRI of the risks of more abrupt change. True to the observation that protest was more likely in political systems that were neither totalitarian nor pluralistic (Tarrow 1998, 77), PRD activists sought to exploit opportunities presented by Mexico's gradual opening. But the Mexican government repressed many early PRD demonstrations violently, granting them use of "the potent weapon of outrage" (Tarrow 1998, 84).

Unlike the PAN, which had a fifty-year history of interacting with the PRI-state before the PRD was even formally constituted, the PRI-state had little reason to believe the PRD would consolidate out of the Cardenista Front (FDN) of tiny parastatal parties, which served largely as the registration vehicle for the Cárdenas 1988 presidential bid. As seen in Chapter 2, there was no reason for the authoritarian incumbents to believe the FDN would last, and hence no anticipated future relationship existed of any depth or duration, in terms of Ellickson's (1991, 94) hypotheses of recurrence to legal norms of conflict resolution. As soon as the PRI's national legislative alliance with the PAN was formalized in congressional certification of the 1988 presidential election, the national PRD was dispensable as a legislative group, and its ineptitude in defending the vote in local and state races made the party easy prey at the subnational level too. With the exception of Cárdenas's personal leadership, which waned after 1988 until he won the Mexico City mayor's sash in 1997, there existed little for the PRI-state to fear in the PRD, nor a rational reason for the PRI-state's repression. Recall from Chapter 5 that 80 percent of the 200 fatalities nationwide attributable to postelectoral conflicts were in PRD-PRI conflicts (with most of the remainder visited upon the smaller leftist parties that in 1988 had allied with the movement later formalized as the PRD).

For its part, the PRD had neither the legal preparation of the PAN nor the conservative opposition's willingness to seek legal compensation for PRI electoral misconduct by "externalizing losses to a third party" (again, Ellickson's term), that is, going to court as a means of exposing either the vulgar levels of PRI fraud or the utter dependence of Mexico's electoral institutions on the ruling party. The grassroots PRD, unconvinced of legal strategies' utility, had only one initial strength against its PRI tormentors in local elections. This strength emerged out of the PRD's overwhelming weakness. Great resource asymmetries in bargaining with the PRI-state made PRD threats of mobilization credible and their aversion to risk much lower, and led them to adopt an "all or nothing" approach characteristic of heavily discounted future interactions (Knight 1992, 129). In other words, they had nothing to lose, especially in regions where the police, the military, the local Interior Secretary representative, or other government agencies actively repressed them anyway.

How did the PRD overcome resource shortages and repression to construct and consolidate a viable leftist challenge to the regime during its short existence? This question can perhaps best be informed by work from the new social movements literature, as well as by that on party behavior. More specifically, I refer to a new interpretation of the causes of social action, intersecting political agents, and the "dimensions of political systems which structure collective action" (McAdam et al. 1996, 10). Contrary to prior approaches emphasizing identities of movement members rather than their political consequences and accomplishments, these new theorists are informed by microanalytic rationality. Their movement activists may be motivated by endogenous identities, but they are also shrewdly rational, seeking to compensate for their lack of conventional resources (money, specialized training, information, influence with elites, etc.) through appeals to construct such identities and "frame" urgent messages at society's margins. Movement leaders seek to convey such a desperate need for collective action that they justify departure from the authoritarians' rule of law through memorable, deviant, and even violent acts highlighting injustices by the status quo.

This "process framing" approach locates preferences for change in the preferences of the opposition party/movement, rather than in those of the incumbent. While McAdam et al. (1996) do not develop a full theory of institutional formation, one might, in extending their reasoning, assume that any rule-of-law consensus established by the incumbents (in conjunction with opposition or independently) would be honored only in the breach. Shortcomings of the authoritarian regime, such as egregious human-rights abuses, would be showcased and framed by transition-seeking opponents in search of political opportunity. I consider this interpretation in explaining how such an amalgamation of squabbling little groups coalesced as a national party-movement. I also demonstrate, amplifying evidence presented in Chapter 5, that they often failed to unify or even communicate between towns. Indeed, the spontaneous nature of PRD movements – in response to local conditions more than national imperatives – limited the consolidation of these movements as a national party.

In the beginning, the leaders of the PRD had little choice, due to their own inexperience and organizational weakness, but to steer their party's relations with the regime "decision by decision." It was not until mid-1995 that the radical and reformist visions of the party came into direct confrontation, with the reformists winning. This chapter first analyzes the national context of that showdown through the lens of the divergent strategies under consideration toward elections and postelectoral conflict. Then, I consider local case studies of postelectoral conflicts as a means of directly contrasting PAN and PRD behavior. Unlike the case of the PAN, however, I do not study individual cases of postelectoral mobilization; rather, I consider three statewide networks of PRD postelectoral mobilization. These three case studies are the Michoacán 1992 local elections that characterize the party's conduct of electoral politics during its confrontational era; the Chiapas 1995 local race, demonstrative of the PRD's inability to control some local mobilizations even after taking the national decision to favor negotiation over mobilization; and the Veracruz 1997 local elections, illustrative of both the potential and the pitfalls of taking the post-1995 conciliatory electoral strategies to their extremes.

PRD'S ELECTORAL OPENING GAMBIT: DEBATE, DISCORD, AND ANTIREGIME TENDENCIES

The *segunda vuelta* period, that is, the PRD's first six years of existence, were marked by dismal electoral failures punctuated by a few postelectoral successes. Unlike the tiny leftist parties that historically negotiated plural local administrations after postelectoral riots, the PRD did actually manage to parlay some consolation prizes into displays of decent governance (at least up to the standards of PRI small-town municipal administration), which in turn increased the national party's local presence and helped the party grow. Furthermore, to "win" a run of these municipal council proportional-representation seats or "co-mayorship" positions, the party grew increasingly adept at wrecking postelectoral havoc prior to negotiating these seats and by publicizing authoritarian reprisals in the national and international media. At its best, then, the PRD's postelectoral strategy was not so different from that of the PAN. However, unlike the PAN, where the party remained united even through its most severe battles, the PRD was always divided and rarely achieved its aspirations.

From its inception, the PRD was a political Tower of Babel formed from every leftist political party legalized in the 1970s and 1980s, as well as a large number of PRI dissidents. Initially, party leadership was skewed toward ex-*PRIístas*, although this did balance out with time. Some 54 percent of the party's first forty-eight-member congressional delegation, for example, were members of the PRI's Democratic Current (the PRI dissidents led by Cárdenas and Porfirio Muñoz Ledo), 19 percent were members of the "electoral left" (the Communist Party [PCM], the Mexican Socialist Party [PMS], the Party of United Mexican Socialists [PSUM], etc.), and some 21 percent came directly from social movements and had little or no party experience. In the 1991 Congress, however, only 10 percent of the forty-one members were former *PRIístas* from the Democratic Current, while 32 percent claimed "old left" roots and 44 percent came from affiliated social movements (Prud'homme 1996, 16).[3] These "currents" were almost immediately labeled within the party: "the rainbow" of "old leftists" whose support was credited with winning Muñoz Ledo the party presidency in 1994 and who included Amalia García (party president from 1999 to 2001); the "Democratic Current" of urban social movement activists, particularly in Mexico City, comprising Cárdenas's support base; and a more independent group of regional activists, initially from Veracruz and Michoacán (but now dispersed nationally), headed by PMS leader Heberto Castillo until his death in 1997. As noted in the party's convocation, "it will be an alliance converging over great common

---

[3] The remaining 6 percent in 1988 and 15 percent in 1991 were independent politicians, members of the "parastatal" FDN parties (the Authentic Party of the Mexican Revolution [PARM], Popular Socialist Party [PPS], and Party of the Cardenista Front for National Reconstruction [PFCRN]) who defected to the PRD, and congressional members whose past affiliations could not be identified.

principles, different currents of ideas, none of which is exclusive of the others: democrats and nationalists, socialists and Christians, liberals and ecologists" (Cano 1995b, 6). With the accommodation of these groups by the early 1990s, it became clear that two overarching currents existed within the party (as within many leftist parties), the Cárdenas-led idealists and the Muñoz Ledo–led pragmatists.

This alphabet soup of tiny leftist fronts, coalitions, and parties faced two critical dilemmas: first, maintaining "antisystem" purity while finding a place in Mexico's democratic transition, and secondly, respecting the broad spectrum of opinions within the party while forging a discipline that would enable a unified party to advocate for political change. Unlike the PAN, which started as a tiny and homogenous group and added members sharing core beliefs over half a century, the PRD started as a popular protest against the regime, attracted by the "antiregime" common front candidacy of Cuauhtémoc Cárdenas but sharing little else. As the momentary coalition of 1988 dissipated, it became quite clear, in the PRD's dismal federal electoral performances of the early 1990s, that the 1988 pro-Cárdenas groundswell had been an electoral outburst against the regime, but not a mandate on how to change it.

The final radical-reformer showdown came in August 1995 at the PRD's third national congress. The radicals, under Cárdenas, proposed the party delegitimize Zedillo just as it had Salinas, even though Zedillo had clearly won the 1994 election and Salinas may well have lost in 1988. Calling for the resignation of Zedillo, Cárdenas acknowledged that the PRD did not possess the "correlation of forces" needed to prompt this resignation so that the PRD could assume power. Hence, Cárdenas called for a pacted "government of national salvation," allowing Zedillo to negotiate his own removal and naming a plural interim administration from the country's social groups to preside over a transition.[4] Having publicly proposed this vague "government of national salvation" on two other occasions, Cárdenas conceded at Oaxtepec that Zedillo's resignation was not "the central point of my demand" and that until the PRD had sufficient strength to execute his plan, "we will not lose ourselves in sterile discussions" (Cárdenas 1995). However, even with this minor

---

[4] The wording of Cárdenas's speech was so controversial when penned two months before the Oaxtepec meeting that Muñoz Ledo vetted several versions before acceding to the radical tone calling for a "new political regime, substantial modification of economic policies, and the rescue of national sovereignty" (Cano 1995a, 11). Muñoz Ledo raised his dissent again at Oaxtepec and afterward, quitting the party in 1999.

qualification, Cárdenas's proposal failed to curry favor with the sitting president.

Muñoz Ledo's counterargument, in direct contradiction with Cárdenas, was that "we cannot sit down to negotiate with the government and tell them that the first thing is, 'I want you to leave.' We need to pact reforms so that change occurs in the direction desired by the majority of Mexico, and not according to a list..."(Muñoz Ledo 1995). Cárdenas's judgment was defeated in the vote to determine the party's platform by a three-to-one margin. The radicals accepted this vote, ceased planning a "government of national salvation," and set about building the party's electoral base, which had been dwindling steadily since its creation. Indeed, the electoral consequences of maintaining the extreme "national salvation" position might have been dire, but given the PRD's electoral misfortunes, the stakes did not seem so high. The more realistic Oaxtepec reformists were fighting – at least in the short term – for scraps from the table of power: proportional-representation seats in Congress, state legislatures, and municipal councils – the stuff of postelectoral conflicts.

CONSOLIDATION (1995–1998): FAVORING THE FIRST ROUND (ELECTIONS) OVER THE *SEGUNDA VUELTA*

Tenaciously clinging to the *segunda vuelta* strategy, Cárdenas told supporters immediately after the 1994 election that he had erred in believing that systemic corruption could be defeated by the popular vote. But unlike in 1988, Cárdenas's call for a postelectoral reckoning rang false in 1994, as the popular leader continued "charging" the regime for injustices committed six years earlier (Aguilar Zinzer 1995, 447). Transition-seeking advisors in 1994 warned of the need to place electoral performance over the harvesting of past PRI-state injustices, but a powerful faction led by PRD electoral advocate Samuel del Villar refused to accept the 1994 results and filed hundreds of postelectoral "knock-off" electoral court complaints, still notorious among Mexico's electoral justice literati (see Chapter 3), and cast protest votes at PRD Executive Council meetings in an effort to dissuade his colleagues from accepting defeat.

In the absence of a recognized victory, Cárdenas had in 1988 settled for mobilization as a proxy for the popular vote. And in public opinion, he had triumphed in 1988, in a campaign where "filling the *zocalo* [the central square]" was synonymous with PRD victory because vote tallying was crooked and could not faithfully represent a candidate's support. By

1994, however, after three electoral reforms and the birth of mass-media electoral campaigns in Mexico, filling the *zocalo* was no longer enough. To Cárdenas's credit, he did modernize his campaign strategies for his 1997 bid to be mayor of Mexico City, which he won by a fraud-proof margin in the first round (the election), becoming Mexico City's first popularly elected mayor ever.[5] Cárdenas conveyed his message through the mass media, rather than just "filling the *zocalo*," and combined forces with the post-Oaxtepec pragmatists in the party's legislative wing and, as of 1996, the modern electoralist strategists of new party president López Obrador (Mexico City's mayor from 2000 to 2003). As stated by moderate Jesús Ortega, the PRD diagnosed its fatalist tendency of "bearing witness" to regime authoritarianism and recognized the need to instead "start acting like a party in government" (Sotelo 1997). López Obrador openly met with Zedillo in November 1997, hoping to soften the party's image and reverse its electoral fortunes. Running as incumbents, the early 1990s PRD mayors lost 60 percent of their local governments in reelection, as "the citizenry wants a constructive government, not a confrontational one" ("Pierden perredistas...").

The consolidation of the PRD as a loyal opposition party at the federal level is clearly traceable to mid-1995. However, there has been a tremendous lag at the state and local levels, as the so-called "Syndicate of Governors" exists as a collection of repressive holdovers from the Salinas era who oppose distributing public resources to opposition-held municipalities. As seen in the case of the PAN and as will be demonstrated for the PRD with case studies from Michoacán and Chiapas, electoral institutions to resolve postelectoral conflicts could be "rigged" in various fashions, and local PRD activists, usually acting independently of national leadership, frequently responded by mobilizing first and asking questions later. Unfortunately for the PRD, their mobilizations – unlike those of the PAN – did not help unify the party. Rather, the series of postelectoral demonstrations merely exacerbated internal contradictions and reinforced a lack of discipline also displayed in the party's own fraudulent internal elections in 1996, 1999, and, to a lesser extent, in 2002.[6]

---

[5] The post had previously been filed by presidential appointees.

[6] In 1996 and in 1999, the PRD's internal electoral service found irregularities in between 30 and 40 percent of the *casillas* in the internal balloting for party president won by Andrés Manuel López Obrador and Amalia García, respectively (Hidalgo and Guerrero 1999, Delgado and Monge 1999).

MICHOACÁN 1992: RIGGED INSTITUTIONS AND VIOLENT
CONFLICTS ON CÁRDENAS'S HOME COURT

Postelectoral violence broke out in Michoacán in 1989 as well as in 1992, stemming from divisions within the state's political elites. In exchange for Cárdenas's "embarrassment" of Salinas by defecting from the PRI while governor of Michoacán in 1987, Salinas punished Cárdenas and the PRD in the 1989 Michoacán legislative elections, widely viewed as among the most fraudulent state elections ever (Rivera Velázquez interview; Beltrán del Río 1993, 91).[7] Following this debacle in which the PRD was denied its majority by PRI-controlled electoral institutions, some PRD leaders adopted a more conciliatory stance (at least locally). According to former Michoacán Congressman José Alfonso Solórzano Fraga (interview), the PRD negotiated with the Michoacán PRI, vowing to accept mayoral race outcomes without protest or bloodshed (or disruption of the governor's forthcoming "state of the state" address) if electoral results were respected. Indeed, the PRD won 52 of 113 municipalities in 1989, including Morelia, the state capital and by far the PRD's most important municipal victory prior to 1997.

But the electoral certification was conducted in a ragtag manner for the 1989 mayoral races. The Electoral College agreed not to rule on any of the mayoral races until after a political bargaining table had reached as many postelectoral agreements as possible. The bargaining table was composed of several high-level state PRI and PRD leaders, national delegates from each party, and the governor. Cases were handled thirty at a time, with the wide-margin victories agreed upon first and closer races saved to the end, with an impasse reached over the last thirty cases. "The PRI wanted to win the majority, that is at least 57, for strictly political reasons" (Solórzano Fraga interview). After all the "resolvable" conflicts were settled, violence broke out in the rest, with nineteen slayings and dozens of violence-related injuries, and, finally, after the federal government lost its patience four months later, "hard-liner" federal authorities removed, arrested, and detained 103 PRD activists.[8]

---

[7] Stripped of legal pretensions, the governor-controlled state electoral commission annulled 161 ballot boxes, mostly in PRD-won districts, subtracting votes from the opposition on the preposterous grounds that "none of the ballots show signs of having been folded when placed into the ballot box," and "because the vote total is unlikely given that all ballots are marked in the same manner," etc. (Beltrán del Río 1993, 91).

[8] Journalist Pascal Beltrán del Río offers the best summary of events. He reported fatal violence in the following municipalities in the three months following the December 1989 elections: Jungapeo (two PRD activists), Jacona (municipal police officer and a PRD

Michoacán possessed no autonomous electoral court in 1989–90; post-electoral legal complaints were handled by the Michoacán Electoral Commission, an arm of the state executive. In fact, at the end of December 1989, when some seventeen city halls had been taken by PRD activists (bringing the tally of "occupied" towns to over thirty including those occupied after the preceding legislative races), the electoral commission resolved to stop meeting for a "lack of material." The director of the body denied the existence of any unresolved disputes, stating that "all have been attended to" (Beltrán del Río 1993, 131). After a dozen postelectoral slayings, the state legislature convened a multipartisan commission in January 1990 to resolve the thirty-three last, heated disputes. This commission won legislative permission to disregard a half-dozen electoral outcomes and replace them with "plural" electoral councils, but this was a pittance to impatient federal Interior Secretary Fernando Gutiérrez Barrios. The PRD leadership, under increasing pressure but without success, sought to convince municipal leaders to stop occupying town halls. But, "the [PRD's] collective leadership waffled, fell into contradictions, and even attacked their own fellow party members" (Beltrán del Río 1993, 143). The forced removal of the *PRDístas* on April 5, 1990, was denounced by Cárdenas as a conspiracy proving Salinas's unwillingness "to dialog or negotiate" (Beltrán del Río 1993, 148). Indeed, the incident demonstrated the limits of Salinas's patience with his presidential rival on Cárdenas's home court, patience that would also wear thin in 1992.

The 1992 elections transpired under different electoral rules, as the Michoacán PRD negotiated electoral reforms directly with Gutiérrez Barrios, in violation of the federal pact, ostensibly to minimize conflicts in the 1992 governor's race (see Chapter 4), which preceded the mayoral elections. The PRD sought an autonomous magistrate to head the newly created electoral court but instead received José Solórzano Juárez, who as president of the State Supreme Court in 1989 had rejected all PRD complaints on appeal from the electoral commission in those blatantly fraudulent local races. If the PRD (as well as the PAN and the PRI) were disappointed with the naming of Solórzano Juárez prior to the election,

---

activist), Turicato (PRD mayoral candidate and his brother), Apatzingán (PRD mayoral candidate, PRD activist, PRI activist), Zitácuaro (two police officers), Tuzantla (PRI mayoral candidate), Huandacareo (PRD mayoral candidate), Tacámbaro (two PRD activists), and Benito Juárez (three PRD activists, one police officer). Additionally, there were dozens of non fatal shootings, kidnappings, beatings, and other melees (Beltrán del Río 1993, 130–47).

all three parties (including the PRI) were even more dismayed after the elections, when they all roundly criticized the court's performance (Gurza 1992).

Some twenty-two election-related slayings were reported through mid-1993 in thirty town hall takeovers by the PRD and, for the first time, by the PRI.[9] State PRD leaders, stalemated in bilateral negotiations within Michoacán, took the matter to the federal Interior Secretariat, where, according to Beltrán del Río (1993, 385), the party demanded concessions in twenty-seven municipalities in exchange for vacating twenty-four town halls. The Interior Secretary, represented by Sub-Secretary Arturo Núñez, is said to have asked PRD leader Jesús Ortega to rank order the party's priority municipalities in conflict. The Interior Secretary then ordered the electoral court to reverse PRI victories in favor of the PRD in seven of the thirteen PRD priority towns (Beltrán del Río 1993, 384).[10] Even more than in other cases, the electoral court here was explicitly used as another bargaining chip.

After these concessions were apparently "legalized" through the electoral court, talks broke down between the Interior Secretary and the PRD. Having reached a dead end in federal negotiations, the *PRDístas* wanted another multipartisan legislative group to resolve the Michoacán crisis. The state PRI refused, but personnel changes at the Interior Secretary were conducive to reopening talks.[11] However, the second round did not advance either, as the state government was persuaded to reconsider only six of the thirty-two contested municipalities. Extended negotiations did yield a settlement in which six PRI mayors-elect resigned to make way for three PRD mayors and three more "acceptable" *PRIístas* (Beltrán del Río

---

[9] The 1992 postelectoral slayings were reported as follows: Turicato (PRD town council member and ten PRD activists), Jungapeo (PRD activist), Aguililla (PRD activist), Charapan (PRD activist), Paracho (PRD activist), La Piedad (PRD activist), Uruapan (PRD activist), Yurécuaro (two PRD activists, two PRI activists), and Zitácuaro (PRD activist). In addition, some fifteen opposition partisans were injured during the January 1 changing of the guard in Apatzingán y Uruapan (Beltrán del Río 1993, 382–90).

[10] Núñez acknowledged participation in the Michoacán postelectoral negotiations but did not discuss details (Núñez interview). All three major parties strongly censured what they perceived as the electoral court's partiality (Gurza 1992). Solórzano, who received a lucrative gubernatorial appointment as a notary public after stepping down from the electoral court, had no comment.

[11] Michoacán PRI leader Martín Julio Aguilar publicly attributed the reassignment of Interior Secretariat negotiator Beatriz Paredes to her "losing control of the negotiations in favor of the PRD" (Gómez and Resillas 1993).

1993, 389). The remaining postelectoral conflicts lingered for months, however, as PRD leaders sought to persuade local activists to keep their word and abandon municipal buildings.

A CASE-BASED ANALYSIS OF MICHOACÁN'S 1992 WHITEWASH COURT

Under extreme political pressures, the electoral court ruled erratically, but usually with a protective "cloak of legality" that gave the outward impression of conforming to the state's election laws. The Michoacán 1992 court annulled many more races than any electoral court before or since, as one of the first state electoral courts in Mexico to annul more than one race, let alone seven (representing 6 percent of all municipalities).[12] Individual cases did not reveal inconsistencies in the annulments as glaring as the 1989 Michoacán legislative elections had, although the tools of judicial discretion seem to have been applied unevenly. I briefly review two cases that appear to have been discretionarily "returned" to the PRI with revocation of PRD victories – in Jungapeo and Charapán – and the case of Cotíja, one of those allegedly on the list submitted by the PRD to the federal Interior Secretariat for annulment by the state electoral court in a "whitewash" arrangement, whereby institutional cover was given to a political decision.[13]

The PRI had alleged general violence in Jungapeo, where three ballot boxes had been burned, apparently by activists from the victorious PRD. The electoral court summed votes from the burned ballot boxes (apparently taking totals from an *unofficial* electoral commission report the PRI produced), adding disproportionately to the PRI tally and throwing a declared PRD victory to the PRI. The court failed to mention why it accepted these unofficial documents when dozens of other complaints had been rejected from consideration because the court had refused to accept evidence other than formal "public documents" (i.e., official government or nonofficial but notarized acts), as per Michoacán Electoral Code Article 193 (Michoacán Electoral Tribunal R.I.M. resolution 85/92, 3–5). Had the court formally accepted complainants' unofficial "acts," it

---

[12] The known pre-1992 state electoral-court annulments include San Juan del Rio, Queretaro (population 154,700), in 1991, and Santa Catarina, Nuevo León (population 202, 100), in 1988.

[13] For comparison of this case to several other "whitewash" electoral court cases of institutional failure, see Eisenstadt (2002).

would have had to accept scores of the cases it had summarily rejected on the same grounds.

A second verdict of dubious judicial merit, that of Charapán, yielded another PRI victory by annulling a PRD win. This case was decided on one electoral magistrate's admittedly extralegal reasoning that "the complaints alleged by the complainant are insufficient; however, *given that they relate to issues of public security and social interest*, this institution will supplement the complaint" (Michoacán Electoral Tribunal resolution R.I.M. 70/92 and 82/92, 9, italics mine). The legal basis for such intervention was Article 214 of the state constitution, which did indeed authorize the court to "supplement evidence and arguments," although none of the thirty-five other complaints reviewed received such lenience.[14] Charapán was accorded priority by the electoral court due to allegations that PRD supporters violated the sanctity of the municipal electoral committee during vote tallying and forced that committee to annul two ballot boxes illegitimately, changing the outcome to favor the PRI. Supplementing the complainant's case, the electoral court revalidated the two ballot boxes, reverting the PRD victory back to the PRI (R.I.M. resolution 70/92 and 82/92, 5–13).

Unlike in Charapán, the court's interpretation of "public security and social interest" may have been served by reverting the PRI's victory in Cotija to the PRD, as per the alleged "orders" from the federal PRI-state. The latitude argued in the verdict gives credence to the depiction of the 1992 Michoacán electoral court as a "whitewash" institutional failure. Like most complaints seeking to cover all bases, this one alleged a potpourri of charges: illegal PRI roundups and transport of voters from polling station to polling station in government vehicles to cast multiple votes; offerings of cash bribes or government largesse for votes; employment of ineligible poll workers; "theft" of polling station documents; posting of official party propaganda; and crooked tallying (R.I.M. complaint 41/92, 1–6).

Two reasons were given for determining that the complaint was partially founded. First, it was "discovered" that one of the polling station presidents was the sister of one of the candidates on the PRI slate, and one ballot box was annulled because the magistrates argued, invoking Article 72 of the state electoral code, that fraternal ties created conflicts of interest (R.I.M. resolution 41/92, 6). Article 72 mentions nothing about

---

[14] For a discussion of the effects of "supplementing the complaint" in federal law (the basis for Michoacán's electoral code), see Chapter 3.

family relationships and specifies only that potential poll workers must be registered voters, of recognized integrity, who possess "the knowledge to fulfill the duties" (Ley Electoral del Estado de Michoacán, 27). The other two PRD-victory-clinching ballot boxes were annulled because one of the town regents "kidnapped" ballot box installation acts (R.I.M. resolution 41/92, 6–7). While the state-appointed town electoral council acknowledged that one of the regents did take the acts, these sheets were not those used to tally votes; their only legal purpose was to certify that polling stations had opened on time and were properly composed. Perhaps, by the narrow dictates of the law, such a procedural violation was sufficient to annul the ballot boxes (although there was no proof of any late polling booth openings or incomplete compositions), but such formality is inconsistent with the "loose" acceptance, in the Jungapeo case, of a party's copy of the vote tally in place of the burned official vote count.

These cases reveal bias, especially coupled with the court's blatant admission of nonlegal reasoning in the Charapán case, where individuals' subjective definitions of "public security and social interest" seemed to outweigh strict definitions of the law. Indeed, democratic elections should pertain to the "social interest," and in early 1990s Michoacán, given the brutality exercised against the opposition, all the elections related to "public security." If the postelectoral bargaining tables did not function equitably, the formal legal courts seemed just as biased against the PRD. The party's advantages in Cárdenas's home state were its overwhelming strength (despite internal division) and its desperate persistence. As it became clear to the PRI-state that the PRD in Michoacán would not be deterred, cooperation by the regime became more likely, especially with the emergence of a moderate faction led by gubernatorial candidate Arias by 1992, which the PRI-state could prop up as a wedge against the extreme left. So sheer numbers and their translation into credible threats finally won maneuvering room for the PRD in Michoacán's local elections. The party's Chiapas chapter had less luck, even after the national PRD's strategy change at Oaxtepec, as social fragmentation, both within the party and in its broader base, was overwhelming.

LEVIATHAN IN THE TROPICS: STRIVING TO BUILD ELECTORAL INSTITUTIONS IN CHIAPAS

In Mexico's poorest state, where a third of the population qualifies as "seriously malnourished," only 38 percent of the municipalities have paved roads, 70 percent of the population has no electricity, and

40 percent has no water, it was perhaps no surprise that rectifying biased electoral institutions was not the most urgent public policy challenge
(Monroy 1994, 20–35). Unlike Michoacán, where social conflicts were
played out through elections (at least partially), in Chiapas, social deprivation ran much deeper. Postelectoral conflicts were rampant through the
1970s and 1980s, but they were usually just skirmishes in long-standing
battles between landowners and peasants, between Protestants and
Catholics, and between members of the state's scores of indigenous groups
in a half-dozen major linguistic groups. Rightist "white guard" vigilante
militias and leftist Zapatista *guerrillas* cordoned off PRI-state access to
half a dozen municipalities each, where, as of the mid-1990s, they were
the unquestionable authorities, having seized power with little recourse
to parties or elections. Land-tenure disputes in Chiapas have for cen-
turies produced human-rights abuses dwarfing social conflicts in most of
Mexico's other states, but elections also yielded tensions, especially with
the advent of political competition in the 1990s. That the norm of electoral
justice could even acquire any standing among the state's conflict-savaged
society – and it did, but years later – is testimony to the success of electoral
institutions.

Electorally, Chiapas had been eminently *PRIísta* since the party began.
The state had been a solid reservoir of PRI votes – nicknamed "the green
vote" – in all national elections as rural peasants were considered mal-
leable and less sensitive to fraud than educated urban voters. During the
state's pre-1991 PRI monopoly, election-related disputes took the form of
intra-PRI squabbles over mayoral candidate selection. Absolute PRI hegemony – in which the PRI vote in some cases exceeded 100 percent (Aziz
and Molinar 1990, 166–70) – held in federal elections as late as 1991,
when in 49 out of 113 municipalities, 100 percent of the voters cast ballots for the PRI in local elections, despite the presence of other candidates
on most ballots. The state's long history of postelectoral mobilizations
extended back at least to 1946, when allegations of PRI electoral fraud in
Tapachula ended in several protesters' deaths (Arreola Ayala 1985, 335). In
the 1980s, several municipal councils resulted from scores of postelectoral
conflicts and dozens of city hall "takeovers." But these municipal councils
either resulted from factional fights within the PRI (Burguete interview),
or from independent leftist social movements only loosely affiliated with
opposition parties, if at all.[15]

---

[15] Legislative records were not printed before 1991, and half the municipal councils formed
   that year were never properly approved by the state legislature. Chiapas has only small
   newspapers and no archives extending back to the 1980s. Hence quantitative analysis

Prior to 1991, elections were largely irrelevant as channels for political or social discontent. Those outside the system struggled through nonelectoral means, prompting a history of *guerrilla* movements even before the Zapatista rebellion of 1994. Dozens of postelectoral conflicts after the 1991 elections rendered the creation of over twenty municipal councils, reasserting the precedent for such power-sharing arrangements.[16] So when the federal government granted the Zapatista rebels a wide political berth after their shocking January 1994 insurrection, over a dozen social movements and parties took town halls, demanding a share of local governance spoils in less violent "copycat" acts. The federal government, fearing the spread of Zapatista influence to these more benign social forces, obliged, creating dozens of plural municipal councils with PRD participation in 1994 and well over forty since 1992.[17]

Although electoral courts were described as legal figures in the 1988 and 1991 electoral codes, the first functional electoral courts on record in Chiapas were created in the 1994 reforms by a consensus among the PRI, PRD, and PAN in time for the gubernatorial contest between Amado Avendaño (PRD) and Ernesto Robledo Rincón (PRI). Avendaño, an independent newspaper columnist and Zapatista spokesman, was not a PRD member and made political differences widely known to the party. After the election, the PRD debated whether Avendaño's losing vote was worth defending, or whether to concentrate their postelectoral effort on Cárdenas's behalf by filing federal electoral court complaints regarding the presidential race instead. While most of the Chiapas state PRD leadership concentrated on Cárdenas, a last-minute decision was made to file complaints on Avendaño's behalf, although the PRD prosecutors, in a dramatic show of inefficiency, arrived to file complaints with the state electoral commission minutes after the filing period had expired (Guzmán, Luna interviews).

Avendaño's bitter loss and subsequent proclamation that he was "Governor in Exile," internal financial scandals, and disagreement over

---

is extremely limited. Arreola Ayala (1985) does write that in 1983 there were nineteen postelectoral conflicts resulting in seventeen municipal building takeovers.

[16] The PRD fielded only thirty-two mayoral candidates in 1991 (as compared to 100 in 1995) and won only one mayorship outright. But the party quickly became the state's second electoral force, even as the PAN also developed important constituencies in middle class trade-based towns such as Huixtla. The PAN's winning of Chiapas capital Tuxtla Gutiérrez in 1995 signaled the party's full entry into electoral contention.

[17] The exact number is hard to discern. Only twenty-six were approved by the state legislature, but several protagonists interviewed insisted on numbers over forty: for example, forty-eight (Gómez Maza interview) and close to sixty (Jarquin interview).

party objectives favored two new splinter parties, the Chiapas Demo-cratic Party (PDCH) and the Party of the Chiapas Popular Civic Front (PFCPCH), formed earlier in 1994 by *PRDístas* dissatisfied by local can-didate impositions by the party's national headquarters. The PRD's short-comings in 1994 were exacerbated by a structural problem that continued to afflict the party in 1995. The PRD, which made its first statewide elec-toral showing in 1991 mayoral races with 7 percent of the vote, was not organizationally prepared to be a strong second force after garnering 17 percent in 1994. Composed of social activists of various ideological currents – from radical *guerrilla* leaders to center-left social democrats – the party was extremely short on resources and electoral expertise.[18] In short, the Chiapas PRD magnified the shortcomings of the national party.

This disarray was most vividly reflected in the breakaway factions of the PRD, the PDCH and PFCPCH, and in the internal PRD dissent in selecting candidates in 1995 for 11 of the 113 municipalities, yielding five postelectoral conflicts *inside* the PRD (Gómez Maza and Toledo inter-views). A rift also grew between the national and state chapters of the PRD over relations with the Zapatistas. The national leadership sought to pact with the Zapatistas, a natural ally against the federal government, while the state PRD chapter wanted little contact with the insurgents, especially after the Zapatistas boycotted the 1995 elections altogether (Luna, Gómez Maza interviews).[19]

THE 1995 POSTELECTORAL BAZAAR: PAPER-SHUFFLING JUDGES AND AUCTIONEER LEGISLATORS

None of the sixty-eight complaints submitted to the Chiapas Electoral Tribunal in 1995 were even accepted for magistrate consideration. The

---

[18] Most of the party's destitute rural followers in Chiapas never finished grade school, and close to half spoke Chiapas's three main indigenous dialects rather than Spanish.

[19] The Zapatistas themselves divided over whether to accept the PRD as their electoral agents, create a new party to wage the electoral "front" of the Ejército Zapatista de Liberacíon Nacional's (EZLNs) battle, or just ignore elections altogether. In a straw vote at the EZLN's Aguascalientes "platform-writing" convention (August 1994), Zapatista strategists and hundreds of sympathetic observers gathered at five thematic round tables, including one on "the democratic transition and the role of political parties," where eleven out of twenty-six speakers pronounced in favor of the electoral route to democ-racy (with four of these actively endorsing the PRD or its candidates), eight advocated "alternative routes to power," and seven did not take a clear position (Valdés Vega 1995, 11 fn. 21). While Marcos and the EZLN ideologues make constant references to both "democratic" and "revolutionary" transitions, their true preferences remain unclear.

PRD, having complained about the lack of electoral institution independence prior to the election certification (López and Matías 1995), viewed the electoral court as compromised from the inception.[20] Electoral court president José Espinoza Castro argued that his court went out of its way to consider party complaints, even registering late complaints, and that "bad faith" provoked parties to extralegal mobilization (interview).[21] In a few cities, notably Soyaló, Acapetahua, and Villacomaltitlán, passion-seized activists confirmed this "bad faith" hypothesis, burning official ballot tallies and hence all evidence of possible fraud, to the open dismay of PRD state leadership (Gómez Maza, Luna interviews).[22]

However, in at least some of the sixty-eight contested elections, PRD leaders argued that they had sufficient proof to raise doubts about electoral fairness and to warrant electoral court consideration. An author-supervised review of over fifty cases provided by local PAN and PRD chapters concluded that several presented allegations worthy of consideration.[23] The greatest inconsistency was in the weight accorded to the protest writings – descriptions of violations filed by dubiously trained party poll representatives "marking the place" for formally argued complaints elaborated by lawyers back at party headquarters within three days of the election.[24] In a few instances, appeals court magistrates implied that minor deficiencies in protest writings should have been

---

[20] The PRD categorically refused to sign the governor's political party "pact for peace and democracy," which would have bound opposition parties to the results in exchange for no tangible concessions from the PRI. The PAN conditioned its signature (never actually given) on removal of the biased presidents of the electoral court and electoral commission, and on the governor's promise not to campaign for the PRI (López and Matías 1995, 30).

[21] Espinoza Castro would not release any information on cases heard by his court, but a summary of the court's verdicts, published in 1996, confirmed that *not one* vote was annulled in the 1995 local races (Chiapas Electoral Tribunal 1996, 89).

[22] Gómez Maza (interview) said the burning of "fraudulent" ballots was based on a 1991 precedent. In that local election, protesters burned electoral material in Pueblo Nuevo Salistahuán and Mazatán, forcing the state Interior Secretary to negotiate municipal councils.

[23] The review was assisted by former UNAM law student Amilcar Peleaz Valdés, who also ably assisted the author in reviewing the Michoacán cases and the federal electoral court filings from 1988 through 1997.

[24] Before being eliminated as a requirement in several states and then by the federal electoral court in 2000, the filing of protests was the single greatest obstacle to opposition-party electoral justice access. Party election-day poll witnesses often lacked the formal training (or basic literacy) needed to complete the document. While national electoral lawyers filled in gaps by filing the formal complaints, these lawyers were rarely present at the polls.

supplemented by the lower court (R.A. resolution 74/95, 16), and the lower court did accept complaints with flawed protest writings (R.Q. resolution 37-A/P/34/95, 2). In most cases, however, disparities between protest writings and subsequent complaints resulted in immediate rejections.

The Chiapas electoral court filings were certainly inferior to the PRD's federal electoral court filings in presentation and arguments (despite consultation with three PRD federal legal advisors who participated in the local "defense of the vote" campaign), but they would seem to have warranted a nonzero rate of magistrate consideration, which merely entitles a case to consideration of a verdict of "founded" or "unfounded." In the 1994 federal elections, by contrast, fully 50 percent of the PRD's cases were at least accepted for consideration (with "founded" verdicts accruing to at least one ballot box in 34 percent of the half accepted for consideration). Whatever the legal principles guiding magistrate rulings, the electoral court was an utter failure in its broader mission of processing postelectoral tensions through legal channels. While her wording was quite strong, Chiapas PRD legislator Emma Toledo justifiably questioned the electoral court's verdicts, which she said lacked "reason, objectivity, professionalism, or legality" (Toledo 1995, 2).

True to the "dueling focal points" competition between formal and informal institutions, a jugular formula for postelectoral mobilization was conceived and aptly referred to by the equation: "*mobilization + storming of town halls = municipal council*" (Domínguez Torres and Granda Montalvo 1996). Some of the earlier "municipal councils" had been approved by Chiapas's unicameral legislature as per law, providing state authorities with a legal veto on allowing these institutional deviations. However, Chiapas Speaker of the House Juan Carlos Bonifaz Trujillo publicly decreed in 1994, with the apparent authority of the entire PRI-state, that no more municipal councils would be created, as acceding to even one municipal council would prompt the immediate proliferation of dozens more, and that through such plural city councils, the Zapatista rebels would gain political footholds through PRD representatives (Burguete, Jarquin, Gómez Maza interviews).

Bonifaz's dramatic "slippery slope" argument notwithstanding, no connection actually existed between the PRD and the Zapatista rebels. The Zapatistas had in fact boycotted the 1995 local races in the five municipalities they then controlled or greatly influenced: Las Margaritas, where the official results gave a narrow victory to the PRI; Nicolás Ruiz and Ocosingo, where political unrest postponed elections; El Bosque, where divisions within the PRD led to construction of a parallel municipal government; and San Andrés Larráinzar, where indigenous customs for selecting leaders yielded results different from the election, prompting judicial debate on the proper conduct of local elections. The state government's strategy, actively supervised by the national Interior Secretary, was to prevent further encroachment by the Zapatistas on government sovereignty through the creation of plural municipal councils, which could include a Zapatista presence. As has been seen, there was little positive contact between the PRD and the rebels.

In fact, after the 1995 election, PRD National President Porfirio Muñoz Ledo publicly accused Zapatista Sub-Commander Marcos of obfuscating the choice between ballots and bullets. Marcos replied that his group was "not the military arm of the PRD" and that in fact, the PAN represented the most effective national alternative to the PRI (Caballero 1995, 9). And if relations between the national PRD and the Zapatistas soured after the local elections, they remained largely nonexistent at the local level in Chiapas, where the PRD accused Marcos of having "cost" the PRD dozens of municipal races by calling for an election boycott.[25] Even in 2001, when the Zapatistas put down their guns and marched to Mexico City in support of autonomy-enhancing indigenous rights legislation, the PRD divided over whether to support the rebels, who, after all, had come to prominence through a violent episode in 1994, killing dozens of people.

Contrary to demonstrable facts, the federal and state governments in the mid-1990s worried about a possible "domino effect" spreading Zapatista influence. Conceding that a PRI-state presence had been lost in the five EZLN-controlled towns, the state and national interior secretariats concerned themselves with maintaining sovereignty over Chiapas's 108 other municipalities. They faced a bind. On the one hand, they feared Zapatista-PRD collusion (albeit groundlessly) and wished to maximize PRI control to ensure the most "impermeable" local governments possible. However, on the other hand, state and federal government agents wished to appease opposition parties and depoliticize postelectoral conflicts to avoid provoking Zapatista sympathies (Jarquin interview). It was a delicate balance, achieved through the ad hoc creation of a

---

[25] Gómez Maza (interview) said that instead of winning only eighteen municipalities, the PRD had aspired to win some forty-eight, and that close losses in twenty-five to twenty-eight municipalities could be attributed to divided loyalties of supporters who ultimately followed Marcos rather than the PRD out of fear of reprisals.

postelectoral bargaining table by moderate PRI and PRD state legislators (but not formally part of legislative business) and state Interior Secretary representatives.

It remains unclear who launched the bargaining table,[26] but the PRD may have made the greatest sacrifice by subjugating antiregime tendencies for transition-seeking stability. Emma Toledo, the PRD negotiator, stated that her party's moderates felt a responsibility to distinguish themselves from Zapatista scare tactics "to demonstrate that the PRD was contributing to the social peace in Chiapas" (interview). Carlos Alonso, the PRI legislator, said the PRD refused to submit towns it had won to arbitration, considering only PRI victories for negotiation (interview). Even with grandstanding by both sides, some fifty-six postelectoral conflicts were negotiated, while twelve postelectoral conflicts remained unsolved. Most of the unresolved cases involved mobilizations under the PRD banner, but which could not be controlled by PRD state legislators or the leadership council (Gómez Maza interview).

In a bargaining table similar to that described by Solórzano Fraga in 1989 Michoacán, state leaders from the PRD and the PRI, accompanied by the winning and losing local candidates, proposed plural administrations for each, starting with the most resolvable cases and ending with the most intractable ones. "It was like an auction," said Toledo, in which the losing party bid was countered by the victorious party in a self-binding process that lasted until the two sides concurred. According to Toledo's minutes (the PRI negotiators denied having kept records), only one mayorship was "traded," but scores of lesser nonelected positions were negotiated. These ranged from city manager posts (in a couple of towns) all the way down to town drivers (five towns), janitors (four towns), cemetery caretakers (three towns), clerical workers (three towns), and one librarian's assistant (author correspondence with Toledo).

Immediately after the election, the state PRD sent "Postelectoral Situation" questionnaires to dozens of conflictive municipalities (Figure 7.1), asking "What do the PRD supporters want?" and "If there was a possibility of creating a plural municipal government, would you accept posts in

---

[26] Protagonists from all three participant groups claimed to have initiated the bargaining table (Córdova, Toledo, Jarquin interviews). It was apparent, however, that the negotiation was a case of second-party contracting between the PRI and PRD, rather than third-party enforcement by the PRI-state, which was largely a bystander to the process, neither setting the agenda nor enforcing agreements.

Partido de la Revolución Democrática

Situación pos-electoral

MUNICIPIO: *Chiapilla* Chiapas
Municipality

REPRESENTANTE:
Representative

¿SE HAN REALIZADO PLÁTICAS CON EL GOBIERNO U OTROS PARTIDOS PARA BUSCAR UNA SOLUCIÓN A LA IMPUGNACIÓN DE LA ELECCIÓN? SI___ NO **X**
Have you conducted talks with the government and other parties to seek a solution to the election you are contesting?

1. ¿CON QUIÉN SE HA HECHO? *Ninguno*
Who have you talked with?

2. ¿QUÉ RESULTADO HAY? *Ninguno*
What have been the results?

3. ¿QUÉ PROPONE LA AUTORIDAD O LA GENTE DEL PRI?
__ What do the authorities and the PRI propose?

What do our PRD colleagues want?
4. ¿QUÉ QUIEREN LOS COMPAÑEROS DEL PRD?
Negociar con el Partido del PRI los puestos administrativos, que sean repartidos entre ambos Partidos conforme a derecho.

5. DE EXISTIR LA POSIBILIDAD DE HACER GOBIERNOS MUNICIPALES PLURALES ¿ACEPTARÍAN PUESTOS EN LA ADMINISTRACIÓN PÚBLICA? SI **X** NO
If the possibility exists of forming plural municipal governments, would you accept positions?

6. ¿CUÁLES SEAN Y A QUÉ PERSONAS PROPONEN?
What are the positions and who are the candidates you propose to fill them?

PUESTO / POSITION	NOMBRE DE LA PERSONA PROPUESTA / NAME OF THE PERSON PROPOSED TO FILL IT
Secretaria Municipal	Adán Vargas Estrada
Director Obras Públicas	Patricio Mangua Rincón
Regidor	José Luis CHACÓN Barrientos
Juez Municipal	Juan López García Vargas
Encargado de Registro Civil	Pedro Silvano Arcute
Director del D.I.F.	Genaro Gómez Díaz
Presidente Suplente	Rubén Chacón Barrientos
Chofer	Emanuela Pérez Domínguez
Chofer	José Manuel Vásquez Pérez

FIGURE 7.1 1995 Chiapas PRD "Postelectoral Situation" Questionnaire.

the administration?" Collecting information for their starting gambit at the state capital bargaining table, the state PRD activists further queried local affiliates: "Which posts [does the local PRD demand], and who do you propose to occupy each one?" Electoral courts were regarded as trivial from the beginning. Three case studies show how even the shadows of extralegal conflict-resolving institutions were often lost in Chiapas's dark and lawless jungles.[27]

THE CHIAPAS PRD'S FORMULA: MOBILIZATION PLUS STORMING OF TOWN HALL EQUALS MUNICIPAL COUNCIL

The conflict in San Andrés Larráinzar (population 15,100) exemplified the challenge posed by indigenous communities seeking to maintain judicial autonomy in the face of conflicting state and federal law. This rural economic backwater was catapulted to notoriety as the Zapatista-controlled town where peace talks between the EZLN and federal government stalled in 1996.[28] Acknowledged as a true judicial lacuna and "as Chiapas' most genuine post-electoral conflict" (Arias interview), it stemmed from a contradiction in outcomes of traditional *usos y costumbres* and the Chiapas electoral code. During the generations of PRI-state dominion, the community selected leaders through *usos y costumbres* and "ratified" the selection by running the mayor designee with the PRI as the town's unanimous "candidate of consensus" (Jarquin, Arias interviews). Until the mid-1990s, *usos y costumbres* were never recognized but often practiced in hundreds of indigenous municipalities in ethnically heterogeneous states. While not legally recognized in most states, *usos y costumbres* were legalized in the mid-1990s in regions of Oaxaca and Sonora.[29]

Four months prior to the 1995 local races, a massive "straw poll" plebiscite in Larráinzar's town square proclaimed Juan López González as mayor. López González was declared mayor in a nonbinding declaration fingerprint-signed by town officials, and, for the first time ever, he

---

[27] The two not further explored are EZLN-influenced Ocosingo, where a municipal council was formed in lieu of elections after it was decided that elections represented a threat to the area's social peace, and Chilón, where a "white guard" of *PRIísta* ranchers killed several peasants over a long-standing property dispute reopened by the election.

[28] The Larráinzar Accords, granting increased indigenous autonomy, were signed by the federal PRI-state and by the Zapatistas in February 1996, but had still not been enacted in March 2001, when hundreds of Zapatista rebels marched to Mexico City. The accords were thought by many to extend beyond constitutional limits.

[29] In 1995, Oaxaca's electoral law accepted *usos y costumbres* in 412 municipalities (out of 570), where since local authorities wielded absolute control over administration changes, they argued that partisan postelectoral conflicts (as defined by external authorities) were no longer possible. However, unofficial accounts depicted some two dozen conflicts, only one of which was resolved within the parameters of the state electoral code. In Sonora, *usos y costumbres* are also recognized in the state electoral code but only practiced on the Yaquí Reservation (Gutiérrez and Matías 1998).

registered with the PRD rather than with the PRI in the October elections. The disgruntled losing slate in the *usos y costumbres* "straw poll," empowered by a legitimate means of challenging the victor, registered with the PRI and won the election by surprising López González, who, faithful to tradition, neglected to campaign for the "meaningless" party-based election. Without even bothering to file electoral court complaints, the PRD-registered clan took city hall and occupied the building for over two years. The flow of state revenues into Larráinzar stopped, as did the provision of state services there.

The postelectoral crisis in Soyaló (population 7,100) resulted from PRD activists' burning of fraudulent vote counts. The town's state electoral commission representatives (responsible for distributing ballots to precinct heads, tallying them, and reporting results to the state electoral commission) divided over whether to invalidate the results from a ballot box where fraud was widely suspected. When a deadlock was reached over how to proceed, PRD sympathizers burned their party's copy and the official electoral commission copy of the controversial ballot box tally. The PRI representative disappeared into the woods with his copy, reappearing hours later at the state electoral commission, where the party's copy was accepted in lieu of the irretrievable official tally (Luna, Jarquin, Gómez Ruiz interviews, R.Q. resolution 57/A/95, 4–6). Unlike the Larráinzar conflict, the Soyaló case was taken to the state electoral court, where it was procedurally dismissed for lacking an individualized protest writing (Chiapas Electoral Tribunal 1996, 42, 73).

The legal straightjacket of either accepting improper evidence (mere copies of acts required in original form), or encouraging future destruction of such acts by partisans willing to burn the rule of law to win cases on its ashes, was discomforting to electoral court authorities (Espinosa Castro interview). But the net result was still that the electoral court was unequipped to address social tensions enveloping Soyaló. State PRD leaders lamented this evidence tampering, but it was not surprising that individual PRD supporters stooped to such tactics, which had produced two local election annulments in 1991 yielding plural municipal councils that the electoral arsonists hoped for in 1995 (Gómez Maza interview). However, this time the PRD won nothing but instability in the town, where work stoppages, government services shutdowns, and factional animosities prevailed during the three-year town administration (Luna, Jarquin, Gómez Ruiz interviews).

Tensions in Venustiano Carranza (population 51,700) had already escalated by the October elections due to a land tenure conflict between

PRIísta ranchers in a "white guard" vigilante group and a radical peasant organization, called the House of the People (*La Casa del Pueblo*), which had provoked two deaths and three injuries earlier in the year and over a dozen slayings since the 1960s (Harvey 1998, 105, 145, 157). The PRD and House of the People leaders disavowed any real connection, except that the peasant group appropriated the PRD party label to register its candidate. The House of the People conducted a radical postelectoral strategy, taking city hall and risking clashes with the dangerous vigilantes already suspected of involvement in several acts of preelection violence. As lamented by former PRD state president Arturo Luna:

They don't coordinate with us, but only borrow our registry. After the election, they launch their own movement without consulting us, and then, only after it gets them into trouble, do they come to us. How is the party supposed to represent them? This party lacks a lot of formal organization and political culture, but what can we do? (interview)

The state PRD did finally intervene on the House of the People's behalf in postelectoral negotiations with Chiapas's governor, but with little credibility, as government negotiators too understood that the PRD was not party to the House of the People's actions. An electoral court complaint was filed by the PRD, but – characteristically – it was declared unfounded (Chiapas Electoral Tribunal 1996, 40, 81).

House of the People representatives admitted reticence about letting Luna and the PRD represent them, claiming to be more radical than conventional parties and too particular to be understood by outsiders (Abarca interview). Since 1976, when peasants occupied the municipal building for two months before settling for municipal council representation (Harvey 1998, 105), the House of the People had routinely managed their own postelectoral conflicts. But at the national and local levels, the capability of independent (i.e., non-PRI-affiliated) peasant organizations to negotiate with the regime reached their limits in the 1980s, when the House of the People and other local peasant groups formed the Emiliano Zapata Peasant Association (OCEZ) and a national "Plan de Ayala" Coordinating Committee (CNPA) umbrella of thirty such regional groups. Through land takeovers and protest mobilizations to redistribute land, "its actions succeeded in postponing the end of agrarian reform, but it [the CNPA] was unable to articulate an alternative set of proposals to confront the impact of austerity policies, and the reduction of public spending on health and education" (Harvey 1998, 137). While the House of the People's problems ran too deep for electoral solutions, the PRD accepted their cause, albeit reluctantly.

In Chiapas 1995, as in Michoacán 1992, electoral justice was still an oxymoron. However, if a projected future of extensive interaction between the PRD and PRI in Michoacán forced the authoritarians to accept the PRD's existence and end the repression, the PRD in Chiapas had no such strength. Lacking organization and administrative capacity, the PRD in Chiapas managed to bring the PRI to the bargaining table only because of the extrinsic value to the PRI-state of stabilizing municipal governments to avoid Bonifaz's nightmare of Zapatista dominos falling throughout the jungle. No matter that PRD relations with the Zapatistas were even worse than the PRD's poor relations with many of its constituent social movements. The Zapatista rebellion had created a small sovereignty crisis and an epic public-relations disaster both domestically and internationally. Any risk of fanning the flames of local public discontent (equated through this faulty "zero sum" logic with pro-Zapatista sympathy) had to be averted by the PRI-state, even if this meant "auctioning" janitor and librarian's assistant posts to the PRD. Intrinsic party strength, such as in the party's Michoacán stronghold, or extrinsic intangibles, such as the party's perceived moderating influence in Chiapas, were required in the PRD's preconsolidation years to overcome overall weakness, internal divisions, and authoritarian repression. However, I now turn to one of the PRD's greatest post-Oaxtepec local success stories, the Veracruz elections of 1997, distinguished by electoral success and relatively innocuous postelectoral proceedings. But while the PRD's "growing pains" in Chiapas and Michoacán led to that party's eventual consolidation into electoral forces sufficient to win governorships in Chiapas 2000 and Michoacán 2001, apparent party gains in 1997 Veracruz actually divided the party in the medium term.[30]

DEMOBILIZING FOR SUCCESS: THE PRD ADAPTS TO THE ELECTORAL ROUTE IN VERACRUZ

After a slight improvement in postelectoral efficiency during the early 1990s, the post-1995 PRD failed to win more than "symbolic" municipal or state positions at the bargaining table for several reasons:

  1. the ascendancy of post-Oaxtepec reformism rendered *segunda vuelta* threats obsolete (or at least less credible);

---

[30] The Chiapas victory came in coalition with the PAN, which had long coattails after winning the presidential election just two months earlier, but the candidate – while not joining either party – was clearly sympathetic to the "leftist" opposition. In Michoacán, Cuauhtémoc Cárdenas's son won the governorship in late 2001.

2. President Zedillo shut down postelectoral negotiating tables, demonstrating once and for all in the Tabasco governor's race that he was unwilling and/or unable to continue the Salinas tradition of forcing local PRI postelectoral sacrifices for the national PRI (see Chapter 4);

3. The ill-prepared PRD failed on several occasions to judicially defend its own electoral victories, reducing the credibility of electoral fraud in postelectoral negotiations and showing partisans that they needed to defend their votes judicially.

This decline in postelectoral strategy was initially offset by improvements in the party's electoral strategies. In a bitter blow to the antiregime "movement side," the transition-seeking "party side" under Muñoz Ledo's successor, López Obrador, recruited gubernatorial and mayoral candidates among dissatisfied *PRIístas* in numbers unprecedented since the PRD's founding. In 1996, the party assimilated hundreds of high-level former *PRIístas* in the Democratic Convergence, initiated by former Veracruz governor Dante Delgado[31] and including a pool of former PRI activists that produced nearly half of the PRD's two hundred 1997 Veracruz mayoral candidates (including those of Veracruz's twelve largest cities). Former *PRIísta* Layda Sansores, the PRD's 1997 gubernatorial candidate in Campeche, was also recruited to the Democratic Convergence. Registered as an external PRD candidate, she ran a close second to the PRI and launched perhaps the last distended postelectoral conflict of Mexico's protracted transition (lasting some eight months in late 1997 and early 1998).[32] The PRI hemorrhaging to the PRD appeared even more severe in early 1998, as the leftist opposition acquired popular gubernatorial candidates, including Ricardo Monreal Avila, who, until being passed over in January 1998 by the PRI in that party's search for a gubernatorial candidate in the state of Zacatecas, was the highly regarded majority whip for the PRI's federal Chamber of Deputies caucus (Correa and Chávez 1998).

---

[31] Delgado was jailed on corruption charges shortly after leaving the PRI but was released on an appeal in November 1997, after almost a year of organizing the Democratic Convergence from prison.

[32] The gubernatorial election in Tlaxcala 1998 provoked a two-month postelectoral conflict by the losing PRI, and the governor's race in Guerrero 1999 resulted in a two-month postelectoral conflict by the losing PRD. The preelectoral conflict in Yucatán 2001 lasted almost eight months, while the Tabasco 2001 gubernatorial conflict lasted only a few months.

Besides the Mexico City mayors Cárdenas and López Obrador, the PRD's greatest pre-1998 mayoral election success with *PRIístas*-turned-PRD candidates was in Xalapa, Veracruz (capital city of Mexico's third largest state [population 336,300]), the only capital besides Mexico City won by the party since Morelia, Michoacán in 1989. The victorious mayor of Xalapa, a former university rector and *PRIísta* state Interior Secretary running in the Democratic Convergence, was succeeded by another PRD mayor in 2000. Several of the "new PRD's" candidates were tainted by corruption allegations against Delgado. However, former Veracruz PRD state president Domingo Alberto Martínez Reséndiz said that under the party's new pragmatic leadership "elections are to win power, not to exercise morality" (interview). Martínez Reséndiz acknowledged that perhaps better background checks must be performed on external candidates not known to the party but that, overall, the well-received policy has been to field candidates who could win elections, whatever their backgrounds.

Veracruz, where a coalition of pre-PRD leftist parties first endorsed Cárdenas's 1988 presidential bid, spawned dozens of postelectoral conflicts and several municipal councils in the 1980s and 1990s. Several legitimate electoral victories were denied the PAN in the 1980s, and several more were denied the PRD and other leftist parties in the early 1990s (Yuñez Linares interview). Moreover, there existed a strong tradition, predating the PRD, of placating the left with minor administrative posts, such as those negotiated at the Chiapas 1995 bargaining table. In 1988 Veracruz, for example, there were an "infinity" of postelectoral changes in most of the 207 municipal "tickets" (Murguía Velasco 1988) with electoral winners conceding to last-minute substitutes (including some who never even made the ballot) just before taking office, in what came to be known as *gazetazos* (see Chapter 4).

While PRD activists defended their pragmatism as the only way to defeat electoral fraud, critics accused the Veracruz PRD of "selling out" to the party's national headquarters. The national PRD was said to have imposed the Democratic Convergence candidates on Veracruz as per a new national strategy of fortifying electoral results even at the expense of recruiting candidates from outside the party. A partisan of Muñoz Ledo's transition seeking, Martínez Reséndiz lauded the Veracruz PRD's turn to electoral rather than postelectoral victories, even if with dubious candidates from outside the party. He did state, however, that differences existed between the national and state leaderships, exacerbated by national leaders' visits to the state even prior to the 1997 elections and threatening the *segunda vuelta* if electoral laws were not respected. "They can come, make their brash declarations and then go back to Mexico City," Martínez Reséndiz complained. "We have to live with the consequences" (interview).

As in Chiapas, the Veracruz PRD was a hodgepodge of sectors and sects, mixing *segunda vuelta* advocates and more institutional players. Echoing the national PRD's early crises, the state party was so disorganized in 1992 that when native son and former PMS head Heberto Castillo was nominated gubernatorial candidate by Cárdenas and the PRD national leadership, the elder statesman of the Mexican left initially turned his party down, on the grounds that "there are terrible problems in the struggle for local leadership in almost all the state's municipalities... I do not see how, in such an internally divided party, it will be possible to win the governorship" ("Heberto no Quiere").[33]

In the early 1990s, strong local PRD delegates from the indigenous mountain region of the state near San Andrés Tuxtla (population 125,000) ran the party effectively with an emphasis on postelectoral mobilization. Upon "winning" a plural municipal council in 1991,[34] San Andrés Tuxtla and surrounding communities bordering Tabasco launched postelectoral conflicts after the 1994 state and federal elections. Modeled after López Obrador's successful 1991 "Caravan for Democracy," in which scores of peasants from Tabasco and Veracruz marched hundreds of miles to Mexico City, the 1994 local Veracruz mobilizations were more traditional; the PRD took over city hall and formed a "parallel government" ("Instalará el PRD"). In the 1994 federal election, the existence of widespread and provable irregularities in the San Andrés Tuxtla congressional district, challenged by federal PRD "defense of the vote" lawyers, led to annulment of that race in the federal electoral court. The PRD won a special election in 1995, sending the leading *segunda vuelta* radical to Congress and leaving state leadership to the reformers.

Most PRD leaders viewed the San Andrés Tuxtla congressional race annulment as a victory for the legal adjudication of disputes rather than for the extralegal route of contestation that accompanied the filing of the Federal Electoral Tribunal (TFE) complaints. Of the mobilization route, Martínez Reséndiz quipped, "We've been through that," and while it may

---

[33] Castillo did finally accept the nomination, but lost the race by a wide margin.
[34] The Veracruz PRD also "won" membership in the creation of three other plural councils in rural southern Veracruz after 1991, in Angel R. Cabada, Las Choapas, and Filomeno Mata. But these postelectoral victories were largely due to spontaneous local conflicts, rather than to any "trickle down" from Tabasco.

be a stage through which every party must pass, Veracruz has been one of the most successful PRD chapters, based on shifting from "all in a bunch" mobilizing[35] to careful candidate selection, meticulous "defense of the vote," and perfection of the electoral playing field (Martínez Reséndiz interview). However, Martínez Reséndiz's vision turned out to be a noble objective more than a factual description.

In 1998 the PRD was widely accused of imposing "leftovers" from other parties on its militants (e.g., see Musacchio 1998, 39), such as Sansores and Monreal, who, while former PRI stalwarts (like most of the PRD's national leadership), were popular candidates for the PRD to appropriate, especially in states without a prior PRD constituency. Hence Cárdenas, López Obrador, and the PRD national leadership were able to impose external candidacies on fledgling local chapters, which stood only to gain in proportional representation seats and public campaign funding from the presence of such vote draws on gubernatorial tickets. The national leadership drew the line at Veracruz, however, where Cárdenas personally vetted the popular Salinas-era Attorney General Ignacio Morales Lechuga (also a Democratic Convergence member) as 1998 gubernatorial candidate, despite his strong support within the Veracruz PRD. In Cárdenas's view, Morales Lechuga was allied with the PRI-state during its worst anti-PRD transgressions. The controversial candidate was also, according to the Veracruz pragmatists, the only possible PRD candidate who could compete against the PRI's candidate, son of former president Miguel Alemán and part owner of the powerful and unapologetically *PRIísta* Televisa media conglomerate. Morales Lechuga had lost the PRI internal selection and, like Monreal in Zacatecas, approached the PAN before turning to the PRD. He ultimately landed on the ticket of the tiny Worker's Party (PT) and the Mexican Green Ecologists's Party (PVEM), where he lost decisively but drew votes from the PRD. The Morales Lechuga episode left doubt about whether the federal PRD had acted in the best interests of Veracruz, doubts raised prominently even in 2001 during the ongoing rounds of *mea culpas* over the party's poor performance in the 2000 federal elections.[36]

The *segunda vuelta* was largely discontinued by 1997. Rather than denying the opposition victories from state or national headquarters, or

---

[35] This is Mártinez Reséndiz's term "*todos en bola*" (interview).

[36] The PRD's total vote shrank in Veracruz from 680,000 in the 1997 local elections to 320,000 in the 2000 local elections, and the party's growing anti-Cárdenas factions blamed this on the "historical leader's" autocratic decision in the Morales Lechuga case (Jiménez 2001).

storming town halls in the municipalities, the PRI accepted its resounding defeat in the state's half-dozen major cities and more than half of the state's 200 towns. State PRI president Miguel Ángel Yuñez Linares accepted blame for the defeat of what had been the official party, and resigned his post. The electoral court accepted for consideration seventy-four of the eighty-nine cases of inconformity presented by the parties (the vast majority by the PRI and PRD) and issued nineteen "partially founded" or "founded" resolutions. The PRD, not surprisingly, judged the electoral court as having performed its job fairly and there were no harsh recriminations from the PRI or the PAN either. Multiparty competition had arrived in Mexico's third most populous state and was reinforced in 2000, when the PRD and PAN again made important inroads in the state's municipalities, and with only a half-dozen PRD postelectoral conflicts. However, as in much of the country, the PRD lost electoral ground in 2000, blaming negative coattails of Cárdenas's uninspired presidential bid.

CONCLUSIONS: PARTY CONSOLIDATION AS THE BINDING OF THEIR FATE TO BALLOTS

The PRD electoral and postelectoral successes were largely guaranteed in Michoacán, home of some 80 percent of the party's National Executive Committee, even as late as 1990. Cárdenas ruled with a firm grip over the party of followers whose leaders "all worked for him when he was governor" (Yanner 1992, 86). However, the party's dispersion in other regions at that time was quite thin, as observed by former Federal Deputy Leonel Godoy:

When Cárdenas was a [presidential] candidate there was no problem; we could get tens of thousands of votes. But during the local elections when the party had to stand on its own strength, there wasn't enough organization and mobilization to do anything.... (quoted in Yanner 1992, 86)

The party was beset by resource shortages, lack of a core constituency, inexperienced leaders, abysmal communication, and fraud committed in their own internal elections. Yet, as evidenced from Tables 2.1, 2.2, 4.3, 4.4, and Appendix B, the party steadily increased its share of congressional and presidential votes, congressional and mayoral candidate registrations, and election-day poll coverage by party representatives. In addition to offering a place where dissident *PRIístas* and old-time radicals could co-exist, the party provided an alternative to those disenfranchised in the hinterlands of the despotic "old" PRI's strategic vote reserve, galvanized by Cárdenas's Michoacán following and Mexico City residents.

Cárdenas's stubborn but principled insistence on the *segunda vuelta* did not always convince his more patronage-seeking followers, such as Congressman Félix Salgado Macedonio, who revealed the sometime hypocrisy in party strategy after Guerrero's 1989 conflictive elections: "We accept the proposal of shared municipal administrations. But where we have resounding proof of victory, we will not submit ourselves to the capriciousness of the government" (Rueda 1990).[37] In other words, the PRD's postelectoral strategies ultimately could not resolve the PAN's "partial restitution" conundrum either. More bluntly, PRI-state offers of compensation for electoral fraud transgressions would be accepted, but only in cases where the PRD would not have won anyway. Where the PRD won using clean balloting, there would be no negotiation of the "votes of the people," but where the PRD was not certain, its activists would traffic in ballots. This PAN-like pragmatism was effective in very few cases, notably the López Obrador negotiations with the Interior Secretary over Tabasco's 1991 municipal races. Mostly, the PRI-state tolerated human rights–abusing local party bosses and refused outright to negotiate with their electoral enemy. The PRI-state strategy toward the PRD trickled down to local levels in socially conflictive states, where electoral commissions were stacked by the governor, and inaccessible electoral courts denied partisans any recourse to electoral fraud.

Parallel to the national PRD's insistence on the *segunda vuelta*, local party chapters, only loosely connected to federal headquarters, launched their own postelectoral conflicts, almost always under the direction of local social movement leaders rather than national PRD instructions.[38] If the PAN was known for theatrical, federally led, and highly controlled postelectoral mobilizations to draw publicity and pressure the PRI-state in parallel negotiations, PRD mobilizations were spontaneous, locally based, and often quite severe. As noted by a PAN activist in Oaxaca, "The PAN always notifies occupants of building takeovers and leaves a

---

[37] Salgado Macedonio was the PRD's unsuccessful 1999 Guerrero state gubernatorial candidate and postelectoral conflict leader. In 2000 he was elected to the Chamber of Deputies.

[38] Some of the prominent social movements associated with the party have been the Democratic State Assembly of the Chiapanecan People (ADEPECH) and the Rural Collective Interest Union (ARIC) in Chiapas; the Coalition of Workers, Peasants and Students of the Isthmus (COCEI) in Oaxaca; and the Peasant Organization of the Southern Mountains in Guerrero.

back door open so that government employees may exit at any time. The PRD arrives unannounced and takes building occupants hostage, sometimes for weeks" (Moreno Alcántara interview). It was as if there existed one PRD in Mexico City with satellite offices in a few states with party organizations (such as Michoacán and Veracruz) and a set of outposts (such as Chiapas and Oaxaca) where social movements appropriated the party's banner (sometimes without even consulting the party bureaucracy) for their own ends. Former PRD electoral affairs secretary Javier González Garza (interview) said as much: "there are hundreds of actions taken around this country every day in the name of the party which we [the national office] will never even learn of." Which was the real PRD? This was a truly troubling question during the party's founding, but one that grew less important as the party's national headquarters consolidated lines of communication, if not hierarchical control, after Oaxtepec, and especially during López Obrador's party presidency between 1996 and 1999.

If pursuing electoral justice through legal channels did not initially work for the PRD, the extralegal route did not ultimately fare much better nationally nor in state and local elections. Meager municipal council administrative positions were of little consolation, especially when the party's proportional-representation council member or town driver was obstructed from doing his or her job, persecuted, or even killed (recall the more than 150 *PRDista* slayings mentioned in Chapter 4). The PRD's insiders made their discontent clear, voting decisively at Oaxtepec to end Cárdenas's continuous revival of 1988. The entire country may have made it clear in 2000. While the post-2000 search for scapegoats has led to further internal division, especially within the former "rainbow" faction – abandoned by PRD deserter Muñoz Ledo in 2000 after Cárdenas blocked his bid for the party's presidential candidacy.[39] This internal bickering has not led, as in 1988 and 1994, to extended efforts to undermine election

---

[39] The rivalry between former fellow "rainbow" faction members Amalia García (descended from the former communist subfaction) and her 1999 challenger for the PRD presidency, Jesús Ortega, the PRD's Senate leader and Federal Electoral Institute (IFE) representative (still head of the "*chuchos*" subfaction), broadened in October 2000, when he founded the "New Left" faction, vowing to win the party's leadership. The PRD hierarchy's number two leader, Jesús Zambrano, who negotiated the Tabasco 2000 interim governorship after García failed (Garduño Espinosa 2001), joined Ortega, as did longtime electoral pragmatist Villavicencio. García's faction, the *amalios*, came away from the PRD's Sixth National Congress in 2001 fortified but was succeeded in the presidency in 2002 by Rosario Robles, of Cárdenas's faction. Ortega again came in second place.

credibility based on claims ranging from factual to fanciful. Dozens of increasingly pragmatic PRD leaders offered mea culpas and diagnoses of the party's shortcomings in the year after their miserable 2000 performance, but for the first time ever, none blamed their failures on Mexico's electoral institutions.[40]

Rather than looking to the *segunda vuelta*, the more pragmatic among PRD's emergent post-2000 factions placed their stock in the *primera vuelta* or first time around. According to Villavicencio (2001 interview), the PRD learned to respond to complaints filed by other parties as the party started to win local elections by garnering more votes. In 2000, strategists seeking to avoid the embarrassment of 1994 inaugurated classes for activists on documenting electoral irregularities, stepped up efforts to cover all the ballot boxes of important municipalities, and implemented a policy, similar to the PAN's policy, of sending observer notables (national party leaders and legislators) to monitor particularly conflictive races. Rather than promoting social tensions, "we should contain them, and foster more confidence in institutions" (Villavicencio 1998 interview). The rationality of PRD federal electoral complaint filing strategies in 2000, as compared to the "knock-off" barrage in 1994 (see Tables 3.3 and 3.4), substantiates Villavicencio's claim. Indeed, as demonstrated in Chapter 5, the PRD's main obstacle to courting democracy was not failure to adhere to any national democratization pact, nor the weakness of electoral institutions. Rather, the identified cause of PRD postelectoral conflicts was the national party's inability to halt locally originating conflicts or otherwise control local fronts. The party was simply not sufficiently disciplined or farsighted to concern itself with the credibility of institutions, until the party leadership's all-or-nothing antisystem behavior was tempered at the Third National Congress in Oaxtepec and then moderated again with its realization – in scores of separate movements around the country in the late 1990s – that the *segunda vuelta* was not working. At the doctrinal level, the pragmatic legacy of Muñoz Ledo, who quit the party

---

[40] Many leaders offered advice in an unprecedented spirit of self-criticism. Just to cite a few examples: Cárdenas, in joining with political rising star Rosario Robles, his interim Mexico City mayoral successor in January 2001, to launch the "Regeneration" current, accused García of failing to register new PRD members, to which García answered that it was the quality of the members, not numbers, that mattered most (Guerrero 2001). García blamed an antiquated media campaign (Hidalgo and Guerrero 2000), while longtime activist Pablo Gómez argued that factionalism and Cárdenas's stranglehold on the party had ruined its chances (Hidalgo 2000), and Robles told a U.S. think-tank audience that the PRD had lost touch with voters ("Robles Critica en Washington al PRD").

upon having his ambitions repeatedly blocked by Cárdenas, was taken up by López Obrador and by 1999–2002 PRD President Amalia García, in defiance of Cárdenas and post-2002 President Rosario Robles, and was again ratified at the party's Sixth National Congress in 2001, where the party validated negotiations with the rightist Fox administration, but on an issue-by-issue basis.

Formidable internal obstacles to strong PRD electoral showings remain, as exemplified by the extensive fraud in its 2002 and 1999 internal elections,[41] by the party's inconsistency in external candidate selection, by its inefficient coalition building for the 2000 federal elections,[42] by the persistence of Cárdenas as the party's immovable eminence, and, most recently, in the party's post-2000 finger pointing. The PRD threats of postelectoral mobilization in Tabasco 2001 and accusations that the party negotiated the 2001 Morelía, Michoacán mayorship (García 2001) betray PRD claims of having fully abandoned informal institutions as a route to power. But for all its travails, the PRD has established a consistent electoral niche and can develop one in policy making if leaders accept Jesús Ortega's challenge of defining PRD strategies to make it an attractive electoral and governance option – recognizing that it must confront the PAN and the PRI rather than just defining itself as not-the-PRI (Vega 2002b).

If before 2000, the PRD responded to criticism by falling back on pre-Oaxtepec threats and marches when the legal route failed them, the post-2000 PRD has assumed a more responsible role in courting democracy in Mexico, to the point that the party is moving beyond its primordial conflicts over whether to abide by electoral results and institutions. The *segunda vuelta* has rung increasingly false, especially given that improved organization allowed the PRD newfound success in postelectoral complaint filing even before PRD lawyers initiated proceedings that led to

[41] In the PRD's March 2002 internal election, Robles won despite the fact that 17 percent of the voting booths were never opened (Saúl Rodríguez 2002). Despite allegations by Robles's opponent, Jesús Ortega, and others that the election should have been annulled, Robles was declared victor, and Ortega immediately created a training center within the party to make his New Left current "the best prepared for the 2003 federal elections" (Vega 2002a). Despite its irregularities, the 2002 internal balloting was not nearly as corrupt as in 1999, when Ortega lost to García in a second election after the first was annulled due to irregularities that were even more prevalent (Torre 2002).

[42] Undoubtedly the worst decision the party made in the run-up to 2000 was to join forces with several tiny parties that cost them 35 percent of their proportional-representation seats (fourteen of their forty) but that probably added less than 10 percent to the ticket's vote total.

resounding judicial path successes in 2000 Tabasco and Yucatán. The PRD's 1988 intransigence catalyzed Mexico's protracted transition, but that social movement lost momentum upon being formalized as a party. The cunning authoritarian incumbents effectively discouraged a PRD-PAN grand coalition, although as the next chapter illustrates, the PRI-state came apart anyway without one.

8

Dedazo from the Center to Finger Pointing from the Periphery: PRI Hard-Liners Challenge Mexico's Electoral Institutions

> We came in by bullets and will not be removed by votes.
>
> Fidel Velázquez (PRI labor head from 1949 until 1997) (cited in del Collado 2000, 271)

It was the best case scenario from the National Action Party's (PAN) hypothetical *concertacesión* playbook. The sitting Party of the Institutional Revolution (PRI) president congratulates the PAN challenger on the very night of the election, preempting any need to press their postelectoral case through the courts or in the streets. While Vicente Fox's defense of the vote team and the PAN relished their victory and reveled in the fact that they would not have to engage in their usual three-day postelectoral complaint-filing marathons, the *PRIístas* were not so pleased with Zedillo's announcement. Rumors circulated in the days after the election that Zedillo had betrayed his party for a place in history as Mexico's great democratizer. And while being a gracious loser may have been part of Zedillo's bid to be the hero of courting democracy in Mexico, it was viewed as disloyal by a party that held power for generations precisely by valuing loyalty as the highest trait.

If the PRI bureaucracy's immediate response to Zedillo's recognition of Fox was simmering contempt, it boiled over in the following months in a PRI-on-PRI postelectoral conflict in Mexico State claiming dozens of lives and in protests by outgoing governors in Tabasco and Yucatán against the federal electoral court's unprecedented interventions in state elections. Fisticuffs broke out in the Tabasco State Legislature and separatist T-shirts appeared on the streets of Yucatán's capital as frustrated PRI hard-liners attenuated the growing divide between the PRI's dinosaur "vote-getters" and its technocratic state policy makers. The PRI had imploded, leaving hard-liners without incentives to "behave" on the promise of future career advancement. The fissure between the party side and the government side, broadening since technocrat Carlos Salinas's first *concertacesiones* in the late 1980s sought to add the *PANístas* to his political constituency at the expense of PRI traditionalists, had been subjected to increasing stress since 1997, when the PRI lost its Chamber of Deputies simple majority. But even by the mid-1990s, the government's linkage of electoral and policy issues in negotiations with the PAN had grown so pervasive that every *PANísta* vote for a PRI initiative prompted media speculation about which upcoming local election Salinas had ceded in return. Zedillo tried to reverse these trends, but his position had already been weakened by his predecessor's horse trading, by the slaying of Salinas's chosen successor, Colosio, and by the *guerrilla* uprising in Chiapas.

Zedillo's acceptance of Fox, while inevitable, nonetheless caught the PRI traditionalists by surprise. The president seemed to have penned the concession speech without consulting the party's bases, and with a detachment anathema to diehards in "the revolutionary family." Moreover, it demonstrated not only that the party had lost the presidency, but also that the outgoing president, who had distanced himself from the PRI throughout the campaign, seemed to show no remorse about failing to use the full weight of the PRI-state on behalf of its 2000 presidential candidate, Francisco Labastida. The national PRI and its dependent regional and local machines entered a tailspin of finger pointing and mea culpas. Violent internal conflicts resumed, reminiscent of those that had characterized the PRI during its pre–World War II consolidation. In the absence of a strong central authority or stakes to play for, *PRIístas* in the municipality of Chimalhuacán, Mexico State, launched the most potent postelectoral conflict since Michoacán 1992, and the most lethal in-fighting among *PRIístas* since the 1940s. So, ironically, just as the opposition parties had finally traded placards for briefcases, the PRI – formerly the staunch rule-of-law champions – took to the streets in conflicts prompting a dozen deaths among *PRIísta* "dinosaurs" from different clans.

But worst of all, two December 2000 decisions by the Electoral Tribunal of the Judicial Power of the Federation (TEPJF) – one annulling the PRI's narrow 2000 Tabasco gubernatorial victory and the other repelling the intervention of Yucatán's powerful *cacique* governor in that state's 2001 gubernatorial election – turned PRI hard-liners against the very electoral institutions they had stewarded to creation. Throughout

Mexico's impoverished south, where the most recalcitrant PRI governors continued to maintain clientalist ties, the PAN and Party of the
Democratic Revolution (PRD) formed unlikely coalitions to overthrow
the *caciques*. The PAN predictably defended the federal electoral court
against the Yucatán governor's defiance, making states' rights his battle
cry against the *PANístas'* familiar rule-of-law advocacy. Less expected was
the PRD's waving of the rule-of-law banner and declarations that electoral
courts were the first and final means to electoral justice.

This chapter reconsiders changes in PRI-state/opposition relations in
Mexico's protracted democratic transition, but mostly from the *PRIísta*
perspective. I document the bifurcation of the post-2000 PRI into
transition-seeking technocrats (previously the "state" in PRI-state) and
patronage-seeking regional hard-liners still struggling to avert federal intervention and prevent opposition alliances from dismantling their clientalist machines. Adding agency to structural theories of PRI party development focusing on the "traditionalist-technocrat divide" exacerbated
by economic crisis (Centeno 1994, Hernández Rodríguez 1991, Langston
1999), I identify the PRI-state's propensity for *concertacesión* as a catalyst
of this split and as the consequence of two long-standing tendencies that
converged in the 1990s, presidential discretion and PRI-state clientalism,
as the basis for winning support.

I trace the growing breach within the PRI and argue that while all-out
battles among *PRIístas* did not surface until 2000, vestiges of intraparty
division were evident as of 1989, when the first publicized post-1988
concertacesiones were granted to the PAN in the Mazatlán local race. Open
defiance of electoral institutions was evident starting in 1998, when the
party abandoned its seat on the Federal Electoral Institute (IFE) General
Council, and culminated in the 2001 Yucatán executive and legislative
branches' defiance of federal electoral court orders. I review differences in
PAN and PRD strategies vis-à-vis the now-deposed authoritarian incumbent and conclude by considering an issue fundamental to the modality
of the transition, how the opposition parties were able to form a de facto
coalition against the ruling party after years of separately courting democracy in Mexico, but only after an alternation in power had already taken
place. Finally, I consider the evolution of the independent ombudsmen
and electoral courts to the point of attaining an autonomy uncommon
in Mexico's nascent democracy and that has adversely affected desperate
PRI efforts to restore the *status quo ante*.

Amidst the chaos wrought by disgruntled *PRIístas* even back in the
1990s, it was almost easier for presidents Salinas and Zedillo to negotiate

with the PAN's credible leaders than to take their chances with their party's disillusioned rural and sectoral activists. Having signed his "letter of intent" to ally with the PAN in 1989, Salinas sealed this fate repeatedly, as intractable local conflicts increasingly reverberated upward to national negotiating tables. As the PAN extracted escalating costs for joining coalitions with the PRI, the authoritarians faced increasing constraints on choice. As late as 1994, Salinas was thought to possess an almost irrational fear of Cárdenas and the PRD,[1] and the party's Oaxtepec declaration that Zedillo resign so that the PRD might lead a "government of national salvation" did not improve relations. The choice was clear to the authoritarian incumbents. Either they would have to take their chances on further reforming the electoral institution "monster" they had created, and at least gain a partner with whom to finalize Mexico's neo-liberal economic reforms, or they would have to rely on their increasingly belligerent regional PRI machines to defeat the antiregime PRD. The PRI-state consciously chose the former in 1989 and did not renege, even after realizing, some two years before the 2000 electoral watershed, that its era of complete hegemony was over.

Even after its electoral drubbings of 2000, the PRI remained powerful. Although no party possessed a majority in the Chamber of Deputies (and the PRI maintained only a narrow majority in the Senate), the PRI retained a plurality in both houses of Congress, and the *PANista*-led executive branch was acutely aware of its limitations.[2] The PRI in 2001 held more of Mexico's thirty-two governorships than the PAN and PRD combined, and while its gubernatorial losses accelerated after July 2000, the party still retained the most penetrating local networks. The election in 2002 of notorious "dinosaur" leader Roberto Madrazo (the former Tabasco governor who encouraged 1995 and 2000 post-electoral conflicts there) as national PRI president virtually assured that the former "catchall" party would regroup and establish a greater ideological consistency on the center-left. The PRI President Dulce María Sauri, who inconsistently defended the federal cause in the 2000 Tabasco

---

[1] Boylan (2001, 16) quotes longtime Salinas confidant Manuel Camacho as stating: "My impression is that the president never stopped worrying about the possibility that Cárdenas' popularity might grow and that he might win in 1994.... This was true even after 1991 and continued right until the very end."

[2] IFE Citizen Counselor–turned–Assistant Interior Secretary Juan Molinar may have said it best (interview): "We want to turn our situation of divided government – in which no party has a majority in Congress – into one of shared government.... It's hard to say whether we are being generous or just realistic.... We have no choice."

crisis but defended states' rights in the concurrent Yucatán challenge, acknowledged that without a president heading the PRI-state, a large power vacuum existed (Vargas and Méndez 2001). This power vacuum was finally filled in February 2002 by the ubiquitous Madrazo, whose popularity inside the party was attributable to his electoral success (Tabasco 2001 was the first PRI-won governorship after 2000), his decisive – if controversial – leadership, and his time-tested vote-harvesting skills.

The PRI's historic emphasis on discipline was already under siege during the 1980s when the party-state's previously endless use of public resources was cut back with the advent of neo-liberalism, conditioning the regional bosses' loyalty, which had implicitly been traded for ample federal patronage. The PRI's emphasis on rule-of-law institutionalism, long the pillar of its defense of the status quo, started to fray after the party's 1997 mid-term loss of its Chamber of Deputies majority, and came completely unhitched with the party's embarrassing showing in July 2000. Like the PRD during its years as party and movement, the PRI lost control of its followers. No longer restrained by prospects for glorious careers in a national party hierarchy unfettered by resource constraints or electoral competition, regional PRI *cacique* governors all around Mexico – but especially in the clientalistic and impoverished south – unbound themselves, deciding to go it alone. Nowhere was this more evident than in the Tabasco and Yucatán rebellions against federal electoral institution intervention, which also had national-level implications, as even apolitical technocrats and partisan moderates sought to obstruct the disobedient independent electoral institutions they had created. After establishing long-term patterns of executive discretion and clientalism conducive to the Salinas-era logic of *concertación*, I evaluate the direct challenges to federal authority by Tabasco Governor Roberto Madrazo and Yucatán Governor Victor Cervera Pacheco. Then I turn to the national PRI's more subtle recent efforts to discredit the electoral institutions of its making and roll back its own electoral reforms.

PRI-STATE DISCRETION AND PATRONAGE: SHORT-TERM BENEFITS, LONG-TERM LIABILITIES

Recall from Chapter 4 that the president's *dedazo* nomination of governors (who frequently were not even elected), combined with the postrevolutionary norm of no reelection for all elected offices, granted the president extraordinary "metaconstitutional" powers.[3] These powers, consolidated under Lázaro Cárdenas's powerful reign in the 1930s, were legitimized by a series of formal constitutional amendments, some extending back to 1917, as well as through informal practices that evolved during the *maximato* and *cardenista* eras. The president's discretion in selecting who would govern extended from the most lowly village mayor to the presidential successor.[4] And the extension of this discretion to the legislative branch prompted legislator loyalty to their formal and informal nominators in the ruling party, rather than to their constituents or any abstract notion like representation.[5]

No president since Alemán used this discretion as extensively as Salinas, the last PRI president with the strength to use such powers. After the PAN's "near miss" gubernatorial and mayoral candidacies of the 1960s and 1970s, that party was finally "allowed" to win a governor's race in 1989 and was even encouraged to claim mayoral and gubernatorial posts not won at the ballot box, such as the notorious *concertacesión* of Guanajuato in 1991, which Fox ceded to a third-party *PANísta*, Carlos Medina Plascencia, also one of the party's most powerful national leaders. The PRD also sought to exploit the PRI-state's willingness to negotiate, but soon found that this goodwill extended only to the PAN. As elaborated later in this chapter, postelectoral negotiation after postelectoral negotiation distorted the incentives of local and national *PANístas* as well as of local *PRIístas*, undermining the national PRI's unity and local chapter efforts to compete electorally with the opposition. By itself, this trend may not have been so adverse to the PRI. But in tandem with the PRI-state's post–1980s economic crisis resource shortage, the blow was powerful indeed.

---

[3] Garrido actually codifies nine "metaconstitutional" powers (1989, 422–5), including: "establish himself as ultimate authority on electoral matters," "designate successor of his presidency," "designate state governors, members of the PRI majorities in Congress, and most state representatives and mayors," "remove governors, mayors, and legislators at the federal and state levels," and "hold sway over municipal governments, overriding local government autonomy as set forth in Article 115 of the Constitution."

[4] While Zedillo abdicated this power, apparently realizing his party needed the unity derived from picking the most popular presidential candidate through an open primary, Salinas and all PRI presidents before him exercised this power, rigorously documented by Castañeda (1999).

[5] In a revealing survey of members of Mexico's Chamber of Deputies, respondents consistently ranked supporting their president, their party, and their careers as their most important motivations, and fulfilling voter demands and overseeing the executive branch as their least important motivations (Ugalde 2000, 132, 151–6).

The PRI had built its dynasty on loyalty and discipline. While early legitimacy resulted from its initial ideological mission of institutionalizing the Mexican Revolution's objectives of land reform, labor rights, and political enfranchisement, that platform was diluted by the 1940s into symbolism and rhetorical claims without the accompanying public policy. The promise of co-optation of clever opponents, and the threat of punishment if they refused, is widely known to have propelled the PRI-state. As long as the party-state could afford to offer constituency services – albeit discretionary and conditional – citizens would actively support the PRI, especially at election time, or at least acquiesce. As in other protracted transitions, voters in Mexico traded their votes for bicycles, roof laminate, nonperishable bulk foods, or sewing machines.[6]

If PRI recruitment started faltering in urban areas by the late 1980s and early 1990s, when the PRD became a viable alternative for PRI defectors and the *PANísta* volunteers started accepting public funds and professionalizing staffs, the destruction of long-time clientalist practices in rural and impoverished backwaters was much more gradual. Recall that the PRI-state's size shrank drastically in the 1980s, first because of the debilitating Debt Crisis of 1982 and the subsequent years of recession and hyperinflation mentioned in Chapter 2, in which the public sector's share of gross domestic product (GDP) dropped from 44 percent in 1982 to just 31 percent in 1987 (Cypher 1990, 161). Second, the PRI-state continued to shrink even after the economy recovered in the mid- and late 1980s because the solution prescribed by the emerging neo-liberal consensus, increasingly shared by domestic technocrats and international lenders after 1985 as oil revenues fell, was that Mexico's economic growth would have to be financed by external capital. By Thacker's sweeping account (2000, 85), there was still no overwhelming consensus for opening to outside markets in 1985, but it was clear to de la Madrid, who faced increasing electoral challenges and needed new sources of capital, that business support and investment had to be recaptured. By Salinas's term, the alliance between business and the PRI-state included advocates of trade liberalization, privatization of hundreds of state-owned companies, and continued decreases in public spending. De la Madrid had launched

---

[6] All of these examples are from the Yucatán 2000 federal election alone. For other examples of the historical pervasiveness of exchanging goods for votes throughout Latin America, see Posada-Carbó (2000). For more contemporary examples, see Cornelius (1975) and Fox (1994) on Mexico, von Mettenheim (1998) on Brazil, Barkan and Okumu (1978) on Kenya, and Rigger (1994) on Taiwan.

the North American Free Trade Agreement (NAFTA) trade coalition, and provoked the first ideological debate within the ·"catchall" PRI in generations, referred to in the political economy literature as pitting apolitical policy-maker "*técnicos*" against machine-boss "*políticos.*"

But the breach also had profound electoral implications, as partisans were reminded with each *concertacesión.* It forced a confrontation between a new ascendant national PRI directorate – epitomized by the Salinas and Zedillo economic policy secretariats and valued for formal education and technical skills – and the state and local electoral activists. Once rewarded with high-visibility government posts and positions of responsibility with the party, the PRI's electoral activists were being cast aside between elections and disdained by the new elites as political "hacks." Except for the Salinas-Zedillo appointments to the Interior Secretariat and traditionally clientalist secretariats like agriculture, labor, agrarian development, and patronage-granting parastatal companies (mostly headed by partisan ex-governors), commitment to scientific models was prized over practical experience by the *técnicos,* who wielded considerable authority even beyond the executive's dictates (Williams 2002, 407). Aside from Salinas's realization that the PRI's damaged electoral machine needed immediate attention, epitomized by his selection of the ill-fated bridge-builder Colosio, the kudos all went to the economic reformers, whose dominions even extended to traditionally "political" secretariats like education and social development. These social service provision ministries were "ground zero" in the battle between the clientalism-driven *PRIístas* and those pursuing technical rationality.

In social policy, a direct contradiction arose between the technocrats' desire to target cost-effective welfare programs where they would have the greatest impact, and the PRI's traditional imperative of pork-barreling largesse for votes. While the clever implementers of Salinas's trademark social program, Solidarity, seemingly reconciled the dilemma by efficiently targeting well-programmed spending, but in areas of greatest PRI electoral need rather than in those of highest economic marginality (Molinar and Weldon 1994), Jonathan Fox argues that by the late 1980s policy makers did seek to ameliorate poverty using technocratic tools. "State managers replaced their traditional crude insistence on ruling party control with more subtle forms of controlling access to the system," Fox writes, warning that they were still not pluralistic because they "discourage any questioning of the government's broader socioeconomic policies and its controversial electoral practices" (Fox 1994, 160).

Furthermore, Jonathan Fox allows that programs designed to replace PRI-state discretion with objective needs assessment may actually have increased local *PRIísta* reliance on electoral fraud to offset the diminishment of direct clientalism by the nationally directed program managers (Fox 1994, 160–1), a hypothesis consistent with the early 1990s escalation of local PRI postelectoral conflicts and internal strife. Indeed, in a plausible extension of this reasoning, Fox proposes that the downgrading of exchange relations from clientalistic to semiclientalistic (in which deals are unenforceable) may actually have made electoral fraud even more credible to opposition parties and the electorate more broadly (Fox 1994, 161). The reason is that coercion previously used by the PRI-state to violate the secret ballot was no longer available, thus increasing uncertainty among those who welshed on deals with the PRI about whether their neighbors were also violating unenforceable agreements.

CONCERTACESIÓN AS ORIGINAL SIN: PRIMORDIAL WEDGE BETWEEN LOCAL AND NATIONAL *PRIÍSTAS*

Whatever the size of the national PRI-state's coffers, resourceful PRI machine bosses with supporters loyal to them rather than to the national party were unwilling to mothball their clientalist networks until election time while their careers withered and the party was taken over by professional bureaucrats who had never held public office and had few if any stakes in the party. Furthermore, they were increasingly frustrated by national PRI-state decisions to confront the PAN and Cardenísta threats through *concertacesión* rather than through patronage, heightened electoral campaigning, and the reduced margin for "patriotic fraud," the traditional PRI's strong suit. Starting in 1989 with President Salinas's tolerance of Ernesto Ruffo's Baja California victory in the first PAN governorship permitted ever, local PRI leaders in "victimized" areas blamed the PAN and their own national PRI leadership for forcing them to grant *concertacesiones* throughout the 1990s. These costs were perhaps most vividly evident in the 1995 Tabasco "Rebellion of the PRI," where the local PRI actually took up arms against the PRD. But the national PRI apparatus paid a much higher price overall for its negotiations with the PAN, commencing with the 1989 Mazatlán mayor's race and escalating with the Guanajuato governor's race and the Sonora mayoral races in 1991. Throughout the early 1990s there were dozens of PRI-PAN *concertacesiones*, but they did taper off after 1995.

The annoyance of local PRI activists upon winning elections only to have their victories stripped away did little for local PRI chapter morale or for the promotion of electoral competitiveness among the ranks. Contradictions between the PAN's calls for state electoral autonomy and threats to blackmail national policy making whenever their local electoral fancies were not tickled were not lost on savvy PRI activists (see interviews with Manjerrez, Martínez Escobar, Moreno Uriegas, Núñez, Sandoval, etc.). Indeed, these contradictions offered a window on tensions between the PAN's transition-seeking advocates of strong institutions and the party's pragmatic patronage seekers. The division within the PAN was seized upon by the national PRI, which also divided with local chapters on whether to consummate *concertacesiones*. The PRI's ironclad discipline, epitomized by the oft-cited quote "whoever moves does not come out in the picture" (Camargo 1998a),[7] came apart precisely over this issue.

The *PRIístas* most disturbed by the national party's penchant for negotiating away their turf were without a doubt the powerful "syndicate of governors."[8] Governors like Bartlett in Puebla, as well as Cervera Pacheco in Yucatán and Madrazo in Tabasco, were not used to having their wills vetoed, legally or otherwise, especially not by their party's highest member and his presidential cabinet. Several of these governors met on occasion, with the topic of *concertacesiones* always high on their agenda. In fact, at the height of the 1996 Huejotzingo controversy, a half dozen of these governors issued a statement that rather than encouraging negotiations that circumvented the law, postelectoral conflicts needed to be resolved "at the local level, because we are believers in state sovereignty, that there exist laws and authorities at that level" (Sánchez and Castellanos 1996).

These governors and other regional bosses had increased their power within the party bureaucracy since the PRI's 14th Assembly in 1990, when, reacting against the party's traditional corporatist pillars, the National Executive Committee redistributed votes from these pillars to the states, according to a new "territorial" logic that was supposed to make the party more electorally accountable (Hernández Rodríguez 1998, 82). In practice, this reform merely fortified the governors, especially when complemented, at the PRI's 16th Assembly in 1996, by another reform requiring

---

[7] This quote is originally from Fidel Velázquez, the PRI's labor sector *cacique* for over forty years (see del Collado 1998, 4), but has been adopted into the party's lexicon.

[8] Bartlett repeatedly denied the existence of any organized "syndicate of governors" under his leadership, until his own exploratory campaign for the PRI's 2000 presidential candidacy led him to acknowledge the existence of such a group and announce their endorsement of his candidacy (Chávez Cruz 1998).

all gubernatorial or presidential aspirants to have served ten years in the party and have held prior electoral office (Hernández Rodríguez 1998, 91). By requiring its highest officials to have culled electoral bases, the PRI fortified career politician governors and their networks of mayors and local activists at the expense of the "technocratic" policy makers who had dominated national government since the mid-1980s.

The traditionalists tried – but failed – to insert a clause in the PRI's internal statutes, at the party's 16th National Assembly in 1996, that would expel party officials who cut *concertacesión* deals ("Rasuran Acuerdos"). While the governors' influence in the PRI's National Executive Committee grew in the 1990s, local activists were increasingly frustrated by actually having to compete in and win elections. And if that was not bad enough, they found themselves campaigning and winning only to be "burned" at the bargaining table. They launched postelectoral conflicts of their own, numbering over 180 during the twelve years studied. Postelectoral conflicts by *PRIístas* were not unheard of in earlier decades, but they were usually quarrels between *PRIístas* over internal candidate selection, not to be underemphasized, because, as per V. O. Key's dictum for the one-party-dominant U.S. South, "the primary's the election" (1994, 407).

Battles between PRI factions over local candidate nomination, either between local *caciques* or between the dictates of the center and a local *cacique*, grew increasingly belligerent with the advent of political competition after 1977. In 1979, the army intervened after losing faction *PRIístas* burned a half-dozen city halls in Chiapas (Guillén 1998, 195). Dozens of PRI candidate selection feuds erupted between national party delegates and local political machines in Oaxaca during the early 1980s (Martínez Vázquez and Arellanes Meixueiro 249–50), and organized internal opposition to PRI candidate selection was quite common in 1980s Guerrero, Hidalgo, México State, Puebla, Tabasco, Tlaxcala, and Veracruz (Alonso 1985, 356–7), to name a few. In the late 1980s and the 1990s, these feuds still found expression, such as in Oaxaca 1989, where some forty of the state's municipalities contested the party's candidate selection; Tabasco 1991, where dissident *PRIístas* burned their party's own municipal headquarters; San Luis Potosí 1992, where the internal selection losers staged hunger strikes; and Veracruz 1991, Hidalgo 1994, Yucatán 1995, Chihuahua and Mexico State 1996 and 2000, and Morelos 1997, where dissidents from the ruling party also occupied government buildings.

However, compared to previous decades, when intra-PRI rivalries prompted hundreds of preelectoral conflicts rather than mere scores of them, the 1990s were a decade of moderation. In the era of multiparty competition these intra-PRI quarrels were complemented by bona fide PRI postelectoral conflicts when they lost local elections. Hence, they protested losing in a myriad of ways and places, from Sonora 1991, where they ransacked a town and burned down city hall, to the Tabasco 1995 standoff against the removal of a governor, to Yucatán 1998, where PRI state legislators traded blows with the PRD on the floor of the state legislature rather than admit a federal electoral court–mandated extra PRD legislator. At the postelectoral level, over two-thirds of the 186 conflicts by *PRIístas* between 1989 and 2000 were with other parties, while nearly half of the close to fifty attributable to internal PRI dissent were launched by extremist "white guard" vigilantes only loosely affiliated with the party, such as *Antorcha Campesina* and *Paz y Justicia*. While such groups conducted marches, building takeovers, and even shootings under the PRI's banner, the formal party organization did not sanction such acts.

SOUTHERN POLITICS, MEXICAN STYLE

In the mid-1990s, *concertacesión* agreements with the PAN started to trickle down, as PRI-state loyalists found that they could "whitewash" adverse electoral results through crooked subnational electoral institutions. Indeed, the Huejotzingo controversy in Puebla 1995 (Chapter 6) was an important antecedent to the 2001 Yucatán standoff. Then-governor Bartlett pressured Puebla's electoral court to let a fraudulent but close PRI victory stand in a small town where economic interests sought to construct a new airport. Inspired PAN leaders with extensive legal evidence and serendipity stalled broad roundtable talks in the national Congress, linking a return to negotiations to the "stealth" resignation by the declared PRI victor in favor of a *PANista* interim mayor. This *cause celebre* of the PAN led directly to the 1996 electoral reforms giving the federal electoral courts appellate jurisdiction over local elections (Ojesto 2001 interview). But the case also improved Bartlett's national standing, making him an advocate for "true federalism" who sought to increase local control over affairs of his state, even when – as in most cases – resources were federally generated. It was hardly surprising that defeated 2000 PRI presidential-primary candidate Bartlett emerged as one of the strongest supporters of Cervera Pacheco's battle to ignore the federal electoral court.

The other important precursor to the Yucatán showdown was the TEPJF's watershed decision scant days earlier, when it annulled the 2000 PRI gubernatorial victory in Tabasco based on extensive circumstantial evidence rather than on a singular "smoking gun." The electoral court credited several "indicators of electoral fraud" in annulling that election: electoral authorities' insistence on opening all the preliminary results statewide without justification, the dramatic electoral authority–recognized PRI monopoly on television publicity and news coverage, the location of contraband electoral materials such as ballots at a PRI-contracted survey research firm, and compelling but circumstantial evidence that Madrazo had mobilized public resources for the campaign.[9] While the electoral court magistrates argued that they had been gradually amassing tools of judicial activism to render the powerful verdict (Reyes Zapata interview), the political parties and especially the PRI, accustomed to a servile electoral court, were shocked.[10] The antielectoral court hostility, combined with pro-Yucatán and anti–Mexico City bias, made for a compelling populist appeal, which Yucatán House Speaker Myrna Hoyos and Governor Cervera Pacheco immediately seized upon, positing themselves as patriot decentralizers.

Governors such as Mario Villanueva Madrid in Quintana Roo had publicly opposed federal intervention in local races at least since its implementation in 1996, but never with the firmness of the Yucatán PRI.[11] Governor Cervera Pacheco's argument, that the electoral court's intervention in December 2000 to select a slate of state electoral commission citizen counselors was a violation of the federal pact, was unsubstantiated. Contrary to claims widely circulated within Yucatán by venerable constitutionalist Ignacio Burgoa Orihuela that the federal electoral court overstepped its bounds by selecting Yucatán's citizen counselors in Mexico City, the federal electoral court was empowered to do so under Mexico's constitution. Judicial authorities (Orozco 2001 interview) insisted that unchallenged precedents did exist for direct federal interpretation of

---

[9] The decision reached was a 4–2 split vote (with one abstention). The dissenting opinion did not dispute the patterns of irregularity but questioned whether they were sufficiently grave so as to annul the election (Barba and Medina 2001). Tribunal President Ojesto, having stated in a regrettable and highly publicized offhand comment to a reporter that the Tabasco race seemed fair, decided to abstain.

[10] The federal court had just granted the PRI additional proportional-representation seats in the Mexico City Council, and the party expected similar treatment in other matters. In truth, the electoral court had reached many prior anti-PRI verdicts, but none of grave consequence.

[11] Villanueva, who went on the lam before being arrested in early 2001 on drug trafficking charges, fanned the flames of state sovereignty in a speech to inaugurate the IFE and TEPJF's Third International Conference on Electoral Law before 600 electoral law specialists (Moncisbays Ramos 1998).

state electoral laws and of election-related state legislature acts. The original violation of the Yucatán electoral code was self-evident; the electoral commission ombudsmen required approval by a four-fifths majority (or twenty of twenty-five members of the unicameral body), and only fifteen legislators approved the initial slate.[12] In October 2000, the TEPJF ruled that the Yucatán legislature had selected its electoral commissioners illegally and called for a new selection.

The Yucatán legislature, led by Speaker Hoyos, who had committed the first act of open defiance of the TEPJF ever in 1998,[13] agreed initially to uphold the electoral court decision, reselecting the same slate of electoral commissioners, but with the needed twenty votes. However, irregularities in this process prompted the electoral court to intervene again – requesting stricter adherence to the original verdict, which the Yucatán legislators were no longer willing to undertake. The contradiction of first accepting the electoral court decision and then backtracking and declaring it unconstitutional was not lost on legal analysts, and Hoyos and Cervera Pacheco were not deterred by their inconsistency. Nor was PRI national president Sauri, the Yucatán ex-governor who resigned over the 1993 *concertacesión* of Mérida to the PAN (Chapter 6), and who sided with Cervera Pacheco against the Mexico City electoral authorities.

Waving a banner of state autonomy and even threatening succession from the union, Cervera Pacheco found political resonance in defying the electoral court verdict. His "*Yucatecos* versus the Mexico City bureaucrats" campaign, resoundingly endorsed by 95 of the state's 106 mayors, boosted the governor's popularity and even spurred the printing of "Republic of Yucatán" T-shirts, which tapped resentment of the region's

---

[12] The Yucatán state legislature consisted of fifteen *PRIístas*, eight *PANístas*, and two *PRDístas* (Lujambio 2000, 161).

[13] In that case, the Yucatán legislature initially refused to grant the PRD its last proportional-representation seat in the state legislature. The seat was significant as it overturned the PRI majority in the legislature, immediately opening the possibility of impeachment proceedings against Cervera Pacheco (which never materialized). After losing in a suspicious midnight Yucatán appeals circuit session and amid cries of "Another embarrassing *concertacesión!*" (Quintal 1998), the PRD filed an appeal to the federal electoral court, which ruled in the PRD's favor and forced the local PRI to "stand down." A classic "whitewashing," the reversal came after days of federal pressure from the PAN's legislative faction. The party threatened withdrawal from national legislative-executive negotiations over a PRI-proposed banking system bailout for which PAN congressional support was needed. Immediately after the pro-PAN Yucatán court decisions, the *PANísta* legislators returned to the bargaining table, conditioning their cooperation on continued Yucatán government compliance (see "Regresan, Luego de Concertacesión," and Camargo 1998b).

historical subordination to the center.[14] Moreover, he caught the federal electoral authorities between two poor options – ordering enforcement of their verdict using public force or failing to intervene, losing credibility, and opening future decisions to second-guessing by emboldened *caciques*. The Interior Secretariat, long the final bargaining table where conflicts were resolved, hesitated to get involved; its functionaries argued that rather than resorting to strong-armed "good cop, bad cop" tactics of the past, it should be merely a "negotiating space."[15] Even President Fox, himself a veteran of the 1991 Guanajuato *concertacesión*, did not want to intervene. After establishing his noninterventionist position in the Tabasco crisis,[16] Fox insisted that the Yucatán legislature was responsible for following the federal electoral court's dictates and that his government planned not to intervene because "the *yucatecos* have the ability to resolve their own issues and I'm sure they are going to do so" (Olvera Aguirre 2001).

The proposed solution, which allowed federal authorities to bide their time while Cervera Pacheco played out all options short of violence, was for the federal electoral court to name a "legal" Yucatán electoral commission to compete with the "illegal" Yucatán legislature–ratified electoral commission. Not unlike the Puebla 1983 "Peoples' Tribunal" to publicize electoral fraud, the Chihuahua 1986 "Peoples' Jury," and the 1994 "Electoral Defender of the People of Chiapas," dueling institutional focal points were found to be the best means of distending conflict. However, the overwhelming difference between the Yucatán 2001 electoral commissions and the Puebla, Chihuahua, and Chiapas "peoples'" electoral courts was that this time the legal authorities had opted for the duality as a means of stemming conflict, whereas in the prior cases, the opposition parties and other societal interests had initially chosen to vent conflict through those institutions.

[14] Cervera Pacheco himself cited a celebrated 1840 effort by Yucatán to win independence from Mexico, but then insisted that "this does not mean, as tomorrow you [the media] will say, that we are preparing to separate . . ." (Mendoza 2000).

[15] Molinar (interview) noted that with the legal reform that stripped the Interior Secretariat of much of its intelligence-gathering and coercive functions, it had been left primarily as a negotiating space. Furthermore, he said that the demise of the PRI greatly reduced the role of his office. "There used to be two PRIs, the one which won elections from party headquarters and the one which governed the country from this building. That is no longer the case."

[16] In one of the new president's more colorful quotes, Fox announced, "This is an issue for Tabasco to decide and not for the Federal Executive, which has powers clearly delineated in the constitution, which nowhere states that we should go around sticking our noses to see what happens in the states. Other presidents were accustomed to doing that, but it is not happening now, nor will it" (Garduño 2001).

The duality was intended to demonstrate the credibility of government institutions, rather than detract from this credibility. With the electoral court's selection of the second Yucatán electoral commission, institutional credibility in Mexico had graduated to a second intermediate step, recourse to the PAN's "partial restitution" logic, but by electoral court authorities. The solution to the Yucatán conflict was political, as the commission appointed by the legislature received the $4 million budget for conducting the May 2001 elections, but the electoral court–appointed commission received the nominal list of voters, which was routinely provided by the IFE to each state's electoral commission. Because each side had something to offer, a political deal had to be cut so that the federal electoral court could save face. But Cervera Pacheco did not desist until the Mexican Supreme Court finally ruled in April 2001 that combining the two electoral commissions into one "super-commission" was illegal. The Cervera Pacheco–backed commission (formally named by the PRI-dominated legislature) finally "stood down" to allow the naming of a compromise electoral commission to organize elections some six weeks hence.

The significance of the Yucatán standoff against the federal electoral court was not only the sudden clout it ascribed to the long-ignored electoral court, but also that it was the most important articulation of anti–Mexico City "federalism" in a decade. Disenchanted electoral losers had challenged the imposition of *PRIísta* "winners" through similarly extended protests after gubernatorial contests in Tabasco 1994, Michoacán 1992, Guanajuato 1991, San Luis Potosí 1991, and of course Chihuahua 1986. But in each of those other cases, the opposition challenged impositions by the PRI-state on the localities. In conflicts with *PANístas* prior to Yucatán 2001, the discontented could be classified into two groups, the disaffected local *PANístas* disturbed by the often outrageous levels of electoral fraud, and the even more agitated local *PRIístas*, upset at being "sold out" to national-level PAN/PRI *concertacesiones*. Conflicts with the PRD were usually less complex, involving only frustrated local *PRDístas* irritated at their inability to counter the PRI-state's electoral fraud and even repression, and further distraught by their inability to open informal negotiations with the PRI-state, as they lacked the PAN's conduits.

The Yucatán conflict altered all of these patterns in several important ways. First, the protesters who occupied the state electoral commission for two months were all *PRIístas*, breaking the opposition-led protest dynamic of the past. Second, the hard-liner-led national PRI was united with the local Cervera Pacheco machine in opposing the federal electoral court ruling, against the PAN-led federal government and PRI moderates. Third, contrary to past patterns of Interior Secretary intervention, the national government was loath to take sides. Fourth, the protesters' ire targeted a legal decision, justified by an emerging field of law and legal institutions, rather than the usual arbitrary *concertacesión* (or lack thereof, in PRD cases).

The electoral court's decision to select its own Yucatán Electoral Commission was all the more powerful coming on the heels of the landmark Tabasco gubernatorial case. While national PRI president Sauri inconsistently accepted the federal electoral court's annulment of the Tabasco governor's race while refusing to allow federal electoral court meddling in her home state's gubernatorial race, the national PRI largely heeded her position. A few moderates bucked the PRI, but most remaining supporters unquestioningly toed the party line. Contradictions with all those decades of PRI rhetoric praising law, reason, and constraint by those who had stewarded the development of autonomous electoral institutions – even while seeking not to actually use them – were exposed. At their worst, the PRI's new leaders appealed to base instincts of mob rule and threatened their clientalist bases; at their best they enlisted the populist anti–Mexico City themes of regionalism, federalism, and sovereignty to justify disobeying federal mandates. While their strong and defensive post–July 2000 stance conveyed surprise and desperation, many in the PRI perceived, as early as 1997, that their electoral institutions were reforming themselves beyond the control of their creators. Before their institutional attention shifted to refuting the TEPJF after 2000, *PRIísta* hard-liners focused their efforts on repealing the autonomy of the IFE.

CONCERTACESIÓN BUT WITH NO DEAL CLOSER: THE POST-1997 PRI EFFORT TO DISCREDIT IFE

The new electoral authorities noted immediately after being named late in 1996 that a split was occurring between the electioneering PRI and the governing PRI. One of the IFE's new "citizen counselor" ombudsmen noted that the PRI-state's expectations for the unknown scholars-turned-ombudsmen were deceivingly low (Cárdenas interview) and that the PRI-state had approved their nominations precisely because of their apparent malleability. However, the IFE's policy makers immediately dispelled such notions, investigating campaign spending violations against the PRI's most controversial machine boss, Governor Madrazo.

In perhaps its most significant pre-2000 verdict, the federal electoral court validated the IFE's inquiry in principle. However, in practice the electoral court, following a logic described by critics as highly political, ruled that the statute of limitations had expired. The IFE was correct in investigating Madrazo's alleged improprieties, but time had run out on its ability to do so. The ruling faintly hinted at the electoral court's soon-to-emerge independence, blown wide open in the 2001 Yucatán case and in 2002 and 2003 rulings to support rigorous IFE investigations of campaign finance improprieties by both Fox and Labastida. But unlike the IFE, which was freed from partisan bonds to the PRI-state with the multiparty nomination of the 1997 ombudsmen, the electoral court's uncoupling from the PRI-state awaited defeat of the magistrates' *PRIísta* nominators in 2000. A broad collegial policy-making council presided over by entrepreneurial ombudsmen rather than a legal court of narrow jurisdiction, the IFE was predictably the first electoral institution the PRI rejected. Reminiscent of the PAN's successful departures from the bargaining table in 1995 over Huejotzingo, the PRI withdrew its party representative from the IFE General Council in November 1998.

The PRI's five-month IFE walkout was the beginning of the PRI's transformation from confident rulers to beleaguered loyal opposition.[17] In a strategy suggestive of an opposition party more than of the dominant party that had presided over the IFE's very creation, the PRI-state exacted a heavy public-relations cost. How could an electoral institute established to mediate party interests function without the presence of the largest party? The PRI's boycott dissipated in March 1999, when party moderates, seeking to bolster the electoral institutions they still thought would legitimize their 2000 victory, realized that the party's interest was in reinforcing the IFE's authority. As summarized by Labastida advisor Sandra Fuentes-Berain in the run-up to 2000 (interview):[18] "We don't want to shoot our own foot by discrediting IFE."

Contemporary to its emerging difficulties in controlling the IFE, the PRI lost its absolute majority in the Chamber of Deputies, grew increasingly

---

[17] Schedler (2000, 388) traced the PRI's discontent back to October 1997, when several of the new ombudsmen – opposed by the ruling party – challenged the objectivity of Executive Secretary Felipe Solís. Suspicions of Solís's partisanship was warranted; in late 2000, PRI Congressman Felipe Solís was named the party's Secretary for Electoral Action.

[18] This group interview was conducted by the author and three other members of the Carter Center's preelectoral mission, headed by Robert Pastor, then of Emory University.

defiant of the new electoral rules, and increased its postelectoral partic
ipation both in the courts and on the streets. In a national-level pattern
replicated in many states, the PRI went from the least-frequent filer of
complaints in 1988 to the most-frequent filer in 2000 (see Table 3.4).
Starting in the early 1990s, the PRI had established a national office to
coordinate defense of the vote campaigns, publish "defense of the vote"
guides, and mobilize teams of attorneys nationwide for postelectoral pro
cesses. But it was really not until 2000 that the party fully mobilized its
legal structure to file electoral complaints and "loose cannon" partisans
in Mexico State launched the party's most severe postelectoral conflict
in generations. As demonstrated, the PRI's outward reactions were quite
evident starting in 1997 to the end of the party's monopoly over electoral
institution control. Less empirically evident, but even more important,
was the growing breach between the local *PRIístas* and the national PRI-
state, exploited so masterfully by Cervera Pacheco in 2001 but which had
already begun to widen more than a decade earlier.

COMPLIANT PARTIES AND RISK-TAKING MAGISTRATES CONSOLIDATE DEMOCRATIC GAINS

Disembodied from the state apparatus that had nourished it for seventy-
one years, the PRI grew even more desperate in the mea culpa months of
late 2000. Casting aside the electoral institutions they had tolerated – and
even promoted – as PRI-state, the PRI's national leadership backpedaled
strategically to the heyday of *concertacesión* with the PAN, behaving as
if their "price" for placidly accepting Labastida's defeat was the governorship of Jalisco, Mexico's fourth most populous state. Reminiscent of
the PAN's threats to boycott Zedillo's inauguration if the *PANista* mayor
of Monterrey was not recognized, the PRI threatened to diminish Fox's
legitimacy by not attending his inauguration if the *PANistas* did not agree
to a ballot-by-ballot recount of the Jalisco election. Also true to the *concertacesión* era, the PRI and the PAN sat down at a bargaining table with the
outgoing Interior Secretary to hammer out a deal. However, the *PANistas*,
entering office in a matter of days, did manage to stall negotiations and de-
fer the angry national PRI leadership to the federal electoral court, where
they began to pressure for "relief." However, Castillo Peraza's hypothetical *concertacesión* playbook had been written with the assumption –
which no longer held for the *PANistas* – that they were the underdogs. No
matter that Salinas had conceded such deals from a position of strength;
they would not make such errors of judgment.

The federal electoral court refused to whitewash the Jalisco gubernatorial election, increasing the vast political distance between Jalisco 2000
and Monterrey 1994. After months of verbal recriminations, the PRI's
poorly argued case – in which the party violated the appeals process by
changing its argument between the initial hearings in the Jalisco electoral court and the federal appeal – was ruled as mostly unfounded in
February 2001, leading to further – unfounded – attacks against the electoral court (Granados Chapa 2001). By the admission of its own legal
advisor (Zazueta Félix interview), the *PRIístas* were the last to realize that
the electoral courts had become real, whatever the PRI-state's intentions
when they allowed the creation of these institutions.

The PAN had used the idealized norm of electoral justice and parliamentary persistence to push for electoral court creation for over fifty years.
The PRD had finally learned to use the courts masterfully as a check
against the most heinous regional PRI machine bosses. Despite progress
by the regime's opponents, many in the PRI – even in 2000 – still perceived
the federal electoral court as another accouterment to disguise their authoritarian regime. But the electoral court justices – after a decade of
developing electoral law, increasing their autonomy from the PRI-state
one dissenting vote at a time, and, ultimately, achieving total independence in July 2000 when their nominators lost reelection – had always
envisioned a more important fate. The federal electoral court's inscrutably
legally and politically dispassionate Jalisco ruling (disseminated over the
Internet at www.trife.gob.mx) confirmed the electoral court's professionalism and exposed the widening breach between the diehard *PRIístas'*
efforts to cling to the past and the moderates' escalating embarrassment
with their own party. Rather than being pulled together by an emerging leader, the internal division only pushed PRI partisans further apart,
prompting postponement of the election of new national leadership (originally slated for 2000) to 2002.

The federal electoral court in May 2002 ruled in favor of the PRI in
a ruling every bit as significant as the precedent-setting annulment of
Tabasco, the governor's challenge over Yucatán, and the national PRI's
blackmail threats over Jalisco. The TEPJF ruled that the IFE had the right
to follow the money trail of Fox's campaign expenditures to its origin. The
IFE's investigation, first launched by a PRI complaint in June 2000 and
still continuing three years later, had landed early in 2002 at the doorsteps
of several private businesses, which had sought cover behind Secretary of
the Treasury "bank account privacy" statutes. The electoral court over-
ruled these allegations – demonstrating its fortitude and independence yet

again – and gave the IFE authority to investigate the allegations against Fox's campaign. While suspicions had not yielded formal allegations yet in early 2003, this enhanced authority to investigate was also applied to federal investigations that Labastida had received illegal campaign funds laundered through Petróleos Mexicanos (PEMEX). And in 2003, this IFE investigation did culminate in a fine against the PRI of some U.S. $10 million. Through all of these verdicts, the federal electoral court established itself – along with the IFE and perhaps Mexico's human rights ombudsman – as the premier formal institution stewards of Mexico's democratization. The electoral court, still presided over by Magistrate Ojesto Martínez Porcayo, a holdover from the original 1988 court, had gone from being a laughingstock to a formidable guardian of democratic rights. The PAN and the PRD had lived the consolidation of electoral court authority. The PRI was only forced to reckon with this fact after 2000.

PORK-BARRELING WITHOUT THE CHOPS: A DOWNSIZED PRI FACES ELECTORAL COMPETITION

While the PRI's legendary federal-level discipline broke down only recently, local-level PRI affiliates frequently took matters into their own hands well before 2000. Local leaders increasingly turned to postelectoral mobilization,[19] especially during local affiliates' initial experiences with losing elections in areas where postelectoral conflicts were successful, such as in Oaxaca, where work stoppages and building takeovers in Juchitán 1992 led to a plural municipal council with PRI participation, and in Tlaxcala 1998, where *PRIístas* shut down public administration for weeks after losing the governorship to a former *PRIísta* in the PRD. Recall that there were over four PRD postelectoral conflicts for every one by the PRI, and that the PRI's postelectoral conflicts caused 18 fatalities while those by the PRD yielded 152 deaths. Between 1989 and 2000, even the disciplined PAN had launched more postelectoral conflicts than the PRI (203 to 186). Unlike the other parties, the PRI presumably could squelch postelectoral mobilization by pressuring its corporatist bases.

But even before 2000, the sacrosanct relationship between the CNC (the National Peasants Confederation) and the PRI came unglued.

---

[19] PRI postelectoral conflicts can be hard to differentiate from PRI internal candidate selection conflicts where the loser then moves to the PRD.

"Whenever an uncontrolled mobilization happens, I call the head of the peasant confederation (the CNC)," confirmed Oaxaca's PRI subsecretary for electoral affairs (Cortés López interview) in a pre-2000 interview. "But sometimes there is nothing they can do either." In Puebla too, the 1990s CNC negotiated postelectoral conflicts on behalf of the PRI (García García 1995, 194). These *PRIísta* corporatist networks bent under political competition throughout Mexico, but perhaps nowhere more than in opposition-governed states, where the lack of a customary PRI hierarchy lent itself to the "chicken with its head cut off" metaphor, such as in Guanajuato (Sandoval interview). And increasingly, as in Oaxaca 1989 (Chávez and Yescas 1989) and 1992 ("Se Divide la CNC"), the PRI's corporatist peasants were the postelectoral propagators. Indeed, these former pillars of the corporatist PRI-state had grown so unruly by 2003 that they bargained more like tentative coalition partners seeking guarantees of congressional seats and resources than like "revolutionary family" patriarchs (Herrera Beltrán interview).

At the first signs of multi-party competition in the early 1980s, the PRI had legally constructed a vast network for basic food-product distribution (González Compeán and Lomeli 2000, 533).[20] However, the 1980s economic crisis forced cutbacks in patronage offerings at all levels and transfer of these captivating programs into federal jurisdiction, where Salinas – at least – kept his social welfare Solidarity Program true to the PRI's electoral ends (Molinar and Weldon 1994). Traditional machine bosses in the regions also continued the PRI-state's preelectoral works, fixing roads, extending electrical systems, and giving out bicycles, lottery tickets, grade school "scholarships," and food "care" packages on the eve of elections.[21] But the PRI-state's influence diminished over the 1990s due to a economic crisis–driven decrease in available patronage, the escalating "bidding" for side payments by grassroots loyalists being courted by real opposition parties, and an increasingly independent electorate, which heeded calls by opposition parties and electoral authorities alike to take PRI-state gifts and then vote their consciences (Cornelius 2002).

---

[20] The national PRI at that time established an extravagant nationwide network of supplies to fulfill requests by 3,153 local groups. They set up 274 "flea market" *tianguis*, 422 popular sector stores, 778 union stores, 112 mobile stores, 155 butcher shops, 35 consumer cooperatives, 15 bakeries, 15 supply depots, and 1 pharmacy (González Compeán and Lomeli 2000, 533).

[21] In one of the first formal surveys of electoral patronage, one-third of Mexico State's 1999 gubernatorial election voters said they had received handouts, and 80 percent of them voted for the PRI (Dillon 1999).

Despite the emerging patterns of PRI-state diminution, genuine electoral competition, and a more independent electorate, the local *PRIístas* tended to focus their ire on what they viewed as the most tangible acts of PRI-state betrayal, the *concertacesiones*.

Besides endorsing *PRIísta* post-*concertacesión* rebellions in Yucatán 1990; Guanajuato, San Luis Potosí, and Sonora 1991; Michoacán, Oaxaca, Puebla, and Sinaloa 1992; Guerrero, Mexico State, and Yucatán 1993; Nuevo León and Tlaxcala 1994; Puebla, Tabasco, and Zacatecas 1995, to name a few, national hard-line leaders sought to include an anti-*concertacesión* clause in their party statutes (such as at the 16th National Assembly) and consistently voiced opposition to such fruits of negotiation. At the sixty-seventh anniversary of the PRI, six governors, including Puebla's Bartlett and Oaxaca's Diódoro Carrasco Altamirano (later Zedillo's last Interior Secretary), issued a statement calling for greater coherence between "what we say and what we do" in the conduct of postelectoral negotiations (Sánchez and Castellanos 1996). Tacit admission of past sins by interventionist PRI local bosses also came as pleas by the national PRI president that "*PRIísta* governors and mayors should abstain from participating" in the selection of the party's candidates in 1998 (Medina 1998). As a deterrent to would-be negotiators in their own party as well as to concession-starved opposition leaders, state PRI leaders still routinely announced that the party would no longer negotiate victories. Prior to the 2000 federal elections too, the PRI's Labastida, the PAN's Fox, and the Interior Secretary all issued such declarations as part of this ongoing ritual, also indulged in Campeche 1997 (Ochoa 1997) Michoacán 1998 (Morales 1998b), Puebla 1998 (Ramos 1998), and Guanajuato (Gachuzo 2000) and Tabasco ("Descarta Sauri") in 2000 among others. Such proclamations have proven true over the last couple of years (e.g., see Cázarez 1998 and Morales 1998) but carried a hollow ring in the early 1990s, such as in Guerrero 1993, where the governor disavowed participation in postelectoral negotiations with the PRD immediately before submitting to such negotiations (Pérez 1993). Local PRI political operatives – and their national bosses – continued seeking to "win at all costs" by waving the banner of patriotic fraud, laundering campaign expenditures, and offering dispensations for votes.

The PRI "dinosaur" cronies sought to harness state largesse for partisan ends, but since the mid-1990s these throwbacks to the days of impunity often were exposed by an increasingly watchful press, and even chastised by PRI moderates such as Zedillo and the Mexican electorate in

2000.[22] The "sane distance" policy may have turned the other cheek to Madrazo's abuses, but the cronyism was nothing like the PRI-state's heyday under Salinas, when the president convoked the country's wealthiest entrepreneurs in one room and raised $500 million for the 1994 presidential race (Oppenheimer 1996, 97–101). Zedillo did seem to back off of his distancing policy as 2000 approached and the pressure mounted for him to assist his floundering colleagues. Zedillo inaugurated twice as many public works in the first months of 2000 as over the same period in 1999 (Medina 2000), PRI operatives such as Cervera Pacheco traveled their states regaling voters with washing machines,[23] food, and other patronage (Turati 2000), and PRI-state parastatal companies such as PEMEX, the public oil monopoly, mobilized their "get out the vote" networks (Marí and Núñez 2000). The president's staff argued that initiating public works, and publicizing them in a nonpartisan manner, was evidence of government effectiveness rather than "electoralism" (Barros Horcasitas interview). The IFE sought to curb PRI-state excesses by exhorting the president and all governors to cease publicizing public works one month before the federal elections, but only a half-dozen states (most governed by the PAN) announced their compliance (Irízar and Barajas 2000).

While no evidence was ever found in the 2000 federal election that the PRI would invoke "Plan B," a 1988-style massive fraud if the party fell behind in the polls, a PAN-PRD alliance was forged to denounce fraud, reminiscent of the historic Clouthier-Cárdenas postelectoral alliance twelve years earlier. Ultimately, the unfounded perception that the PRI-state was reverting to excesses of the past may have cost the PRI the presidency. The lesson drawn by Labastida advisors (Bernal interview) was that Labastida, a left-of-center "new *PRIísta*," lost his way after the first presidential debate, when, after a weak showing, the campaign brought in "dinosaurs" such as Bartlett and Carlos "Hank" Gonzalez, who represented "the old PRI" and conjured images of corruption, assassinations, and electoral

---

[22] Cornelius (2002) even argues from survey data that voters were repelled in 2002 by coercive tactics, as employed by the PRI and, to a lesser extent, by the other parties.

[23] On his campaign swings for Labastida (and for his 2001 successor), Cervera Pacheco gave away thousands of washing machines and other durable goods at a rate of nearly $3,000 per minute. When asked whether he was buying votes, the Yucatán governor replied, "If the vote is secret, then how am I buying votes?" (Turati 2000). More clandestine PRI storage areas were discovered in Guerrero, containing letters from local *PRIístas* requesting groceries, Labastida propaganda, flour, beans, plastic sandals, children's games stamped with the PRI logo, and candy (Flores and Guerrero 2000).

fraud (Miranda Ayala interview). Introduction of the "dinosaurs" into the campaign's high levels immediately sent Labastida's public approval ratings – which had been higher than those of Fox through much of the spring – on a downward spiral (Bernal interview).

Even before 2000, the retrograde *PRIístas'* lives had been complicated by campaign spending limits and nonpartisan electoral institute ombudsmen. Since then, circumstances have grown increasingly "deplorable" in local and regional PRI headquarters accustomed to opulence but learning austerity. They just wanted to continue practicing their craft – winning elections – without concerning themselves with "good government," electoral competition, or making payroll. Counterbalancing the dinosaurs within the ruling coalition were the technocrats, whose highest preference was for continuing to enact their neo-liberal economic policies – largely opposed by the dinosaurs – while maintaining at least a facade of democracy. Since 1997, negotiating a legislative coalition grew easier for the ruling technocrats than making deals with the dinosaurs of their own party. A decade before they reached the 2000 break point, tensions between these two factions within the PRI were directed against the *concertacesiones*. At the height of the national PRI's credibility erosion in the early 1990s, PRI strategists sought to resolve their party's crisis through more formal institutional channels. But they proposed too little, too late.

LUBRICATING THE POLITICAL MACHINES: THE PRI'S STRUGGLE FOR COMPETITIVENESS

Mexico's parties have grown predictable since the severing of PRI-state unity in the mid-1990s, as all three parties increasingly undertook electoral (as opposed to postelectoral) campaigning. The mystery of the Mexican case is not party behavior over the last several years, but rather the dynamic of PRI-state and opposition bargaining during the first twenty years of the country's protracted transition. How could the dominant party perpetuate its monopoly for so long, despite the existence of viable regime opposition? The threat of the "grand coalition" (*à la* Chile, the Philippines, or Spain) certainly motivated the PRI-state to carefully manipulate electoral opening. But how could they maintain so much control for so long?

Even without the added stimulus of reelection (at the national level or in local elections), the post-2000 PRI began adapting to the electoral connection, taking pages from the PAN's postelectoral playbook. Desperate to regroup in states where they were out of power, "PRI as opposition" leaders felt sandwiched by unresponsive national directorates used to resolving all partisan political problems through simple triangular communications ("*telefonazos*" in colloquial Spanish) among four groups: aggrieved local partisans (from the PRI or opposition); the governor and/or state Interior Secretary; the president and/or federal Interior Secretary; and the national PRI. These local leaders were adept at using their apparatus to corral support and votes, but not so accustomed to gaining votes the hard way, by convincing voters one by one. The national PRI, to assure continued attention to the states where the hegemonic party no longer governed, established a national liaison with opposition-governed states, dubbed the "Secretariat for Orphan States," and fortified its system of regional delegates (Orozco Loretto interview). Locally, accountability was inserted into campaigning, such as in Veracruz 1997, where PRI state president Miguel Ángel Yunez adopted an unprecedented strategy of making lower members of the mayoral ticket, the regents, accountable to the party by assigning them to a portion of the district. Yunez divided responsibility for mayoral campaigning among the regent candidates too, and insisted the party would base decisions of which regents would assume office off of the party's list on whose zones delivered the most votes, rather than just granting the usual free rides on mayoral candidate coattails or postelectoral negotiator savvy (interview).

Perhaps the most significant adaptation by PRI moderates to the new competitiveness was the party's acquiescence to holding internal primaries, thereby ensuring selection of the party's most popular candidates rather than merely the political prodigy of the governor or other high-level party operatives. Recall from Chapter 4 that the installation of such primaries had been under consideration since the 1960s, but was never properly executed. While the PRI's 1998 experiments with internal gubernatorial primaries, the first in over thirty years, were held only where the party no longer governed and thus had little to lose, the strategy did bring an impressive PRI reclamation in Chihuahua, which had been "lost" to the PRI since 1992.[24] Starting in 1998, the PRI adopted open primary voting in a majority of its gubernatorial candidate selections, and suffered

---

[24] Langston (2000a, 11) attributes the Chihuahua recovery to three factors, which were not all present in three other states studied (Baja California, Guanajuato, and Jalisco). Those factors were opposition weaknesses (PAN or PRD); strong ties between state and national PRIs; and interest by national PRI in winning the state back. Langston's observations were valid through July 2000.

more defections in cases where the candidate was selected through delegate conventions or political council meetings (González Compeán and Lomeli 2000, 770–5). Open primaries to select competitive candidates were also utilized to select other candidates, in legislative and municipal elections, and in 1999 the PRI ended the presidential *dedazo*. An open presidential primary was held for the first time ever, in which Labastida defeated a discontented Madrazo, alienating him from party moderates but rallying the faithful behind Labastida. And although the party after 2000 postponed planned internal reorganization for over a year, in May 2001 the PRI conducted an internal election among some 350 party notables to select the party's new secretary general (the number two position), and, to their credit, they elected a moderate known to get along with all the major factions.

The Labastida-Madrazo open primary was followed in February 2002 by a Madrazo victory in a nationwide open election for party president, after which Madrazo and the PRI accepted their new opposition party status. The PRI's internal balloting, like that of the PRD, was rife with fraud, embarrassing partisans with claims of ballot stuffing (Rendón, Marí, and Pensamiento 2002), handouts of canned foods (Díaz 2002), and trafficking of votes (Hidalgo 2002). Madrazo's victory united remaining PRI loyalists (detractors such as Mexico State's PRI structure had openly dissented but prior to the election), and soon after assuming the party's leadership position, former "dinosaur" Madrazo met publicly with Fox, in a controversial move to bring back moderates, and announced the return to the party's economic team of technocrats like Pedro Aspe, Salinas's Treasury Secretary. Addressing internal polls in which those surveyed cited the PRI as Mexico's "worst party," César Augusto Santiago, the Madrazo PRI's secretary for electoral affairs, admitted that his party had deserved that perception, and that he hoped to overcome the party's reputation as "*mapaches* [literally "raccoons" but Mexican slang for electoral bandits] and ballot box stealers" by clamping down on wrongdoers and demonstrating a new electoral administration that focused only on winning elections. Santiago acknowledged that the PRI's reputation was not being helped by the federal investigation of whether PEMEX laundered millions of dollars that illegally wound up in Labastida's presidential campaign, but promised that the guilty would be punished in the party as well as in the penal system (Guerrero 2002).

Even years before their rude awakening in 2000, PRI strategists sought to replace patronage connections with an electoral connection to improve the chances that their candidates could win without the PRI-state's habitual "extra help." Local *PRIístas* undertook grassroots consultations to establish real ties with popular sectors (i.e., those transcending the traditional and dysfunctional corporatist ties), but with only mixed effects. Once the hemorrhaging began in the mid-1990s, it only accelerated as "passed over" *PRIísta* leaders aspiring to quick governorships learned that there was also life outside the PRI, and that the PRD in particular was anxious to improve its electoral fortunes by "importing" PRI defectors wholesale, such as in the Campeche gubernatorial race in 1997; the Veracruz 1997 local elections; the Baja California Sur, Tlaxcala, and Zacatecas 1998 gubernatorial contests; and the Chiapas and Tabasco 2000 gubernatorial elections. In particular, the party hemorrhaged interlocutors between the technocrats and hard-liner "dinosaurs" such as long-time PRI careerists Arturo Núñez, a valuable former PRI caucus leader in the Chamber of Deputies until he quit the party in 2000 upon being passed over as Tabasco's gubernatorial candidate; Ricardo Monreal, former PRI congressional leader; and Manuel Camacho, former Mexico City mayor who exited the party after being denied Zedillo's candidacy in 1994 and now heads a tiny center-left party. Perhaps the most damaging case of PRI defection (since the Cárdenas–Muñoz Ledo wave in the late 1980s) was that of Monreal, who won the PRD's first governorship outside Mexico City in 1998 and immediately started proselytizing the viability of the PRD to his *PRIísta* friends (Caballero 1998).

When they ran close but could credibly claim victory, local PRI chapters launched preemptive victory mobilizations to avert opposition postelectoral displays and to raise the ante of *concertacesión*. Such was the case of the governor of Colima's March of the PRI Triumph in 1997. At the march, held four days before the electoral institute certified the close election between the PAN and the PRI, the soon-to-be *PRIísta* governor-elect proclaimed that his thousands of gathered supporters would use "all legal means" to ensure recognition (Barrera 1997). *PRIístas* also started engaging in their first "serious" defense of the vote campaigns ever, after prior postelectoral campaigns consisted of "trotting out a 'sacred cow' lawyer to inaugurate the defense of the vote, who we knew was not going to do anything because we always won and by a wide margin" (Zazueta Félix interview). The PRI also started to utilize tactics unheard of in the late 1980s but common by the mid-1990s, by actually using the electoral courts they had created merely as a "window dressing" concession. As the PRI learned how to defend its votes through formal institutions, the PAN and PRD learned the limits of postelectoral cooperation. Although they failed several times in the 1990s to unite under a common front, the two former regime opponents did find common ground in post-2000 efforts to break PRI bosses' holds over Mexico's impoverished south.

NO GRAND TRANSITION COALITION, BUT A SHORT-LIVED PAN-PRD ALLIANCE TO BREAK THE PRI

The 1988 election was the closest the PAN and the PRD (then the Cardenista Front [FDN]) ever came to forging a significant alliance against the PRI-stacked deck until 2001, when the two opposition parties decided that ending the reigns of southern PRI *caciques* like Madrazo and Cervera Pacheco was more important than their considerable policy differences. While the PAN and the PRD had managed cooperation during some 1990s local elections, their efforts were usually thwarted after the election, when the PAN sought to negotiate and the PRD tried to mobilize. Like many characteristics of Mexico's democratization, the pattern extended back to the postelectoral conflict of 1988.

During the summer of 1988, the PAN's Clouthier submitted to Cárdenas's postelectoral campaign, but the PAN's disciplined apparatus was inattentive to Clouthier's renegade activities. As pointed out by Loaeza (1999, 429), the PAN's frustration with the regime's blatant fraud was surpassed by the conservative opposition's disdain for Cárdenas[25] and the left, and its unwillingness to agitate for ingovernability, which would threaten their interests as much as those of the *PRIístas*. Cárdenas's supporters felt that as the primary victims of the regime's shameless electoral fraud, citizen revulsion at the magnitude of the injustice against them would carry the day, and they did not worry excessively about tending bridges with the rest of the opposition. Clouthier, as the third-place "spoiler" and a maverick neo-*PANísta*, did initially support Cárdenas, until his party abandoned him with a "letter of intent" to serve as the PRI's legislative coalition partner. The PAN-Cárdenas alliance ultimately went nowhere, not unlike subsequent, more localized efforts to unify the opposition.

Early 1990s PAN-PRD alliances were forged for regional elections, notably in the 1992 Durango and Tamaulipas state gubernatorial and mayoral contests.[26] The alliances endured the elections, but consistent with

---

[25] Recall that the PAN was born in part as a reaction against the populism of Cárdenas's father.

[26] In the San Luis Potosí gubernatorial race the two parties also joined a common front, headed by a third regional party, the Potosino Civic Front (*Frente Cívico Potosino* [FCP]).

evidence presented throughout this book, they parted in irreconcilable differences over postelectoral strategies. In Durango, the PAN broke ranks after the PRD accused the PAN of characteristically negotiating away mayoral and state legislator victories in exchange for "favorable consideration" in the gubernatorial contest, which the party eventually lost to the PRI (Maldonado 1992). In Tamaulipas's fraudulent and violent 1992 elections, the rupture was less formal, but the two parties' strategic differences were even more pronounced. The PAN and the PRD announced the creation of a "Caravan for Democracy," but the PAN backed down, calling for citizen restraint, while the *PRDístas* concentrated their marches in towns where they felt most wronged. The *PANístas* "peeled away" from PRD marchers and took their complaints to legal instances (the state electoral commission and legislature), while the PRD occupied town squares and bore down. The PAN acknowledged that they had negotiated with the federal Interior Secretary, but only for the liberation of the sixty-five postelectoral violence arrestees in exchange for their voluntary dispersion from the Ciudad Victoria city square (Rivera 1992). Clearly, these alliances served the interests of neither party, rather than the interests of both. The parties' positions were just too far apart. Courting democracy in Mexico would just have to be achieved incrementally, hampered by a divisible and conquerable opposition, at least for the time being.

The failure of opposition grand coalitions during the height of the postelectoral contestation period offers yet further evidence of the differences in postelectoral negotiation strategies of the PAN and the PRD. The PAN's coalitional position vis-à-vis the PRI and its formal institution contestation are attributable to 1988 strategy changes by status quo–favoring actors comprising the party's base and its high endowment of legal expertise, giving the PAN a comparative advantage in legal contestation over social mobilization. The PRD, contrarily, has no pre-1988 history of electoral contestation and its local activists run the spectrum from recalcitrant antisystem *guerrillas* to moderate PRI defectors. That party's blackmail strategy was its comparative advantage, given the PRD's strength of mobilizing peasants and workers and its lack of lawyers.

Even given these differences, however, both major opposition parties relied somewhat on mixed strategies. The PAN sought federal dialogue and *concertacesión* to resolve local problems, but deployed Active and Passive Civil Resistance (RECAP) where perceived as necessary. The PRD

This case is not further considered because both of the major opposition parties were clearly subordinated to the FCP's leader, Salvador Nava.

mobilized first but also sought where possible to maintain connections with federal authorities, even when state and local contacts broke down. Advisors for both parties had similar comments about the need to deploy multiple strategies. The PRD president, López Obrador, for example, called for simultaneous legal and extralegal strategies, while the PAN leadership expressed essentially the same sentiment, articulated by PAN judicial advisor Germán Mártinez as "total politics" – documenting irregularities when filing complaints, but bolstering this approach with political pressure. The differences between these positions are nuanced, but perceptible. The PAN's total politics always caught the PRI-state's attention, while the PRD's double strategy was roundly ignored until passing entirely to the extralegal stage.

For Mexican politics, the distinction is growing moot, however, as with the passage of time, these opposition parties are ceasing to rely on postelectoral strategies and converging in their reliance on formal institutions, the regime of electoral courts. Also of note, as of the mid-1990s, the summation of forces, formerly assessed by the election itself, has been increasingly possible through the conduct of public opinion polls. *Concertacesión* and the *segunda vuelta* are turning out to have been transitional tactics, improvised for use with moribund formal institutions to pressure their reform into serviceable ones. The implications of this change for theorizing judicial institution development cannot be understated. The difference between success and failure has not been the institutions themselves, but rather how the actors used them.

The resort to extralegal tactics exerted an extreme cost, causing fatigue and even violence among opposition partisans and contempt among local PRI leaders for agreements made by their national leadership that invariably promoted national stability at the cost of hard-fought local victories. But a review of the evolution of postelectoral strategies by both parties demonstrated that postelectoral behavior may be sorted into three categories: brutal postelectoral conflicts without viable legal recourse prior to the 1988 watershed; competing mixed legal and extralegal strategies from 1989 to about 1995 (the focus of this study); and most recently, the post-1996 primacy of reformed formal institutions for resolving conflicts within the rule of law. Indeed, while electoral magistrates cited the law, however labyrinthine, as justification for their actions, political actors drew their own conclusions about the cost-effectiveness of submitting complaints, and sometimes still opt out of participation in cases like the notorious paper-shuffling courts of Chiapas, Oaxaca, and Tabasco of the mid-1990s. However, in these most recalcitrant of the PRI machine's states, and especially in the rural southern states that tend toward bi-partisan competition (as opposed to the more urban center and north, where all three major parties have tended to have a larger presence over the last few years), gubernatorial coalitions, modeled on the successful PAN-PRD alliance in Chiapas 2000, threaten to unseat the PRI.

More specifically, in the wake of 2000 the fledgling Yucatán PRD offered to back the large PAN base there, and the PAN, in exchange, initially offered to throw its small Tabasco base behind that powerful state PRD structure (although the PAN later reneged, apparently due to local resistance). While representatives from both parties acknowledged that it was easier to sacrifice candidacies where they had little hope anyway, they nonetheless insisted that even being able to reach an alliance across an extensive ideological divide meant that each of them highly prioritized ridding Mexico's south of the PRI *caciques* and establishing a rule of law above partisanship (Nava interview; Villavicencio 2001 interview). With the collapse of the Tabasco accords, this trend toward cooperation proved circumstantial rather than enduring,[27] but it was still significant. While Cervera Pacheco and new Tabasco Governor Eduardo Andrade (and his mentor Roberto Madrazo) may have benefited from their "bread and circuses" federalism, the PRI may have been the ultimate loser here too. In the run-up to the 2003 congressional mid-term elections, interest in coalitions resumed. This time the PRI allied with the tiny PVEM against the PAN. With little help from the PVEM, the PRI dominated the July 2003 mid-term elections. While failing to win a congressional majority, the PRI (and PRD) gained Chamber of Deputies seats at the PAN's expense, as voters punished Fox for policy failures. But the PAN had forever distanced Mexico's parties from the state.

ZEDILLO CUT OFF A FINGER; FOX CUT OFF HIS ARM: *PANÍSTA* RESTORATION OF THE FEDERAL PACT

Winning office offered little guarantee of taking office during the last decade of Mexico's protracted transition, especially for opposition party victors in backwater towns with no history of sharing power. Sometimes, local PRI mayors stooped to violence to quiet critics within their

---

[27] Even as the PAN and PRD discussed a Tabasco-Yucatán alliance, these two opposition parties divided over proper postelectoral tactics in a half-dozen Veracruz towns, where as per well-established patterns, the PAN sought to use legal channels and negotiation, whereas the PRD, which had occupied five town halls, refused to vacate its positions (Meza 2001).

administrations, such as in Meztitlán, Hidalgo in 1991 and Tezoatlán, Oaxaca in 1989 where National Human Rights Commission inquiries found municipal police officers guilty of slaying PRD town administrators, although charges were never pressed in either case (National Human Rights Commission 1994, 236–7, 422–4). More often, PRI-governed municipalities merely excluded the opposition's proportional-representation city council members from participating in town meetings or collecting paychecks (see Chapter 4).

The best means of neutralizing opposition input into public administration has been to just ignore them, as unlike in Mexico's several "divided government" state legislatures, opposition city council members are powerless to second-guess executive decisions. Throughout Mexico, opposition party regents in *PRIísta* administrations lamented their relegation to minor posts – like caretaker of the municipal graveyard or park – rather than to positions as city treasurer or supervisor of public works. This trend reached new lows in the Chiapas PRD's acceptance, at the 1995 postelectoral bargaining table, of a proportional-representation position as part-time town librarian's assistant (Chapter 7). It was not even uncommon for outgoing mayors, even from the same party as the incoming mayor, to leave public works unfinished and abscond with records, prompting transition period newspaper headlines such as "Disorganized Municipal Administration" (Gaxiola 1998), "Mayors Responsible for Concluding Projects" (Guarneros 1998), and "Mayors-elect Denounce the 'Dismantling' of Their Towns" (*Diario de Yucatán* 2001). One of the first publicized municipal audits ever revealed public-spending irregularities in 86 percent of Veracruz's 210 municipalities (Jiménez 1999).

While he did not actively campaign against heinous abuses by his local machine affiliates, Zedillo did encourage *sana distancia* (distancing of the state from the PRI). While the president generally refused to challenge the machine-boss governors[28] (at least not compared to Salinas's *dedazos*), his administration at least publicly opposed crooked campaigning and the other forms of renegade governance that had characterized state and

---

[28] While Zedillo refused to follow up on opposition complaints against "syndicate" mainstays Bartlett, Cervera Pacheco, and Madrazo, his administration did pressure for resignations of three less powerful governors implicated in scandal: Rubén Figueroa of Guerrero, Sócrates Rizzo of Nuevo León, and Carrillo Olea of Morelos. Mario Villanueva of Quintana Roo finished his term on the lam, as U.S. Drug Enforcement Agency investigators sought to question him in April 1999, but were unable to locate Villanueva, who attended to the final days of his administration's business using a facsimile machine but was captured in 2001.

local government since well before the Avíla Camacho regime in Puebla epitomized PRI cronyism for all time. The PRI "dinosaur" cronies still sought to harness state largesse for partisan ends, but since the mid-1990s these throwbacks to the impunity era often were publicized by an increasingly watchful press and even chastised by PRI moderates (in word if not in deed). The PRI moderates were actually relieved under Zedillo to concern themselves with the good of the party, without balancing these preferences against their frequently conflicting interest of running the government. For example, Arturo Núñez, Interior Sub-Secretary during several of the worst postelectoral conflicts, said that from a partisan perspective, the *concertacesión* agreements were deplorable, as they violated the public will, and in cases where his party had won (or at least been officially declared as victors). Núñez insisted that negotiating *concertacesiones* was sound public policy, however, because "political negotiations are always better than violence" (interview). So even as collusion with the PAN made local machine *PRIístas* reel, it also divided the party's moderates.

No one was as familiar with these detrimental effects on party morale as Vicente Fox, who came to power vowing never to sell out his own party and the electorate by cutting such deals without them. In resolving the Tabasco and Yucatán election-related conflicts locally, with the federal government striving to lower its profile and serve only as a third-party mediator, the PAN's administration may have made the PRI's post-2000 regrouping efforts more difficult. Cervera Pacheco's rhetoric aside, there were no arbitrary interventions from the center to rally against (despite the Yucatán governor's best effort to provoke some). The remaining moderates in the PRI had to continue striving to improve electoral performance by unifying local party chapters, building an ideological identity to help recruit members, and selecting the most popular candidates available. But in many instances, the moderates were still outbid by the party's *caciques*.

Prospects for PRI-PAN cooperation did improve as Fox's approval ratings fell from their postelectoral peak back to atmospheric levels after his promises of reform got mired in congressional politics. For all the hype surrounding the meteoric rise of the no-nonsense maverick in cowboy boots, Fox's tax reforms were mangled. His boastful promise of reaching a peace accord with the Chiapas rebels in "15 minutes" and his proposed changes in the constitution, the electoral system, education, labor, and energy policy all languished in Congress for three full years. A tripartite Chamber of Deputies and PRI-dominated Senate blocked passage of all but a handful of Fox-sponsored bills (notably an important freedom of information act) and unprecedented tensions arose between Fox and the

PAN's more conservative congressional delegation. The nadir in Fox's relations with Congress was the Senate's April 2002 prohibition of a planned presidential trip to Canada and the United States as punishment for the dismantling of Mexico's traditionally independent foreign policy by Fox's controversial International Relations Secretary Jorge Castañeda (who resigned several months later). Accused of submitting excessively to United States dictates on U.S.-Mexico border security, immigration policy, and relations with Cuba (long the pride of Mexico's independent foreign relations), the revolutionary family's remaining senators interceded. Soon afterward, Fox invited the PRI to govern with him, and a Fox-Madrazo meeting gave substance to this declaration. However, new schemes of interparty relations were easier for leaders to promise than to deliver. Just as Fox was defining "sane proximity" with the PAN, Madrazo was seeking to undo decades of *PRIísta* political practices.

The turn to internal primaries had not stopped retrograde *PRIísta* governors from falling back on proven incentives and threats to ensure continued loyalty from those who lose internal primaries. For example, in Guerrero 1996 interim Governor Angel Aguirre Rivero is said to have stood before the three PRI candidates for mayor of the important tourist destination Taxco, colorfully promising that "I will make the second place finisher the vice-mayor, and the third place finisher a state legislator [ignoring, as in the old days, that these were elected posts]. But this only if you remember that if you do not comply, I will break your a – " (Cano 1996). The finger pointing and dirty campaigning in the PRI's 2002 internal election, reminiscent of the most retrograde PRI performance in Tabasco or Yucatán, underscored the difficulties faced by party reformers. The PRI governors' continued insistence in "weighing in" on these decisions took its toll on candidate selection in the late 1990s, and after the 2000 deluge, the traditionalists grew even more belligerent. Indeed, while the party now embraces open primaries, it may in practice be backsliding. The corporatist pillars of the PRI-state, now free agents who negotiate their support for seats and resources (much like other PRI coalition allies like the Green Party or PVEM), are said to be imposing candidacies from below, as the governors used to from above.

Before 2000, finite limits existed to the PRI's willingness to compete, and to compete as a mere party rather than as a party-state. Tabasco 1995 represents a line in the sand drawn by local PRI bosses unwilling to tolerate the removal of their governor to placate opposition. That mobilization defined the limits of Zedillo's intervention. The president apparently was unable to control *cacique* rebellions in the PRI (invoking the "new federalism" as their banner), and lost control over his party's hard-liners. But while the regions run by the PRI's most intransigent machine bosses continued to tolerate electoral fraud and other corruption, they did not seem – Madrazo and Cervera Pacheco scandals aside – to trickle up to the national PRI any more. As the PRI-state's clients evolved into autonomous citizens, courting democracy in Mexico claimed its greatest casualties of all, the PRI moderates who had conceded in the late 1980s to opposition party pressures and built electoral institutions that the PRD and especially the PAN had successfully turned against them. Courting democracy had meant courting disaster for the world's longest reigning dominant party. However, if the 2003 mid-term congressional elections were any indication, the PRI's reformers had managed to start turning the former electoral machine into a responsive opposition party, demonstrating that the wounds of 2000 – while crippling – were not mortal.

9

A Quarter Century of "Mexicanization": Lessons from a Protracted Transition

> The proper tactic should not be to boycott the election but to create an
> alternative program or alternative structure through the election.
> Guideline on the [South Korean Assembly 1985] General Election[1]

While a few of the early electoral courts of Mexico's political opening
packed courtrooms for public hearings, most were never heard from. A
few featured a full slate of contentious cases and no-nonsense judges who
overturned municipal elections with resounding gavels. Many were empty
chambers except for the magistrates and the echoes of their rubber stamps
of governors' commands. Institutional failure pervaded Mexico's first experiments with electoral justice, which was not surprising in one of the
world's most fraudulent electoral systems. In fact, fewer than a third of
the country's first institutional arbiters of electoral fraud successfully adjudicated postelectoral disputes by preventing disagreements from spilling
out of the courtrooms and onto the streets.[2]

Far from mere "second thought" reactions by losing parties, postelectoral conflicts were a bona fide informal institution and, arguably, were
more important than the elections themselves during much of Mexico's
protracted transition to democracy. This work has documented their existence in some 15 percent of Mexico's local elections between 1989 and
2000, but my numbers no doubt underrepresent their frequency. The
pattern of extensive postelectoral conflicts during the first six years of

[1] Cited in Im (1989, 227).
[2] For a systematic assessment of electoral court failures in fourteen of Mexico's states, see
Eisenstadt (2002), which argues that only four of these did not fail in the early 1990s.

270

the sample period and tapering off during the final six years is no doubt much more pronounced than my representation of them, due to improvements in news coverage during the final years of the study. As the media professionalized and national newspaper coverage improved, the media's ability to penetrate even the most rural areas improved dramatically, but only in the late 1990s. There is no way to estimate the underreporting of postelectoral conflicts during the early years of my study (and the years prior to those studied), but it is worth considering that the evidence presented is incomplete and that full information would have rendered an even more compelling story.

The quantitative evidence presented was complemented by colorful case studies of informal institution successes. Governorships and mayoral elections were thrown to the sabotage-threatening National Action Party (PAN), while the Party of the Democratic Revolution (PRD), repeatedly testing their unabashedly candid "mobilization + storming of town hall = municipal council" formula, settled for proportional-representation *gazetazos* in Veracruz, hydra-headed mayoral power sharing in Oaxaca, and cemetery caretaker and village driver jobs in Chiapas. Formal institution failures were equally graphic. Statements from a Michoacán electoral judge were reproduced arguing verdicts on "issues of public security and social interest" rather than on legal merits. None of the scores of complaints presented in Jalisco 1992, Tabasco 1994, or Chiapas 1995 was even accepted for electoral court consideration, and no evidence could be found in Campeche 1991, Chiapas 1991, and Michoacán 1989 – even after dozens of interviews and extensive archive searches – that the electoral courts codified in law ever even received any complaints at all. And perhaps the exemplar of electoral court failure for all time was Zacatecas 1992, where the electoral court was established but received no complaints, while wary parties simultaneously contested scores of elections in the state legislature's electoral college in a visceral realization that even in the formal institution realm, political contingencies trumped legal arguments every time (see Zacatecas State Electoral Commission 1992, Eisenstadt 2002).

This surreal melding of the informal and the formal did start in the mid-1990s, as federal codifications of electoral justice norms started trickling into the states and dueling focal points melding formal and informal institution rules allowed political actors to bridge the gap between the construction of formal institutions and compliance with them. But the single most important finding of this book is that before this mixing of formal and informal institutions, the *concertacesión* and *segunda vuelta* had been institutionalized as informal rules agreed upon by relevant actors from the Party of the Institutional Revolution (PRI), the PAN, and, ultimately, by the PRD too. These bargaining tables were the institutional "training wheels" of Mexico's protracted transition to democracy, the mechanism of a gradual transition from clientalism-driven authoritarianism toward democratic consolidation. In the emerging literature on informal institutions, they were "substitutive informal institutions," which evolved to compete with – and even subvert – their formal institution counterparts (Lauth 2000; Helmke and Levitsky 2003).

The state and local dueling-focal-point extremes followed upon a gradual evolution of electoral justice at the federal level. The 1988 federal elections witnessed a Kafkaesque competition between electoral magistrates who rendered verdicts without examining evidence because the Congress would not trust them with the electoral acts they later burned, and the electoral college of congressional members-elect who disregarded electoral court verdicts and horse-traded seats and "elected" popular vote losers in exchange for certifying the Salinas presidency. Burned figuratively in 1988, the nascent federal electoral court built up credibility slowly but continuously, case by case, jurisprudence by jurisprudence over more than a decade. However, even after having weathered political purges in 1993 and 1996, and being incorporated into the conservative judicial branch, it was not clear to anyone in 2000 that the court could fare any better in a repeat of the postelectoral chaos of 1988. The electoral court's public relations campaign, which stooped to ads on television and in consumers' phone bills extolling the institution's independence, indicated that the electoral court did not trust that the political parties would respect its verdicts. While more subdued than in 1988 and 1994, Cárdenas issued warnings to respect the vote, which betrayed faith in the electoral courts – whatever the glossy phone bill inserts said. The left's longtime icon perceived that his personal credibility was yet again stronger than public confidence in formal institutions. But even Fox, conveying the anti–formal institutions bias of a cynical partisan who had seen one electoral fraud too many, speculated pre-2000 about what fraud margin the PRI-state could still get away with, and what level of postelectoral mobilization would be needed to counter it. Only after being freed from their nominators by Fox's election did the federal electoral magistrates grow into their discretion, issuing enough path-breaking verdicts between 2000 and 2003 that they seemed at several points to upstage the Supreme Court as Mexico's principal agents of courting democracy.

Luckily for the legal system, even partially autonomous electoral courts during the 1990s had generated slow acceptance of formal institution adjudication of electoral disputes, especially by the PRI-state, which never thought their electoral livelihoods would depend upon these courts they had originally created as window dressing. Loser consent with electoral outcomes had been mostly attained by the late 1990s, exemplified, ironically, by PRI presidential candidate Francisco Labastida's stoic acceptance on July 2, 2000, of Mexico's first alternation of power in seventy-one years. In the formative decades of courting democracy in Mexico, however, the PRI-state's hopes that the increasing use of electoral courts would lead to a decreasing resort to extralegal mobilizations were not immediately fulfilled. In fact, the use of electoral courts actually increased the propensity of opposition party election losers to mobilize, at least initially. The introduction of autonomous institutions to channel Mexico's severe and even lethal postelectoral conflicts off the streets and into the courtrooms actually had the opposite effect. What were the institution builders doing wrong?

Parting from this idea that elections in transitional Mexico were for much more than counting votes, this book had three broad aims. First, it specified the role of postelectoral mobilizations – informal institutions – in advancing Mexico's electoral opening even before the advent of formal institution electoral courts. Second, it argued that contrary to the pacted democratization model, protracted transitions may occur when authoritarian incumbents seek to divide and conquer opponents, negotiating incrementally with patronage-seeking opponents. Third, it demonstrated that even when credible formal institutions (in this case, electoral courts) existed, political parties initially responded more to structural social grievances than to the codification of formal electoral institutions. That is, the causes of postelectoral mobilizations occurring in 15 percent of Mexico's local races over the last twelve years ran much deeper than just elections. The "electoralist fallacy" described by Schmitter and Karl, whereby observers erroneously consider nations to have democratized solely on the basis of having staged apparently free and fair elections, must be applied in "electoral authoritarian" regimes as well as in consolidating democracies. The finding that historical grievances matter more than electoral laws is important for scholars of democratization and specialists in economic and political development alike. In authoritarian Mexico, local elections and postelectoral conflicts were indicators of deeper social problems, rather than solutions to these problems.

Courting democracy in Mexico has been a story of emboldened opposition parties coming to accept electoral courts, and of the courts vesting themselves in their own authority over time. It has been only partly the story of formal institutional changes, crucial for defining the limits of these powers. Informal institutions and party strategies have been at least as important. As the PAN and even the PRD accepted and embraced the norm of electoral justice as articulated by the emboldened Electoral Tribunal of the Judicial Power of the Federation (TEPJF), traditionalist remnants of the PRI-state have proven to be the most resistant to acceptance of this norm. This chapter summarizes the party strategies taken by the three main actors in Mexico's protracted transition and considers the policy implications of the primacy of structural/historical factors over formal institutional constitutions in mitigating postelectoral conflicts. Finally, it reconsiders the broader implications of the Mexican experience for studying informal institutions, political party strategies, and protracted transitions to democracy.

THE PRI UNDER SALINAS-ZEDILLO: FROM FACTIONS TO PARTY AND BACK AGAIN

This book has sought to explain protracted electoral opening as a continuous series of bargains struck between the authoritarian incumbents and their opponents over electoral outcomes. But underneath the PRI-state's unitary bargaining position, I identified varying preferences among leaders within the party-state's three constituencies: the ruling coalition, the regime opposition, and the international community. The opposition parties perhaps have been more complex than the simple one-dimensional model of compliance with authoritarians specified in Chapter 1, ranging from "antiregime" at one extreme to "patronage seeking" at the other. For the most part, the moderated but often ineffectual post-1995 PRD has preferred transition seeking to antiregime radicalism or regime co-optation. The more nuanced PAN has broadly pursued transition-seeking gradualism, but with a patronage-seeking policy alliance with PRI-state technocrats in the 1990s for enactment of PAN-PRI economic policies. This patronage seeking was complemented by the *PANistas'* vigorous transition seeking, bordering on antiregime tactics in places like Huejotzingo, against the PRI local *caciques* – sometimes even in alliance with the PRD. Over two decades, the PAN shrewdly positioned itself as the fulcrum of the balance between the increasingly technocratic PRI-state, its internal local dissent, and the more antiregime left. And while the PAN's monumentous *concertacesiones* originated locally, they reverberated throughout PRI chapters all around Mexico with a much greater impact than their mere numbers, as they served to fortify the PAN and the PRI-state technocrats at the expense of the local PRI bosses.

Stark differences between PRI-state responses to PAN and PRD postelectoral conflicts – presented here using both quantitative and qualitative evidence – demonstrate this pattern. Ranking PAN leaders acknowledged a "special relationship" between the PAN and the PRI during Salinas's term, considered at length in Chapter 6, in which the PAN privileged itself as the regime's loyal opposition. National PAN officials also admitted conducting direct communications with national PRI leaders, the Interior Secretary, and in some cases with Salinas in the pursuit of national solutions to local problems. In all of its most notorious *concertacesiones* such as the governorships of Guanajuato and San Luis Potosí 1991 and mayoral races in Mazatlán 1989, Mérida 1993, Monterrey 1994, and Huejotzingo 1996, the national PAN negotiated with the national PRI-state leadership, finding "gentleman's agreement" solutions that "washed" PRI victories through political (rather than judicial) institutions – such as state legislatures or bipartisan bargaining tables – to find compromises acceptable to the PAN.

The PRD experienced nothing close to the good fortune of the PAN in negotiating postelectoral conflicts. The PAN managed to persuade the national PRI to pressure local PRI chapters to resign electoral victories so the PAN could claim the wins (and maintain the PAN-PRI national policy alliance intact). The PRD, contrarily, until recently had nothing valuable to offer the PRI at the national level. The PRD consistently opposed PAN-PRI economic and social policies and, for the first several years of Salinas's term, did not even recognize the PRI's candidate as the proper winner of the 1988 balloting. So where the PAN received backdoor access to the regime's power elites, the PRD had to play threats of ingovernability from the grass roots as attention-grabbing postelectoral cards. The PRD did manage, after systematically fraudulent elections such as local races in Michoacán 1992 and Chiapas 1995, to receive concessions of "plural" local governments, involving regents from the PRD as well as the PRI. But as PRD activists bitterly acknowledged, they usually just received "token" regencies, such as village graveyard caretaker rather than city manager. Unlike the PAN, which managed through its dual strategy to promote both electoral justice and *concertación*, the PRD's single-pronged *segunda vuelta* provoked only backlashes from the PRI-state, prompting injuries and even deaths. Before Tabasco 2000, which marked the arrival of the PRD as a legitimate postelectoral contender in the electoral justice realm, the party had won no PRI-state postelectoral concessions in any gubernatorial or even important mayoral contests.

A near exception, the PRD's successful negotiation of the departure of the official PRI victor in the 1994 Tabasco governor's race, which might have significantly altered Zedillo administration relations with the opposition, was "called back" at the last minute as local PRI leaders reneged on their deal to sacrifice their governor in exchange for a national-level truce between the PRI and the PRD. The local PRI machine bosses under Zedillo were able to reclaim some of the power they had lost to the PAN under Salinas, but it was too late for them to preserve control over enough local machines that when aggregated together, they still added up to the world's longest-reigning one-party state. As the local machines were loosely joined together by personalistic ties during the 1920s and 1930s, so they had begun to disband from the party-state in the early 1990s under the encouragement of their own president, who cared more about uncoupling economic policy from political patronage than about maintaining the flow of clientalism to his local affiliates. The electoral playing field had been leveled for national elections by 1996, and was being leveled in even the most *PRIísta* local bastions in the years that followed, based on the empowerment of the federal electoral court as final arbiter of local elections that same year. So even though local *PRIístas'* relative positions in the party improved after Tabasco 1995, and especially after the party's recognition of its need to restore the political bases after a poor showing in the 1997 mid-term congressional elections, they had already given up their competitive advantage.

The distinctions drawn in Chapter 2 among interests of the three constituencies of formal institutional reforms – PRI-state moderates, opposition parties, and international critics – do not hold in considering the informal realm of *concertacesión*. Contrary to the more transparent interests arrayed behind electoral law reforms, the interests of the first two constituencies – the domestic actors – are intertwined. The differing actor incentives in negotiating formal and informal institutional changes prompted a crucial gap, empirically evidenced in Chapter 5 as the breach between sub-national electoral institution autonomy and local postelectoral conflicts. Informal institution negotiations revealed the existence of a crucial third domestic actor – local PRI extremists – whose conflicts of interest with the PRI-state moderates accelerated the PRI-state's downward electoral spiral. These local PRI activists, unaccounted for in most analyses of Mexico's protracted transition to democracy, were – along with the oft-studied opposition parties – the lynchpins of the transition. Viewed case by case, the changes in PRI-state behavior were subtle. But they added up to a clear pattern, when assessed in relation to PAN and PRD strategies, which forever altered the balance of power between the PRI-state and opposition.

The international community's preferences have been considered less in the course of this work, as they were significant only as filtered through the interests of the PRI-state. While considered independently in Chapter 2, the international community was elsewhere treated as an important additional pressure upon the technocrats running the federal PRI-state, who sought to attain at least the outward trappings of democracy in Mexico, even if the internal reality was different. Actual pressures by international actors – and especially the North American Free Trade Agreement (NAFTA)–negotiating United States – were diffuse and somewhat inconsistent. That is, anti-NAFTA congressional members would periodically chastise Mexico's "democracy deficit" for their own political ends, but there was no sustained government-to-government pressure on Mexico to open its political system. Salinas's explicit decision to liberalize the economy before the polity revealed the assumption, also true in U.S. support for other undemocratic but stable allies worldwide (elaborated in Schmitz 1999), that provided Mexico did not embarrass the United States by committing wholesale human-rights atrocities, the U.S. would not influence PRI-state domestic policies. The PAN and PRD did successfully expose authoritarianism in Mexico by recounting electoral fraud to international institutions such as the United Nations and the Organization of American States (OAS), but the impact of these gestures in the 1990s was fleeting, and, again, they were only significant inasmuch as they shamed PRI-state moderates.

BOTTOM-UP LOCAL OPPOSITION PARTY STRATEGIES: A CRUCIAL CAUSE OF POSTELECTORAL CONFLICTS

Chapter 5 yielded counterintuitive findings that stronger state electoral institutions did not reduce the frequency of PRD postelectoral conflicts, while high levels of social conflict increased their frequency. The findings point to a broader conclusion, taken for granted in much of the literature on political development and institutions, that the social/political context in which an institution is created is far more significant than the institution itself. Appending pure structural arguments, this finding augurs for the role of individuals and party agents in deciding how to handle structural conditions like economic deprivation or past histories of social conflict, but allows that these structural contexts do constrain. Evidence also directly disconfirms "pure" institutional explanations, confirming that Mexico's transition-era postelectoral conflicts are reducible neither to economic indicators nor to codifications of electoral institution autonomy. Rather, the postelectoral conflicts of Mexico's protracted transition were the product of rational party activists maximizing their organizational strengths and political leverage against the PRI-state in calculations based on past successes and future objectives as well as on the constraints posed by economic conditions and institutions' formal constitutions. Evidence presented in Chapters 5 and 7 confirmed that for the PRD, preexisting social conflicts were a great cause of locally originating postelectoral conflicts, while Chapter 6 highlighted national leverage as the principal motivation for PAN conflicts.

In the 1980s, the PAN, burdened for decades by an antielectoral bias, finally overcame the doctrine of its late 1940s consolidation, achieving electoral success by veering to the ideological center, from transition seeking to patronage seeking. While the PRI-state began fearing the neo-*PANísta* upstarts and their economic clout, the PRI-state also needed to cultivate a loyal opposition, and allowed some initial electoral reforms that actually fostered competition, hoping that these would benefit the PAN over the newly legalized left. The *PANístas* stuck to the rule-of-law advocacy that had become their trademark, but complemented it, especially after 1986, with aggressive street demonstrations and civil disobedience. Ultimately, however, the PAN posed little threat to the PRI-state and was actually embraced when an antiregime party arose on the left.

Cárdenas nearly cost Salinas the presidency in 1988, and the PRD founder clearly cost Labastida the presidency in 2000, even though third-time-around Cárdenas placed a distant third in balloting. Cárdenas's direct impact in 2000 was minimal; the effect he had was from 1988 to the mid-1990s, when he and the PRD channeled regime opposition and brought out the PRI-state's authoritarianism, provoking further distancing by many citizens from the PRI. Most importantly, the PRD provoked the PAN-PRI alliance that made the Fox victory possible. Since the 1995 Oaxtepec meeting, the PRD has shed its radical mantle, but without fully consolidating a moderate identity until 1997–8, when ex-*PRIístas* started winning governorships for the PRD, fully supporting federal electoral reforms and proficiently using the formal institutions of electoral justice. For a brief period in 2000 and 2001, the PRD joined the PAN in an informal alliance against the PRI in Mexico's *cacique*-governed southern states, the most recalcitrant holdouts against Mexico's transition. But that informal alliance had dissipated by 2003, when rumors started to circulate about a national legislative coalition between the PRD and a recentered PRI.

Formal institutional reforms increased electoral uncertainty by legalizing the outlaw leftist parties and channeling them toward elections in 1977, and mandating increases in proportional-representation seats on city councils in 1983. However, the new uncertainties about local electoral outcomes did "trickle up" to the federal level in the late 1990s, but after the PRI's electoral machines had already started falling into disrepair. Contrary to elite-driven transition models, frictions between the technocrats and the moderates within the federal PRI-state were subordinate to pressures between national party headquarters and the local chapters asked to concede to the PAN. Important ideological and strategic tensions between national technocrats and *políticos* did exist, but the biggest friction was between national and local party organizations.

The dismantling of clientalist patterns complemented the evolution of formal institutions toward greater electoral uncertainty and, initially at least, sparked numerous postelectoral conflicts. The gradual reduction in the PRI-state's ability to resort directly to clientalism also had a dramatic impact, especially in rural areas, as electoral reforms made the secret ballot a reality and ruined local *PRIístas'* abilities to reward PRI supporters and chastise opposition voters. The opposition-led enforcement of voter safeguards combined with the increasing viability of non-PRI parties and campaigns by the PRD and the PAN – exemplified by the PAN's jingle, *"toma lo que dan, y vota por el PAN"* (take what they give you and vote for the PAN) – to increase uncertainty about electoral outcomes and postelectoral conflicts, at least initially.

The "tapering off" of opposition postelectoral conflicts at the end of the 1990s is attributable to three causes, only one of which was the development, finally, of credible electoral institutions Mexico's political parties could accept. The other two causes of this key indicator of courting democracy in Mexico were party strategies caused by opportunity structures generated by informal institutions. The PRD's 1995 realization of the limits of its antiregime tactics and subsequent evolution toward transition seeking was also instrumental, even though this policy was inconsistently implemented in localities with demand-based mobilizations, and where factions loyal to the historic left remained strong. The reduced PAN interest in postelectoral mobilization and *concertacesión* after Zedillo proved unable to enforce such deals was also an important reason why opposition postelectoral conflicts diminished. In short, the incremental reforms of state electoral institutions did constrain the opposition party's range of options, but they did not enable the transition. Only party strategies could do that.

Given both opposition parties' increasing use of judicial (rather than political) routes for resolving disputes, the differences in strategy between them (and indeed between them and the PRI) has diminished. Distinctions still do exist between the PAN and the PRD. For example, recall PRD activist Javier González Garza's statements that "the PRD is an optical illusion rather than a party" and that "every day, there are 100 acts in the country in the name of the party about which the national directorate knows nothing." González Garza, the party's electoral affairs director in the early 1990s, summed up the differences between PAN and PRD postelectoral strategies in two concrete distinctions. First, he said that unlike the PAN, the PRD never possessed sufficient discipline to guarantee the execution of agreements negotiated for spoils with state PRI chapters or state or national governments. Second, he said the PRD never benefited from the PAN's agreement with President Salinas that if PAN election losers could demonstrate fraud with electoral acts and documentation, then the Salinas administration would accept adverse results. While the second point has been addressed extensively, the implications of the first warrant further consideration.

FROM CLIENTALISM TO MERE "PORK BARRELING": ELECTORAL INSTITUTIONS AND DEVELOPMENT

The PRD activists say that without proportional-representation seats on municipal councils in the early 1990s, local leaders would likely never have gotten the chance to govern (Gómez Maza interview). Indeed, as the human rights abuses cited in Chapter 4 against *PANísta* and *PRDísta* local officials attest, ensuring opposition city-council seats was no trivial matter in the early 1990s. However, by the late 1990s, the debate has moved beyond the opposition parties' seat entitlements to the question of whether they were being allowed to serve. As stated recently by a PAN activist in Oaxaca, "The proportional representation *regidurias* are now given by law.... It is not a matter of getting an extra position or two, but of giving our regents a real voice in local government, rather than pushing them aside" (Ramales 1998). Rather than being charged with care for parks and village graveyards, opposition party regents want a say in municipal finances and service delivery.

Concertacesión has cost the PAN and PRI credibility. Even now, whenever the PAN votes with the PRI in national congressional chambers, the cry of *concertacesión* is heard, with PRI activists nationwide speculating about what was traded away by the PRI in exchange for the PAN's support. The $60 billion banker bailout in late 1998 was a good example. The PAN initially exposed the PRI-state's lax regulation of a bailout fund for debt-strapped banks and joined the PRD for several months in denouncing the double standard of bailing out bankers who had made bad loans with taxes from the burdened middle classes. However, as interest on the bad loans increased the public deficit, the PAN parliamentary delegation did an about-face and voted with the PRI at the last minute, largely exonerating the bankers and authorizing the executive to pay uncollected debt from federal coffers. Critics at the time saw the PAN-PRI complicity as a replay of their Salinas-era cooperation, with the PAN accorded the Sinaloa governorship (which the party eventually lost, disconfirming that hypothesis) or even the 2000 presidency ("El Blanquiazul Concertacesionó...").

For the PAN, this credibility loss has merely been a manageable transaction cost to be dutifully borne; to the PRI it has been a monumental loss. The PRI has paid dearly for negotiating the voters' will. Since the mid-1990s, national and state party leaders, and outgoing *PRIísta* governors, have had to proclaim prior to each local election that there would be no *concertacesiones*. Such proclamations seem to have proven true over the last year or so, but carried a hollow ring in the early 1990s. The PRI, long a nonideological "catchall" party, also needs to acquire a reputation for consistency and needs to stand for something beyond vague "revolutionary ideals." Only then will the party be able to offer more than clientalism.

Recent research questions whether the provision of particularistic goods is inherently a collective "bad." Drawing from studies of the U.S. Congress (Cox and McCubbins 1993) demonstrating that party leader "whips" are designated to ensure that an electorally optimal mix of collective and particularistic goods are allocated by the party, Lyne (2000, 29) argues that for the developing world too, "what has been so pejoratively labeled pork or particularism is in fact the grease that allows the collective goods policy wheels to turn" even in logrolls where national legislative votes are traded for "pork" in a legislator's district. While combining collective and particularistic goods provision no doubt enhances the capacities of politicians – both to enhance social welfare and maximize career advancement – the provision of collective goods in Mexico requires uncoupling the clientalist networks linking ruling elites, which for decades precluded the provision of any collective goods whatsoever.

The PAN partially overcame the high transaction costs of participating in elections by maintaining consistent programmatic positions, reinforced by an active legislative agenda promoting democratic opening, and other salient, symbolic, and nonexcludable goods that united regime opponents, such as transparent electoral justice. While the PRD struggled to even organize means of distributing goods to constituents and debated how to turn its legacy of social conflict into credibility as Mexico's true democratizers, the PAN outflanked the bickering *PRDístas*. However, the PAN was in the unique position, by virtue of credible self-promotion as the champions of courting democracy, to extract particularistic *concertacesión* gains from the PRI-state and market them as collective goods outcomes. The PRI-state, meanwhile, sacrificed the particularistic side of the delicate balance, thereby hampering their own future, in favor of providing a more collective good, the technocrats' economic policy. The PRI-state misdirected its particularistic means toward collective ends as PAN support for neo-liberal policies was only an indirect effect of *concertacesión* (especially because the PAN would have supported many of these reforms even without the side payments). The direct effect was local PRI discontent leading to internal rebellion within the PRI. Neither party fostered a collective goods public domain, as both the PAN and the PRI were motivated toward particularistic ends, the Mexican polity's only established rewards.

The establishment of a public domain – politician incentives for collective goods provision – was perhaps the greatest public-policy challenge of courting democracy in Mexico. Executive and legislative branch reelection would no doubt foster an electoral connection, where current incentives favor only politicians' ties to their party, which determine their political fate. The former PRI-state's discretion in allocating resources and corrupting elections has been dismantled at the national level, and whatever the failings of Fox's relations with the PAN, the sitting president has not allowed his party to construct a PAN-state. However, this more neutral model for distributing state resources has not entirely trickled down to the states. "Bartlett's Law," advocated by the Interior Secretary–turned–PRI Puebla governor, actually increased gubernatorial discretion over congressionally mandated revenue sharing between state and national governments. The law was a significant boost to the *PRIístas*' interpretation of Zedillo's "new federalism" even after 2000, as the party's remaining local machines still controlled two-thirds of Mexico's governor's mansions.

TOP-DOWN PARTY LEGAL STRATEGIES AND THE ASCENDANCE OF ELECTORAL COURTS

The 2001 test – in which a demagogue PRI governor in Yucatán rose up against the judicial system in the "old PRI's" swan song of defiance – consolidated the authority of Mexico's TEPJF beyond reproach. Already fortified by its bold annulment of the 2000 Tabasco governor's race, won by Madrazo's candidate,[3] the electoral court staved off this brazen challenge while the executive branch watched from the sidelines. Unlike the Salinas era, when the president was known to intervene in local postelectoral conflicts with regularity, Fox and Interior Secretary Creel refused to intervene, at least overtly. Mexico's opposition-turned-government argued that the principle of local autonomy demanded that they not intervene. But having watched the PRI weaken under the weight of *concertacesión*, Fox no doubt also sought to avoid additional wedges between his maverick presidency and the PAN's party and congressional leadership that was already disenchanted with Fox's failure to involve the party more extensively in his administration.

By 2003 the federal electoral court, which in the foreboding summer of 2000 had resorted to stuffing phone bills with glossy ads attesting to the institution's independence and professionalism, was widely viewed as perhaps Mexico's most autonomous "ombudsman" institution, especially after its verdict allowing the Federal Electoral Institute (IFE) to follow the money trails of the 2000 Labastida and Fox campaigns into previously "off limits" domains. The construction of a strong, autonomous electoral institution was no doubt made possible by the confluence of circumstances early in the new millennium. The continuance of a politically plural judicature named by Zedillo and ratified by the PRI-majority Senate, but under the "hands-off" Fox administration, allowed the body to thrive. So did the independent leadership of the IFE's bold ombudsmen and of electoral court presidents like Ojesto Martínez Porcayo, one of the first magistrates to annul PRI-won congressional races in the early 1990s, when rumors floated that PRI bosses held sway with the electoral court and when the presiding magistrate was rewarded by Zedillo after 1994 with a political appointment as Sub-Secretary of the Interior. The rapid evolution of electoral dispute case law, covered in Chapter 3, also facilitated the court's self-sufficiency after 2000, as did its apparent agreement

---

[3] Madrazo's candidate did win a cleaner special election nearly a year later and did take office as governor.

with the Supreme Court, which at least initially upheld the electoral court verdicts hinting at constitutional interpretation.[4]

However, this book has argued that the greatest inducement of all to the fortification of the rule of law in the electoral realm was the persistence of the opposition, and particularly the PAN, in keeping electoral court reform on the legislative agenda since 1947. That party's vision of a legalistic and plural electoral system, combined with the declining PRI's need for a legislative ally starting in 1989, allowed for the construction of autonomous formal legal institutions, even before Mexican democracy was ready for them. The decade-long realignment of political actor postelectoral expectations around these new institutions allowed for a smooth conclusion in the new millennium to Mexico's protracted democratic transition.

While they have died out in most of Mexico, postelectoral conflicts remain the last, best arena for negotiation in Mexico's forgotten hinterlands like Chiapas, Oaxaca, and Tlaxcala. These lingering conflicts, albeit in more benign forms than their lethal antecedents, attest to the persistence of underlying social conflicts, socioeconomic disparities, and desperate citizens who are still not being heard, despite ongoing but often electorally targeted social spending and Fox administration promises. But given the convergence of formal and informal postelectoral dispute adjudication in Mexico's electoral courts, the nature of these conflicts has changed drastically. In the 1980s and early 1990s, the postelectoral process was often an ill-targeted, bloody, and continuous confrontation from election day until the final protesters were dragged away from the buildings they had occupied for months after administration changes. By the late 1990s, and especially in the new millennium, postelectoral conflicts in states with credible dispute resolution mechanisms consisted of a few demonstrations precisely timed to crucial moments in the judicial chain of events – the official vote count and the electoral court ruling.

Where sustained mobilizations used to be provoked by credible allegations of brutality, fraud, and corruption, contemporary sporadic

---

[4] Electoral court magistrates initially complained that the 1996 integration of the electoral court into the Judicial Power of the Federation – with an appeals court more closely integrated into the federal judiciary – had curtailed the discretion they possessed during the mid-1990s, when the electoral court was an independent ombudsman commission. But the previously conservative appeals court, which previously overturned almost all substantive electoral court decisions, has become the most active chamber during the Fox administration. The Supreme Court's May 2002 verdict stripping the electoral court of its ability to interpret the constitution may have ended this fleeting "golden era" of Mexico's electoral court.

protests are held over candidate spending and formulas for allocating proportional-representation seats. Problems relating to the conduct of Mexico's elections have changed by an order of magnitude in just a decade, and the country has gone from having one of the world's most corrupt electoral systems to possessing one of the cleanest. Mexico's meteoric ascendance to electoral transparency is instructive to other democratizing nations, and in areas well beyond the mere technicalities of electoral administration.

THE SIGNIFICANCE OF INSTITUTIONAL LAGS
IN PROTRACTED TRANSITIONS

The "institutional lag," that is, the period between the initial creation of institutions and their acquisition of credibility, seems in Mexico's states to have lasted two electoral processes for Mexico's reluctant formal institution users in the PRD. As demonstrated rigorously in the institutional failure cases, the electoral courts served early on more as a proxy for whether the PRD felt wronged than as a functional dispute-resolving mechanism. By 1995, the electoral court had started to supplant postelectoral mobilizations and bargaining as the principal vehicle for contesting results. Numerous case-study examples also confirm this pattern for other states with crucial (albeit statistically insignificant) precedents of informal institution postelectoral settlements and highlights differences between PRD and PAN strategies in those cases.

Obviously, electoral courts and party compliance with them are far from the only institutions important to the increasing electoral competitiveness of opposition parties and their acceptance of the regime's liberalizing "rules of the game." As elaborated in Chapter 2, reforms mandating greater opposition proportional representation; increased transparency of the electoral lists and balloting stations; the creation of a more plural and autonomous national electoral commission (and subsequent reforms in the states); and limits on campaign contributions and media exposure have had profound positive impacts on parties' decisions to participate in elections and "run to win." The advent of accurate exit polls and voter preference surveys also gave parties better information about their standing, and conditioned expectations. In fact, electoral court reforms were among the last and arguably least important electoral reforms. However, acceptance or contestation of their rulings remains the single best proxy for whether the opposition accepts the "bundle" of practices represented by the official results. Hence this work focused on the endpoint of the electoral decision tree, rather than looking further up for institutional violations of "free and fair elections." As always, the ultimate – albeit subjective – measure of electoral transparency is loser compliance.

The broader point, that opposition party participation in formal electoral institutions leads eventually to these parties' acceptance of their rules, reflects not just on the courts themselves, but on electoral institutions more broadly. Institutions matter, certainly, but so does the "demand side," opposition parties' acceptance of them. While this fundamental point was not lost in the Moncloa model transitions, these pacted transitions did proceed so quickly that it was impossible to meaningfully disaggregate them into component processes. Democracy was not courted, but rather ushered in. After the smoke cleared in these transitions, actors were either "in the system" and compliant, or "outside the system" and rebellious. Democracy was a matter of maintaining a ruling coalition with more "ins" than "outs." This book has argued that in Mexico's protracted transition, opposition compliance was much less automatic.

While the PRI-state was largely able to control the rhythm and pace of Mexico's protracted transition and to prevent an all-out ruptured transition, the opposition parties also impacted the transition and, in fact, generated the impetus for change. The modality of change in the Mexican case bears striking similarities to the means by which transformations came about in Brazil, Kenya, South Korea, and Taiwan, to cite just a few. In such transitions, the authoritarian incumbent's behavior is crucial, to be sure. In all of these cases, tacticians of the ruling elites sought to liberalize the participation of nonthreatening opponents so as to "decompress" the regime and thereby avoid broader opening. But while this authoritarian starting gambit was necessary for political opening, it was far from sufficient. I have argued that the key to understanding the transition was the iterated bargaining of the authoritarian incumbents and their challengers, and that the establishment of competing legal and informal institutions for resolving conflicts, such as over the outcome of elections, was the hallmark of protracted transitions such as Mexico's.

This work has sought to demonstrate, in one of the most important but highly specific arenas of transition, the postelectoral bargaining space, that divergent strategies by the PAN and PRD were instrumental in maintaining pressures for liberalization while simultaneously collecting sufficient electoral spoils to keep alive their internal aspirations of sharing power. While they occupied different positions along the "antiregime to transition-seeking to patronage-seeking" continuum, these parties' positions were constantly shifting in response to intrinsic and extrinsic factors.

Rigorous demonstration that compliance with electoral laws was not automatic or even significant in Mexico's nonpacted transition, and that comparisons of opposition votes with those of the PRI were not decisive, refuted standard explanations of postelectoral mobilization and demonstrated the inadequacy of standard explanations. I introduced local party strategies as the significant missing variable by demonstrating that opposition parties frequently overstepped national and state leadership demands (regardless of PRD policy not to storm town halls before receiving electoral court verdicts). The divergence of the two opposition parties' relations with the PRI-state made cooperation between them all but impossible and reinforced the pivotal role of the authoritarian incumbent as arbiter between them. Contrary to most studies describing internal party organization or opposition party-regime relations in a single grand moment (i.e., a pacted transition), I argued that in studies of protracted transitions, greater emphasis is needed on the interplay between internal party organization, interparty relations, and relations between the opposition and authoritarian incumbents over iterated rounds of bargaining.

My most significant finding offers an important rejoinder to conventional theories, that opposition-party compliance with "rules of the game" is far from automatic, even if those rules appear to be equitable. Formal rules are at best only part of the story. Informal practices, typified here as backroom postelectoral bargaining tables, often illuminate more of the actors' behavior than does merely reviewing court dockets visible in broad daylight. The dominance of extralegal bargaining over legal proceedings was predictably evident in my statistical sample during "period one" (before the introduction of autonomous electoral courts). However, not so predictably, the dominance of the extralegal over the legal also prevailed in "period two," when the opposition parties exploited both paths of dispute resolution, maximizing their side-payment settlements rather than any norm of electoral justice. Only in "period three" was the predictable pattern of formal institution dominance firmly established over informal bargaining. These findings have implications for future research both in microinstitutional studies of judicial institutions generally and in macrolevel research on democratic transitions.

THE NEED FOR A MICROINSTITUTIONAL BASELINE OF JUDICIAL BEHAVIOR

In general, judicial institutions in established rule-of-law polities are difficult to model as political actors. As Gillman appropriately points out

(1997, 11), the difference between rational judges adhering to strong individual preferences and those adhering to norms of principled behavior in a set social order is difficult to ascertain. Unlike reelection-maximizing legislators or budget-maximizing bureaucrats, judges tend to be appointed for extended terms and into positions where the resources or discretion available for their maximization defy parsimonious models of rational politician incentives. However, in still-consolidating judiciaries, where judges' gowns may not yet be long enough to cover executive branch incursions into judicial decision making, magistrate incentives may still be laid bare, as they were in Mexico's electoral courts throughout this work. Studying preconsolidation judicial institutions alone is insufficient for getting to the bottom of magistrate motivations, although it is an effective start toward understanding authoritarian courts (Toharia 1975) and newly democratic ones (Epstein and Knight 1996). However, a means of empirically measuring judiciary institutional success must still be derived.

Judicial "success" is unobservable in broad political (as opposed to strictly legal) terms except as the affected parties' compliance with decisions. Hence, the answer suggested in this work has been to measure judicial success as the null hypothesis of judicial failure. Hence, postelectoral conflicts, an observable occurrence of judicial failure, became the proxy for establishing success. This sleight-of-hand measurement technique, defining "working" judicial institutions as those that do not fail, may only be feasible under very specific conditions, where all or most incidents of noncompliance are observably manifested. But when such conditions exist, such as in "period two" protracted transitions when actor compliance with formal institutions is possible but not given, this method can powerfully assess judicial institution effectiveness.

I maintain that this novel means of assessing judicial failure may be extended, within limits, to other issue areas where noncompliance with the law carries observable manifestations. Of course, sufficient variance must exist within the sample of cases to make such measurement meaningful. The mere 16 percent occurrence of postelectoral conflicts even in the most varied of my samples (period two) barely approached the minimum threshold of outcome variance (postelectoral mobilization versus no mobilization) discernible by most statistics programs. More generally, the dynamic of dueling focal points, derived from work on informal institutions by authors like Ellickson and Knight, merits further refinement, but with greater reference to concrete cases where formal and informal institutions for dispute adjudication compete head-on.

What of the lag between the creation of electoral courts and compliance with them, the enigmatic "second period" (T2) of my study? This specification of the period required for the actors to decide to comply is a necessary consideration, one that I assert may be factored into most studies on the transition to a rule of law (separate but often collinear with democratic transitions). I contend that past studies of judicial institution building and democratization have failed to formally measure actor compliance for two reasons: they assumed actor compliance because in the abrupt pacted transitions they studied, such compliance was largely granted by all actors in the elite settlement pact, and there existed no subtle means of measuring partial compliance anyway. Such compliance was "all or nothing," just like the pacted transition itself.

COURTING DEMOCRACY – THE ART OF INDUCING
PROTRACTED TRANSITIONS

Lamounier cites the lack of scholarly attention to Brazilian electoral politics under the military "electoral" dictatorship as one of the principal reasons why the Brazilianists collaborating on *Authoritarian Brazil: Origins, Policies and Failure* (1973) failed to anticipate the electoral decompression that began immediately after the book's publication. Certainly they were not the only prognosticators to miss the subtle signs of the increasing importance of elections in Brazil. Lehoucq laments the opinion of many social scientists that "the history of dictatorship, civil war, coups d'etat and the like in Latin America make a study of electoral competition irrelevant, outside a few places like Chile, Costa Rica, and Uruguay ... " (1997, 18). Scholars of Eastern Europe (excepting Dinka and Skidmore) also ignored the electoral affirmation of communist governments until 1989. Indeed, perhaps the only serious treatment of elections in authoritarian regimes, *Elections Without Choice* (1979), was unable to reach generalizable conclusions.

The mere existence of elections, however, generates a demand for opposition. In authoritarian regimes, the demand for an opposition willing to continuously lose but continue to compete must somehow be addressed by the authoritarian incumbents. The frequent answer, as Chapter 6 demonstrates with respect to the co-optation of the PAN by the PRI, is in side payments. But patient and savvy opponents able to constantly up the ante of their participation can sometimes parlay small gains into bigger ones at crucial moments. Hence the emphasis here has been on prefounding elections and on changes in opposition compliance, as these register significant changes not just in the conduct of elections (an issue of merely technical interest at best), but in the entire incentive structure of authoritarian state–opposition relations.

The literature on Brazil's and South Korea's electoral transitions referred to the possible "Mexicanization" of those countries[5] as a choice not made at the juncture when the military leaders performed their Dahlian (1971) calculations of whether to liberalize or repress. The "Mexican solution" was considered to be the hardening of one party dominance to permit only a token cosmetic opposition. At that moment, Mexico was at its apex of great economic growth and tremendous regime stability with only minor transgressions against Mexican citizens.[6] Brazil's decision not to Mexicanize but rather to allow genuine opening allowed opposition victories at the state and local levels, which eventually diminished the military's party, the National Renovation Alliance (ARENA), raised opposition Brazilian Democratic Movement (MDB) expectations, and, most importantly, afforded the MDB rewards to loyal activists, who became governors, mayors, and bureaucrats rather than remaining antiregime banner wavers. Furthermore, as presciently noted by Cammack (1988), the conversion of the PRI from electoral machine into a mere administrator of neo-liberal policies that were not of the party leaders' making has increased similarities with the authoritarian ARENA, which was also responsible for implementing policies designed outside the party bureaucracy.

The exaltation of 1970s authoritarian Mexico as a model that Latin American and East Asian authoritarians could aspire to makes the achievements of the PAN and the PRD (as well as the PRI moderates) all the more impressive. Slowly opening the world's longest continuous one-party system to the 2000 crescendo of transition was a remarkable achievement by the opposition parties, almost despite themselves. The issue for further research then, particularly as other longtime one-party systems such as Indonesia, Nigeria, and the People's Republic of China gesture toward the protracted transition model, is what can

---

[5] On Brazil, see Lamounier 1989 (60, 70) and Cammack 1988. On South Korea, see Im 1989 (228).

[6] Certainly the 1968 massacre of students by federal police at Tlatelolco was not considered "soft repression" by the families of the hundreds of victims, nor by the survivors of the 1970s *guerrilla* movements who were widely persecuted and even forcibly "disappeared." However, compared to the regimes' complicity in the wholesale disappearances of hundreds of regime dissidents in the Southern Cone's "Dirty Wars," Mexico was not a major human-rights abuser. It was only in the 1980s, when South America democratized, that Mexico's less glaring but long-standing human-rights abuses became more conspicuous by comparison.

"Mexicanization" in the twenty-first century mean for regime oppositions in these liberalizing regimes?

This question must be addressed with a caveat about the limits of my
claims. This book has not sought to prove that opposition party behavior causes democratization. My argument has been more nuanced. I have
sought only to argue that such parties have often been underestimated in
empirical studies of Third Wave democratization and offer a corrective to
this omission. Nor have I engaged in an ontological debate about which
came first, the cracks within the authoritarian incumbent regime or an
organized opposition. I have demonstrated, however, that Mexicanization proponents in Brazil and South Korea, for example, erred by merely
studying the PRI-state rather than also considering the crucial role of
the PAN and PRD. The authoritarian incumbents cannot be understood
in a vacuum. Much more attention is needed to the relations between
the authoritarians and their organized opponents, and the implications
of these relations for courting democracy, political party behavior, social
movements, and the new institutionalism.

A normative concern arises in relation to the typology of transitional
opposition parties briefly mentioned here. Which opposition strategy –
"antiregime," "transition-seeking," or "patronage-seeking" – is more
likely to propel a protracted electoralist transition into all-out democratization? Patronage-seeking parties are frequently placated with side
payments from the authoritarian incumbents, rendering them electoral-
victory "poor" but side-payment "rich" in sinecures, proportional-
representation seats, public financing, etc. However as in the Mexican
case, patronage-seeking oppositions can be temporarily induced out of
this duplicity by transition-seeking parties, prompting a realignment of
opposition forces and united opposition. Such patterns of authoritarian-
opposition behavior have characterized several pacted transitions arising
from the acceleration of protracted transitions. Revisiting cases such as
the Philippines and Chile, but with these types of questions, might afford greater appreciation of Mexican authoritarians' prowess at maintaining a divided and conquered opposition for decades through a selective incentive system for dispensing consolation prizes to electoral
runners-up. This sort of "postelectoral connection" between patronage-
seeking opposition and its constituency served the authoritarian
incumbents and patronage-seeking PAN, but only until the antiregime
PRD also committed to transition seeking. Indeed, it took them decades,
but for cases meeting the specified preconditions, the PAN, the PRD, and
the PRI's moderates have finally given "Mexicanization" a good name.

Appendix A

Coding the Postelectoral Conflict Dependent Variable

The sample states slightly overrepresent both opposition-party registration of candidates and postelectoral conflicts, but in most cases, the sample does not overrepresent the universe of all of Mexico's municipalities by more than 5 percent (Table A.1). Postelectoral conflicts were coded from a wide range of media sources, including those listed in Appendix B.1 with regard to coding of the independent variable "localized social conflicts," as well as the national and local newspapers cited in the bibliography. Multiple opposition-party mobilizations in one municipality were rare, but when they occurred, in every case I entered only the mobilization by the non-PRI contender (PAN or PRD), as there were not enough PRI or third opposition-party mobilizations to allow for the model to retain statistical significance when they were included as separate dependent variable categories. In the dozen or so cases with mobilizations by both the PAN and the PRD, the higher vote-getter among the runner-up parties was credited with the conflict, as I considered that party to be the main postelectoral contender (and usually there was a large margin between second- and third-place finishers). Just as electoral contention was either PRI-PAN or PRI-PRD but almost never PAN-PRI-PRD (at least not until the late 1990s), postelectoral contention also followed this pattern during the period under study. The selection of the ten sample states and specification of the time periods is addressed in Chapter 5. Postelectoral conflicts were coded as follows: 4 = conflicts resulting in deaths; 3 = conflicts producing serious injuries or building occupations longer than one month; 2 = multiple-event mobilizations lasting less than one month; and 1 = single-iteration (one-day) mobilizations.

TABLE A.1 *Comparison of National Postelectoral Conflict Trends with Those of Ten-State Sample*

Period/Descriptor by Year	PAN National	PRD National	PAN 10-State	PRD 10-State	Period/Descriptor by T1, T2, T3
1st period 1989–91 total N	2,388	2,388	1,005	1,005	T1 1989–91 total N
1st period candidates run	1,030	1,134	468	564	T1 candidates run
1st period percent w/ candidates	43%	47%	47%	56%	T1 period percent w/ candidates
1st period postelectoral conflict	72	206	54	118	T1 1 postelectoral conflict
1st period percent conflictive	7%	18%	12%	21%	T1 percent conflictive
2nd period 1992–4 total N	2,393	2,393	1,005	1,005	T2 period 1992–4 total N
2nd period candidates run	1,399	1,316	736	712	T2 period candidates run
2nd period percent w/ candidates	58%	55%	73%	71%	T2 percent w/ candidates
2nd period postelectoral conflict	85	269	24	162	T2 postelectoral conflict
2nd period percent conflictive	6%	20%	3%	23%	T2 percent conflictive
3rd period 1995–7 total N	2,005	2,005	1,005	1,005	T3 period 1995–7 total N
3rd period candidates run	1,679	1,744	937	926	T3 period candidates run
3rd period percent w/ candidates	84%	87%	93%	92%	T3 percent w/ candidates
3rd period postelectoral conflict	27	162	7	51	T3 postelectoral conflict
3rd period percent conflictive	2%	9%	1%	6%	T3 percent conflictive
4th period 1998–2000 total N	2,009	2,009	N/A	N/A	Post-T3 1998–2000 total N
4th period candidates run	1,663	1,741	N/A	N/A	Post-T3 candidates run
4th period percent w/ candidates	83%	87%	N/A	N/A	Post-T3 percent w/ candidates
4th period postelectoral conflict	19	91	N/A	N/A	Post-T3 postelectoral conflict
4th period percent conflictive	1%	5%	N/A	N/A	Post-T3 percent conflictive

Note: Changes in the total number of municipalities from the first period base (from 2,393 in 1989 to 2,427 in 2000) are due to the addition of new municipalities, most of which are given at www.inafed.gob.mx/numeros/recien.htm. The "Ten-State" samples strictly follow the timeline given in Chapter 5 and generally follow the time periods of the national samples presented here. Some 413 municipalities were subtracted from the second period's total number of municipalities (2,418), because these municipalities were removed from partisan contention as in 1995 the elections in Oaxaca were transferred to *usos y costumbres* (which also reduced the fourth period total by 418 from 2,427). The following municipalities are missing from the "Ten-State" sample because elections were not held or the author was unable to obtain them: first period – Nicolas Ruiz, Chiapas, Almoloya del Rio, Mexico State, and Abasolo, Nuevo León; second period – Nicolas Ruiz and Ocosingo, Chiapas, Almoloya del Rio, Mexico State, Vista Grande, Michoacán, Abasolo, Nuevo León, and Rio Grande, Zacatecas. Vista Grande, Michoacán, is missing from all three periods. The "percent conflictive" comes from dividing the number of conflicts by the number of elections with candidates running from the given party.

294

Appendix B

Coding of Independent Variables

Social Conflicts Index

This variable was an index composed of: (1) human-rights assessments for the middle years of the period under study (measured by state), (2) agrarian conflicts per capita as taken from the November 1998 "cut" of complaints filed to the federal Attorney General for Agrarian Issues, measured starting in 1992, and (3) from compilation of "citizen demands" for the six months preceding each election.

1. The human-rights assessments were compiled from national media (*Reforma/El Norte,* and *El Financiero* on CD-ROM) and an April 1999 "cut" of the "Heriberto Jara" Center for Municipal Services (CESEM) *Base Hemerográfica de Acontecer Municipal de México, 1994–1998.* While none of these sources continuously covered the period under study (leading me to a more specific municipality-by-municipality measure using local press), there was sufficient overlap for the years 1993 through 1995 for me to average them. Incidents of human-rights abuses (excluding prison uprisings and domestic violence) were coded as follows: one for intimidation, violent confrontation (but without serious injury), or detainment, as of a journalist; two for disappearance, serious injury, and reports of torture; three for one death; four for multiple deaths; five for five to twenty deaths; ten for more than twenty deaths. An effort was made not to duplicate incidents across sources. This state-level measure was weighted as 50 percent of the value of the "Social Conflicts Index."

TABLE B.1 *Local and National Newspapers Used*

State/Period	Local Press	National Press	Election Date	Start of Coding
Chiapas 1991	No newspaper[1]	CD-press compilation	8/18/91	2/18/91
Chiapas 1995	No newspaper	Infosel-Reforma	10/15/95	4/15/95
Chiapas 1998	No newspaper	La Jornada	10/04/98	4/04/98
Edo. de México 1990	*El Sol de Toluca*	El Norte/Reforma	11/11/90	5/11/90
Edo. de México 1993	*Demócrata de México*	El Norte/Reforma	11/14/93	5/14/93
Edo. de México 1996	*Demócrata de México*	Infosel-Reforma	11/10/96	5/10/96
Guanajuato 1991	*El Heraldo de León*	El Norte/Reforma	12/01/91	6/01/91
Guanajuato 1994	*El Heraldo de León*	El Norte/Reforma	12/04/94	6/04/94
Guanajuato 1997	*El Heraldo de León*	El Norte/Reforma	7/06/97	1/06/97
Jalisco 1992	*El Informador*	CD-press compilation	2/09/92	8/09/91
Jalisco 1995	*El Informador*	El Norte/Reforma	2/12/95	8/12/94
Jalisco 1998	*El Informador*	La Jornada	11/10/97	5/10/97
Michoacán 1989	*La voz de Michoacán*	No CD source	12/03/89	6/03/89
Michoacán 1992	*El Sol de Morelia*	CD-press compilation	12/06/92	6/06/92
Michoacán 1995	*La voz de Michoacán*	El Norte/Reforma	11/12/95	5/12/95
Nuevo León 1991	No newspaper	CD-press compilation	11/10/91	5/10/91
Nuevo León 1994	No newspaper	El Norte/Reforma	8/21/94	2/21/94
Nuevo León 1997	No newspaper	El Norte/Reforma	7/06/97	1/06/97
Sonora 1991	*Diario del Yaqui*	CD-press compilation	8/18/91	2/18/91
Sonora 1994	*El Imparcial*	El Norte/Reforma	8/21/94	2/21/94
Sonora 1997	*El Imparcial*	El Norte/Reforma	7/06/97	1/06/97
Veracruz 1991	*Diario de Xalapa*	CD-press compilation	11/10/91	5/10/91
Veracruz 1994	*Diario de Xalapa*	El Norte/Reforma	11/13/94	5/13/94
Veracruz 1997	*Diario de Xalapa*	El Norte/Reforma	10/19/97	4/19/97
Yucatán 1990	*Diario de Yucatán*	No CD source	11/25/90	5/25/90
Yucatán 1993	*Diario de Yucatán*	El Norte/Reforma	11/28/93	5/28/93
Yucatán 1995	*Diario de Yucatán*	El Norte/Reforma	5/28/95	11/28/94
Zacatecas 1992	*Momento*	CD-press compilation	8/02/92	2/02/92
Zacatecas 1995	*Momento*	El Norte/Reforma	8/06/95	2/06/95
Zacatecas 1998	*Momento*	La Jornada	7/05/98	1/05/98

Upon scaling and averaging the values across three years to a five-point scale to reduce the range of values, I obtained the following values: Chiapas – four, Guanajuato – one, Jalisco – one, Mexico State – five, Michoacán – two, Sonora – one, Veracruz – two,

---

[1] Indicates that there was no local newspaper available at the National Library or online for this period, and hence national press was relied upon exclusively.

Yucatán – two, and Zacatecas – one. Aside from a higher valuation for Mexico State than for Chiapas (due no doubt to the Mexico City and suburbs bias of the national media), the results are consistent with expectations. I previously gathered complaints filed with local state human-rights commissions, hoping this would offer a more localized assessment of human-rights abuses, but found that during the period of the study, state human-rights commissions were just being implemented and in many cases received few complaints because citizens either were unaware of them, did not trust them, or did not think them to be effective.

2. Authorities resolved some 90 percent of the 89,667 collective agrarian conflicts in my ten-state sample, but having no measurement of intensity of the conflicts, I counted them all equally, dividing them by population estimates to establish agrarian conflicts per capita. The fifty-year legacies of these agrarian divisions offered a useful proxy for social unrest that could be "framed" by political entrepreneur opposition activists. This local measure was weighted as 25 percent of the index's value. I scaled the values to reduce the range to within the following limits: zero to one conflicts per capita was scaled as zero; one to three conflicts per capita was scaled as one; three to six conflicts per capita was scaled as two; and above six was scaled as three.

3. Municipal citizen demands, coded by research assistants from local and national press for the six months between each of the three electoral cycles and then averaged together into one measure, were taken from the newspapers listed in Table B.1.

Events were coded by the following scale, with each event receiving a singular entry (from start to finish) from each media source. In other words, if a citizen demand[2] was mentioned in both sources, it was counted twice (to highlight its importance). The citizen demands at the municipal level were coded as follows: one for demands lasting only one day without any of the following – violence, detainees, injuries, deaths, or property damage; two for demands lasting at least a week or in which there was

---

[2] The principal key words used for CD-ROM searches, and issues sought in text analysis, included the following: blockade, corruption, credit, debtors, demand, electricity, human rights, indigenous, mobilization, movement, pavement, peasants, police, protest, squatters, stoppage, security, street vendor, sewage, strike, takeover, violence, and water. Any protests relating to elections were stricken from the sample.

violence that did not result in serious injury nor material damage; three for demands lasting between a week and a month, or that involved detainees, injuries, and/or material damage; and four for events lasting longer than a month or that resulted in deaths. Scores (ranging from one to forty-five) were doubled for cities over 100,000 except for state capitals, which are known to host more than their share of demonstrations. Upon being divided by T2 population to render citizen demands per capita and transformed by a factor of ten the resulting numbers were scaled as follows: values of zero to one were coded as zero; one to four were coded as one; four to eight were coded as two; and above eight were coded as three.

The final "Local Conflicts Index" formula was: [2(Indicator 1) + Indicator 2 + Indicator 3]/4

Prior Electoral Conflicts (PRD and PAN)

This variable was obtained by recoding the dependent variable (explained in Appendix A) as a "dummy variable" for which a value of one represented a postelectoral conflict by the given party during the prior period, while a value of zero represented no conflict. Postelectoral conflicts during period T0 (1987–9) were also considered.

Strength of Institutions

This variable was coded from state electoral laws in effect during the electoral process (see Bibliography). See Table B.2 for the index.

PRD and PAN Organization (Poll Watchers)

First, using IFE data[3] on the percentage of precincts "covered" by PAN and PRD poll workers on the election day of the 1988, 1991, 1994, and 1997 federal elections, and extrapolating data for the years between these elections, I used these indicators as proxies for state PAN and PRD organization levels. The values during election years, with "between-election" years extrapolated, are as follows in Table B.3.

---

[3] I tried to collect more localized data from the electoral commissions of the ten sample states but quickly found that it was spotty and did not cover the entire time period of the study.

Ratio of PRD/PAN-to-PRI Votes

For each opposition party, this variable is a ratio of the party's vote to those officially obtained by the PRI. This is more informative than comparing the election winner (the PRI in over 80 percent of the races during the study) and first runner-up, because as a rule the PAN and the PRD did not contest elections won by other parties besides the PRI (and the overwhelming pattern of two-party competition meant that, for example, where the PAN won, there would be no real PRD organization to challenge them in any case). In one T2 case and three ALL T cases, there were no PRI candidates, and hence this measure was impossible (and indeed the cases were excluded from analysis because the variable called for division by zero).

Pct. Earning Subminimum Wages

Indicator 9 of the National Population Council and National Water Commission's (CONAPO) marginalization index, this variable measured the percentage of households in each municipality earning fewer than two minimum wages. For T1 data was used from the 1990 census, for T3 the data was from the 2000 census, and for T2 an average was taken of the other two values.

Municipal Income Per Capita

Taken from the Interior Secretary's Center for Municipal Development data (available at www.segob.gob.mx), this shows each municipality's total income during the election year (from federal and local sources) divided by that year's population (from official census data in 1990, 1995, and 2000, and from official projections and author projections using the standard growth curve for intervening years).

Population (Natural Log)

Here I took official census data in 1990, 1995, and 2000, and used 1995 official projections for intervening years in the late 1990s, and author projections using the standard growth curve for intervening years in the early 1990s. The natural log of the population was taken to transform the variable into a range more consistent with the other variables.

TABLE B.2 *State Electoral Institution Autonomy from Executive Branch. State electoral codes' rankings on scale of autonomy from executive branch range from zero (unspecified or no autonomy) to three (full autonomy) in each category.*

State and Year	Election Council Makeup	Election Council Selection	Limit on Party Legislators	Electoral Observer Role	Electoral List Audited?	Campaign Spending Regulation	Poll Worker Selection	Electoral Court Autonomy	Executive Magistrate Selection Role	Acceptable Evidence Range	Overall Average Autonomy (0 to 1)
Chiapas 1991	1	0	0	0	1	0	1	1	3	0	.23
Guanajuato 1991	1	0	3	0	2	1	2	2	2	0	.50
Jalisco 1992	1	0	2	0	2	1	1	1	3	0	.37
Mexico 1990	1	0	0	0	1	0	1	1	2	0	.20
Michoacán 1989	1	0	0	0	1	0	0	0	1	0	.10
Nuevo León 1991	1	0	3	0	1	2	3	2	3	1	.53
Sonora 1991	1	0	0	0	0	1	0	1	3	0	.20
Veracruz 1991	1	0	2	0	1	1	0	1	3	0	.30
Yucatán 1990	1	0	0	0	1	0	0	0	0	0	.07
Zacatecas 1992	1	1	2	0	2	0	1	1	3	0	.37
T1 Avg.	1.00	0.14	1.21	0.00	1.14	0.57	0.93	0.30	1.64	0.07	.25
Chiapas 1995	3	3	3	0	2	3	3	3	3	1	.80
Guanajuato 1994	1	2	3	1	3	1	2	3	2	2	.67
Jalisco 1995	3	3	3	3	2	3	2	2	2	2	.83
Mexico 1993	1	0	1	0	2	3	2	2	2	2	.50
Michoacán 1992	1	1	0	0	0	1	3	2	3	1	.40
Nuevo León 1994	3	1	3	0	2	3	3	2	2	2	.70
Sonora 1994	0	2	2	3	2	2	2	2	2	1	.60

Veracruz 1994	3	3	2	2	1	2	2	2	2	.67
Yucatán 1993	1	2	2	0	1	2	2	1	1	.53
Zacatecas 1995	2	2	3	3	2	2	2	2	2	.73
T2 Avg.	2.07	1.93	2.07	1.50	1.71	2.36	2.14	1.79	1.79	.65
Chiapas 1998	3	3	3	0	2	3	3	3	1	.80
Guanajuato 1997	1	2	3	1	3	1	3	3	2	.67
Jalisco 1997	3	3	3	3	2	3	3	3	3	.97
Mexico 1996	3	3	3	3	1	2	2	3	3	.83
Michoacán 1995	3	3	2	3	1	2	2	3	3	.73
Nuevo León 1997	3	3	3	3	2	3	3	3	3	.93
Sonora 1997	3	3	3	3	2	3	2	2	1	.83
Veracruz 1997	3	3	2	3	1	2	3	3	2	.80
Yucatán 1995	3	2	2	3	2	2	2	2	2	.83
Zacatecas 1998	2	3	2	3	3	3	3	3	2	.87
T3 Avg.	2.78	2.93	2.71	2.36	2.14	2.57	2.79	2.71	2.29	.85

Coding Electoral Institution Autonomy

1. *Electoral Council Makeup*

0 = no ombudsmen (all executive named)

1 = some executive appointments/some legislator- or party-named

2 = mostly legislatively selected ombudsmen (possible exception of executive-named president)

3 = all ombudsmen selected by judicial branch, parties, or civil society, as well as legislature

2. *Election Council Head Selection*

0 = minister of interior oversees elections directly

1 = governor names head directly

2 = executive nominates, but subject to legislative confirmation

3 = executive has no role (judicial or legislative nomination and legislative confirmation)

3. *Limits on Legislators per Political Party*
0 = no specification
1 = "governability clause" inflating seats of highest vote getter, fabricating majority
2 = no governability clause, but no limit on a party's representation
3 = no governability clause and limits on maximum number of seats accorded to one party

4. *Electoral Observer Role*
0 = no specified role for observers
1 = observers mentioned but rights not specified
2 = observers mentioned, rights specified, but no official role
3 = observers mentioned, rights specified, and role accorded to report irregularities

5. *Electoral List Audited?*
0 = no mention of electoral list
1 = use of federal electoral list without audits
2 = use of federal electoral list with party access for audits
3 = use of federal electoral list with external (corporate) audit

6. *Campaign Spending Regulation*
0 = no mention of campaign expenditures, or only that parties' expenses are tax deductible
1 = provision of public funds on a partially proportional basis, but favoring larger parties
2 = provision of public funds on a fully proportional basis
3 = provision of at least partially proportional public funds; limits on privately raised funds

7. *Poll Worker Selection*
0 = unspecified
1 = local electoral commission names poll workers directly
2 = lottery of registered voters, plus training, yields poll workers
3 = lottery of voters, training, and vetting of list by parties or "vigilance committees" yields poll workers

8. *Electoral Court Autonomy*
0 = no electoral court exists; election certification by electoral institute or legislature
1 = "administrative" court exists but only advises certification by electoral institute or legislature
2 = electoral court has authority, but outcomes may be altered by an electoral college, if only in governors' races
3 = electoral court is the final authority on electoral outcomes

9. *Executive Role in Magistrate Selection*
0 = same officials preside over dispute settlement as over election
1 = special judges appointed directly by executive, even if only some of them
2 = special judges appointed indirectly by executive (subject to approval by legislature)
3 = judges appointed by branches or parties with no direct ties to executive

10. *Acceptable Evidence Range*
0 = no specification of rules governing evidence presentation
1 = rules allow presentation only of "official" documents
2 = rules allow presentation of "official" documents and "private" and technical proof at magistrate discretion
3 = rules allow public, private, technological evidence

TABLE B.3 *Estimated Opposition Party Poll Workers by State and Year*

State	1991 Midterm Races			1994 Presidential Races			1997 Midterm Races			Three-Election Average by State		
	PRI	PAN	PRD	PRI	PAN	PRD	PRI	PAN	PRD	PRI	PAN	PRD
Chiapas	9	22	12*	97	42	78	100	96	93	69	53	61
Guanajuato	92	70	42*	100	100	68	99	99	85	97	90	65
Jalisco	94	35	14	100	96	58	99	98	87	98	76	53
Mexico State	93	20	28*	100	68	90	97	92	94	97	60	71
Michoacán	98	23	84	100	68	99	100	90	99	99	60	94
Nuevo León	85	38	11	100	96	66	100	99	86	95	78	54
Sonora	100	30	10	100	87	68	98	96	95	99	71	58
Veracruz	89	11	41	100	55	94	100	98	93	96	55	76
Yucatán	87	60	1	100	99	37	100	100	92	96	86	43
Zacatecas	86	11	20	97	71	86	99	92	90	94	58	65
Average	86	29	17	100	77	75	99	95	93	95	68	64

Note: *denotes a coalition between the PRD and the PPS.

Sources: Author calculations based on data given by Federal Electoral Institute (1993) 87, 285; Federal Electoral Institute (1995) 307–9; Executive Directorate of Electoral Organization of the Federal Electoral Institute (1997). The given 1991 data for the number of ballot boxes had to be multiplied by three to establish a proper proportion of poll workers to ballot boxes (three representatives from each party were allowed at a given poll). The adjustment was already made for 1994 and 1997. No conclusive data was available for the 1988 federal elections, so the 1991 data was extrapolated backward using the growth formula: $\exp[\ln(t + 1 / t)/10] - 1$.

Pct. Population in Municipal Seat

Taken from the National Center for Municipal Development's 1998 CD-ROM (*Los Municipios de México – Información Para el Desarrollo*) for 1990 and from 2000 census data, this was each municipality's "municipal seat" population divided by that year's total population. For the 2000 census figures, contained on the CD-ROM *Principales Resultados por Localidad* (2001), the municipal seat was taken to be the first community listed within in each municipality. For T1 I used the 1990 census, for T3 I used the 2000 census, and for T2 I averaged these together.

Indigenous Language Speakers

This variable was a percentage calculated by dividing the population of indigenous language speakers by the total population over the age of five (as given by the census). Data was used from the 1990 census for T1, data was used from the 2000 census for T3, and an average was taken of the other two values for T2.

Municipal Population Density

I divided population by the total surface area of the municipality (given in square kilometers).

State Governor National Profile

Using official biographies gathered from several sources, including Web sites and Camp (1995), I coded governors by the following scale, based on their career trajectories before assuming the governorship:

4 = repeat federal congressional member, secretary of state, subsecretary, national ruling party leadership

3 = one-time congressional member, federal bureaucrat for more than ten years (but never reached any position listed in number 4)

2 = any federal experience at all (less than ten years, and not including positions listed in number 4)

1 = no federal experience

Period

This dummy variable was coded one for T1, two for T2, and three for T3.

ADDITIONAL VARIABLE TESTED IN T2

Index of Electoral Fraud

Measured for T2 only (data was not available for every state in T1 and hence could not be used in the ALL T model), this was an average of two indicators: the number of parties submitting electoral court complaints during the days after each election, and the total number of complaints submitted. On those occasions – uncommon by T2 and T3 – that activists launched postelectoral conflicts *before* their lawyers filed complaints (not uncommon in T1 and in previous PRD mobilizations), it may appear inconceivable to consider electoral court complaint filings as a cause of postelectoral conflicts. However, the filings are used still, as they are the best single indicator of exactly how rigged opposition parties perceived the elections to be.

Bibliography

Primary Sources

Attorney General for Agrarian Concerns. 1999. Provision of data by Chief of Advisors Maribel Méndez de Lara on collective agrarian conflicts registered by that office between April 1992 and November 1998 in seventeen of Mexico's states in correspondence with author (February 23).

Bartlett Díaz, Manuel. 1996. *Huejotzingo: Hechos y Razones*. Puebla: Gobierno del Estado de Puebla.

Calderón Hinojosa, Felipe. 1996. Text of April 28 Puebla Speech on Electoral Justice. Typescript.

Campeche Electoral Tribunal. Adjudication records for 1994 and 1997 local elections. Obtained with assistance of Federal Electoral Institute library.

Campeche Superior Tribunal of Justice. 1996. *Revista del Honorable Tribunal Superior de Justicia del Estado de Campeche Numero XIV*. Campeche: Tribunal Superior de Justicia del Estado de Campeche.

———. 1998. Correspondence with Elvia Arzate Estrada of the Federal Electoral Institute Library, March 16, 1998, listing 1994 and 1997 state electoral court case submissions.

Cárdenas, Cuauhtémoc. "Tercer Congreso Nacional del Partido de la Revolución Democrática – Segunda intervención del ingeniero Cuauhtémoc Cárdenas Solórzano en la sesión vespertina de la mesa uno," text of August 25, 1995, speech in Oaxtepec, Morelos. Typescript.

Chamber of Deputies. 1987. *Diario de Debates*, LIII Legislature, Year 1, Number 21, May 22, 1987, 13–31 and 1988 passim.

Chiapas Electoral Council. 1995. *Código Electoral del Estado de Chiapas*. Tuxtla Gutiérrez: Consejo Electoral de Chiapas.

Chiapas Electoral Tribunal. 1995. Chiapas Electoral Council and Electoral Tribunal Records for 1995 Local Elections. Typescripts obtained from Party of the Democratic Revolution archives in Tuxtla Gutiérrez and corroborated by official records.

————. 1996. *Memoria del Proceso Electoral 1995 en Chiapas*. Tuxtla Gutiérrez: Chiapas Electoral Tribunal.

Chiapas Governor's Office. 1988. *Código Electoral del Estado de Chiapas*. Tuxtla Gutiérrez: Chiapas State Governor's Office – Diario Oficial.

Chiapas State Electoral Council and Electoral Tribunal Records for 1998 Local Elections. Typescripts and notes sent to author in electronic correspondence with Magistrate Miguel Zenteno Orantes (January 11, 1999).

Chiapas State Legislature. 1995. *Memoria Legislativa, 1991–1995*. Tuxtla Gutiérrez: Chiapas State Legislature.

————. 1997. *Código Electoral del Estado de Chiapas*. Tuxtla Gutiérrez: Chiapas State Legislature.

Díaz Vazquez, José Luis. 1998. "Comparativo del Presupuesto de Egresos de la Federación Autorizado al Tribunal Electoral del Poder Judicial de la Federación de 1991 a 1997 Dentro del Ramo 22 'Organos Electorales' y Desde 1998 en el Ramo 03 'Poder Judicial,'" included in author correspondence with administrative secretary of Electoral Tribunal of the Judicial Power of the Federation.

"Dictamen del jurado popular," in Lau, Rubén. 1989. *Cuadernos del Norte: Las Elecciones en Chihuahua (1983–1988)*. Chihuahua: Universidad Autónomo de Chihuahua. 82–7.

Editorial Porrúa. 1988. *Código Federal Electoral*. Mexico City: Editorial Porrúa.

Encinas Rodríguez, Alejandro. 1995. "Informe al III Congreso Nacional del Partido de la Revolución Democrática Sobre el Estado que Guarda la Organización del Partido," presented in Oaxtepec, Morelos on August 23. Typescript.

Federal Electoral Institute. 1993. *Cuadro Comparativo del Código Federal de Instituciones y Procedimientos Electorales y Reformas de las Que Fue Objeto en Septiembre de 1993*. Mexico City: Instituto Federal Electoral.

————. 1993. *Memorias del Proceso Electoral Federal de 1991, Tomo IV, Vol. I – Organización, Jornada, y Resultados Electorales*. Mexico City: Instituto Federal Electoral.

————. 1995. *Memorias del Elección Federal de 1994: Tomo IV, Volumen 4*. Mexico City: Instituto Federal Electoral.

————. 1997. Electoral results by district, mimeo, Executive Directorate of Electoral Organization, Instituto Federal Electoral.

Federal Electoral Tribunal. 1992. *Memoria 1991*. Mexico City: Tribunal Federal Electoral.

————. 1994. Complaint of Appeal (from IFE) 400/94 (resolution). Mexico City: Tribunal Federal Electoral.

————. 1995. *Memoria 1994*. Mexico City: Tribunal Federal Electoral.

Federal Electoral Tribunal of the Judicial Power of the Federation. 1996a. Constitutional revision electoral complaint 1/1996 (complaint and resolution).

————. 1996b. Constitutional revision electoral complaint 48/1997 (resolution).

————. 1997a. "Informe Anual 1996–1997." Typescript by the Electoral Tribunal of the Judicial Power of the Federation.

————. 1997b. *Ley General del Sistema de Medios de Impugnación en Materia Electoral*. Mexico City: Tribunal Electoral del Poder Judicial de la Federación.

————. 1998. "Documento de Respuesta a la Solicitud de Información Formulada por el Profesor Todd Eisenstadt, del Centro de Estudios Internacionales del Colegio de México." Typescript with electoral court budget data by José Luis Díaz Vazquez, administrative secretary.

————. 1998a. *Ejecución de Sentencias en los Juicios de Revisión Constitucional Electoral (Caso Yucatán)*. Mexico City: Tribunal Electoral del Poder Judicial de la Federación.

————. 1998b. *Memoria 1997 – Tomo II*. Mexico City: Tribunal Electoral del Poder Judicial de la Federación.

————. Division of Statistics and Jurisprudence. 1999. Synthesis of 1998 Constititutional Revision Judgements Typescript. Mexico City: Tribunal Electoral del Poder Judicial de la Federación.

Federal Electoral Tribunal of the Judicial Power of the Federation. 1988, 1991, 1994, 1997, 2000. Systematic review by the author and a research team of 25 percent of all complaints of inconformity and all complaints annulling ballot boxes filed during these same federal elections (documents stored in the National Archive).

Federal Secretary of the Interior. 1990. *Código Federal de Instituciones y Procedimientos Electorales Comentado*. Mexico City: Secretaría de Gobernación.

————. 1996. "Relación de Concejos Municipales Instalados en el País Durante los Ultimos Tres Periodos de los Ayuntamientos." Typescript. Mexico City: Secretaría de Gobernación.

Federal Tribunal of Electoral Contention. 1988. Systematic review by research team of 25 percent of all electoral complaints filed during the 1988 federal election.

————. 1989. *Informe de Actividades del Tribunal de lo Contensioso Electoral Federal*. Mexico City: Tribunal de lo Contensioso Electoral.

————. 1989. *Revista del Tribunal de lo Contencioso Electoral Federal – 1989*. Mexico City: Tribunal de lo Contencioso Electoral Federal.

Guanajuato Electoral Institute. 1994. *Código de Instituciones y Procedimientos Electorales para el Estado de Guanajuato*. Guanajuato: Instituto Electoral del Estado de Guanajuato.

Guanajuato Electoral Tribunal. 1996. Guanajuato Electoral Institute and Electoral Tribunal Records for 1991 and 1994 Local Elections. Typescripts and notes accessed by author in electoral court archive.

————. 1997. *Informe del Proceso Electoral Correspondiente al Año de 1997*. Guanajuato: Tribunal Estatal Electoral de Guanajuato.

Guanajuato Executive Branch. 1988. *Código Electoral para el Estado de Guanajuato*. Guanajuato: Periódico Oficial de Guanajuato.

Guanajuato State Legislature. 1991. *Código Electoral para el Estado de Guanajuato*. Guanajuato: Legislatura del Congreso de Guanajuato.

"Heriberto Jara" Center for Municipal Services. 1999. *Base Hemerográfica de Acontecer Municipal de México, 1994–1998*. Mexico City: Centro de Servicios Municipales "Heriberto Jara." Typescript.

Jalisco Electoral Council. 1996. *Memoria del Proceso Electoral 1994–1995 en Jalisco*. Guadalajara: Consejo Electoral de Estado de Jalisco.

Jalisco Electoral Tribunal of the Judicial Power. 1998. "Tribunal Electoral del Poder Judicial del Estado de Jalisco – Medios de Impugnación." Typescript.

Jalisco Interior Secretary. 1988. *Ley Electoral del Estado de Jalisco.* Guadalajara: Secretaría General de Gobierno.

———. 1997. *Ley Electoral del Estado de Jalisco.* Guadalajara: Secretaria General de Gobierno.

Jalisco State Government. 1994. *Periodico Oficial del Estado* – August 30, 1994 (Ley Electoral del Estado de Jalisco). Guadalajara: Gobierno del Estado.

Madríd Mulia, Hector. 1996. Correspondence with author. Decree 072/96 of General Archive of the Nation, February 12, 1996.

Mejía González, Adolfo. 1998. Personal correspondence with author, Michoacán Electoral Tribunal Document P-197/98, April 30, 1998.

Mexican Congress. *Diario de Debates.* Mexico City: Camara de Diputados.

México State Electoral Court. 1991. *Memoria e Informe de Labores.* Toluca: Tribunal Estatal de lo Contencioso Electoral.

———. 1993. *Ley de Organizaciones Políticas y Procesos Electorales del Estado de México.* Toluca: Tribunal Estatal de lo Contencioso Electoral.

———. 1994. *Cronologia Jurisdiccional Electoral Noviembre 1990 – Diciembre 1993.* Toluca: Tribunal Estatal de lo Contencioso Electoral.

———. 1996. *Revista del Tribunal Electoral del Estado de México – Genesis de la Reforma Político Electoral de 1996.* Toluca: Tribunal Electoral del Estado de México.

México State Legislature. 1984. *Ley Electoral del Estado de México.* Toluca: Congreso del Estado de México.

———. 1996. *Ley Electoral del Estado de México.* Toluca: Congreso del Estado de México.

Michoacán Electoral Tribunal. 1996a. *Compilación 1995.* Morelia: Tribunal Electoral del Estado de Michoacán.

———. 1996b. Michoacán Electoral Institute and Electoral Tribunal Records for 1992 and 1995 Local Elections. Typescripts and notes accessed by author in electoral court archive.

Michoacán State Legislature. 1984. *Ley Electoral del Estado de Michoacán de Ocampo.* Morelia: Congreso Estatal de Michoacán.

———. 1992. *Ley Electoral del Estado de Michoacán de Ocampo.* Morelia: Congreso Estatal de Michoacán.

Miguel Agustin Pro Juárez Human Rights Center. 1989, 1990, 1991, 1992, 1993, 1994, 1995. *La Situación de los Derechos Humanos en México.* Mexico City: Centro de Derechos Humanos Miguel Agustin Pro Juárez.

Morelos Electoral Institute. 1997. *Memoria Proceso Electoral Morelos 1997.* Cuernavaca: Instituto Estatal Electoral de Morelos.

Moscoso Pedredo, Jorge. 1995. "Discurso de Jorge Moscoso Pedrero, Presidente del PRD en Chiapas, en la Apertura de la Reunión de Presidentes Municipales y Funcionarios del PRD." Typescript, November 18.

Muñoz Ledo, Porfirio. 1995. "Tercer Congreso Nacional del Partido de la Revolución Democrática – Palabras del Presidente Nacional del PRD, Porfirio Muñoz Ledo, en la Mesa Uno." Text of August 25 speech in Oaxtepec, Morelos.

National Action Party. 1990. *Iniciativas de la Ley Presentadas por el Partido Acción Nacional.* Mexico City: Partido Acción Nacional.

———. 1995. *The Democratic Plea of PAN in Yucatán.* Mexico City: Partido Acción Nacional.

———. 1996a. *The Democratic Reason of the PAN in Huejotzingo.* Mexico City: Partido Acción Nacional.

———. 1996b. Internal party archive on electoral results in Mexico City headquarters.

———. 1996c. "Tribunal Estatal Electoral: Un Nuevo Tipo de Fraude." April 29 press release.

———. n.d. *How PRI in Mexico Commits Fraud in Elections.* Mexico City: Partido Acción Nacional.

National Center for Municipal Development, Interior Secretariat. 1997. *Los Municipios de México: Información para el Desarollo.* Mexico City: Centro Nacional de Desarollo Municipal, Secretaria de Gobernación. CD-ROM.

———. 2001. *Sistema Nacional de Información Municipal.* Mexico City: Centro Nacional de Desarollo Municipal, Secretaria de Gobernación. CD-ROM.

National Human Rights Commission. 1994. *Informe de la Comisión Nacional de Derechos Humanos sobre las 140 Quejas Presentadas por el Partido de la Revolución Democrática.* Mexico City: National Human Rights Commission.

National Institute of Statistics, Geography, and Information Processing. 2001. *XII Censo General de Población y Vivienda.* Mexico City: Instituto Nacional de Estadística Geografía e Informática (INEGI) CD-ROM.

National Population Council and National Water Commission. 1993. *Indicadores Socioeconómicos e Indice de Marginación Municipal, 1990.* Mexico City: Consejo Nacional de Población y la Comisión Nacional del Agua (CONAPO).

———. 2001. *Indicadores Socioeconómicos e Indice de Marginación Municipal, 2000.* Mexico City: Consejo Nacional de Población y la Comisión Nacional del Agua.

Nuevo León Electoral Appeals Court. 1994. Appeal Decision to Complaint of [Election Day] Inconformity 65/94 (complaint and resolution). Monterrey: Sala de Segunda Instancia Electoral del Estado de Nuevo León.

Nuevo León Electoral Commission. 1989. *Las Elecciones en Nuevo León/1988.* Monterrey: Comisión Electoral Estatal.

———. 1992. *Elecciones Municipales en Nuevo León/1991.* Monterrey: Comisión Electoral Estatal.

———. 1994. *Elecciones de Ayuntamientos y Diputados Locales en Nuevo León.* Monterrey: Comisión Estatal Elelectoral.

———. 1995. *Elecciones de Ayuntamientos y Diputados Locales en Nuevo León/1994.* Monterrey: Comisión Electoral Estatal.

Nuevo León Electoral Tribunal. 1994. Complaint of [Election Day] Inconformity 65/94 (complaint and resolution). Monterrey: Tribunal Estatal Electoral.

———. 1996. Nuevo León Electoral Institute and Electoral Tribunal Records for 1988, 1991 and 1994 Local Elections. Typescripts and notes accessed by author in electoral court archive.

———. 1997a. *Proceso Electoral de 1997: Memoria Jurisdiccional Electoral.* Monterrey: Tribunal Electoral del Estado de Nuevo León.

————. 1997b. *Relación de Expedientes – Tribunal Electoral del Estado de Nuevo León* [CD ROM version]. Monterrey: Tribunal Estatal Electoral.

Nuevo León Executive Branch. 1988. *Ley Electoral del Estado de Nuevo León.* Monterrey: Edición Oficial.

Nuevo León State Legislature. 1994. *Ley Electoral del Estado de Nuevo León.* Monterrey: Congreso del Estado de Nuevo León.

Oaxaca State Electoral Institute. 1996. *Memoria de los Procesos Electorales de Diputados y Concejales 1995.* Oaxaca: Instituto Estatal Electoral de Oaxaca, 1996.

Oaxaca State Legislature. 1993. Registry of Legislative Decrees, vol. 13, 1992–5. Typescript.

Organization of American States. 1991. *Informe Anual de la Comisión Interamericana de Derechos Humanos – 1990.* Washington: Organización de los Estados Americanos, 101–28.

————. 1994. *Informe Anual de la Comisión Interamericana de Derechos Humanos – 1993.* Washington: Organización de los Estados Americanos, 345–80.

————. 1995. Case 10.180: "Complaint Presented in October 12, 1987 before the Interamerican Human Rights Commission and Resolutions Including the February 22, 1991 Report 8/91." Typescript compiled by National Action Party, Nuevo León.

Party of the Democratic Revolution. 1994. *En Defensa de los Derechos Humanos: Un Sexenio de Violencia Política.* Mexico City: Parliamentary Group, Partido de la Revolución Democrática.

Party of the Democratic Revolution, Secretariat for Municipal Affairs. 1995. *Carpeta de Información al Comité Ejecutivo Nacional.* Mexico City: Partido de la Revolución Democrática.

Party of the Democratic Revolution, Secretariat for Organization. 1998. *Brigadas del Sol – Manual 1998.* Mexico City: Partido de la Revolución Democrática, Secretaria de Organización.

Party of the Institutional Revolution, Puebla. 1996. *Huejotzingo.* Puebla: Partido Revolucionario Institucional.

The People of Chiapas' Attorney General. 1994. "Informe de la Sociedad Civil Que Organizó las Elecciones 1994 en la Zona de Conflicto." Typescript.

Puebla Electoral Tribunal. 1995a. Complaint of [Election Day] Inconformity 9/95 (complaint and resolution). Puebla: Tribunal Estatal Electoral.

————. 1995b. Complaint of [Election Day] Inconformity 10/95 (complaint and resolution). Puebla: Tribunal Estatal Electoral.

————. 1995c. Complaint of [Election Day] Inconformity 47/95 (complaint and resolution). Puebla: Tribunal Estatal Electoral.

Puebla Executive Branch. 1996. *Periodico Oficial de Puebla – 16 de mayo, 1996.* Puebla: Gobierno de Puebla, 8–11.

Puebla State Electoral Commission. 1995. *Código Electoral del Estado de Puebla.* Puebla: Comisión Estatal Electoral.

————. 1996. Puebla Electoral Commission and Electoral Tribunal Records for 1992 and 1995 Local Elections. Partial records provided by Puebla Electoral Commission and supplemented by National Action Party Puebla headquarters.

de Remes, Alain, ed. 2000. *Elecciones Municipales en México, 1980–1998.* Mexico City: Centro de Investigación y Docencia Económicas. CD-ROM.

Sonora Electoral Commission. 1991. *Ley Electoral para el Estado de Sonora.* Hermosillo: Comisión Estatal Electoral.

———. 1998. Correspondence with Elvia Arzate Estrada, head of the Federal Electoral Institute Library, August 11, 1998, listing 1994 and 1997 state electoral court cases.

Sonora State Government. 1994. *Ley Electoral del Estado de Sonora.* Hermosillo: Gobierno Estatal.

———. 1997. *Código Electoral para el Estado de Sonora.* Hermosillo: Gobierno Estatal.

Toledo Vila, Emma. 1995. December 5 speech to the Chiapas state legislature, typescript. Caucus of the Party of the Democratic Revolution, Chiapas State Legislature.

Treasury Secretariat. 1998. "Gasto Programable del Sector Público Presupuestal 1980–1997." Typescript. Secretaría de Hacienda y Control Presupuestal.

Vargas Manríquez, Fernando and Guadalupe Moreno Corzo. 1994. "Legitimación Jurídica de la Procuraduría Electoral del Pueblo Chiapaneco y el Valor Jurídico de sus Actuaciones y Resoluciones." Typescript.

Veracruz Electoral Commission. 1997. *Código de Elecciones y Derechos de los Ciudadanos y las Organizaciones Políticas.* Xalapa: Comisión Estatal Electoral.

Veracruz Electoral Tribunal. 1994. Log of all cases received in 1994 local elections. Typescript.

———. 1997. "Recursos de Inconformidad Interpuestos en el Proceso Electoral Municipal 1997." Typescript.

Veracruz State Government. 1991. *Gaceta Oficial – December 28, 1991 (Eleccion de Ayuntamientos).* Xalapa: Goberino Estatal de Veracruz.

———. 1994. *Gaceta Oficial – October 6, 1994 (Codigo de Elecciones).* Xalapa: Goberino Estatal de Veracruz, 29–182.

———. 1998. Sixth State of the State Report. Xalapa: Gobierno Estatal de Veracruz, 83–97.

Veracruz Tribunal of Electoral Controversies. 1989. *Criterios y Resoluciones – Elecciones Municipales 1988.* Xalapa: Tribunal de lo Contencioso Electoral del Estado de Veracruz.

del Villar, Samuel. 1996. April 16 dissent from National Executive Committee vote. Typescript.

Yucatán Electoral Institute. 1998. *Código Electoral del Estado.* Mérida: Instituto Electoral del Estado.

Yucatán Electoral Tribunal. 1998. Correspondence with author of November 27, 1998, listing 1995 state electoral court case submissions.

Yucatán Executive Branch. 1990. *Ley Electoral de Yucatán.* Mérida: Gobierno del Estado.

———. 1995. *Código Electoral del Estado de Yucatán.* Mérida: Gobierno del Estado, Poder Ejecutivo.

Yucatán Legislature. 1993. *Diario de Debates del Estado de Yucatán, 21 de diciembre, 1993.* Congreso Estatal de Yucatán.

Zacatecas Electoral Commission. 1992. *Memoria del Proceso Electoral 1992.* Zacatecas: Comisión Electoral del Estado de Zacatecas.

Zacatecas Electoral Institute. 1998. *Codigo Electoral del Estado de Zacatecas.* Zacatecas: Instituto Electoral del Estado de Zacatecas.

Zacatecas Electoral Tribunal. 1998. Electoral Tribunal records for 1995 and 1998 local elections. Typescripts provided by Zacatecas State Electoral Court in correspondence with author (document number P/347/998).

Zacatecas State Government. 1995. *Codigo Electoral del Estado Libre y Soberano de Zacatecas.* Zacatecas: Gobierno del Estado de Zacatecas.

Interviews

Over 200 interviews were conducted in some twenty states in researching this book. Those cited in the text are listed, giving the source's position at the time of the interview. A more inclusive list, encompassing all "on-the-record" interviews during the predissertation stages of the research, may be found in Eisenstadt (1998).

Abarca, Eliasur, former PRD Carranza mayoral candidate, May 24, 1996, Tuxtla Gutiérrez.

Alcántara, Juan Miguel, PAN faction member in Guanajuato State Legislature and national coordinator of state legislators, PAN Executive Committee, June 17, 1996, Guanajuato.

Alonso Hernández, Carlos, PRI chair of Standing Municipal Issues Committee, Chiapas State Legislature, May 29, 1996, Tuxtla Gutiérrez.

Álvarez, Luis H., former national PAN president and Chihuahua senator, August 15, 1996, Mexico City.

Álvarez Monje, Fernando, electoral affairs secretary, PAN Chihuahua, July 26, 1996, Chihuahua.

Arce Macías, Carlos, director, Mexican Association of Municipalities, June 19, 1996, León.

Arias, Jacinto, director, Chiapas State Government Secretary for Attention to Indigenous Issues, May 27, 1996, San Crístóbal de las Casas.

Barros Horcasitas, José Luis, chief presidential advisor for internal and external affairs, with Carter Center delegation on June 13, 2000, and July 21, 2000, Mexico City.

Bernal, Horacio, former Coordinator of Public Opinion Polls for the Labastida Campaign, July 27, 2000, Mexico City.

Burguete Constantino, Jesús, staff coordinator, Grand Commission of the Chiapas State Legislature, May 30, 1996, Tuxtla Gutiérrez.

Cárdenas, Jaime, Federal Electoral Institute citizen counselor, July 19, 2000 (conducted with Paloma Bauer de la Isla), Mexico City.

Castillo Peraza, Carlos, former national PAN president, August 16, 1996, Mexico City.

Coindreau Garcia, José Luis, president, PAN Nuevo León, July 29, 1996, Monterrey.

Colome Ramírez, Delio, president, Tabasco State Electoral Tribunal, January 19, 1996, Villahermosa.

Córdova, Ángel, judicial affairs adviser, PRI Chiapas, May 31, 1996, Tuxtla Gutiérrez.

Correa Mena, Luis, former Mérida mayor and Yucatán PAN gubernatorial candidate, January 30, 1996, Mexico City.

Cortés López, Elías, Oaxaca PRI sub-secretary of elections, November 26, 1998, Oaxaca.

de la Madrid Hurtado, Miguel, former president of Mexico, July 26, 2000, Mexico City.

Espinosa Castro, José Gilberto, president, Chiapas State Electoral Tribunal, May 21, 1996, Tuxtla Gutiérrez.

Fernández de Cevallos, Diego, PAN national executive committee member and former presidential candidate, March 5, 1996, Mexico City.

Flores Cruz, Cipriano, president of Oaxaca Electoral Institute, November 25, 1998, Oaxaca.

Fox, Vicente, PAN presidential candidate, June 13, 2000 (with Carter Center delegation).

Fuentes-Berain, Sandra, PRI International Coordinator, June 14, 2000 (with Carter Center delegation).

García de Madero, María Teresa, PAN Secretary, City of San Pedro de la Garza García, August 7, 1996, San Pedro de la Garza García.

García Moreno, Víctor, former substitute magistrate in the Federal Electoral Tribunal, December 11, 1995, and April 28, 1998, Mexico City.

Gómez Maza, Jesús Gilberto, coordinator of PRD faction, Chiapas State Legislature, May 23, 1996, Tuxtla Gutiérrez.

Gómez Ruiz, César Luis, PRD activist in Soyaló, May 24, 1996, Tuxtla Gutiérrez.

González Garza, Javier, federal deputy (proportional representation), and former national PRD director of electoral affairs, August, 25, 1996, Mexico City.

González Verduzco, Roberto, president of appeals circuit, Nuevo León Electoral Tribunal, July 31, 1996, Monterrey.

Guzmán, Edgar, electoral affairs director, PRD Chiapas, May 23, 1996, Soyaló.

Herrera Beltrán, Fidel, federal senator and PRI representative before IFE, February 5, 2003.

Jarquin Gálvez, Uriel, sub-secretary, Chiapas State Secretariat of the Interior, May 30, 1996, Tuxtla Gutiérrez.

Lamadrid, José Luis, Jalisco senator and former PRI electoral affairs director, August 27, 1996, Mexico City.

López Obrador, Andrés Manuel, PRD Tabasco formal gubernatorial candidate, January 14, 1996, Villahermosa.

Luna Luján, Jorge Arturo, president, PRD Chiapas, May 21 and 23, 1996, Tuxtla Gutiérrez.

Manjarrez Rivera, Jorge, ex-PRI candidate for mayor of Monterrey, July 30, 1996, Monterrey.

Manzanera, Jorge, national PAN electoral affairs secretary, August 15, 1996, Mexico City.

Martínez, Germán, judicial affairs director, PAN National Executive Committee, December 8, 1995, Mexico City and director of the PAN's Preciado Hernández Foundation, May 29, 2002.

Martínez Escobar, Miguel Angel, former state legislator and PRI candidate for mayor in Huejotzingo, August 23, 1996, Puebla.

Mártinez Reséndiz, Domingo Alberto, president PRD Veracruz, October 18, 1997, and November 29, 1997, Jalapa.

Martínez Valero, José, judicial sub-director, PAN National Executive Committee, January 17, 1998, Mexico City.

Medina Plascencia, Carlos, former Guanajuato governor and member, PAN National Executive Committee, June 19, 1996, León.

Mejía González, Adolfo, president, Michoacán State Electoral Tribunal, July 10, 1996, Morelia.

Méndez Fernández, Melba Angelina, president, Yucatán State Electoral Tribunal, June 26, 1996, Mérida.

Miranda Ayala, Alejandro, former strategy advisor for the Labastida Campaign, July 27, 2000, Mexico City.

Molinar Horcasitas, Juan, sub-secretary for political development, Interior Secretariat, January 19, 2001, Mexico City.

Moreno Alcántara, Carlos, representative of the PAN to the Oaxaca electoral institute, November 24, 1998, Oaxaca.

Moreno Uriegas, María de los Angeles, senator and former PRI national president, February 19, 1996, Mexico City.

Nava, Cesár, PAN federal deputy and former director of judicial affairs, January 19, 2001, Mexico City.

Núñez Jiménez, Arturo, former director of the Federal Electoral Institute and sub-secretary of government, Interior Secretariat, August 18 and 28, 1996, Mexico City.

Ojesto Martínez Porcayo, Fernando, president of the Appeals Circuit of the Electoral Tribunal of the Judicial Power of the Federation, November 14, 1995, and September 6, 1996, Mexico City and president of the Federal Electoral Court of the Judicial Power of the Federation, January 16, 2001.

Orozco Henríquez, José de Jesús, magistrate on the Appeals Circuit of the Electoral Tribunal of the Judicial Power of the Federation, January 23, 1998, and January 18, 2001, Mexico City.

Orozco Loretto, Ismael, District XI Jalisco congressional member, and national adjunct secretary for states not governed by the PRI, PRI National Committee, August 20, 1996, Mexico City.

Paredes, Orlando, Yucatán gubernatorial candidate and former Mérida mayoral candidate, May 25, 2001, Mérida.

Pérez Noriega, Fernando, PAN federal deputy and president, Justice Commission of the Chamber of Deputies, August 21, 1996, Mexico City.

de la Peza Muñoz Cano, José Luis, president of the Electoral Tribunal of the Judicial Power of the Federation, December 14, 1995, Mexico City.

Rebollo Fernández, José Luis, magistrate on the Sala Guadalajara circuit of the Electoral Tribunal of the Judicial Power of the Federation, January 23, 1998, Mexico City.

Reyes Zapata, Mauro Miguel, magistrate of the Electoral Tribunal of the Judical Power of the Federation, January 16, 2001, Mexico City.

Rivera Pérez, Eduardo, electoral affairs director, PAN Puebla, April 25 and August 22, 1996, Puebla.

Rivera Velázquez, Jaime, former adviser to two-time PRD Michoacán gubernatorial candidate Cristobal Arias, July 12, 1996, Morelia.

Rodríguez Lozano, Amador, former national PRI electoral affairs secretary and Baja California senator, August 12, 1996, Mexico City.

Romero Bolanos, Hector, PRD judicial advisor at the Federal Electoral Institute, July 11, 2000, Mexico City.

Romero, Juan, associate director, PRD Secretariat of Judicial Affairs, April 30, 1996, Mexico City.

Ruffo Appel, Ernesto, former governor of Baja California, May 16, 1997, Chula Vista (USA).

Sandoval Pierres, Armando, president, PRI Guanajuato, June 17 and 21, 1996, Guanajuato.

Santos de la Garza, Luis, attorney and former PAN Nuevo León legislator, August 7, 1996, San Pedro de la Garza García.

Schleske Tiburcio, Jorge, notary public and former Federal Electoral Tribunal Magistrate of the Veracruz Circuit, March 22, 1998, Cancún, and April 30, 1998 by telephone from Mexico City.

Solís Martínez, Juan Carlos, judicial advisor to the PRD, August 18, 1996, Mexico City.

Solórzano Fraga, Alfonso, former PRD minority leader in Michoacán state legislature and federal deputy (proportional representation), August 15, 1996, Mexico City.

Toledo Vila, Emma, PRD coordinator of "ad hoc" postelectoral negotiations and member of PRD legislative faction, Chiapas State Legislature, May 29, 1996, Tuxtla Gutiérrez.

Tuñon, José Luis, assistant director, PRD Secretariat of Judicial Affairs, March 23, 1996, Mexico City.

Vargas Manríquez, Fernando, PRD judicial affairs advisor, January 17, 1998, Mexico City.

del Villar, Samuel, director, PRD Secretariat of Judicial Affairs, April 18, 1996, Mexico City.

Villavicencio, Lorena, PRD judicial advisor to the Electoral Affairs Secretariat, August 27, 1996, PRD representative before the Federal Electoral Institute, January 17, 1998, and PRD Secretary for Political Relations and Alliances, January 12, 2001, Mexico City.

Yuñez Linares, Miguel Ángel, Veracruz PRI president, October 18, 1997, Jalapa.

Zazueta Félix, Marco A., PRI representative at the Federal Electoral Institute, July 18, 2000, Mexico City.

Secondary Sources

Acedo Argüelo, Blanca. 1998. "Sistema electoral: hacia una agenda." *Ciudades – Análisis de coyuntura, teoría e historia urbana* 39, July–September: 7–13.

Aguayo, Sergio. 1998. "Electoral Observation and Democracy in Mexico," in Kevin J. Middlebrook, ed. *Electoral Observation and Democratic Transitions in Latin America*. La Jolla: Center for U.S.-Mexican Studies, University of California, San Diego, 167–86.

Aguilar Camín, Héctor, and Lorenzo Meyer. 1993. *In the Shadow of the Mexican Revolution: Contemporary Mexican History, 1910–1989.* Austin: University of Texas.

Aguilar Zinzer, Adolfo. 1995. *Vamos a Ganar: La Pugna de Cuauhtémoc Cárdenas por el Poder.* Mexico City: Oceano Editores.

Alcocer V., Jorge. 1995. *Elecciones, diálogo y reforma México, 1994/I.* Mexico City: Editorial Nuevo Horizonte.

Alemán Alemán, Ricardo. 1993. *Guanajuato: Espejisimo Electoral.* Mexico City: La Jornada Ediciones.

Alianza Cívica. 1994. *Las elecciones presidenciales de agosto de 1994: Entre el escepticismo y la esperanza.* Mexico City typescript.

Alonso, Jorge. 1985. "Micropolítica Electoral," in Pablo González Casanova, ed. *Las Elecciones en México – Evolución y Perspectivas.* Mexico City: Siglo Veintiuno Editores, 349–74.

Alonso, Jorge. 1993. *El rito electoral en Jalisco (1940–1992).* Guadalajara: El Colegio de Jalisco.

———. 1995. *El cambio en Jalisco – las elecciones de 1994 y 1995.* Guadalajara: Universidad de Guadalajara.

Alonso, Jorge, and Jaime Tamayo, eds. 1994. *Elecciones con alternativas: Algunas experiencias en la República Mexicana.* Mexico City: Ediciones La Jornada.

Álvarez de Vicencio, María Elena. 1995. *Municipio y Democracia – Tesis y prácticas de gobierno del Partido Acción Nacional.* Mexico City: Epessa.

Amezcua, Adriana, and Juan E. Pardinas. 1997. *Todos los Gobernadores del Presidente.* Mexico City: Grijalbo.

Anderson, Roger Charles. 1971. "The Functional Role of the Governors and Their States in the Political Development of Mexico, 1940–1964." Ph.D. dissertation, University of Wisconsin, Department of Political Science.

Arreola Ayala, Álvaro. 1985. "Elecciones Municipales," Pablo González Casanova, ed. *Las Elecciones en México: Evolución y Perspectivas.* Mexico City: Siglo Veintiuno Editores, 329–48.

Arteaga Nava, Elisur. 1995. *La Controversia Constitucional y la Acción de Inconstitucionalidad – El Caso Tabasco.* Mexico City: Monte Alto Editores.

Assad, Carlos Martínez, and Alicia Ziccardi. 1988. *Política y gestión municipal en México.* Mexico City: Instituto de Investigaciones Sociales de la Universidad Autónomo de México.

Avendaño Villafuerte, Elia. 1998. "Repercusiones Jurídicas del Caso Chiapas." Ph.D. dissertation, National Autonomous University of Mexico, Law School.

Aziz Nassif, Alberto. 1987. "Elections in Chihuahua, 1985," in Arturo Alvarado Mendoza, ed. *Electoral Patterns and Perspectives in Mexico.* La Jolla: Center for U.S.-Mexican Studies of the University of California, San Diego, 181–206.

Aziz Nassif, Alberto, and Juan Molinar Horcasitas. 1990. "Los Resultados Electorales," in Pablo González Casanova, ed. *Segundo Informe Sobre la Democracia: México el 6 de Julio de 1988.* Mexico City: Siglo Veintiuno Editores, 138–71.

Báez Rodríguez, Francisco. 1994. "Las piezas perdidas," in Arturo Sánchez Gutiérrez, ed. *Elecciones a Debate: 1988 – las actas electorales perdidas.* Mexico City: Editorial Diana.

Bailey, John. 1987. "Can the PRI be Reformed?" in Judith Gentleman, ed. *Mexican Politics in Transition*. Boulder, CO: Westview Press, 63–95.

Bailón, Moisés Jaime. 1984. "Elecciones locales en Oaxaca en 1980." *Nueva Antropologia* VII, no. 25: 67–98.

Ballard Perry, Laurens. 1978. *Juárez and Díaz: Machine Politics in Mexico*. DeKalb: Northern Illinois University Press.

Barba, Carla, and María Elena Medina. 2001. "Tabasco y Yucatán ¿Competencía del Tribunal Electoral del Poder Judicial de la Federación?" in Todd Eisenstadt and Luis Miguel Rionda, eds. *Democracía Observada – las Instituciones Electorales Locales en México*. Guanajuato: Universidad de Guanajuato, 407–54.

Barkan, Joel D. 2000. "Protracted Transitions among Africa's New Democracies." *Democratization* 7, no. 3, Autumn: 227–43.

Barkan Joel D., with John J. Okumu. 1978. "'Semi-competitive Elections, Clientalism, and Political Recruitment in a No Party State: The Kenyan Experience," in Guy Hermet, Richard Rose, and Alain Rouquié, eds. *Elections Without Choice*. New York: Macmillan Press.

Barkin, David. 1990. *Distorted Development – Mexico in the World Economy*. Boulder, CO: Westview Press.

Basañez, Miguel. 1990. *Pulso de los Sexenios – 20 años de crisis en México*. Mexico City: Siglo Veintiuno Editores, 1990.

Beltrán del Río, Pascal. 1993. *Michoacán: Ni un Paso Atrás – La Política como Intransigencia*. Mexico City: Proceso.

Benomar, Jamal. 1993. "Justice after Transitions." *Journal of Democracy* 4, no. 1, January 1993: 3–19.

Bermeo, Nancy. 1997. "Myths of Moderation: Confrontation and Conflict During Democratic Transitions." *Comparative Politics* 293, no. 3: 305–22.

Bezdek, Robert Raymond. 1973. "Electoral Oppositions in Mexico: Emergence, Suppression, and Impact on Political Processes." Ph.D. dissertation, Ohio State University.

Boni, Felix G. 1977. "Mexico's Accion Nacional: A Case Study of an Opposition Party." Ph.D. dissertation, University of Pittsburgh.

Boylan, Delia M. 2001. "Democratization and Institutional Change in Mexico: The Logic of Partial Insulation." *Comparative Political Studies* 34, no. 1: 3–29.

Bratton, Michael, and Nicolas van de Walle. 1997. *Democratic Experiments in Africa – Regime Transitions in Comprative Pespective*. New York: Cambridge University Press.

Bruhn, Kathleen. 1997. *Taking on Goliath – The Emergence of a New Left Party and the Struggle for Democracy in Mexico*. University Park: Pennsylvania State University Press.

Buendía, Jorge. 1998. "Economic Reform, Public Opinion and Presidential Approval in Mexico, 1988–1997," *CIDE División de Estudios Políticos Documento de Trabajo No. 98*. Mexico City: Centro de Investigación y Docencia Económicas.

Burgoa Orihuela, Ignacio. 1988. *Dialéctica Sobre el Tribunal de lo Contensioso Electoral "TRICOEL."* Mexico City: Ignacio Burgoa Orihuela.

Calderón Alzati, Enrique, and Daniel Cazés, eds. 1996. *Las elecciones presidenciales de 1994*. Mexico City: La Jornada Ediciones and Centro de Investigaciones Interdisciplinarias en Ciencias y Humanidades/UNAM.

Calderón Mólgora, Marco Antonio. 1994. *Violencia Política y Elecciones Municipales*. Zamora, Michoacán: El Colegio de Michoacán.

Cammack, Paul. 1988. "The 'Brazilianization' of Mexico?" *Government and Opposition* 23, no. 3: 304–20.

Camp, Roderic Ai. 1995. *Mexican Political Biographies 1935–1993*. Austin: University of Texas Press.

Carey, John M. 2000. "Parchment, Equilibria, and Institutions." *Comparative Political Studies* 33, no. 6/7: 735–61.

Carter Center of Emory University. 1995. "The August 21, 1994 Mexican National Elections – Fourth Report." Atlanta: Carter Center Working Papers.

———. 1997. "The Carter Center Delegation to Observe the July 6, 1997 Elections in Mexico." Atlanta: Carter Center Working Papers.

Casper, Gretchen. 2000. "The Benefits of Difficult Transitions." *Democratization* 7, no. 3: 46–64.

Casper, Gretchen, and Michelle M. Taylor. 1996. *Negotiating Democracy: Transitions from Authoritarian Rule*. Pittsburgh: University of Pittsburgh Press.

Castañeda, Jorge G. 1999. *La Herencia: Arqueología de la Sucesión Presidencial en México*. Mexico City: Extra Alfaguara Editores.

Ceaser, James W., and Andrew E. Busch. 2001. *The Perfect Tie – The True Story of the 2000 Presidential Election*. Lanham, MD: Rowman and Littlefield.

Centeno, Miguel. 1994. *Democracy Within Reason: Technocratic Revolution in Mexico*. University Park: Pennsylvania State University.

Chand, Vikram Khub. 2001. *Mexico's Political Awakening*. Notre Dame: Notre Dame University Press.

Chavarría, José Luis López. 1994. *Las Elecciones Municipales en México*. Mexico City: Universidad Nacional Autónoma de México.

Choe, Yonhyok. 1997. *How to Mange Free and Fair Elections – a Comparison of Korea, Sweden and the United Kingdom*. Stockholm: Göteborg University Department of Political Science.

del Collado Fernando. 2000. *Voces Desechables – El Sainte Nacional en las Frases de sus Protagonistas*. Ciudad de México: Editorial Oceano.

Cornelius, Wayne A. 1975. *Politics and the Migrant Poor in Mexico City*. Stanford: Stanford University Press.

———. 1986. "Political liberalization and the 1985 elections in Mexico," in Paul W. Drake and Eduardo Silva, eds. *Elections and Democratization in Latin America*. La Jolla: Center for Iberian and Latin American Studies, University of California, San Diego, 115–42.

———. 2000. "Blind Spots in Democratization: Sub-national Politics as a Constraint on Mexico's Transition," in *Democratization* 7, no. 3: Autumn 2000, 117–34.

———. 2002. "La Eficacia de la Compra y Coacción del Voto en las Elecciones Mexicanas de 2000." *Perfiles Latinoamericanos* 20, June 11–31.

Cornelius, Wayne A., Ann Craig, and Jonathan Fox. 1994. *Transforming State-Society Relations in Mexico – The National Solidarity Strategy*. La Jolla: Center for U.S.-Mexican Studies, University of California, San Diego.

Cornelius, Wayne A., Todd Eisenstadt, and Jane Hindley, eds. 1999. *Subnational Politics and Democratization in Mexico*. La Jolla: Center for U.S.-Mexican Studies.

Cornelius, Wayne A., Judith Gentleman, and Peter H. Smith, eds. 1989. *Mexico's Alternative Political Futures*. La Jolla: Center for U.S.-Mexican Studies of the University of California, San Diego.

Cossío Díaz, José Ramón. 1996. *Cuadernos para la Reforma de la Justicia 4: Jurisdicción Federal y Carrera Judicial en México*. Mexico City: Universidad Nacional Autónoma de México.

Covarrubias Ortíz, Jorge. 1996. *Desarollo Político y Transición Democrática (Nuevo León 1985-1995)*. Monterrey: Ediciones Castillo.

Cox, Gary, and Mathew D. McCubbins. 1993. *Legislative Leviathan: Party Government in the House*. Berkeley: University of California Press.

Craig, Ann, and Wayne Cornelius. 1995. "Houses Divided: Parties and Political Reform in Mexico," in Scott Mainwaring and Timothy Scully, eds. *Building Democratic Institutions: Party Systems in Latin America*. Stanford: Stanford University Press.

Crespo, José Antonio. 1996. *Votar en los Estados – Análisis comparado de las legislaciones electorales estatales en México*. Mexico City: Miguel Angel Porrúa.

Cypher, James M. 1990. *State and Capital in Mexico – Development Policy since 1940*. Boulder, CO: Westview Press.

Dahl, Robert A. 1971. *Participation and Opposition*. New Haven: Yale University Press.

Dalpino, Catharin E. 2000. *Deferring Democracy: Promoting Openness in Authoritarian Regimes*. Washington, DC: Brookings Institution Press.

Dezalay, Yves, and Bryant Garth. 1996. "Building the Law and Putting the State into Play: International Strategies among Mexico's Divided Elite," American Bar Association Working Paper Series, no. 9509.

Diamond, Larry Marc F. Plattner, Yun-han Chu, and Hung-mao Tien. 1997. *Consolidating the Third Wave Democracies – Themes and Perspectives*. Baltimore: Johns Hopkins University Press.

Díaz, Luis Miguel, and Ben Lenhart, eds. 1992. *Diccionario de Términos Jurídicos*. Mexico City: Editorial Themis.

Díaz Montes, Fausto. 1992. *Los Municipios: La Disputa por el Poder Local en Oaxaca*. Oaxaca: Instituto de Investigaciones Sociológicas de la Universidad Autónoma Benito Juárez de Oaxaca.

Dinka, Frank, and Max J. Skidmore. 1973. "The Functions of Communist One-Party Elections: The Case of Czechoslovakia, 1971." *Political Science Quarterly* 88, no. 3: 395–422.

Domínguez, Jorge I., and James McCann. 1996. *Democratizing Mexico: Public Opinion and Electoral Choices*. Johns Hopkins University, 151–210.

Eckstein, Harry. 1980. "Theoretical Approaches for Explaining Collective Political Violence," in Ted Robert Gurr, ed. *Handbook of Political Conflict – Theory and Research*. New York: Macmillan/The Free Press, 135–66.

Eisenstadt, Todd A. 1998. "Courting Democracy in Mexico: Party Strategies, Electoral Insitution-Building, and Political Opening." Ph.D. dissertation, University of California, San Diego, Department of Political Science.

———. 1999. "Electoral Federalism or Abdication of Presidential Authority? Gubernatorial Elections in Tabasco," in Wayne A. Cornelius, ed. *Subnational*

Politics and Democratization in Mexico. La Jolla: Center for U.S.-Mexican Studies.

———. 2000. "Eddies in the Third Wave: Protracted Transitions and Theories of Democratization." *Democratization* 7, no. 3: 3–24.

———. 2002. "Measuring Electoral Court Failure in Democratizing Mexico." *International Political Science Review* 23, no. 1: 47–68.

Ekiert, Grzegorz and Jan Kubik. 1999. *Rebellious Civil Society: Popular Protest and Democratic Consolidation in Poland, 1989–1993*. Ann Arbor: University of Michigan Press.

Ellickson, Robert C. 1991. *Order Without Law: How Neighbors Settle Disputes*. Cambridge, MA: Harvard University Press.

Elster, Jon. 1990. *Ulysses and the Sirens – Studies in Rationality and Irrationality*. New York: Cambridge University Press.

Elster, Jon and Rune Slagstad. 1988. *Constitutionalism and Democracy*. New York: Cambridge University Press.

Epstein, Lee and Jack Knight. 1996. "On the Struggle for Judicial Supremacy." *Law & Society Review* 30, no. 1: 87–120.

Escobar, Saúl David. 1987. "Rifts in the Mexican Power Elite, 1976–1986," in Sylvia Maxfield and Ricardo Anzaldna Montoya, eds. *Government and Private Sector in Contemporary Mexico*. La Jolla: Center for U.S.-Mexican Studies, University of California, San Diego, 65–88.

Fox, Jonathan. 1994. "The Difficult Transition from Clientalism to Citizenship: Lessons From Mexico." *World Politics* 46, no. 2: 151–84.

Galván Rivera, Flavio. 1995. "Calificación Electoral: 1812–1988 y Tribunal de lo Contencioso Electoral – Un Analisis Retrospectivo." Corrdinación Académica de Derecho Procesal, Tribunal Federal Electoral. Typescript.

García Alvarez, Yolli. 1994 "Pruebas Técnicas." Federal Electoral Tribunal. Typescript.

García García, José Raymundo Froylan. 1995. "La Antidemocracia en México: El Caso de las Elecciones Municipales de Puebla 1977–1992." Ph.D. dissertation in Political Science, National Autonomous University.

Garrido, Luis Javier. 1989. "The Crisis of Presidentialismo," in Wayne A. Cornelius, Judith Gentleman, and Peter H. Smith, eds. *Mexico's Alternative Political Futures*. La Jolla: Center for U.S.-Mexican Studies, 417–34.

Geddes, Barbara. 1994. "Big Questions, Little Answers." Paper presented at the American Political Science Association, New York.

Gibson, Edward. 1992. "Conservative Electoral Movements and Democratic Politics: Core Constituencies, Coalition Building, and the Latin American Electoral Right," in Douglas A. Chalmers, Mario do Carmo Campello de Souza, and Atilio A. Boron, eds. *The Right and Democracy in Latin America*. New York: Praeger, 13–43.

Gillman, Howard. 1997. "Placing Judicial Motives in Context: A Response to Lee Epstein and Jack Knight." *Law and Courts Newsletter* 7, no. 2, Spring 1997: 10–13.

Giron López, María del Carmen. 1998. "Autonomía e Independencia de los Tribunales Electorales de los Estados." Typescript presented at the Third International Congress of Electoral Law (sponsored by the Electoral Tribunal of the Judicial Power of the Federation, the National Autonomous University Institute of Judicial Research, et al.) Cancún, Mexico, March 22.

Gómez, Leopoldo. 1991. "Elections, Legitimacy, and Political Change in Mexico, 1977–1988." Ph.D. dissertation, Georgetown University.

Gómez Tagle, Silvia. 1994. *De la Alquimia al Fraude en las Elecciones Mexicanas.* Mexico City: GV editores.

———. 1997. *La Transición Inconclusa – Treinta Años de Elecciones en México.* Mexico City: El Colegio de México.

González Casanova, Pablo, ed. 1990. *Segundo Informe Sobre la Democracia: México el 6 de Julio de 1988.* Mexico City: Centro de Investigaciones Interdisciplinarias en Humanidades, Universidad Nacional Autónomo de México.

———. 1993. *Las Elecciones en México: Evolución y Perspectivas.* Mexico City: Centro de Investigaciones Sociales, Universidad Nacional Autónomo de México.

González Compeán, Miguel and Leonardo Lomeli. 2000. *El Partido de la Revolución: Institución y Conflicto (1928–1999).* Mexico City: Fondo de Cultura Económica.

González Graff, Jaime. 1989. *Las Elecciones de 1988 y la Crisis del Sistema Político.* Mexico City: Editorial Diana.

González Oropeza, Manuel. 1987. *La Intervención Federal en la Desaparación de Poderes.* Mexico City: Universidad Nacional Autónoma de México.

———. 1996. "La Irresponsabilidad de los Gobernadores en México," in Victoria E. Rodríguez and Peter M. Ward et al., "New Federalism, State and Local Government in Mexico: Memoria of the Bi-National Conference." Austin: The Mexican Center of ILAS, University of Texas at Austin, October 25–6, 1996, 67–8.

González Ramos, Joventino. 1996. *Monterrey 400, Avance o Retroceso – La Ilegalidad e Ilegitimidad del Proceso Electoral de Monterrey.* Mexico City: Programas Educativos.

Grofman, Bernard and Arend Lijphart, eds. 1986. *Electoral Laws and Their Political Consequences.* New York: Agathon Press.

Guadarrama, Graciela S. 1986. "Entrepreneurs and Politics: Businessmen in Electoral Contests in Sonora and Nuevo Leon, July 1985," in Arturo Alvarado Medoza, ed. *Electoral Patterns and Perspectives in Mexico.* La Jolla: Center for U.S.-Mexican Studies of the University of California, San Diego.

Guillén, Diana. 1998. *Chiapas 1973–1993: Mediaciones, política e institucionalidad.* Mexico City: Instituto Mora.

Guillén López, Tonatiuh. 1992. *Frontera Norte – Una Década de Política Electoral.* Mexico City: El Colegio de México y El Colegio de la Frontera Norte.

Gurr, Ted Robert. 1971. *Why Men Rebel.* Princeton: Princeton University Press.

Haggard, Stephan and Robert Kaufman. 1995. *The Political Economy of Democratic Transitions.* Princeton: Princeton University Press.

Hansen, Roger. 1974. *The Politics of Mexican Development.* Baltimore: Johns Hopkins University Press.

Harvey, Neil. 1998. *The Chiapas Rebellion: The Struggle for Land and Democracy.* Durham, NC: Duke University Press.

Heidenheimer, Arnold J., ed. 1970. *Political Corruption – Readings in Comparative Analysis.* New Brunswick, NJ: Transaction Books.

Helmke, Gretchen. 2002. "The Logic of Strategic Defection: Court-Executive Relations in Argentina under Dictatorship and Democracy." *American Political Science Review* 96, no. 2: 291–303.

Helmke, Gretchen and Steve Levitsky. "Informal Institutions and Politics in Latin America." Paper presented at "Informal Institutions in Latin America," conference, Kellogg Institute, University of Notre Dame, April 24, 2003.

Hermet, Guy, Richard Rose, and Alain Rouquie. 1978. *Elections Without Choice.* New York: John Wiley and Sons.

Hernández Rodríguez, Rogelio. 1994. "Inestabilidad Política y Presidencialismo en México." *Mexican Studies/Estudios Mexicanos* 10, no. 1: 187–216.

———. 1998. "The Partido Revolucionario Institucional," in Mónica Serrano, ed. *Governing Mexico: Political Parties and Elections.* London: The Institute of Latin American Studies, University of London. 71–94.

Higley, John and Richard Gunther, eds. 1992. *Elites and Democratic Consolidation in Latin America and Southern Europe.* New York: Cambridge University Press.

Holston, James. 1991. "The Misrule of Law: Land and Usurpation in Brazil." *Comparative Studies in Society and History* 33, no. 4: 695–725.

Huntington, Samuel P. 1991. *The Third Wave: Democratization in the Late Twentieth Century.* Norman: University of Oklahoma Press.

Ibarra, Eduardo. 1984. "El PCM y las Elecciones de 1980." *Nueva Antropología* VII, no. 25: 43–66.

Im, Hyug Baeg. 1989. "Politics of Transition: Democratic Transition from Authoritarian Rule in South Korea." Ph.D. dissertation, University of Chicago, Department of Political Science.

International Foundation for Electoral Systems. *Mexico's Mid-Term Elections July 6, 1997, International Visitors' Report.* Washington, DC: International Foundation for Electoral Systems.

Jacobson, Gary C. 1992. *The Politics of Congressional Elections.* New York: HarperCollins Publishers.

Jacobson, Gary C. and Samuel Kernell. 1981. *Strategy and Choice in Congressional Elections.* New Haven: Yale University Press.

Jones Luong, Pauline. 2000. "After the Break-Up: Institutional Design in Transitional States." *Comparative Political Studies* 33, no. 5: 563–92.

Key, V. O. 1984. *Southern Politics in State and Nation.* Knoxville: University of Tennessee Press.

Klesner, Joseph L. 1988. "Electoral Reform in an Authoritarian Regime: The Case of Mexico." Ph.D. dissertation, Massachusetts Institute of Technology.

Knight, Alan. 1992. "Mexico's Elite Settlement: Conjecture and Consequences," in John Higley and Richard Gunther, eds. *Elites and Democratic Consolidation in Latin America and Southern Europe.* New York: Cambridge University Press, 113–45.

Knight, Jack. 1992. *Institutions and Social Change.* New York: Cambridge University Press.

Knill, Christoph and Andrea Lenschow, "'Seek and Ye Shall Find!' Linking Different Perspectives on Institutional Change." *Comparative Political Studies* 34, no. 2, March 2001: 187–215.

Krieger, Emilio. 1994. *En Defensa de la Constitución: Violaciones a la Carta Magna.* Mexico City: Editorial Grijalbo.

Lamounier, Bolivar. 1984. "Opening through Elections: Will the Brazilian Case Become a Paradigm?" *Government and Opposition* 19, no. 2: 167–77.

———. 1989. "Authoritarian Brazil Revisited: The Impact of Elections on the Abertura," in Alfred Stepan, ed. *Democratizing Brazil: Problems of Transition and Consolidation.* New York: Oxford University Press, 43–82.

Langston, Joy. 1996. "Why Rules Matter: The Formal Rules of Candidate and Leadership Selection in the PRI," *Documento de trabajo 66 de la División de Estudios Políticos del Centro de Investigación y Docencia Económicas.* Mexico City: Centro de Investigación y Docencia Económicas.

———. 1999. "Changes in Gubernatorial Candidate Selection in the PRI," *Documento de trabajo 102 de la División de Estudios Políticos del Centro de Investigación y Docencia Económicas.* Mexico City: Centro de Investigación y Docencia Económicas.

———. 2000a. "No More Local Leviathan: Rebuilding the PRI's State Party Organizations," *CIDE División de Estudios Políticos Documento de Trabajo no. 111.* Mexico City: Centro de Investigación y Docencia Económicas.

———. 2000b. "A Patchwork Quilt: Why Different Mexican States Have Different Types of Governors," *CIDE División de Estudios Políticos Documento de Trabajo no. 66.* Mexico City: Centro de Investigación y Docencia Económicas.

Lau, Rubén. 1989. *Cuadernos del Norte – Las Elecciones en Chihuahua (1983–1988).* Chihuahua: Centro de Estudios Libres Ignacio Rodríguez Terrazas, A.C.

Lauth, Hans-Joachim. 2000. "Informal Institutions and Democracy." *Democratization* 7, no. 4: 21–50.

Lawson, Chappell. 2002. *Building the Fourth Estate: Democratization and the Rise of a Free Press in Mexico.* Berkeley: University of California Press.

Lehoucq, Fabrice Edouard. 1995. "Institutional Change and Political Conflict: Evaluating Alternative Explanations of Electoral Reform in Costa Rica." *Electoral Studies* 14, no. 1: 23–45.

———. 1997. "Fraud, Electoral Reform and Democracy: Costa Rica in Comparative Perspective." Paper presented at the 1997 meeting of the Latin American Studies Association, Guadalajara.

Linz, Juan J. and Alfred Stepan. 1996. *Problems of Democratic Transition and Consolidation – Southern Europe, South America, and Post-Communist Europe.* Baltimore: Johns Hopkins University Press.

Liu, Yih-Jiun. 1991. "The Election-Driven Democratic Transformation: A Comparative Perspective." Ph.D. dissertation, University of Chicago.

Loaeza, Soledad, 1989. *El llamado de las urnas.* Mexico City: Cal y Arena.

———. 1994. "Political Liberalization and Uncertainty in Mexico," in Maria Lorena Cook, Kevin J. Middlebrook, and Juan Molinar Horcasitas, eds. *The Politics of Economic Restructuring – State-Society Relations and Regime Change in Mexico.* La Jolla: Center for U.S.-Mexican Studies of the University of California, San Diego.

———. 1999. *El Partido Acción Nacional: La Larga Marcha, 1939–1994 – Oposición Leal y Partido de Protesta.* Mexico City: Fondo de Cultura Económica.

López Chavarría, José Luis. 1994. *Las Elecciones Municipales en México.* Mexico City: Universidad Nacional Autónoma de México.

López Obrador, Andrés Manuel. 1996. *Entre la Historia y la Esperanza – Corrupción y Lucha Democrática en Tabasco.* Mexico City: Grijalbo Editores.

López-Pintor, Rafael. 2000. *Electoral Management Bodies as Institutions of Governance.* New York: United Nations Development Program.

Lujambio, Alonso. 1995. *Federalismo y Congreso en el Cambio Político de México.* Mexico City: Universidad Nacional Autónoma de México.

———. 2000. *El Poder Compartido: Un Ensayo Sobre la Democratización Mexicana.* Mexico City: Editorial Océano.

Luna, Matilde, Ricardo Tirado, and Francisco Valdez. 1987. *Government and Private Sector in Contemporary Mexico.* La Jolla: Center for U.S.-Mexican Studies, University of California, San Diego.

Lyne, Mona. 2000. "Generalizing the Electoral Connection: The Voter's Dilemma, Party Reform, and Democratic Consolidation in Brazil." Paper presented at the American Political Science Association annual meeting, Washington, DC, August 31–September 3.

Mabry, Donald J. 1973. *Mexico's Accion Nacional: A Catholic Alternative to Revolution.* Syracuse: Syracuse University Press.

Machiavelli, Niccoló. 1985. *The Prince.* Harvey C. Mansfield, Jr., trans. Chicago: University of Chicago Press.

Magaloni, Beatriz. 1996. "Dominancia de Partido y Dilemas Duvergerianos en las Elecciones Federales de 1994." *Política y Gobierno* 3, no. 2: 281–326.

Malley, Michael. 2000. "Beyond Democratic Elections: Indonesia Embarks on a Protracted Transition." *Democratization* 7, no. 3: 153–80.

Manzanilla Schaffer, Victor. 1995. *México Falsificado y Devaluado.* Mexico City: Grijalbo Editores.

Martínez Assad, Carlos and Alicia Ziccardi. 1988. *Política y Gestión Municipal en México.* Cuadernos de Investigación Social 18. Mexico City: Centro de Investigaciones Sociales, Universidad Nacional Autónoma de México.

Martínez Vázquez, Víctor Raúl, and Anselmo Arellanes Meixueiro. 1985. "Negociación y Conflicto en Oaxaca," in Carlos Martínez Assad, ed. *Municipios en Conflicto.* Mexico City: Centro de Investigaciones Sociales, Universidad Autónoma de México, 203–38.

Maxfield, Sylvia. 1990. *Governing Capital – International Finance and Mexican Politics.* Ithaca: Cornell University Press.

Mazza, Jacqueline. 2001. *Don't Disturb the Neighbors – The United States and Democracy in Mexico, 1980–1995.* New York: Routledge.

McAdam, Doug, John D. McCarthy, and Mayer N. Zald. 1996. *Political Opportunities, Mobilizing Structures, and Cultural Framings.* New York: Cambridge University Press.

McFaul, Michael. 1999. "What Went Wrong in Russia? The Perils of a Protracted Transition." *Journal of Democracy* 10, no. 2: 4–18.

Middlebrook, Kevin. 1986. "Political Liberalization in an Authoritarian Regime: The Case of Mexico," in Guillermo O'Donnell et al., eds. *Transitions from Authoritarian Rule: Latin America.* Baltimore: Johns Hopkins University Press, 123–47.

———. 1989. "The CTM and the Future of State-Labor Relations," in Wayne A. Cornelius, Judith Gentleman, and Peter H. Smith, eds. *Mexico's Alternative Political Futures*. La Jolla: Center for U.S.-Mexican Studies of the University of California, San Diego, 291–306.

Mizrahi, Yemile. 1994. "A New Conservative Opposition in Mexico: The Politics of Entrepreneurs in Chihuahua (1983–1992)." Ph.D. dissertation, University of California, Berkeley, Department of Political Science.

———. 1995. "Democracia, Eficiencia y Participación: Los Dilemas de los Gobiernos de Oposición en México." *Política y Gobierno* 2, no. 2: 177–205.

———. 1997. "Pressuring the Center: Opposition Governments and Federalism in Mexico." *CIDE División de Estudios Políticos Documento de Trabajo No. 71.* Mexico City: Centro de Investigación y Docencia Económicas.

Moctezuma Barragán, Javier. 1994. *José María Iglesias y La Justicia Electoral.* Mexico City: Universidad Nacional Autónoma de México.

Moe, Terry M. 1990. "Political Institutions: The Neglected Side of the Story." *Journal of Law, Economics, and Organization* 6, Special Issue (Conference on "The Organization of Political Institutions"): 213–66.

Molinar Horcasitas, Juan. 1991. *El Tiempo de la Legitimidad – Elecciones, Autoritarismo, y Democrácia en México.* Mexico City: Cal y Arena.

———. 1996. "Changing the Balance of Power in a Hegemonic Party System: The Case of Mexico," in Arend Lijphart and Carlos Waisman, eds. *Institutional Design in New Democracies – Eastern Europe and Latin America.* Boulder, CO: Westview Press.

Molinar Horcasitas, Juan and Jeffrey Weldon. 1994. "Electoral Determinants and Consequences of National Solidarity," in Wayne Cornelius, Ann Craig, and Jonathan Fox, eds. *Transforming State-Society Relations in Mexico: The National Solidarity Strategy.* La Jolla: University of California, San Diego, Center for U.S.-Mexican Studies.

Monroy, Mario B., ed. 1994. *Pensar Chiapas, Repensar México.* Mexico City: Convergencia de Organismos Civiles por la Democracia.

Moreno, Alejandro. 1999. *Political Cleavages: Issues, Parties, and the Consolidation of Democracy.* Boulder, CO: Westview Press.

Munck, Gerardo L. and Carol Skalnik Leff. 1999. "Modes of Transition and Democratization: South America and Eastern Europe in Comparative Perspective," in Lisa Anderson, ed. *Transitions to Democracy.* New York: Columbia University Press, 193–216.

Nadeau, Richard and André Blais. 1993. "Accepting the Election Outcome: The Effect of Participation on Losers' Consent." *British Journal of Political Science* 23, pt. IV: 553–63.

National Democratic Institute for International Affairs and National Republican Institute for International Affairs. 1989. *The May 7, 1989 Panamanian Elections.* Washington, DC: National Democratic Institute for International Affairs and National Republican Institute for International Affairs.

North, Douglass C. 1990. *Institutions, Institutional Change and Economic Performance.* New York: Cambridge University Press.

O'Donnell, Guillermo. 1997. "Polyarchies and the (Un)Rule of Law in Latin America." Presented at the annual meeting of the American Political Science Association, Washington, DC, August 28–31, 1997.

O'Donnell, Guillermo and Philippe C. Schmitter. 1986. *Transitions from Authoritarian Rule: Tentative Conclusions about Uncertain Democracies*. Baltimore: Johns Hopkins University Press.

Oppenheimer, Andres. 1996. *México: En la Frontera del Caos – La Crisis de los Noventa y la Esperanza del Nuevo Milenio*. Mexico City: Vergara Editores.

Panebianco, Angelo. 1988. *Political Parties: Organization and Power*. New York: Cambridge University Press.

Pastor, Robert. 1999a. "The Role of Electoral Administration in Democratic Transitions: Implications for Policy and Research." *Democratization* 6, no. 4: 1–27.

———. 1999b. "The Third Dimension of Accountability: The Role of the International Community in National Elections," in Andreas Schedler, Larry Diamond, and Marc F. Plattner, eds. *The Self-Restraining State: Corruption and Accountability in New Democracies*. Boulder, CO: Lynne Rienner, 123–44.

Pérez Noriega, Fernando. 1989. "Procedencia del Juicio de Amparo Contra Determinaciones del Tribunal de lo Contencioso Electoral." *El Foro – Organo de la Barra Mexicana* 2, no. 1: 11–22.

Peschard-Sverdrup, Armand B. 1997. *The 1997 Mexican Midterm Elections Post-Election Report*. Washington, DC: Center for Strategic and International Studies.

Posada-Carbó, Eduardo. 2000. "Electoral Juggling: A Comparative History of the Corruption of Suffrage in Latin America." *Latin American Studies* 32, no. 3: 611–44.

Programa de las Naciones Unidas para el Desarrollo. 1997. *Análisis del Sistema Electoral Mexicano – Informe de un Grupo de Expertos*. New York: United Nations Development Program.

Prud'homme, Jean-François. 1996. "El PRD: Su Vida Interna y Sus Elecciones Estratégicas." *CIDE División de Estudios Políticos Documento de Trabajo No. 39*. Mexico City: Centro de Investigación y Docencia Económicas.

———. 1997. "The National Action Party (PAN): Organization Life and Strategic Decisions." *CIDE División de Estudios Politicos Documento de Trabajo No. 57*. Mexico City: Centro de Investigacíon y Docencia Económicas.

Przeworski, Adam. 1991. *Democracy and the Market – Political and Economic Reforms in Eastern Europe and Latin America*. New York: Cambridge University Press.

———. 1996. "Studying Democratization: Twenty Years Later." New York University. Typescript.

Przeworski, Adam, Michaeal E. Alvarez, José Antonio Cheibub, and Fernando Limongi. 2000. *Democracy and Development – Political Institutions and Well-Being in the World, 1950–1990*. New York: Cambridge University Press.

Putnam, Robert. 1993. *Making Democracy Work – Civic Traditions in Modern Italy*. Princeton: Princeton University Press.

Ramírez Bernal, David and Rocío Culebro Bahena. 1993. "El Colégio Electoral," in Silvia Gómez Tagle, ed. *Las Elecciones de 1991 – La Recuperación Oficial*. Mexico City: La Jornada Ediciones. 523–34.

Reyna, José Luis and Richard S. Weinert, eds. 1977. *Authoritarianism in Mexico*. Philadelphia: Institute for the Study of Human Issues.

Reynoso, Víctor Manuel. 1993. "El Partido Acción Nacional: ¿La Oposición Hara Gobierno?" *Revista Mexicana de Sociología*. LV, no. 2, April–June 1993: 133–51.

Rigger, Shelley. 1994. "Machine Politics in the New Taiwan: Institutional Reform and Electoral Strategy in the Republic of China on Taiwan." Ph.D. dissertation, Harvard University, Department of Political Science.

――――. 1997. "Lamounier's Theory of 'Opening Through Elections' Applied to the Taiwan Case." Paper Presented at the 1997 Meeting of the American Political Science Association, Washington, DC.

Rionda, Luis Miguel. 1995. "Elecciones Locales en Guanajuato 1994–1995: El Péndulo Electoral." Paper prepared for presentation at the seventh meeting of Mexico's National Meeting of Researchers in Electoral Studies, November 29, 1995.

――――. 1996. "Guanajuato: Democrácia de Laboratorio." Centro de Investigaciones y Estudios Superiores en Antropología Social Ph.D. dissertation. Guadalajara. Typescript.

Rodríguez, Victoria. 1997. *Decentralization in Mexico – From Reforma Municipal to Solidaridad to Nuevo Federalismo.* Boulder, CO: Westview Press.

Rodríguez, Victoria and Peter M. Ward. 1995. *Opposition Government in Mexico.* Albuquerque: University of New Mexico Press.

Roeder, Philip G. 1993. *Red Sunset: The Failure of Soviet Politics.* Princeton: Princeton University Press.

Rojas Alba, Mario. 1996. *Las Manos Sucias – Violación a los Derechos Humanos en México (1988–1995).* Mexico City: Editorial Grijalbo.

Rubin, Jeffrey W. 1997. *Decentering the Regime: Ethnicity, Radicalism and Democracy in Juchitán, Mexico.* Durham, NC: Duke University Press.

Rueschmeyer, Dietrich, Evelyne Huber Stephens, and John D. Stephens. 1992. *Capitalist Development and Democracy.* Chicago: University of Chicago Press.

Sadek, Maria Tereza Aina. 1995. *A Justiça Eleitoral e a Consolidação da Democracia no Brasil.* Sao Paulo: Konrad Adenauer-Stiffung.

Sánchez, Marco Aurelio. 1999. *PRD: La Elite en Crisis.* Mexico City: Plaza y Valdés Editores.

Sánchez Gutiérrez, Arturo. 1994. *Elecciones a Debate 1988 – las Actas Electorales Perdidas.* Mexico City: Editorial Diana.

Sartori, Giovanni. 1976. *Parties and Party Systems – A Framework for Analysis.* New York: Cambridge University Press.

Schedler, Andreas. 2000. "Incertidumbre Institucional e Inferencias de Imparcialidad: El Caso del Instituto Federal Electoral." *Política y Gobierno* VII, no. 2: 383–421.

Schelling, Thomas. 1980. *The Strategy of Conflict.* Cambridge: Harvard University Press.

Schmitter, Phillippe C. 1992. "The Consolidation of Democracy and Representation of Social Groups." *American Behavioral Scientist* 35, no. 4/5, March/June 1992: 422–49.

Schmitter, Phillippe C. and Terry Lynn Karl. 1991. "What Democracy Is . . . and Is Not." *Journal of Democracy* 2, no. 3: 75–88.

Schmitz, David F. 1999. *Thank God They're on Our Side – The United States and Right-Wing Dictatorships, 1921–1965.* Chapel Hill: University of North Carolina.

Scott, James. 1985. *Weapons of the Weak: Everyday Forms of Peasant Resistance.* New Haven: Yale University Press.

Shane, Donald and Scott Mainwaring. 1986. "Transitions through Transaction: Democratization in Brazil and Spain," in Wayne Selcher, ed. *Political Liberalization in Brazil: Dynamics, Dilemmas, and Future.* Boulder, CO: Westview Press, 175–215.

Shepsle, Kenneth. 1989. "Studying Institutions – Some Lessons from the Rational Choice Approach." *Journal of Theoretical Politics* 1, no. 2: 131–47.

Steinmo, Sven, Kathleen Thelen, and Frank Longstreth. 1992. *Structuring Politics: Historical Institutionalism in Comparative Analysis.* New York: Cambridge University Press.

Stepan, Alfred. 1988. *Rethinking Military Politics: Brazil and the Southern Cone.* Princeton: Princeton University Press.

———. 1973. *Authoritarian Brazil: Origins, Policies, and Future.* New Haven: Yale University Press.

Stokes, Susan C. 2000. "Rethinking Clientalism." Paper presented at the XXII International Congress of the Latin American Studies Association, Miami, March 16– 18.

Strom, Kaare. 1990. "A Behavioral Theory of Competitive Parties." *American Journal of Political Science* 34, no. 2: 565–98.

Tapia, Jesús. 1984. "Elecciones locales en Michoacán en 1983." *Nueva Antropología* VII, no. 25: 125–64.

Tarrow, Sidney. 1989. *Struggle, Politics and Reform: Collective Action, Social Movements, and Cycles of Protest.* Ithaca: Cornell University Center for International Studies.

———. 1998. *Power in Movement: Social Movements, Collective Action, and Politics.* New York: Cambridge University Press.

Tate, C. Neal and Torbjörn Vallinder, eds. 1995. *The Global Expansion of Judicial Power.* New York: New York University Press.

Thacker, Strom C. 2000. *Big Business, the State, and Free Trade – Constructing Coalitions in Mexico.* New York: Cambridge University Press.

Toharia, José J. 1975. "Judicial Independence in an Authoritarian Regime: The Case of Contemporary Spain." *Law and Society Review* 9, no. 3: 475–96.

Ugalde, Luis Carlos. 2000. *The Mexican Congress: Old Player, New Power.* Washington, DC: Center for Strategic and International Studies.

Ungar, Mark. 1996. "Judicial Reform: Inequality, Democratization, and Latin America's Courts." Paper delivered at the 1996 annual meeting of the American Political Science Association, San Francisco, August 29–September 1, 1996. Typescript.

Valdés Vega, María Eugenia. 1995. "Las Elecciones Chiapanecas de 1995." Departamento de Sociologia de la Universidad Autónomo Metropolitana-Iztapalapa. Manuscript.

Valencia Castrejón, Sergio. 1996. *Poder Regional y Política Nacional en México. El Gobierno de Maximino Avila Camacho en Puebla (1937–1941).* Mexico City: Instituto Nacional de Estudios Históricos de la Revolución Mexicana.

Valenzuela, J. Samuel. 1992. "Democratic Consolidation in Post-Transitional Settings: Notion, Process, and Facilitating Conditions," in Scott Mainwaring,

Guillermo O'Donnell, and J. Samuel Valenzuela, eds. *Issues in Democratic Consolidation*. Notre Dame: University of Notre Dame Press, 57–104.

Vázquez Gómez, Gerardo. 1996. "Ahora el Torno es Para el Derecho Electoral Mexicano." La Escuela Libre de Derecho. Typescript.

Velasco Arregui, Edgur. 1989. "Crisis y Reestructuración Industrial en México," in Jesús Lechuga-Fernando Chávez, ed. *Estancamiento Económico y Crísis Social en México, 1983–1988*. Mexico City: Universidad Autónoma Metropolitana, Unidad Azcapotzalco, 249–53.

————. 1993. "Industrial Restructuring in Mexico during the 1980s," in Ricardo Grinspun and Maxwell A. Cameron, eds. *The Political Economy of North American Free Trade*. New York: St. Martin's Press, 165–8.

Villar, Samuel del, 1994. *La Nulidad de la Eleccion Presidencial del 21 de Agosto de 1994*. Mexico City: Party of the Democratic Revolution. Typescript.

von Mettenheim, Kurt. 1998. "Direct Appeals, Political Machines, and Reform: Deepening Democracy in Brazil, 1985–1995," in Kurt von Mettenheim and James Malloy, eds. *Deepening Democracy in Latin America*. Pittsburgh: University of Pittsburgh Press, 123–36.

von Sauer, Franz A. 1974. *The Alienated Loyal Opposition*. Albuquerque: University of New Mexico Press.

Weingast, Barry. 1997. "The Political Foundations of Democracy and the Rule of the Law." *American Political Science Review* 91, no. 2: 245–63.

Weldon, Jeffrey. 1997. "Political Sources of *Presidentialismo* in Mexico," in Scott Mainwaring and Matthew Soberg Shugart, eds. *Presidentialism and Democracy in Latin America*. New York: Cambridge University Press, 225–8.

Wilkinson, Steven L. 1998. "The Electoral Incentives for Ethnic Violence: Hindu-Muslim Riots in India." Paper presented at the 1998 meeting of the American Political Science Association, Boston, September 3–6, 1998. Typescript.

Williams, Mark Eric. 2002. "Market Reforms, Technocrats, and Institutional Innovation." *World Development* 30, no. 3: 395–412.

Yanner, Keith. 1992. "Democratization in Mexico, 1988–1991: The Surge and Decline of Support for the Neo-Cardenistas." Ph.D. dissertation, Washington University of St. Louis, Department of Political Science.

Zakaria, Fareed. 1997. "The Rise of Illiberal Democracy." *Foreign Affairs* 76, no. 6: 22–43.

Zamarripa, Roberto. 1993. *Sonora 91: Historia de Políticos y Policías*. Mexico City: Ediciones La Jornada.

Zenteno Orantes, Noé Miguel. 1998. "Juicio de Revisión Constitucional Electoral y su Homología y Fin Jurídico-Social con el Juicio de Amparo." Typescript presented at Third International Congress of Electoral Law (sponsored by Electoral Tribunal of the Judicial Power of the Federation, the National Autonomous University Institute of Judicial Research), Cancún, Mexico, March 22.

Media Accounts Cited

Newspaper articles (especially from *Reforma* and *El Norte*) with no page number given but the word "INFOSEL" mentioned were downloaded from that multimedia company's CD-ROM. There is no page number reference for those newspapers.

"595 Perredistas Han Muerto en los Últimos 10 Años." *Noticias*, 31 de Octubre de 1998, Oaxaca Electoral Institute news clippings.

Alcocer, Jorge V. "Ernesto Zedillo: Presidente Fuerte; Presidencia Democrática." *Voz y Voto*, no. 36, February 1996: 4–12.

Alemán Alemán, Ricardo. "El PRI se Prepara Para Dejar el Poder, Asegura el PAN." *La Jornada*, October 21, 1989: 1.

Alemán Alemán, Ricardo. "Plazo Pública." *La Jornada*, February 19, 1995: 2.

Alemán, Ricardo and Óscar Camacho Guzmán. "Pide el PRD Anular los Comicios del 18 de Agosto; en México No Hay Elecciones Limpias, Dice el PAN." *La Jornada*, October 16, 1991: 6.

"Anularían Elecciones en Guaymas." *El Norte*, August 29, 1991.

Avilés, Jaime. "Inflar la Votación, Órden en Una Grabación Telefónica, Denuncia – Marchará López Obrador al DF Para Demandar la Anulación de las Elecciones." *El Financiero*, November 22, 1994: 56.

"Balcanización y Caciczgos: Ingobernabilidad en Los Estados." *El Financiero*, May 5, 1996: 52.

"El Blanquiazul Concertacesionó – Quirino." *Reforma*, December 14, 1998: 7-A.

Barajas, Esperanza. "Aún no le Ganamos a la Desconfianza." *Reforma*, July 20, 1998: 6A.

Barrera, Jaime. "Marcha Candidato PRIísta en Colima." *Reforma*, July 11, 1997: 9-A.

Beltrán del Río, Pascal. "Conocí al Sistema Desde Adentro, Traté de Cambiarlo, no Fue Posible y Por Eso Estoy en la Oposición: Cuauhtémoc Cárdenas." *Proceso* 916, May 23, 1994: 6–14.

Benítez, José Manuel. "Niegan las Constancias a Regidores Perredistas en Varios Municipios." *La Jornada*, January 18, 1994: 18.

Caballero, Alejandro. "Intransigente con los Partidos." *Proceso* 990, October 23, 1995: 7–9.

Caballero, Alejandro, Álvaro Delgado, and Armando Guzmán. "Comprobado con Recibos: Madrazo Utilizó Una Casa de Cabal Peniche Como Cuartel de Campaña." *Proceso*, September 4, 1995: 20–5.

Caballero, Sergio. "Promueve Monreal a PRD Entre Candidatos Priístas." *Reforma*, July 24, 1998: 23-A.

Camacho, Carlos. "Ocupan Priístas la Alcaldía de Jaltocan; el Edil, Retenido." *La Jornada*, January 20, 1994: 19.

Camacho Guzmán, Oscar. "La Oposición Presentará en el Colegio Electoral Impugnaciones a 154 Distritos." *La Jornada*, October 15, 1991: 1.

Camacho Guzman, Óscar and Ciro Pérez Silva. "Marcha Atrás de Priístas en los Acuerdos Logrados en Gobernación." *La Jornada*, November 14, 1996: 3.

Camargo, Jorge (a). "Demanda el Blanquiazul Cesar Fraudes y Ataques." *Reforma*, July 1, 1998: 8-A.

——— (b). "Divide a Priístas el Caso Yucatán." *Reforma*, July 9, 1998: 20-A.

——— (c). "El Que Se Mueve Sí Sale en La Foto." *Reforma*, August 4, 1998: 8A.

Cano, Arturo (b). "PRD: Ser o Decrecer." *Enfoque*, March 19, 1995: 3–8.

———— (a). "Cuando la Patria se Salva...¿El Partido Tambien?" *Enfoque*, August 20, 1995: 11.

Cano, Arturo. "Y al que no Cumpla...." *Enfoque*, August 18, 1996: 8–9.

Carrillo Tejeda, Melesio. "De 86 Recursos Interpuestos en el TCE Sólo Dos Fueron Resueltos en Favor de los Demandantes." *El Dictámen de Veracruz*, December 5, 1991: 1-D.

Castillo Peraza, Carlos. "Yo Quiero Ser...No le Temo a Nada Ni Dentro Ni Fuera del PRI: Bartlett." *Proceso* 1135, August 2, 1998: 6–9.

Cázarez, Luz María. "El PRI No Se Prestará a Ningún Arreglo: Frías." *El Debate de Culiacán*, November 25, 1998: 1-A.

Chávez Cruz, Patricia. "Bartlett: Como Precandidato Sí Tengo el Apoyo del Sindicato de Gobernadores." *Síntesis*, November 21, 1998: R-3.

Chávez, Elías. "El Dedo que Zedillo se Cortó en Abril Renació Frondoso en Mayo." *Proceso* 1124, May 17, 1998: 6–10.

Chávez, Elías and Isidoro Yescas. "Dividido, el PRI Enfrenta Problema en 40 Municipios de Oaxaca." *Proceso* 666, August 7, 1989: 10–13.

Cobos, Francisco. "Cambiarían Traxcavo por Alcaldia – Gobierno de Coahuila Ofrece Vehículo a Priístas que Ocupan el Palacio Municipal de Parras." *El Norte*, January 4, 1991, INFOSEL.

del Collado, Fernando. "El Lenguaje del PRI: 69 Años...en Frases." *Enfoque* 215, March 1, 1998: 2–10.

Correa, Guillermo and Elías Chávez. "Se le Desmorona el PRI a Zedillo: Escisiones, Renuncias, Fugas y Cambios de Partido Marcan la Mitad de su Sexenio." *Proceso* 1110, February 8, 1998: 22–8.

Creel Miranda, Santiago and José Augustín Ortiz Pinchetti. "Informe Creel-Ortiz Pinchetti." *Reforma*, January 29, 1995: A10.

Delgado, Álvaro and Armando Guzmán. "El Quien es Quien de los Pudientes Tabasqueños que Retuvieron la 'Inversion Llamada Madrazo.'" *Proceso*, January 30, 1995: 28–33.

Delgado, Álvaro and Fernando Mayolo López. "Muñoz Ledo, de Frente al Futuro del PRD: 'Zedillo No Quire Aplastarnos, Hay Que Correr Riesgos y Optar por un Partido Institucionalizado.'" *Proceso* 946, December 19, 1994: 24–31.

Delgado, Álvaro and Raúl Monge. "El PRD, al Borde de Una Crisis Institucional; Irregularidades en 32% de las Casillas en la Elección Nacional." *Proceso*, no. 1169, March 28, 1999: 14–19.

"Descarta Sauri *concertacesión*." *Reforma*, January 7, 2001: 4-A.

Diario de Yucatán (a). "Crisis Política Crece al Demitir la Gobernadora." *Diario de Yucatán*, September 2, 1993: 1.

———— (b). "Acción Nacional Solicatará Nulidad de las Elecciones." *Diario de Yucatán*, December 1, 1993: 1.

Diario de Yucatán. "Alcaldes Electos Denuncian 'Desmantelamiento' de sus Municipios." *Diario de Yucatán*, June 10, 2001, online at www.yuc.com.mx/ noticias/domingo.

Díaz, César. "Enfrenta a los Priístas la Entrega de Despensas." *Reforma*, February 15, 2002: 4-A.

Díaz, Gloria Leticia and Roberto Zamarripa. "Para Calmar a los Perredistas, el Gobernador Figueroa Regala Diputaciones y Regidurías." *Proceso* 891, November 29, 1993: 30–3.

Dillon, Sam. "In Mexico, Votes Can Be Bought, Study Shows." *New York Times*, July 31, 1999: A-1.

"Dimite Candidato del PRI." *El Norte*, October 12, 1991, INFOSEL.

Domínguez Torrez, Eleazar and Sergio Granda Montalvo. "Pases." *Nuevo Péndulo de Chiapas*, March 20, 1996: 5.

"En el TEE, 14 Recursos de Inconformidad." *Tribuna de Campeche*, August 30, 1991: 1.

"Exigen Anular en Chiapas Comicios para 12 Alcaldias." *El Norte*, August 22, 1991, INFOSEL.

Félix, Edgar. "Aguirre Rivero no Escapa a la Fama de Caciques en Guerrero." *El Financiero*, June 30, 1998: 48–9.

Flores, Sergio and Jesús Guerrero. "Acusa PRD a Alcalde de Violar Ley Electoral." *Reforma*, June 19, 2000: 16-A.

Flores de la Rosa, Nuevo León electoral court president, July 30, 1996, Monterrey.

Flores de la Rosa, Roberto. "Nos Apegamos a la Ley." *El Norte*, September 4, 1994, INFOSEL.

Gachuzo, Germán. "Deslinda a Bartlett Candidato Priísta." *Reforma*, May 11, 2000: A-6.

Garavito, Rosalbina. "La Intransigencia Democrática del PRD y su Modernidad." *El Cotidiano* 44, November–December 1991.

García, Adán. "Descartan Pacto con Ex-Gobernador Priísta – Niega PRD Negociar Candidatura." *Reforma*, August 30, 2001: 18-A.

Garduño Espinosa, Francisco. "Amalia García y Jesús Zambrano Contrastan al Negociar Tabasco." *Milenio Diario*, January 14, 2001: 5.

Garduño, Roberto. "En el Caso Tabasco 'No Andaremos de Metiches,' Expresa Vicente Fox." *La Jornada*, January 3, 2001: 3.

Gaxiola, Yovana. "Desorganizada la Gestión Municipal." *El Sol del Pacífico*, December 25, 1998: 1-A.

Gómez, Manuel. "Definen para Priístas 22 Distritos Impugnados: El PAN y el PRD Protestan Casos Aprobados por el Colegio Electoral." *El Norte*, October 21, 1991, INFOSEL.

Gómez, Manuel and Andrés Resillas. "Afirma Priísta que a Paredes 'Se le Pasó la Mano." *El Norte*, February 4, 1993, INFOSEL.

Granados Chapa, Miguel Ángel. "Sigue Mérida el Camino de Guanajuato." *Reforma*, December 22, 1993, INFOSEL.

———. "El Fallo Regiomontano." *El Norte*, September 26, 1994, INFOSEL.

———. "Huejotzingo y Anexas." *Reforma*, February 20, 1996, INFOSEL.

———. "Jalisco en el Trife." *Reforma*, February 20, 2001: 15-A.

Guardiola, Georgina and Yolanda Hernández. "Pide AN Acelerar Resolución." *El Norte*, September 19, 1994, INFOSEL.

Guarneros, Constanza. "Responsabilidad de los Alcaldes Concluir Obras." *El Sol de Tlaxcala*, December 8, 1998: 1-A.

Guerra, Fidel. "Reconocen Falta de Pruebas: Las Irregularidades Documentadas no Son Suficientes Para Invalidar Elección Presidencial, Indica el PAN." *Reforma*, August 29, 1994, INFOSEL.

Guerrero, Claudia. "Discrepa Amalia con Cárdenas Sobre Incremento de Militancia." *Reforma*, January 24, 2001: 7-A.

———. "Admite Análisis Interno Que PRI es Considerado el Peor Partido." *Reforma*, May 13, 2002: 5-A.

Guerrero, Roberto, Fernando Martínez, and Lucí Calderón. "Descalifican Priístas Examen de Democracia." *Reforma*, July 28, 1998: 17-A.

Gurza, Teresa. "PRI, PAN y PRD Censuran al Tribunal Electoral Michoacano." *La Jornada*, December 29, 1992: 6.

Gutiérrez, Alejandro and Pedro Matías. "En Sonora y Oaxaca Avanza la Autonomía Indígena sin Que Atente Contra la Soberanía o la Unidad Nacionales." *Proceso* 1108, January 25, 1998: 12.

"Heberto no Quiere Ser Candidato Para Veracruz." *Diario de Xalapa*, November 21, 1991: 1.

Hidalgo, Jorge Arturo. "Que Cárdenas no Sea un Dirigente 'Suelto.'" *Reforma*, August 13, 2000: 15-A.

———. "Da el PRI Luz Verde al Acarreo de Votos." *Reforma*, February 21, 2002: 6-A.

Hidalgo, Jorge Arturo and Claudia Guerrero. "Obvian en 1996 Proceso Irregular." *Reforma*, April 3, 1999: 5-A.

———. "Admiten Perredistas Errores en Campaña." *Reforma*, July 22, 2000: 4-A.

Hiriart, Pablo (a). "El PSUM, sin Representantes de Casillas en Juárez y Chihuahua." *La Jornada*, July 2, 1986: 1.

——— (b). "Resoluciones Justas, Pide el Presidente al Colegio Electoral." *La Jornada*, August 2, 1986: 1.

Irízar, Guadalupe. "Estan 'Atrapados' Entre dos Códigos." *Reforma*, December 8, 1996, INFOSEL.

———. "Descarta MAM Negociar Tabasco." *Reforma*, December 10, 1994, INFOSEL.

Irízar, Guadalupe and Esperanza Barajas. "Responden Sólo Siete Estados a Exhorto Sobre Publicidad." *Reforma*, June 7, 2000: 15-A.

Jiménez, Sandra Isabel. "Respaldan a Alemán con Dinero de Pemex." *Reforma*, May 24, 1998: 26A.

———. "Detectan Anomalías a 180 Ediles." *Reforma*, January 13, 1999: 16-A.

———. "Atribuyen a Cuauhtémoc Caída del PRD en Veracruz." *Reforma*, March 20, 2001: 18-A.

Juárez, Miguel Angel and Wilbert Torre. "Enjuiciará Congreso a Madrazo y Cervera." *Reforma*, April 15, 1998: 1-A.

López, Fernando Mayolo. "Defiende Los Pinos activismo de Zedillo." *Reforma*, July 4, 2000: A-1.

López, Julio César and Pedro Matías. "En Medio de un Clima Creciente de Violencia, las Elecciones Locales en Chiapas Pueden Derivar en Nuevos Enfrentamientos." *Proceso* 988, October 9, 1995: 30–1.

López, René Alberto (a). "Cifras Contradictorias y Otro Apagón en el Instituto Electoral." *La Jornada*, November 22, 1994: 64.

——— (b). "Desechó el TEE de Tabasco Todas las Impugnaciones." *La Jornada*, December 10, 1994: 9.

Maldonado, Xóchitl. "Rompe PAN Alianza con Perredistas." *El Norte*, August 21, 1992, INFOSEL.

Marí, Carlos and Guadalupe Irízar. "No Permitirán Dimisión de Madrazo Pintado – Amenazan Priístas Formar Otro Partido." *Reforma*, January 19, 1995, INFOSEL.

Marí, Carlos and Ernesto Núñez. "Exhiben Apoyo Priísta Vía la Red de Pemex." *Reforma*, June 17, 2000: 10-A.

Martínez, Fernando. "Descarta Diego Abandonar Candidatura." *El Norte*, December 16, 1993, INFOSEL.

Martínez, Nestor and Jesús Reséndiz. "Reta el PRI a Que el PAN Pida Que se Abran los Paquetes Electorales." *La Jornada*, August 8, 1992: 3.

Martínez, Nestor, Ricardo Alemán, and Oscar Camacho. "Incapacidad del PAN-PRI Para Probar Fraudes en Guanajuato." *La Jornada*, October 24, 1991: 13.

Martínez, Victoriano. "Aceptan Solicitud de Martínez Corbalá Para Que Regresan a Trabajar a Sus Municipios." *El Norte*, October 22, 1992, INFOSEL.

Matías, Pedro. "Resuelven Ocho de Cada 10 Conflictos Poselectorales." *Cantera*, November 3, 1998, Oaxaca Electoral Institute news clippings.

Medina, María Elena. "Piden a Gobernadores no Influir en Comicios." *Reforma*, May 5, 1998: 21-A.

———. "Entrega Zedillo Obras a $3 Milliones por Hora." *Reforma*, June 3, 2000: A-1.

Mejía, Gerardo. "Critica Oñate Solución Dada a Huejotzingo." *Reforma*, May 18, 1996, INFOSEL.

Mendoza, Luis Armando. "Amenazan Pacto Federal." *Reforma*, December 15, 2000: 20-A.

Meza, Martha. "Se Deslindan PRD y PAN." *Diario de Xalapa*, January 3, 2001: 7-A.

Moncisbays Ramos, Alejandra. "La Federación no Debe Intervenir en Conflictos Electorales Estatales – Villanueva." *Novedades de Quintana Roo*, March 23, 1998: 1.

Morales, Gina (a). "No Aceptará PRI Ningún Tipo de Negociación Electoral." *La Voz de Michoacán*, November 12, 1998: 3-A.

——— (b). "No Habrá *Concertacesiones* en Michoacán, Advierte Rojas." *La Voz de Michoacán*, December 11, 1998, 1-A.

Moreno, Daniel (a). "Quedé Mal con Todos." *Reforma*, March 23, 1998: 8-A.

——— (b). "No Soy Pelele de Nadie." *Reforma*, March 25, 1998: 14-A.

Muñiz, Luis. "La Batalla del Jurásico: Bartlett, Abanderado de los Duros por la Presidencia." *La Crisis* 3, no. 99, November 15, 1997: 6–9.

Murguía Velasco, Victor. "Infinidad de Cambios de Ediles en Casi las 203 Planillas." *Diario de Xalapa*, October 7, 1988: 1.

Musacchio, Humberto. "Carnaval de Veracruz." *Voz y Voto*, no. 62, April 1998: 39–40.

"Ninguna Queja o Recurso en el Tribunal Electoral." *Tribuna de Campeche*, August 25, 1991: 1.

El Norte. "Admite PRI Resolución: Reconoce Pichardo que Resolución en Caso Monterrey es Apegada a Derecho." *El Norte*, September 23, 1994, INFOSEL.

Ochoa, Teresa. "No Vamos a Negociar Ningún Triunfo – PRI." *Reforma*, July 16, 1997: 6-A.

Olmos, José Gil and Armando Guzmán. "Madrazo y Fox 'Negociaron' ya la Elección de Tabasco." *Proceso* 1290, July 22, 2001: 16–19.

Olvera Aguirre, Carlos. "Fox Insta a los Yucatecos a Negociar Como en Tabasco." *Milenio*, January 15, 2001: 5.

Pérez, Miguel. "Descarta Figueroa Negociar Resultados." *El Norte*, October 4, 1993, INFOSEL.

Pérez Rayón, Nora. "González Schmal: Matiz Panista de la Resistencia Civil." *El Cotidiano* 24, Julio-Agosto 1988: 37–8.

"Piden Acabar Resistencia – Llaman en Michoacán Ajustarse a Protestas Dentro de la Ley." *Reforma*, August 30, 1994, INFOSEL.

"Pierden Perredistas 60% de Alcaldías." *Reforma*, December 13, 1997: 6-A.

¡*Por Esto!* (a). "Burla." ¡*Por Esto!*, December 12, 1993: 2.

¡*Por Esto!* (b). "Ultimátum." ¡*Por Esto!*, December 14, 1993: 2.

"Presentó el PRD en Córdoba 165 Recursos de Inconformidad." *La Jornada*, August 5, 1992: 5.

Puig, Carlos. "En un Editorial, *Wall Street Journal* Recomendó lo Que se Hizo en Guanajuato." *Proceso* 774, September 2, 1991: 12–17.

Quintal, Johnny Oliver. "Otra Vergonzosa 'Concertacesión.'" ¡*Por Esto!*, June 30, 1998: La Ciudad 2–8.

Ramales, Rosy. "Suspenden Mesa del Diálogo Entre los Partidos Políticos." *Noticias*, October 17, 1998.

Ramos, Jesús. "Maurer Espera que el PAN no lo Utilice para Concertacesión." in *Síntesis*, November 13, 1998: R-6.

"Rasuran Acuerdos en Documento Final." *Reforma*, September 23, 1996: 1-A.

"Regresan, Luego de Concertacesión." ¡*Por Esto!*, July 1, 1998: La República 3.

Rendón, Iván, Carlos Marí, and Daniel Pensamiento. "Documentan Fraude en Oaxaca – Presentan Pruebas de Casillas 'Zapato' a Favor de Madrazo." *Reforma*, February 28, 2002: 5-A.

Resillas, Andrés. "Acusa TEE a PRI de Cohecho Electoral." *Reforma*, December 19, 1995, INFOSEL.

Rico, Salvador and Víctor Chávez. "Amenaza PAN con Romper el Diálogo si no 'Rectifican' Comicios Yucatecos." *El Financiero*, June 30, 1998: 54.

Rincón Rovelo, Walter. "Habrá Consejos de Vigilancia en 8 Alcaldías." *La Voz del Sureste*, January 2, 1999: 1.

Riva Palacio, Raymundo. "Rebelión en la Granja." *Reforma*, January 23, 1995, INFOSEL.

Rivera, Miguel Ángel. "Deciden PAN y PRD Reiniciar sus Protestas a Principios de Diciembre." *La Jornada*, November 21, 1992: 6.

"Robles Critica en Washington al PRD." *El Financiero*, October 12, 2000: 46.

Rodriguez, Carlos Jesús. "Retoma el PPS Tres Palacios Municipales." *El Dictamen* de Veracruz, December 6, 1991: 1-A.

———. "Ajustes Repentinos en 37 Municipios, Varios Fueron Sacrificados Ante Presiones Políticas." *El Dictamen de Veracruz*, January 3, 1992: 1-D.

Rueda, Adrian. "Rechazan Dialogar Bajo Condiciones." *El Norte*, March 9, 1990, INFOSEL.

Sánchez, Adolfo and Antonio Castellanos. "No Más Negociaciones Poselectorales: Gobernadores." *Excelsior*, March 4, 1996: A-1.

Sánchez, Jesús. "Tregua en la Pugna entre Priistas." *El Financiero*, February 25, 1994, INFOSEL.

Santos de la Garza, Luis. "La Reforma Constitucional Federal: Buenas y Malas." *El Norte*, August 10, 1996: 2A.

Saúl Rodríguez, Lilia. "No se Instaló 17% de Casillas, Informa PRD." *El Universal*, March 19, 2002: A-17.

Schlerer Ibarra, María. "El PAN se Reforma Para Protegerse del Desgaste en el Poder." *Proceso*, no. 1262, January 7, 2001: 18–19.

"Se Divide la CNC en San Lucas Ojitlán." *Noticias de Oaxaca*, November 11, 1992: 3C.

Solís, Georgina. "Es Inaceptable Fallo de Tribunal Electoral." *El Norte*, September 9, 1994, INFOSEL.

Solís Georgina. "Pedirá Diego que PAN Deje Diálogo Nacional." *Reforma*, February 16, 1996, INFOSEL.

Solís, Georgina and Patricia Sotelo. "Gana Terreno la Oposición." *Reforma*, November 14, 1995, INFOSEL.

Sotelo, Patricia. "Fortalecerá PRD a Sus Gobiernos." *Reforma*, December 1, 1997: 11-A.

Torre, Wilbert. "De Marrullerías Priístas a Vicios Perredistas." *Reforma*, January 25, 2002: 6-A.

Turati, Marcela. "Los Regalos de Cervera." *Reforma*, June 28, 2000: A-1.

Ureña, José. "Cotejo de Actas en BC, Propone el PAN al PRI." *La Jornada*, August 8, 1992: 5.

Ureña, José. "Clase Política: Fracasó el PAN al Negociar Chetumal en Febrero Pasado." *La Jornada*, May 12, 1996: 4.

Vargas, Rosa Elvira and Enrique Méndez. "Como Oposición, el PRI ya Entró a la "Pubertad Política." *La Jornada* online, January 23, 2001: 21 (http://www.jornada.unam.mx./012nlpol.htm).

Vázquez, Fermín. "Terminar: El Gran Dilema." *El Norte*, December 5, 1993, INFOSEL.

Vázquez, Luis and Javier Kuramura. "Informa el PAN Caso Huejotzingo a la ONU." *Reforma*, April 23, 1996: 4A.

Vega, Margarita (a). "Pierde Credibilidad PRD y Suma Detractores." *Reforma*, May 5, 2002: 6-A.

——— (b). "Crearán 'Chuchos' su Propia Estructura Dentro del PRD." *Reforma*, May 20, 2002: 15-A.

Veja. "Documento: A Conferencia Secreta da ESG – A Abertura por Golbery." *Veja*, September 19, 1980: 6.

Zamarripa, Roberto. "Triunfo Perredista, Según el Dictamen del Tribunal." *La Jornada*, August 13, 1989: 1.

Zamarripa, Roberto (a). "Ni un Voto ha Negociado el PAN con el Gobierno: Luis H. Álvarez." *La Jornada*, November 9, 1992: 11.

——— (b). "Ya se Agotó el Tiempo de las Soluciones Políticas: PAN." *La Jornada*, November 21, 1992: 11.

——— (c). "Le Falló el *Mayoriteo* al CEN del PAN en su Asamblea Estatuaria." *La Jornada*, November 22, 1992: 12.

────── (d). "Álvarez Decidió que Lozano Fuera Candidato para SLP." *La Jornada*, December 12, 1992: 9.

Periodicals Consulted Systematically (beyond those listed in Appendix A)

Centro de Información y Analisis de Chiapas, A.C. *Resumen Informativo* (San Cristóbal de las Casas monthly), 1988–98 passim.
El Debate de Culiacán (Culiacán, Sinaloa daily), 1998 passim.
Diario Diecisiete (Acapulco daily), 1993–7 passim.
Diario de Morelos (Cuernavaca daily), 1991–2 passim.
El Dictamen (Veracruz, Veracruz daily), 1991–2001 passim.
El Eco de Nayarít (Tepíc, Nayarit daily), 1990–1 passim.
El Financiero (Mexico City daily – CD-ROM), 1989–2001 passim.
El Heraldo de Chihuahua (Chihuahua daily), 1992–2001 passim.
El Hidrocálido (Aguascalientes daily), 1992–3 passim.
El Mercurio de Tamaulipas (Ciudad Victoria, Tamaulipas daily), 1998 passim.
El Meridiano de Nayarit (Tepic daily), 1993–4 passim.
El Momento (San Luis Potosí daily), 1991–2 passim.
El Mundo de Tehuacán (Tehuacán, Puebla daily), 1998 passim.
El Noticiero de Colima (Colima, Colima daily), 1994–5.
Noticias – Voz e Imagen de Oaxaca (Oaxaca daily), 1989–98 passim.
¡Por Esto! (Mérida, Yucatán daily), 1989–2001 passim.
Proceso (Mexico City weekly), 1988–2002 passim.
El Siglo de Durango (Durango daily), 1995–6 passim.
Síntesis (Puebla and Tlaxcala daily), 1998 passim.
El Sol de León (León, Guanajuato daily), 1997 passim.
El Sol de Morelia (Morelia, Michoacán daily), 1989–2001 passim.
El Sol de Pachuca (Pachuca, Hidalgo daily), 1996–9 passim.
El Sol de Puebla (Puebla daily), 1992–8 passim.
El Sol de Sinaloa (Culiacán daily), 1989–90 passim.
El Sol de Tampico (Tampico, Tamaulipas daily), 1989–90 passim.
El Sol de Tlaxcala (Tlaxcala, Tlaxcala daily), 1991–7 passim.
El Sol de Zacatecas (Zacatecas, Zacatecas daily), 1998 passim.
Tribuna de Campeche (Campeche, Campeche daily), 1991–8 passim.
Voz del Sureste (Tuxtla Gutiérrez, Chiapas daily), 1998–2001 passim.

Index